The After Effects
Illusionist, 2nd edition

The After Effects Illusionist, 2nd edition

Chad Perkins

Focal Press
Taylor & Francis Group

NEW YORK AND LONDON

First published 2013
by Focal Press
70 Blanchard Road, Suite 402
Burlington, MA 01803
781-313-8808

Simultaneously published in the UK
by Focal Press
2 Park Square, Milton Park, Abingdon, Oxon OX14 4RN

Focal Press is an imprint of the Taylor & Francis Group, an Informa business

Notices
Knowledge and best practice in this field are constantly changing. As new research and experience broaden our understanding, changes in research methods, professional practices, or medical treatment may become necessary.

Practitioners and researchers must always rely on their own experience and knowledge in evaluating and using any information, methods, compounds, or experiments described herein. In using such information or methods they should be mindful of their own safety and the safety of others, including parties for whom they have a professional responsibility.

Product or corporate names may be trademarks or registered trademarks, and are used only for identification and explanation without intent to infringe.

Library of Congress Cataloging in Publication Data
Perkins, Chad.
   The After Effects illusionist/Chad Perkins.—2nd edition.
      p. cm.
   Includes index.
   1. Adobe After Effects. 2. Cinematography—Special effects—Data processing.
   3. Computer animation. I. Title.
   TR858.P48 2013
   777'.9—dc23
                                              2012028197

ISBN 978-0-240-81898-6 (pbk.)

Typeset in Utopia Regular 10/12
Project Managed and Typeset by: diacriTech

Printed in Canada

CONTENTS

BECOMING AN ILLUSIONIST

Welcome to the second edition of *The After Effects Illusionist!* In this book, we're going to look at every single native effect in After Effects. But this will not be a duplicate of the After Effects help documentation—far from it. This book is not meant to be exhaustively comprehensive in the literal sense, meaning that we won't necessarily cover every single property in every single effect. I think the help documentation does a good enough job of that. We're instead going to focus on the purpose of each effect, and also how to use it creatively. I'll also let you know my opinion on which effects are a waste of time, and if there are any substitutes that might work better.

In this chapter, we're going to get you the foundation you need to understand this book, no matter your skill level. We'll also give you a brief overview of all of the exciting things that have been added in this edition of the book. There also may be some tips and tricks in this chapter that can help you as you begin to dig a little deeper into the world of effects.

Why This Book?

I had the idea to create this book after seeing many After Effects users (with far more talent and skill in this arena than I have) doing things manually that could be easily done with the effects that ship with After Effects. Many times, users of After Effects will go back to Photoshop, or Illustrator, or their video editing application, or their dedicated 3D application to make small changes that could have been done quickly and just as well with effects in After Effects.

The problem is that there are now 189 native effects. Many of them are almost completely worthless. Others might seem worthless or abstract, leaving users to wonder—"When would I ever use this?" This book is my attempt to share with you what I've learned in my studies of these effects. The exercise files on the disc that accompanies this book were specifically geared to helping you discover how these effects might help you in your workflow.

How This Book is Laid Out

In this book, we're going to examine (among other things) every native effect in After Effects, as well as some 3rd party tools that have been included with After Effects for quite some time.

We're going to cover each effect in each category (e.g., Color Correction, Distort, Generate, and so on) in the order in which After Effects lists them in the Effects menu (and the Effects and Presets panel). After Effects organizes the categories alphabetically, and then the effects in that category are also organized alphabetically as well. And this is the same order that we will follow in this book. So, remember that these effects are not listed in the order of importance, or sorted in any other way.

After we've finished covering all of the effects, we'll have a few appendix-type chapters that cover more intermediate and advanced effects topics, such as using multiple effects, using maps to control effect properties, and a brief glance at some of my favorite third-party effect solutions.

What's New in This Edition?

This is always the first question on my mind when a new edition for a book is released. Well, let me tell you. There are MASSIVE updates in this edition. I have to thank Focal Press, who have been so patient with me (because I've been taking forever with this). Focal Press has also believed enough in this book to give me a ridiculously large page count for the first edition, and has upped that significantly in this edition. If this book was done halfway, it wouldn't have worked.

So with that, let me give you a brief heads up as to what is new in this edition. First of all, in Chapter 21, I'll take a look at the Cycore effects. This massive collection of over 70 effects has been shipping with After Effects for a long time now, and it's time to take a look. The Cycore effects extend the functionality of After Effects so much, including adding the best native particle systems, all kinds of transitions, blurs, fast rendering and intuitive distortions, weather systems and more. We'll dig into all of this in Chapter 21.

And while we're adding more support for third-party effects included with After Effects, we also decided to cover Keylight. This keying tool from The Foundry has been included with After Effects since the Reagan administration (give or take), and we're going to see how to make this amazing keying tool work for you, as well as potential roadblocks to avoid.

There have also been a host of great effects added that we're going to look at. Everything from the mind-blowing 3D Camera

Tracker to the Refine Matte effect to Warp Stabilizer, Rolling Shutter Repair, new color-based effects like Black & White, Selective Color, Vibrance, and Apply Color LUT.

I've also gone through and revamped TONS of the old stuff. I've recently purchased a RED Scarlet-X camera, and a lot of the new footage used in this book is coming from this camera. I've also learned so much in the last few years since the first edition was written, and I've used so many more plugins and software tools. So I've gone back and added new tips in almost every single chapter.

I've added several more real world examples, especially in the chapter on Expression Controls (Chapter 8). I also received permission to include footage from Causality, a sci-fi show that I've been doing visual effects on, as a practical application of the Fractal Noise effect (shown in Chapter 12). I've also added a new use for the Colorama effect—making luma mattes for sky replacement (Chapter 6). I've even added a bunch of new audio tips (including an expression from AE guru Dan Ebberts for creating an automatic analog synth riff) in Chapter 3.

And again, this is just a small sampling of what's new. There are loads of new tips, updated exercise files, added explanations, and more all throughout this book. I'm so excited about it.

Why Use Effects?

So, what can effects do? Why use them? First, and perhaps foremost—the effects in After Effects are free, once you have After Effects. They don't need extra installations or additional serial numbers. There are no compatibility issues with the native effects.

Effects have a wide range of functions. We can use them to create remarkable patterns that can captivate an audience, or that simulate real world stuff like fire or water. In After Effects, we also adjust color by using effects. But effects can also create simulations, as if something were blowing up or distorting in an organic way. We can access 3D data using effects, and even enhance (and create!) audio using effects. With 189 choices here, and an almost infinite amount of creative combinations, you're sure to find something to enhance your workflow.

The Great Secret to the Effects

If there were one great secret to effects, and I had to sum this book up into a single sentence, it would be that effects are sometimes at their best when used for purposes that they were never intended for. We'll take the Shatter effect (which "blows stuff up," according to its formal definition), and use it to create volumetric 3D text. In Chapter 7, we'll sharpen edges using a blur effect, as seen in Figure 1.1.

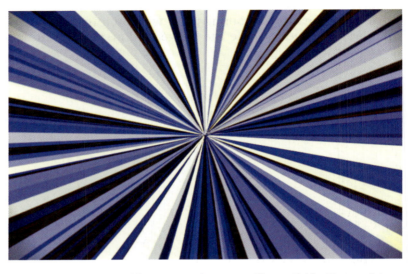

Figure 1.1 These razor sharp edges were sharpened with blur.

In Chapter 5, we'll use an abstract effect (Shift Channels) to relight a scene rendered from a 3D program using 3D data that is stored in the 3D image. In Chapter 16, we'll be creating a sci-fi control panel out of video footage of children running using the Brush Strokes effect. This is seen in Figure 1.2.

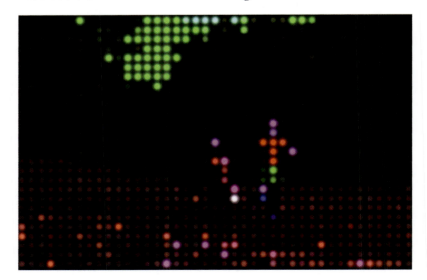

Figure 1.2 Applying an effect called Brush Strokes, we create this 60's sci-fi master computer out of video footage of children playing.

We're going to be creating fireballs and interactive magnifying glasses and lightning and light sabers and armies of objects and realistic flowing chocolate and much more. Of course there aren't any fireball or chocolate effects. We have to get clever to achieve these results. We have to use effects for purposes that have nothing to do with their names. If ever there were a time to reuse the cliché of thinking outside the box, this is it.

Applying Effects

I'm assuming that you are fairly familiar with After Effects. You'll certainly get more out of this book if you know more about other (non-effect) aspects of After Effects, such as color channels and color theory, the names of key panels (such as the Composition panel, Project panel, Timeline panel, etc.), layer blend modes, masks, and so forth. But if you are new to After Effects and want to follow along here, you can still learn a lot. So, in this section, we'll look at how to apply effects.

There are two ways to apply effects—from the Effect menu at the top of the interface, or from the Effects & Presets panel. To apply an effect from the Effect menu, select a layer in the Timeline panel, then go to the Effect menu, find the effect in the effects category that you'd like to apply, and then select it there. The problem with this method is that you have to memorize which effects are in which categories. Why would I want to spend time doing that?

I never use the Effect menu to apply effects. I prefer to use the Effects & Presets panel instead. This panel also has effects grouped by preset, but it also has the added power of a live search field. Start typing in a few letters of an effect, and instantly, all effects that have that combination of letters show up in the search results in the Effects & Presets panel, while all other effects are hidden. To remove the search results and see all effects again, click the X on the right side of the search field.

Once you find the effect in the Effects & Presets panel, you can double click to apply.

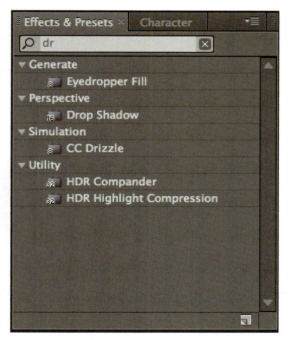

Figure 1.3 Searching for effects in the Effects & Presets panel.

But another benefit of finding effects in this way is that it also gives you drag and drop functionality when applying effects. You can drag and drop the effect from the Effects & Presets panel onto the desired layer in the Composition panel or in the Timeline panel.

Adjusting Effects

Once you've applied the effect, you adjust its various properties in the Effect Controls panel (on the left side of the interface, grouped with the Project panel by default). If your Effect Controls panel isn't showing, you can select it from the Window menu, or press the F3 key on your keyboard. We'll be spending most of this book in the Effect Controls panel, so be familiar with this workflow. Remember that every property that has a stopwatch can be animated.

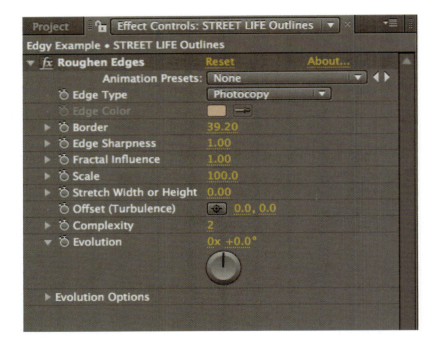

Figure 1.4 The Effect Controls panel; where we go to tweak effect settings.

Resetting Effects and Individual Properties

After experimenting with effects, sometimes you'll want to get back to the default settings. If you click the Reset button at the top of each effect in the Effect Controls panel, you'll reset every setting for that effect back to its default value. However, if you want to only reset the value of one property, right click on its value and select Reset.

Using Effect Presets

Getting the effects settings that are just right can be time-consuming. So, After Effects has provided a way for you to save and reuse your effects settings, using effect presets. Effect presets can store the settings of multiple effects and animation data (including keyframes and expressions). For example, let's say you had created the perfect water texture, comprised of the Fractal Noise effect to make the water texture, the Colorama effect to add color, and you added some expressions to create organic watery movement. You can save all of this work by first selecting all of the effects that you want to save in the Effect Controls panel. You can select multiple effects by holding down the Ctrl(Win)/Cmd(Mac) key while clicking to select them. Then, with the effects selected, open the Animation menu at the top of the screen and select Save Animation Preset. You can then navigate to a location to save the preset, which has a .ffx file extension. To apply an effect preset, simply select the layer(s) to which you want to apply the preset, open the Animation menu and select Apply Animation Preset, navigate to and select the desired FFX file, and click OK. Note that these FFX files are also cross-platform.

Figure 1.5 If you want to clean up the search results in the Effects & Presets panel, deselect Show Animation Presets from the panel's flyout menu.

The Effects & Presets panel can also display effect presets that ship with After Effects, or that are stored in the same folder as the stock presets. That way, when you perform a search, you can use this panel to access presets and apply them quickly. Personally, I find this to be a distraction, especially when teaching. So, I go to the Effects & Presets panel menu and deselect the Show Animation Presets option.

Browsing Effects Presets with Adobe Bridge

Adobe Bridge is a file browsing application that comes with After Effects, and many other Adobe programs as well. It can preview still images (including image sequences!), graphics from Adobe Illustrator, video, audio, PDFs, layered Photoshop documents, and even some 3D files. One of the lesser known features of Adobe Bridge is that it can also preview the animation presets that ship with After Effects. This even includes the ability to preview the text animation presets.

The presets are kinda buried on your hard drive. They're located in the Presets folder in the After Effects folder in the Adobe folder in the Program Files (Win)/Applications (Mac) folder on your computer. However, there's a nifty shortcut for getting Bridge to the presets folder. Go to the flyout menu of the Effects & Presets panel (the same place where we deselected the Show Animation Presets option in the previous section), and choose Browse Presets. This will not only launch Adobe Bridge (assuming it isn't running already), but it will automatically navigate to the Presets folder for you. In Bridge, you'll then see the contents of the Presets folder, which contains a large number of folders of preset categories.

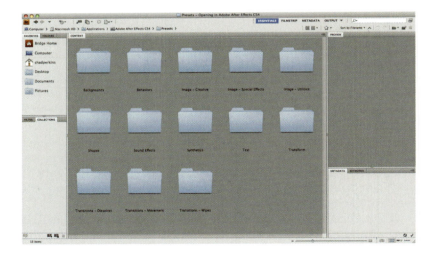

Figure 1.6 The Presets folder, as seen in Adobe Bridge.

If we double click one of the folders—Backgrounds in this case—we'll enter that folder and see previews of all of its animation presets.

Remember that animation presets can contain animation, and so can their previews. Click a preview once in Bridge to select it. It will then display a larger preview in the Preview panel on the right hand side of the interface. It will have its own scrubbable timeline.

To apply an animation preset from Bridge, just double click it in Bridge. This applies to text animation presets as well.

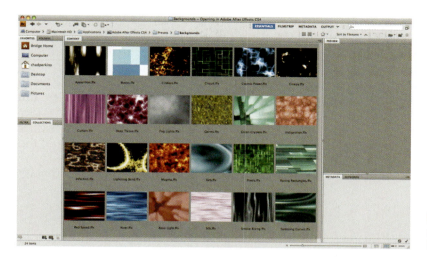

Figure 1.7 Thumbnail previews of the animation presets in the Backgrounds folder.

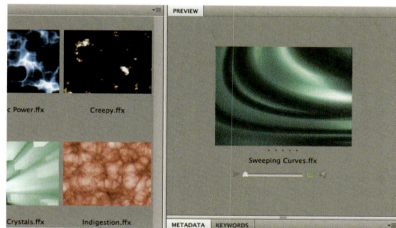

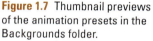

Figure 1.8 When a preset is selected, you can get a larger, animated preview in the Preview panel in Adobe Bridge.

Using Brainstorm with Effects

Introduced in After Effects CS3, Brainstorm allows you to see random variations of settings. This is particularly helpful with effects. You can even select multiple effects in the Effect Controls panel and see random variations of all the properties of both effects. Or, in the Timeline panel, you can select just one parameter of an effect to see random versions of the effect, with only that property changing.

I'm going to create a new solid layer by going to the Layer menu at the top of the interface and choosing Layer>New>Solid. You can also create solid layers by using the keyboard shortcut Ctrl+Y(Win)/Cmd+Y(Mac)—a useful shortcut to memorize for going through this book. I'll then apply the Fractal Noise effect,

Figure 1.9 The Brainstorm icon in the Timeline panel.

followed by the Tritone effect. Next, I'll select both effects in the Effect Controls panel using the Ctrl(Win)/Cmd(Mac) key. Now I'm ready to have Brainstorm create some random results for me. Click the Brainstorm icon at the top of the Timeline panel. Brainstorm used to have the coolest icon of all time (a big brain with a lightning bolt—get it? BRAIN/STORM! Ha! I loved it!), but now it just looks like a thought bubble with a light bulb.

After clicking the Brainstorm icon, the Brainstorm feature opens up, giving you nine variations of these two effects.

Figure 1.10 Opening Brainstorm shows you 9 variations of the parameters in this effect.

By default, the Randomness value is set to 25%. But I want to give Brainstorm more creative license, to I'm going to up that value to 100%. To see nine more variations with our current settings, click the Brainstorm button.

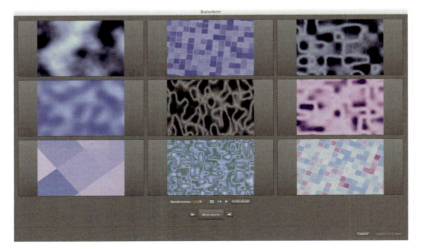

Figure 1.11 After increasing the Randomness value to 100%, Brainstorm returns much wilder results.

You can continue to click the Brainstorm button, which will give you nine more variations each time. Once you've found a pattern you like, hover your cursor over the pattern to get access to four important options.

Clicking the leftmost button will maximize a pattern.

Figure 1.12 Hovering your cursor over one of the results gives you 4 buttons.

Figure 1.13 Maximize a pattern by clicking the first button on the left.

The second button (that looks like a disc icon) is used for when you've found a pattern that you like, but don't want in your current composition. Click this icon to have After Effects create a new composition and a new solid with these effects applied with these settings. When you've completed your work with Brainstorm, you'll find the new comp waiting for you in the Project panel.

The third button from the left (with a checkmark) indicates that you've found the exact settings you're looking for. Clicking this button will close Brainstorm and change the settings of Fractal Noise and Tritone to match the pattern you selected in Brainstorm.

The button on the far right is Include in Next Brainstorm. This is your way of telling Brainstorm that it's getting close to something you like. Click this button, then click the Brainstorm button again to get nine more variations that are similar to the one you've selected. To make the nine variations closer to the one you've selected, take down the Randomness value. You can also include multiple patterns in the next Brainstorm, if you choose.

You can also go back and forth to previous groups of Brainstormed patterns by clicking the back (left arrow) button to the right of the Brainstorm button. Brainstorm also works on animated effects. Click the play button in the Brainstorm window to see what your animations look like with the new patterns.

Figure 1.14 Telling Brainstorm that you want to include a pattern in the next iteration of Brainstorming tends to make other patterns like the one you've chosen. Note that I've also taken down the Randomness value to 20%.

Note that you can also use Brainstorm as a way to learn After Effects. If you're not sure what a certain property or effect can do, simply select it, then open Brainstorm. It will only give you random versions of the properties or effects that you've selected. That way, you can more clearly see what that particular effect or value does.

Common Effect Parameters

Some properties in effects are seen all over the place. Just so we don't have to repeat the same information over and over, let's get familiar with a few of them here.

Effect Control Points

Many effects will have something called an effect control point for certain values. These indicate a point with an XY axis.

Figure 1.15 An effect control point, seen here in the Effect Controls panel for the Twirl Center property.

Effect control points can be adjusted in three ways. You can simply adjust the X and Y dimension hot text values in the Effect Controls panel, as you would any other values. You could also click the effect control point icon in the Effect Controls panel, then click the desired location of the effect control point in the Composition panel. Finally, you can also manually adjust the effect control point in the Composition panel by using the effect control point icon. This icon looks like a circle with a plus in the middle. Note that effect control points can also be targeted by the motion tracking system in After Effects.

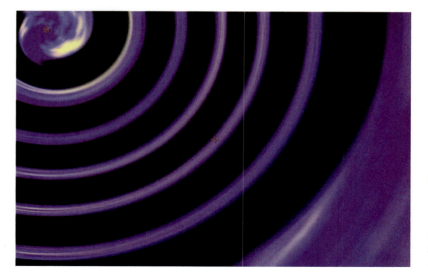

Figure 1.16 An effect control point in the Composition panel is shown. It is the red circle with a plus sign in its center, in the upper left hand corner of the screen. In this instance, it is controlling the center of the twirl.

Random Seed

The Random Seed parameter creates randomization using the same settings that you already have. At first, this may seem confusing. How can it match your exact settings and also be random at the same time?

Think of it this way. Let's say that you and some friends were going to get dinner together. After a few hours of arguing, you decide that you are going to get pizza. Perhaps you even narrow it down to a pizza with some type of meat on it. So, you send out one of your buddies to go get the pizza and bring it back home. Upon their return, they inform you that they brought back a pizza with extra anchovies. Yuck! They followed your instructions to the letter—a pizza with meat. But that's not what you had in mind. So you might send your buddy back to the pizza place to pick up another pizza using your same criteria.

This is a lot like using Random Seed. It keeps all of the settings of the effect unchanged (like your rules for dinner—pizza with meat), and then gives you variations of the effect based on those settings. Random Seed is great if a pattern is created that has an element in the wrong spot, or if you just want to rearrange things a bit.

Composite on Original

Composite on Original settings come in many forms. A similar property might be called Blend with Original, Opacity, or something similar. Basically, this allows the effect to blend in with the original layer. If you applied Fractal Noise to a layer with video to create a fog effect, you might change the blend mode or lower its Opacity value.

Personally, I prefer the power of having effects on their own independent layer, so that I can adjust them as I please without affecting my source footage. This is why I frequently use solid layers, so that I can keep my effects as autonomous layers.

About the Artbeats Footage

The stock video powerhouse, Artbeats.com, has graciously provided some great stock video clips for us to use in this book. They can be found in the Artbeats folder in the Media folder in the exercise files that are on this disc. The versions that I will be using in my screenshots will be at full video resolution. Note that the versions included on the disc are half size (320 × 240 pixels), and are also watermarked. If you care to purchase the full resolution clips, you can find the clips of the same name (and many more) on Artbeats.com.

2

THE 3D CHANNEL EFFECTS

We're going to start out by looking at the 3D Channel effects. Not for any reason, other than they come first alphabetically, and we're covering these effects in the same order they appear in After Effects.

The 3D Channel effects serve a very unique purpose in After Effects. All of them deal with files output from dedicated 3D applications such as Maya, 3DS Max, or Cinema 4D. Note that the 3D Channel effects do not aid in creating 3D objects. Unless you have access to 3D applications like the ones previously mentioned, or files made from such, you may want to skip this chapter.

Most 3D applications can export 2D image sequences using special types of image files that contain additional 3D information, stored in the file almost like metadata is—beneath the surface. This "additional 3D information" can record important details such as how far away from the camera the objects are (the Z depth), information about the objects (such as their object ID), information about their materials (material ID), and so on. The After Effects in the 3D Channel category can access and use this data to do anything from create 3D fog, created a shallow depth of field (blur), isolate individual objects for color correction or mattes, and much more. For example, we'll look at examples in this chapter where it was set up in the 3D file to record the 3D depth of the image. We can then selectively blur (or rack focus) objects that are farther away or closer to the camera; all in a flat 2D layer!

Note that this data is not automatically built into all image renders from 3D applications. Only certain file formats (such as .RPF) can store this type of information, and your 3D program must be set up to render this information.

So, what types of 2D files with 3D data does After Effects understand? To be used in the 3D Channel effects in After Effects, they must be exported in your 3D program. You can store data in RLA, RPF, Softimage PIC/ZPIC files, and in Electric Image EI/EIZ formats. When importing 3D channel data from Softimage and Electric Image, note that you still import only the PIC or EI files, respectively. The ZPIC and EIZ files store

Beware of Uneditable Images

One of the challenges of working with 2D images with 3D data is that Photoshop cannot read, edit, or save them. Because you don't have the luxury of doing any retouching (at least in Photoshop), you'll need to make sure that the render from your 3D application is perfect, or else you're stuck making adjustments to the image in After Effects. With its extensive color correction tools as well as its brushes and clone stamp tool, After Effects is actually pretty good at that kind of thing, but it's certainly something to be aware of.

the depth information, but they cannot be imported into After Effects. However, After Effects will be able to read the 3D data if the ZPIC file is in the same folder as the imported PIC file. The same holds true for EIZ and EI files. Consult the help documentation of your 3D program to learn how to export 3D channel data in the above file formats.

Be aware that some 3D channels are unavailable in certain file formats. And I should also point out that all of the above file formats are still image files. Currently, there aren't any video file formats in After Effects that can store 3D channel data. If you do need to extract data for a series of frames, use an image sequence.

In this chapter, we're going to be using an RPF file created in 3DS Max by a very talented 3D modeler, Kymnbel Bywater from spilledinkanimation.com. Kymnbel meticulously set up this 3D garage scene so that it contains the Z depth of the objects, as well as object IDs, surface normals, and more.

Using the Info Panel

The Info panel is absolutely critical to working well with 3D channel data. It can tell you the Z depth (and other 3D channel information) while your cursor hovers over your image with the effect selected.

Figure 2.1 The 3D garage scene created by Kymnbel Bywater that we'll be using throughout this chapter.

More on 3D in After Effects

You can also import Maya's MA scene format type. Cinema 4D can even output its own type of After Effect project files (AEC files) so that 3D elements in the 3D environment, such as lights and cameras, can be animated and adjusted in After Effects. After Effects CS6 introduced the ability to create truly three dimensional objects, but it still cannot import 3D objects. Using the Trapcode plugin Form (version 2 and later), you can import a 3D object for use with that effect. In this chapter, we'll be looking at how to use 3D data contained within special 2D files.

The 3D Channel Extract Effect

The 3D Channel Extract effect helps you to extract 3D data from a 3D channel. These results are then used in conjunction with another effect.

Let's open up the 3D.aep project I've created as an example for these 3D channel effects. Apply the 3D Channel Extract effect to this layer. The layer is then turned to shades of gray. These shades of gray represent the levels of depth in the 3D file.

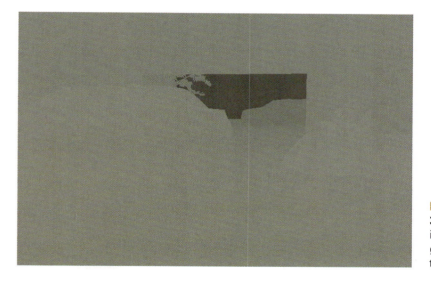

Figure 2.2 After applying the 3D Channel Extract effect, the image is changed to shades of gray that represent the depth of the 3D objects.

Using the default values, it's difficult to see what's going on here. But these grayscale values are supposed to represent the 3D depth of each object, with the objects closest to the camera in white, and the objects furthest from the camera in black. But right now, everything is just gray. Let's fix that.

In the options for the 3D Channel Extract effect in the Effect Controls panel, we have three options. First is the 3D Channel drop down, which specifies which channel from the 3D file to extract. The default setting is Z-depth (i.e., 3D depth), and we'll leave it here for a moment. Next we come to the Black Point and White Point values, which determine the furthest and closest 3D points in this image, respectively. These numbers represent the distance in pixels the 3D objects are from the virtual camera.

But how do we know how exactly how far away they are? The answer is simple—use the Info panel. With the 3D Channel Extract effect active and selected in the Effect Controls panel, click on the spot where the table is on the right hand side of the image.

This table is the object closest to the camera. Once you click in this image in the Composition panel, its Z depth information will show up at the bottom of the Info panel.

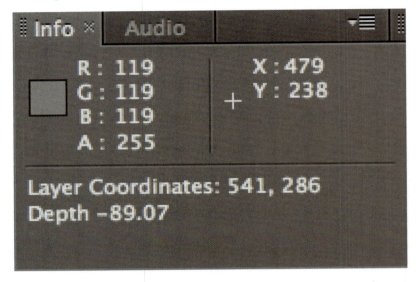

Figure 2.3 After clicking on a 3D object in the Composition panel with the 3D Channel Extract effect selected in the Effect Controls panel, the Info panel tells us the approximate distance the 3D object is away from the camera.

Now we know that we need to set the White Point value to about −89. And although we don't have the shadow information corrected yet, we have more contrast in our depth map.

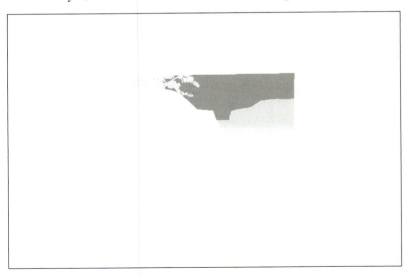

Figure 2.4 The results of changing the White Point level to −89.

Next, let's repeat the same procedure, but we'll use the background this time. With the 3D Channel Extract effect still selected in the Effect Controls panel, click on the darkest point of this image in the Composition panel. Then look in the Effect Controls panel to discover its Z depth.

The Info panel tells us that the background is about –4125 pixels in relation to the camera. Use this value for the Black Point property to complete the settings of this depth map.

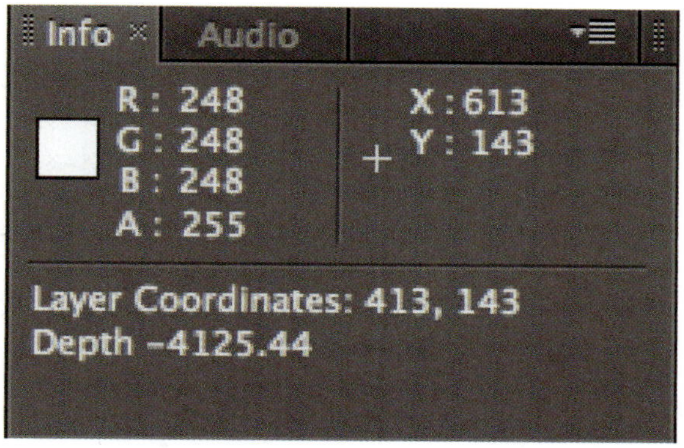

Our depth map looks great. But what do we use it for? We can now use this effect as a luma matte for other effects, such as blurs. Or we could use it as a map to control other effects, such as Displacement Map. You can also use this effect to find out the Z depth values of objects throughout this image for use in other effects in this chapter, such as the Depth Matte and Depth of Field effects.

Figure 2.5 The Info panel displays the distance from the camera to the background.

Figure 2.6 The corrected depth map.

All of the work we've done so far with this effect has been to create a great map of the Z depth in this image. But this is only one of the many channels that we can extract with this effect. In the 3D Channel drop down, change the value to Object ID. Now, when you click on one of the 3D objects in this scene (such as the car or the table), the Info panel will display the Object ID of that object.

Object IDs are identifying numbers assigned to objects by a 3D program. If you did not assign Object IDs in your 3D program, or if you did not export your file with those Object IDs, or if your

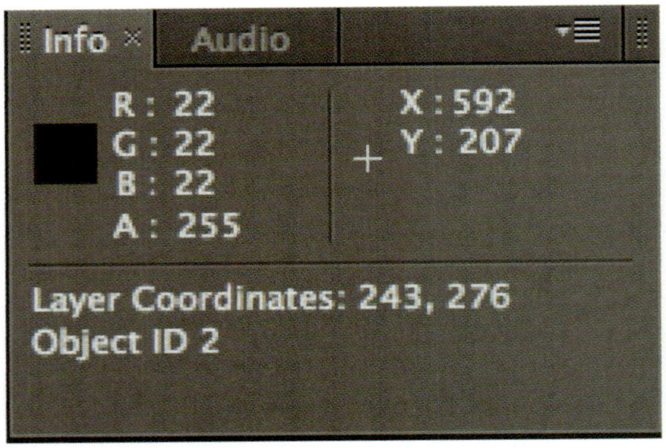

Figure 2.7 With the 3D Channel drop down set to Object ID, the Info panel will now display the Object ID of objects in the Composition panel that you click on.

file format does not support them, this feature will not work. Later on in this chapter, when we cover the ID Matte effect, we'll use these Object ID numbers to quickly isolate different objects in our 3D scene.

Now change the 3D Channel drop down to Surface Normals. Surface normals display a color value for the direction that each polygon is facing. This may seem like a bunch of random colors at first glance. But when we cover the Shift Channels effect in Chapter 5, we'll use this data to add a new light in this scene as if we had added it in the original 3D scene.

There are several other settings besides the ones that we've covered. But the above listed options in the 3D Channel effect are the most common and helpful, from my experience. Just remember that this effect isn't supposed to do anything visually interesting. But it does extract the key data that you need to control other properties in other effects to help you make the most out of the 3D data in your files. The other effects in this chapter would not be as useful without knowing the Z-depth information in your layer, as extracted by the 3D Channel Extract effect. Note that you do not always need to keep the 3D Channel Extract effect applied to your layer unless you need its results to be used with other effects. In some cases, you might apply this effect to learn what you need about your 3D channels, and then delete it.

The Depth Matte Effect

The Depth Matte effect can mask out (remove) objects in your 3D scene, based on their Z depth, or distance from the camera. This is helpful in an infinite amount of circumstances. Let's say that we want to remove the background added by the 3D artist, and replace it with a matte painting from another artist. Because it's the background, it will have the largest Z depth, making it easy to remove with the Depth Matte effect.

Another trick with the Depth Matte effect, and one that we're actually going use here, is to composite a 2D layer into a 3D scene. This is a great skill to master. You'll probably want to follow along with this exercise, so open up the Depth Matte.aep project from the Chapter 2 folder of the exercise files. This project contains a comp with the 3D garage scene, and a video of my buddy, Paavo (creator of www.malachyte.net) riding a unicycle. I've already keyed out (removed) the background for you. We want to make Paavo look like he's jumping around behind the table, and in front of the garage door.

Figure 2.8 The Depth Matte .aep project.

It might seem like the next step is to apply the Depth Matte effect. But we first need to rearrange the stacking order of these layers. Drag the paavo balancing.mov layer below the garage_ zoom0170.rpf layer. Now we can apply the Depth Matte effect to the garage_zoom0170.rpf layer.

When we first apply the Depth Matte effect in this project, the results are completely black, or in other words, completely masked out. This is because the default Depth value is such that the entire image is removed. Remember from our previous look at this file (when we covered the 3D Channel Extract effect) that the object that is closest to the camera is −89 pixels away. So a value of 0 was high enough to mask out everything. Just so we can see what's going on here, take the Depth value to −250. All depth values farther away than this will be removed.

You can also increase the Feather value to create a smooth transition to transparency. Unfortunately, feathering will not get rid of the undesirable blockiness along the edges of 3D mattes. Besides, only the edges at the exact depth specified in the Depth parameter are affected. In Chapter 11, we'll look at a few ways to clean these edges up a little.

I'm actually going to take my Feather value back to 0. Now we need to find the point in 3D where we want Paavo to be. We want him behind the table but in front of the garage wall. To find this depth range, select the Depth Matte effect in the Effect Controls panel.

Figure 2.9 Taking the Depth value to –250 removes all pixels farther away than this.

Figure 2.10 Increasing the Feather value feathers the edges of the exact bit depth. Notice that the edges of the other depths are still hard.

Then click on the back of the table; the part of the table that is farthest away from you. The Info panel will display a value that should be around –170. Then, click on the garage wall behind Paavo. The Info panel should display a value of about –445.

From this, we learn that our depth value needs to be set to a value between –170 and –445. Thankfully, our example value of –250 fits the bill, but anything safely in this range should work just as well.

The next step is to select the garage layer in the Timeline panel, and press Ctrl+D(Win)/Cmd+D(Mac) to duplicate this layer. Then drag the duplicate below the paavo balancing layer. When you're done, you should have a paavo sandwich, with a garage layer on top of the paavo balancing layer, and another garage layer beneath it.

Figure 2.11 It's important to have your layers set up like this in order for this technique to work.

So far, there's no change in the Composition panel. What we need to do to finish this project off is to select the garage layer at the bottom of the layer stack. Then, in the Depth Matte effect controls, select the Invert checkbox. This causes everything that was hidden to be revealed and vice versa. Now, Paavo appears to be right in between the table and the back wall, right where we want him. If this had been a regular still image, this job would have been much more challenging and time-consuming.

Figure 2.12 Because of the depth mattes we've created, Paavo is now in between the table and garage wall.

The Depth of Field Effect

Depth of field is a beautiful thing. It is a blur effect created by a camera lens at different depths. It might as well have been called "depth blur." Depth of field is used to focus a viewer's attention on a subject, by blurring out details they should be ignoring.

Figure 2.13 A photo showing depth of field. The branch and snow are in focus, while everything in the background is out of focus. This focuses our attention immediately on the branch. Photo courtesy of Heather Perkins.

Depth of field is a very natural effect because our eyes essentially do the same thing. Focus your eyes on something that is close to you—perhaps this book. Everything behind seems to blur away and recede into the distance. Now focus on something far away. The book seems to become blurry.

Depth of field is also beneficial because it helps make video look more like film. If you look at video footage, it will often have a complete lack of depth of field with all depth levels in perfect focus. This doesn't seem as natural because it's not the way our eyes work, and it's not what we're accustomed to seeing in film.

The Depth of Field effect here in After Effects attempts to recreate a natural depth of field by using the depth information in the 3D channel data. To see this in action, open up the 3D.aep project from the Chapter 2 folder of the exercise files. Apply the Depth of Field effect to the layer of this garage scene. The default settings don't create a blur right off the bat. We need to do some setup first. First, let's change the Maximum Radius value to 3. Maximum Radius determines the amount of blur. Its default value is 0, which is why we don't see any blurring when this effect is first applied. Note that a little blur goes a long way in this effect. Small values like this are usually all you need.

Figure 2.14 The result of increasing the Maximum Radius (blur amount) to 3.

The next thing I do with this effect is to adjust the Focal Plane Thickness value. For this value, I usually input the amount of depth in the entire scene. This basically tells After Effects how big my virtual world is, in terms of 3D depth. Earlier, when we looked at the 3D Channel Extract effect, we saw that the closest object to the camera was the table on the right (with a depth value of –89), and the object farthest away from the camera was the background (with a depth value of about –4100). So the total amount of distance from the front to the back is about 4000. Change the Focal Plane Thickness value to 4000.

The blur disappears, but that's okay. We now need to specify where we want the blur in terms of 3D depth. We adjust that with the Focal Plane property. If we take this to 4000, it will blur the background. But we start to see a little problem here. As we blur the background, the rest of the image starts to blur a little as well.

What we need to do now is to adjust the Focal Bias parameter. When using depth of field on a real camera, the width of the aperture determines how shallow or deep the depth of field is. Let's say that we only wanted the wrench of the table in focus, and everything else closer or farther away out of focus. That is a small object, so we would need a more open aperture to produce a more shallow depth of field. We can simulate a narrower depth of field by adjusting the Focal Bias property.

I'm going to take the Focal Bias value to 0. Adjusting Focal Bias throws off your blur a little, so now I need to fix my Focal Plane value. I'll take the Focal Plane value to 3600. We now have the entire background blurred, but the blur stops right at the garage door.

Figure 2.15 The result of adjusting the Focal Plane Thickness and Focal Plane properties.

The plant right outside the garage door is blurry while the garage door itself is sharp because of our narrow depth of field.

Figure 2.16 The result of adjusting the Focal Bias and Focal Plane values.

What if we wanted to make our viewers focus their attention on what was happening outside? That might be challenging because there's a table in our way, and a really sexy yellow car, too. Simply change the Focal Plane value to –4800 to make the foreground blurry and the background sharp. It may sound weird, but viewers will ignore everything else close to them, instead focusing on the objects in focus.

Figure 2.17 The eyes are naturally drawn to objects in focus, even if those objects are in the distance.

This illustrates one of the great advantages of using the 3D channel information with the Depth of Field effect, rather than trying to recreate this look with masks and other blur effects. With the Depth of Field effect, we can animate the Focal Plane property to shift viewer focus. You can't do that with masks. Depth of field is a really powerful storytelling tool in video. It makes this effect one of the best reasons to use 3D files with 3D channel data.

The EXtractoR Effect

Several years ago, the famed visual arts studio, Industrial Light and Magic (ILM) created a file format called OpenEXR. OpenEXR is a still image file format that can store 32 bit HDR data, and is akin to the powerful 3D file types mentioned at the beginning of this chapter. The biggest difference, perhaps, is that OpenEXR can store many more layers or channels of 3D data.

Many 3D software programs—such as Cinema 4D, Blender, Lightwave and others—support OpenEXR, as well as Photoshop (since version CS2) and the Mac OS (since 10.4). After Effects has been able to import OpenEXR files since After Effects 7, but it has never been able to access all the various layers of data that can be stored in them. Since CS4, After Effects has included two new effects, the EXtractoR effect (did you catch the capitalized EXR in there?) and the Identifier effect, which can take advantage of layered OpenEXR files.

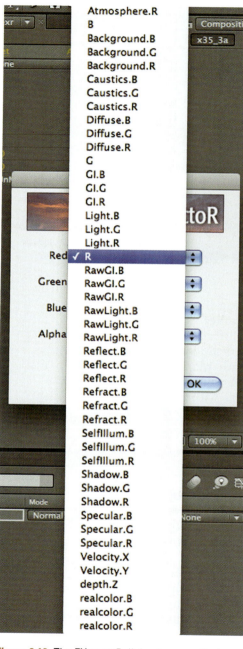

Atmosphere.R
B
Background.B
Background.G
Background.R
Caustics.B
Caustics.G
Caustics.R
Diffuse.B
Diffuse.G
Diffuse.R
G
GI.B
GI.G
GI.R
Light.B
Light.G
Light.R
R
RawGI.B
RawGI.G
RawGI.R
RawLight.B
RawLight.G
RawLight.R
Reflect.B
Reflect.G
Reflect.R
Refract.B
Refract.G
Refract.R
SelfIllum.B
SelfIllum.G
SelfIllum.R
Shadow.B
Shadow.G
Shadow.R
Specular.B
Specular.G
Specular.R
Velocity.X
Velocity.Y
depth.Z
realcolor.B
realcolor.G
realcolor.R

Figure 2.18 The EXtractoR dialog box can display all the layers stored in multi-layered OpenEXR files. You can choose which layer to use for which color channel.

After applying the EXtractoR effect, click anywhere in the Channel Info area in the Effect Controls panel to open a dialog box that will allow you to choose which channel of data that you would like to use for each color channel and the alpha channel.

The OpenEXR format is constantly being improved and developed. Currently, it can store up to 49 channels of data. There are so many in Figure 2.18, that they don't even fit on screen at the same time. Perhaps by the time you read this, it will be able to contain even more. For more information on the EXtractoR and IDentifier effects, visit the website of the developer, www.fnordware.com. On this site, they not only have documentation, but downloadable sample OpenEXR files that contain many channels that you can practice with.

The Fog 3D Effect

The Fog 3D effect creates fog that traverses through a scene in 3D space. Again, this effect uses the Z depth information stored in a file to determine where to put the fog. This effect works well at enhancing the realism of a 3D scene, but the lack of quality in the method used to create the fog is a little disappointing.

To see what this puppy does, open up the Fog 3D.aep project from the Chapter 2 folder. Apply the Fog 3D effect to the garage_zoom0170.rpf layer. The default results turn our entire layer white. To see what the Fog 3D effect is trying to do, adjust the Fog Start Depth value to about −150, and the Fog End Depth value to about −300. This sets the range of fog, and everything behind this is also covered in fog. As with other depth-based effects in this chapter, when this effect is selected in the Effect Controls panel, you can click in the Composition panel to have the Z depth of an object displayed in the Info panel.

The default results really aren't very foggy. The only thing I can imagine using this effect for is for an apocalyptic nuclear explosion.

Figure 2.19 The Fog 3D effect after adjusting the fog starting and ending points.

Thankfully, the Fog 3D allows you to use another layer as a gradient for the 3D fog. We're going to use the other layer in this comp, which is a layer of precomposed fractal fog, created with the Fractal Noise effect. It's important that it is precomposed or the Fog 3D effect will not be able to use the textures generated by the Fractal Noise effect.

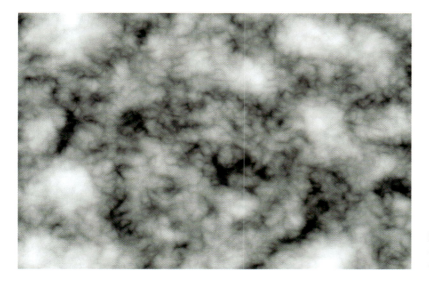

Figure 2.20 The fog pattern created with the Fractal Noise effect.

To use this fractal fog layer as the pattern for our 3D fog, select the PRECOMP fractal noise layer from the Gradient Layer drop down in the Fog 3D effect options in the Effect Controls panel. Make sure the visibility of the fractal fog layer itself is turned off. To blend the layer selected in the Gradient Layer drop down into our for in the Fog 3D effect, increase the Layer Contribution value. I took the Layer Contribution value to 60.

Figure 2.21 After selecting the fractal fog pattern in the Gradient Layer and increasing the Layer Contribution value to 60, we have more believable fog.

One of the things that is making this fog seem so fake is its density. Let's reduce the Fog Opacity value to 25%. This will create a smoky area in the back of the garage, and will look a little more

Figure 2.22 After reducing the Fog Opacity value to 25%, the results are much more believable.

believable than what we've seen with this effect so far. We can also lower the Scattering Density value to make the fog less thick.

The real benefit of the Fog 3D effect is that we can adjust the Z depth of the fog with the Fog Start Depth and Fog End Depth parameters. These properties can also be animated to create the effect of fog rolling in.

Figure 2.23 Here, the Fog Start Depth and Fog End Depth properties have been adjusted to isolate the fog to the outdoors. This would look a lot cooler if we didn't have a bright blue sky in the background, but you get the idea.

The ID Matte Effect

The ID Matte effect can use either object IDs or material IDs to isolate objects, or to remove them. This is helpful if you would like to use one element from an entire scene. In this case, we're going to isolate the car on the left hand side using its object ID. It's quick. It's easy. It beats the heck out of rotoscoping.

Open the 3D.aep project from the Chapter 2 folder. Apply the ID Matte effect to the 3D garage scene. Since this scene was not set up with material IDs (and it was meticulously set up with object IDs), we'll leave the Aux Channel drop down set to Object ID.

With the ID Matte effect selected in the Effect Controls panel, you can click on different objects to isolate them. Or, if you've used the 3D Channel Extract effect to find out an object's ID, you can just type the object ID number into the ID Selection value. I'm going to type in a value of 2, which is the object ID for the yellow car in the front. This isolates the car and removes all other objects.

Figure 2.24 Using the ID Matte effect we can isolate objects, such as this car.

If you wanted to keep the entire garage scene and create a hole where the car is, you can select its object ID, and then select Invert.

Figure 2.25 Selecting Invert will keep the garage scene and remove the car.

You might have noticed some rough edges also. You can increase the Feather value to smooth those out. However, this usually doesn't do the job completely. You'll probably also want to apply an effect like the Simple Choker effect (discussed in Chapter 11) to finish cleaning up those edges.

Figure 2.26 The matte is slightly cleaner with a little bit of edge feathering. Here, I took the Feather value to a modest 1. The results are slightly improved, but nowhere near perfect.

Isolating objects is a great feature of not only the ID Matte effect, but of 3D channels in general. In Figure 2.27, I added some red solids with Gradient Overlay layer styles as a background, painted a shadow, duplicated the car layer to use it as its own reflection, and warped the reflection into place with the Bezier Warp effect (discussed in Chapter 7).

Figure 2.27 Isolating the car allows us to use it as an independent object.

3

THE AUDIO EFFECTS

The Audio effects are meant to be applied to layers with audio. The exception to this is the Tone effect, which actually creates audio and can be applied to any layer, even a solid. There is a smattering of audio tracks included in the Audio folder in the Media folder of the exercise files, if you'd like some practice with these effects. There are a few concepts that are common to many of these effects, so let's look at them briefly before we proceed. Keep in mind that these audio features are not extremely powerful. If you're looking for a more professional audio editing environment, you'll want to use a program like Adobe Audition.

Treble, Bass, and EQ

Audio is created by audio waves at different frequencies. Some of them are low in pitch, like Barry White talking or the pounding of a large, deep drum. These are referred to as bass tones. Some of them are high in pitch, like little children singing or the shrill violin notes from the shower scene in *Psycho*. These tones are generically referred to as treble tones. The range of tones between treble and bass is often referred to as the mids, short for the middle of the range.

Dry and Wet Out

When applying an audio effect to a piece of audio, it's common to use the analogy that we are wetting it; soaking it in effects. So, the audio track on its own is said to be dry. Most audio effects, including several in After Effects, allow you to balance the final mix between the original audio signal, and the audio signal with the effect applied. The original audio signal coming out of the effect is referred to as the "Dry Out", and the effected audio signal coming out of the effect is referred to

Previewing Audio

Remember that you can't preview audio by hitting the spacebar key. If you want to preview video and audio, do a RAM preview by pressing 0 on the numeric keypad. Or, if you just want to preview audio only, you can hit the period key on the numeric keypad. If you're on a laptop, you can still usually access numeric keypad keys by the use of a function key.

as "Wet Out." Think of this like the audio equivalent of opacity. To lower the volume of an applied effect, reduce the Wet Out property, if there is one.

If you've applied an audio effect (such as Backwards) that doesn't have such controls, you can duplicate the audio track and apply the effect to the duplicate, and then balance the Audio Levels property of both layers to achieve the desired balance. If you're applying this effect to the audio on a layer with video, you can duplicate the layer and turn off the visibility of the duplicate.

Left and Right Stereo Channels

Another audio attribute that consistently comes up is that of stereo audio. This refers to audio played in the left channel (or speaker) and in the right channel (or speaker). When an audio clip plays back the exact same audio in both ears, the clip is said to be mono. Most elements in musical recording have some degree of panning applied. Panning is the process of spreading out a sound between the left and right channels. Each instrument can be completely in the left or right channel, or be perfectly mixed between them, or it can be panned to be in one channel more than the others. Having a good stereo mix gives audio tracks a greater degree of realism, as objects in the real world create sounds all around us.

The Backwards Effect

The Backwards effect causes audio tracks to be played backwards. This has the similar sound to grabbing an LP record that is playing, and manually dragging it backwards. This is great for sound effects. Audio clips of snare drums or cymbal crashes with the Backwards effect applied create sweeping swooshes that are great accents for motion graphic elements. There are no properties for the Backwards effect, other than to select Swap Channels, which trades the left channel for the right channel.

The Bass & Treble Effect

The Bass & Treble effect is another very simple audio effect. There are only two parameters: Bass and Treble. You can increase or reduce the volume of low tones using the Bass property. Independently, you can also increase or reduce the volume of high tones using the Treble property. The Parametric EQ effect in this category gives you much more control, but if you're new to working with audio, this effect may be simple enough for you to make the adjustments you need.

The Delay Effect

The Delay effect is a little more complex than what we've looked at so far. The Delay effect creates a repeat of the audio in an audio layer. This effect is useful for creating echoes, or for creating the illusion that audio was recorded in a large, cavernous environment. For a slight audio delay, as if you were talking in a large cathedral for example, it's probably better to use the Reverb effect, discussed later in this chapter.

The Delay Time value determines—in milliseconds—how long the delay is from the original signal. The Delay Amount value determines how loud the first echo is compared to the original signal. The default value of 50% creates an echo that starts off being half as loud as the original audio. Increasing the Feedback property allows some of the echoes to create more echoes. If this get too chaotic, you can reduce this value to create a cleaner delay.

The Flange & Chorus Effect

Flange and chorus are two effects common in the audio world. Although they are different effects, they are created in a similar manner, and so we have access to them both in the Flange & Chorus effect. Both effects are created by creating a slight delay in the audio signal, and duplicating that delay several times. These echoes are referred to as "voices" in this effect.

Flange effects are created by modulating (adjusting) the echo, which usually results in a warbled effect, as if you were a cartoon character saying something underwater. The warbled echo can also be slow and smoother, like the bridge on the Lenny Kravitz song, *Are You Gonna Go My Way*. Chorus is usually a more subtle effect, with the delay only slightly out of phase (usually), which sounds like the audio is being created by multiple sources. You can hear a similar effect in the vocals of songs by The Ramones.

The Voice Separation Time value determines the delay between echoes. Use the Voices value to determine how many echoes are created. The Modulation Rate parameter controls the speed of the warble, while the Modulation Depth controls how much warbling is happening.

If you wanted to create a flange effect with a quick warble (like you were underwater or gargling), try taking up the Modulation Rate value to something like 2 (which creates a faster modulation, or warble), and increase the Modulation Depth value to about 65% (which creates a more intense modulation). To slow the modulation, reduce the Modulation Rate property.

If you wanted to create a chorus-type effect, the first step is to increase the Voices parameter, and then to enable the Stereo Voices checkbox. Selecting Stereo Voices will stagger the voices in each speaker. So, the first voice will play back in the left speaker, the second voice will play back in the right speaker, the third voice in the left speaker, and so on. This goes a long way into creating a realistic chorus effect. Next, I will increase the Voice Separation Time to about 10, then increase the Voices value to about 4, leave Modulation Rate at its default, leave Modulation Depth at its default, and take the Voice Phase Change property to about 90%. This will create a rich chorus effect. Of course, these are just some sample settings. There are many other formulas for creating flange and chorus sounds in the Help, but these are some settings to get you started experimenting with this effect.

The High-Low Pass Effect

The High-Low Pass effect is like a tone filter. It has two modes: high pass and low pass. High pass filters out low (bass) tones, and allows high (treble) tones to pass through. Low pass filters out high tones and allows low bass tones to pass through. The Cutoff Frequency property allows you to fine tune exactly which tones get filtered out, depending on which mode you've selected from the Filter Options drop down.

The High-Low Pass effect is especially good for audio recorded with video. Many times after recording, you might hear a low pitched hum from a generator, or maybe a high-pitched whine from a fan or other device. The High-Low Pass is a great way to eliminate such noise from your audio.

High and Low Pass filters are really helpful in creating realism in sounds. For example, if you had a stock sound effect of the ambience in a night club scene, you might want to apply a low pass filter (by choosing Low Pass from the Filter Options drop down) if the shot takes place outside of the club. If the shot then moves inside of the club, you could animate the Cutoff Frequency property to go from lower to higher. Adding a little Low Pass (and maybe a little High Pass in a separate, additional instance of the effect), can also make sound effects that were recorded close to a microphone (like foley effects) sound like they actually exist in an environment.

The Modulator Effect

The Modulator effect creates an end result similar to flange, but without the additional voices. Without the additional voices, the modulation to audio tone in this effect can create effects ranging from a vibrato, to a more intense tremolo. These effects are reminiscent of the "speed" setting on vintage guitar amplifiers. The important settings in this effect are ones that we've already discussed in the section in this chapter on the Flange & Chorus effect: Modulation Rate (the speed of the modulation) and Modulation Depth (the amount of modulation).

The Parametric EQ Effect

Effects like bass and treble allow you to adjust high and low tones. But what about all the tones in between? And what if there are certain frequencies of the high tones that you want to make louder, and other high frequencies that you want to make quieter? The Parametric EQ effect allows you more control over individual audio frequencies using three different sets, or bands.

Each band gives you precise control over an exact audio frequency. You can adjust up to three bands. To enable a band, select one of the Band checkboxes in the Effect Controls panel. Each band has the same three controls. Frequency specifies which audio frequency you are targeting for that band. The Bandwidth value is almost like feathering the selection. You might want to, say, enhance the volume of the snare drum. You might not know its exact audio frequency. Use the Frequency parameter to make your best guess. Then increase the Bandwidth value to increase the range of values that the band affects. Then, use the Boost/Cut value to increase or decrease the volume of the chosen frequency. The Parametric EQ effect allows you more control over your audio adjustments.

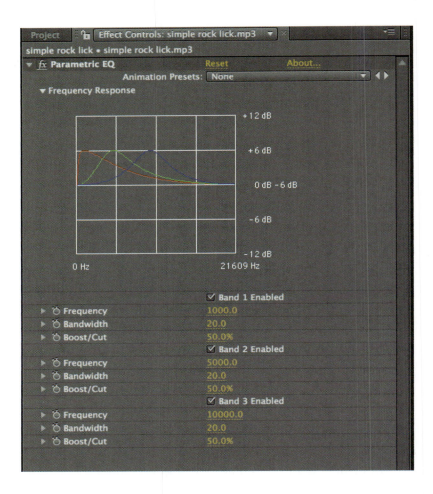

Figure 3.1 The Parametric EQ effect in the Effect Controls panel. Each color represents a different band.

The Reverb Effect

The Reverb effect is one of the most frequently used audio effects in the history of ever, as Spongebob would say. If you've ever heard a song recorded in a recording studio or watched a TV commercial or seen a movie, you've heard an artificially added reverb effect. The purpose of the Reverb effect is to add a slight echo, usually to make audio sound more like it does in real life. In real life, when you speak or play an instrument, the acoustics of the environment (such as walls, or the ceiling) bounce the sound around creating a fullness. Reverb adds that fullness to audio that sounds flat.

The echo added by the Reverb effect is usually much more subtle than the echoes created by the Delay effect. You might think of it this way: If you want the effect to be obvious, use delay. If you want the effect to be imperceptible, use reverb.

The Reverb Time value determines the time (in milliseconds) between the original audio and the echo. Increasing the Diffusion value can create the illusion that the audio was created in a large room. Decay determines how long it takes the echo to fade out. If the sounds takes longer to fade away (which is created by a high Decay value), then it indicates that there is more space in the room. So, a larger Decay value is better for simulating audio in a large space. Brightness refers to the treble values in the echoes. Increase the Brightness value to brighten the reverberating sound.

Reverb is a great effect for blending audio. In the same way that we adjust color to aid in compositing when combining visual elements, it's important to make sure that audio tracks that are supposed to exist in the same scene have the same amount of reverb. This is particularly important when using overdubs from actors in movies.

The Stereo Mixer Effect

The Stereo Mixer effect is the tool to use if you need control over the channels in a piece of audio. This effect gives you control over the volume (level) of the left and right channel independently. Because this effect allows you to adjust volume in terms of percent (instead of by decibels, as in the Timeline panel), it might be more intuitive for audio amateurs to use this effect for basic audio adjustments.

The Stereo Mixer effect also allows you to change the panning for each channel. If you're experiencing any weird audio anomalies because of this effect, you can probably fix it by enabling the Invert Phase checkbox, which ensures that the redistributed audio frequencies don't clash with each other.

The Left Pan control controls what is happening with sound that is panned to the left (similar to the Right Pan panned to the right). By default, Left Pan is panned to −100%, which is all the way left. Right Pan is a positive 100%, which is all the way right. Note that these properties can be animated. To animate the sound of a helicopter going from left to right through a scene for example, you might take the Right Pan value down to 0 (which centers the balance of the right channel), or even all the way down to −100% (which takes the content of the right channel and places it all the way to the left in the stereo spectrum). You can then animate the Left Pan and Right Pan values to be positive later on in the composition. This will cause the sound to go from left to right, creating the illusion that sound is traveling from left to right. Little touches like this can really sell a shot.

The Tone Effect

The Tone effect generates audio tones. It actually makes sounds from scratch. The Tone effect is the only effect in the Audio effect category that does so. You can even apply this effect to a solid layer to create audio on it.

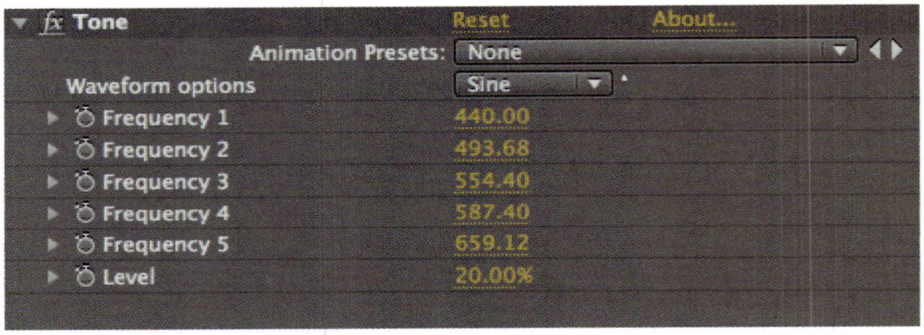

Figure 3.2 The Tone effect in the Effect Controls panel.

The problem with the Tone effect is that it's almost impossible to use. You can select an exact frequency to be played by five different frequency generators in this effect. If you know music and audio frequencies well, you can set these to play a chord. But honestly, it would probably be easier (and faster) to walk away from your computer, learn to play a musical instrument, go to a recording studio, and record yourself playing that chord, than it would be to get the Tone effect to play it correctly. I'm only slightly exaggerating.

So why use it? I actually do use this effect on occasion. Sometimes, I'll have issues playing back audio. I'll apply the Tone effect to a new solid in a new comp to see if the problem is with the audio I've imported, or with my audio hardware configuration preferences.

The great benefit to this effect is that Adobe has included some great animation presets for this effect. You can access these from Adobe Bridge, or from the Animation Presets drop down at the top of the Effect Controls panel. Figure 3.3 shows the list of included presets. The presets are mostly phone related, including a dial tone, dialing, and a busy signal. There's also a sweet laser blaster.

Synth Ramp Up

After Effects legend and expressions genius Dan Ebberts (who, coincidently, did the tech edit for both editions of this book) gave me this sweet little formula for a cool analog synth-sounding wind up. First set the Waveform Options in the Tone effect to Saw. Then take Frequency 4 and Frequency 5 down to 0. Then, for Frequency 3, add this expression: effect("Tone") ("Frequency 1")*1.005. For Frequency 2, add this expression: effect("Tone") ("Frequency 1")*.995. Finally, animate the value of Frequency 1 from 10 to 600 over the course of about 6 seconds. Sounds like the beginning of a 1983 Van Halen concert. Brilliant work, Dan!

And if you ever needed a quick retro laser blast or "fail" tone, just take the Waveform options drop down to Square, zero out each frequency from 2 to 5, and take Frequency 1 down to about 80. Make it a short pulse by animating the Level parameter from whatever volume you want, down to 0. It sounds like an old Atari game from right inside After Effects!

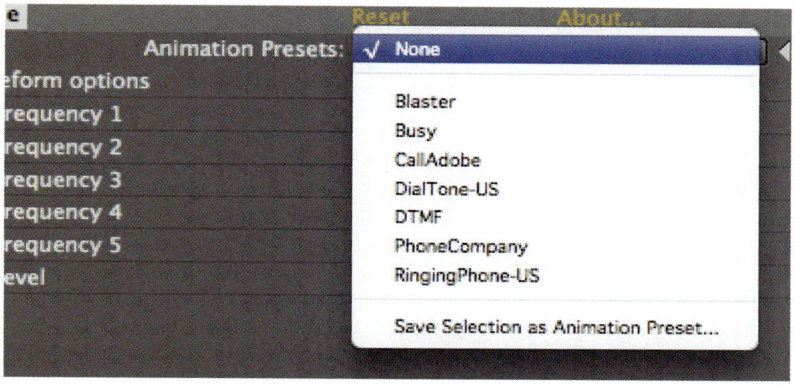

Figure 3.3 The animation presets for the Tone effect that are included with After Effects.

Other Locations for Presets

Instead of choosing these presets from the Effect Controls panel after applying the Tone effect, you can choose them right from the Effects & Presets panel (as long as you've enabled Show Animation Presets from the panel flyout menu). When applying presets in this way, you don't even need to apply the effect first—just apply the animation preset to the layer and it's already applied for you. In this case, the Tone presets are found in the Sound Effects category of the Animation Presets.

4

THE BLUR & SHARPEN EFFECTS

The effects in the Blur & Sharpen category all soften (blur) an image, or make it more crisp and detailed (sharpen). There is a little skew in the balance here, as only 2 of the 13 effects in this category deal with sharpening (and only one of those is any good). The remainder all apply some degree of blur.

Blurring is useful in After Effects for a whole host of reasons. It can soften an image, or parts of an image to create a focal point for the viewer. Blurs are frequently used with motion graphics to create wispy or glowing elements. Blurring is also commonly used with particle effects such as Particle Playground or Radio Waves, when creating objects like snowflakes or glowing sparkles. Blur can be used in compositing, as when you're trying to composite something very pristine (such as objects rendered from a 3D program) with something a little more rough (like live action footage). Blurs (particularly motion blur and the Directional Blur effect) can be used to simulate and suggest motion. Blurs can also be used to smooth out textures that are to be used as maps to control effect properties. And these are only a few of the many things that blurs can be used for. Because there is such a diversity of purpose, it makes sense that there are 11 different blur effects in After Effects. No matter what you use After Effects for, chances are being a master of these blur effects will help.

The Bilateral Blur Effect

The Bilateral Blur effect, introduced in After Effects CS4, is a unique blurring effect. It is similar to the Smart Blur effect that has been in After Effects for a while. Both blur effects attempt to keep edges crisp while blurring surface details, which is also similar to the way that the Surface Blur filter works in Photoshop. But the Bilateral Blur effect allows a slight amount of edge blur, which creates a real dreamy appearance that still appears natural. Like the Smart Blur effect, Bilateral Blur can also be used to smooth out compression artifacts and other surfaces, while keeping edges sharp. Also, contrary to its intimidating name, it's a very simple effect to use and master.

Open the Bilateral Blur.aep project from the Chapter 4 folder of the exercise files. This project contains a photo I took of a ferry in Seattle.

Figure 4.1 The ferry image from the Bilateral Blur.aep project. Interesting fact: this is the first photo that I took that I actually liked.

Apply the Bilateral Blur effect to the ferry image layer. Thankfully, the defaults for this effect have changed to enable Colorize. But if it gets turned off, you'll have a grayscale image, as seen in Figure 4.2.

Figure 4.2 The results of the Bilateral Blur effect with the Colorize check box unchecked.

The Bilateral Blur effect adds an interesting misty effect. The effects are particularly noticeable in the details (or, lack of them) in the clouds.

Figure 4.3 After selecting the Colorize option, the color in the image returns.

The default results create a misty, dreamlike haze over our image. This is great for ethereal dream sequences, or for simulating fog. If we reduce the Radius value, we reduce the amount of blur. Let's take the Radius value to 5. This eliminates the overall hazy look, and just blurs surface textures. You'll notice the grungy texture of the side of the ferry clean up quite a bit, while the edges around the ferry windows remain sharp. Unfortunately, you'll also probably notice how this effect takes forever and a day to render! You'll have to weigh the benefit of the effect's results with the lengthy render time to determine if this effect will work for you.

We know that the Bilateral Blur effect mostly blurs surfaces, while leaving edges intact. But what qualifies as an edge? The Threshold parameter specifies what surfaces are considered edges. For a more blurry image, increase the Threshold value. To keep the images on small details, lower the Threshold value. Using a lowered Radius value of 10 (which localizes the blur) and an increased Threshold value of 10 (which preserves fine details), we get a cartoon-like stylized effect. I actually prefer these results to many of the results from the actual Cartoon effect.

Figure 4.4 After reducing the Radius value to 5, the blur becomes more localized.

Figure 4.5 The image with a Radius value of 10 and a Threshold value of 10. The boat looks especially cartoonish.

As we're seeing, the Bilateral Blur effect has more looks than Derek Zoolander. We've previously covered the Radius parameter, which can blur the colors of layers, while keeping edges intact. We get an edgy desaturated look when we set the Threshold value at 15, and take the Radius value to a ridiculously high value of 2000. Who would've thought that we could create more intensity with a blur effect?

Figure 4.6 The result of setting Radius to 2000 and Threshold to 15.

Sometimes, with "unusual" blur effects such as Bilateral Blur and Smart Blur, it is helpful to compare the results to those of other blur effects. First, let's take a look at this same image blurred with the Fast Blur effect. Take particular notice of what is happening to the edges. Blur effects like Fast Blur universally blur every pixel the same amount, so the edge details are immediately lost.

Figure 4.7 The same image blurred with the Fast Blur effect, with a Blurriness value of 7.

Finally, let's look at this same example blurred by the Smart Blur effect, which is closely related to the Bilateral Blur effect. Notice how the results seem more stylized and artificial than what we've seen with the Bilateral Blur effect.

Figure 4.8 The same image blurred with the Smart Blur effect.

The Box Blur Effect

The Box Blur effect is perhaps the most advanced of the standard blur effects (e.g., Fast Blur and Gaussian Blur). This effect gets its name because all pixels within the Blur Radius get equal weighting, as opposed to something like Gaussian Blur, where each neighboring pixel gets a unique weighting. This basically just means that the blur calculates faster. And as we'll see, this effect can actually achieve smoother results than Fast Blur or Gaussian Blur as well.

Open the Box Blur.aep project from the Chapter 4 folder of the exercise files. This project contains a comp with a simple shape layer that will help us to see what's really happening with the Box Blur effect. Then we'll look at another example of the Box Blur effect using a comp in this project that contains a still image. First, go to the shape layer comp and apply the Box Blur effect to the shape layer.

The default settings of the Box Blur effect don't do very much. Increase the amount of blur by increasing the Blur Radius parameter. If you take this value to small amounts (<5), the blur will seem somewhat similar to a generic blur. Take the Blur Radius value to 50 to see the boxiness of this blur effect.

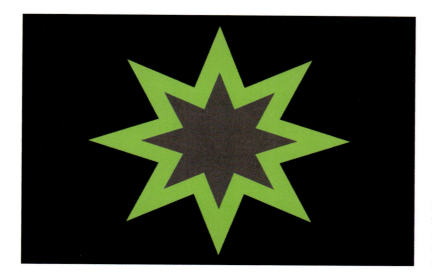

Figure 4.9 The shape layer in the Box Blur.aep project. This simple example will help us to see what the Box Blur effect is doing.

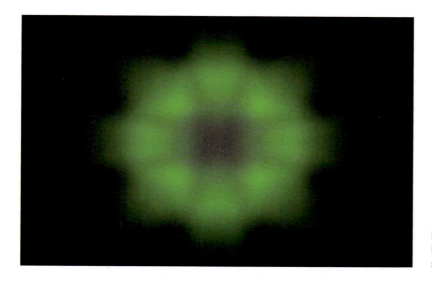

Figure 4.10 Taking the Blur Radius value to 50 allows you to see the boxy results of the blur.

This type of boxy blur can create interesting results with motion graphics. But what if you wanted a smoother blur? One of the paradoxes of the Box Blur effect is that it can create blurs that are both boxier and smoother than standard blur effects like Fast Blur and Gaussian Blur. This is all thanks to the Iterations parameter, which determines how many copies of this blur is applied to the layer. So, if we use an Iterations value of 3, it would be like duplicating the effect three times. This creates a very smooth blur.

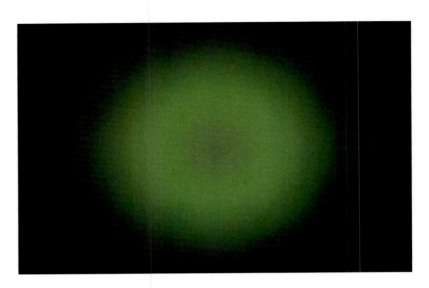

Figure 4.11 The result of taking the Iterations to 3.

Next, let's see what the Box Blur effect looks like on an image. Hop on over to the not intimidated comp, which contains a photo of my daughter going toe to toe with a llama. She really has no fear of animals, even ones 10 times her size.

Figure 4.12 The not intimidated comp.

Apply the Box Blur effect to this layer. The boxy results of the effect are much more difficult to see when applied to actual footage. But the Box Blur effect does create a signature halo around objects. This could be great for creating a dazed and confused POV shot.

Just by way of comparison, I'm going to apply the Fast Blur effect to this layer (making sure to turn off the visibility of the Box Blur effect). I'm also going to take the Blurriness value to 25.

Figure 4.13 I took the Blur Radius value to 25 here. I've zoomed in so you can more clearly see the details.

Notice that the halo created by the Box Blur effect is much more pronounced. The Fast Blur effect smoothes out the blur results more. There isn't a right or wrong way to blur, just different methods that you might prefer in different circumstances.

Figure 4.14 The results of applying the Fast Blur effect with the Blurriness value at 25.

Horizontal and Vertical Blur

Many blur effects in After Effects have a Blur Dimensions drop down that allows you to create only horizontal or only vertical blur. This creates the illusion that the object is moving left and right (horizontal) or up and down (vertical). If you want more control over the precise direction of the blur, use the Directional Blur effect.

The nature of the Box Blur effect creates the most unique results when isolating the blur to a specific dimensions. In Figure 4.15, I took the Blur Radius value to 30, left the default Iterations value at 1, and changed the Blur Dimensions drop down to Horizontal. This only creates blur along the X axis (left and right).

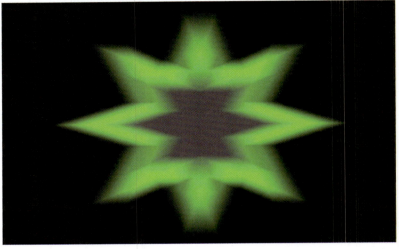

Figure 4.15 The results of changing the Blur Dimensions value to Horizontal.

If we changed the Blur Dimensions value to Vertical, the blur would be along the Y axis (up and down). Again, notice the way that the Box Blur effect makes a boxy blur. This causes the edges of the star to overlap, creating new geometric patterns. You could not achieve this boxy result with other blur effects, although you can alter the blur dimensions in other effects.

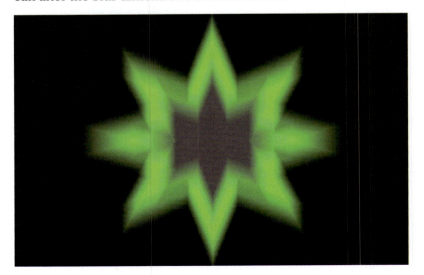

Figure 4.16 The results of changing the Blur Dimensions value to Vertical.

The Camera Lens Blur Effect

The Camera Lens Blur effect is an upgrade from the venerable Lens Blur effect, and is the most powerful and complex of all effects in this chapter. It can be viewed as a cross between the 3D Channel effect, Depth of Field, and Compound Blur. I use this effect because its style of blur resembles true camera blur much more than any other blur effect, especially the way it causes highlights to bloom.

Figure 4.17 shows a clip that I shot that just didn't turn out the way I wanted it to. The colors all kind of blend together, and the subject doesn't really pop. I also spent a lot of time trying to make the background beautiful with all of the glass, mirrors, lights, and reflections in the background. But it just fell flat. You can find this clip and the accompanying project in the Camera Lens Blur.aep project in the Chapter 4 folder of the exercise files.

Figure 4.17 The original shot. Swing and a miss.

So, I did some initial color correction, made some selective adjustments using masks, and I like this much better now. However, the background still doesn't have the magical quality that I was looking for.

What's missing here is more separation between subject and background. In times past, I might have grabbed for the Fast Blur effect (or something similar). But if we apply Fast Blur (to the CAMERA BLUR ADJ LAYER layer—which already has a rough background mask created for you), taking the Blurriness value to about 15 pixels, we do get more separation between the girl and the bottles, but it still falls flat and doesn't have the same realism that would be there if we shot this with a shallow depth of field.

No, this won't work. What this is missing is bokeh, which is a common term for the blooms created in camera by blurry highlights. Bokeh is just magical—in motion graphics and visual

Figure 4.18 The image after some light correction. Background still sucks though.

Figure 4.19 Applying Fast Blur to the background isn't going to get us there.

effects. It's like fog and backlighting in cinematography, or magic wands in Harry Potter land, or pizza to elementary school parties. It just makes everything better.

So, I'm going to delete the Fast Blur effect and apply the Camera Lens Blur effect. The default settings here can be pretty mild, so let's turn up the Blur Radius value to 15. Ooh. That's interesting. We're now seeing some of that beautiful bokeh in the bottles in the background. To make that pop even more, I'm going to increase the Gain value (in the Highlight section) to 60. To increase the amount of stuff that gets that "pop" applied to it, I'm going to decrease the Threshold value to 120 (assuming that, like me, your current project is in 8 bpc mode). These settings are very strong so that you can see them noticeably in Figure 4.20. You may want to dial them back a little to taste. Note that you can also increase the Highlight>Saturation value if you'd like more color in your bokeh.

But all in all, this is amazing. Fast Blur (and other blurs) have a tendency to wash out highlights which, again, is not how things work in a camera. And also, as you increase the blur, the edges of the bokeh (the highlight blooms) will still remain sharp, as they do when recorded with real world optics.

Figure 4.20 Those little hexagons are called bokeh. Notice the realistic way that the blooms overlap each other.

By default, the shape of the bokeh is a hexagon. But you can change this to triangles, diamonds (squares), or other shapes by changing the Shape drop down value in the Iris Properties section. I don't have extremely expensive lenses, and the shape of the bokeh is determined by the components of the lens. So most of my lenses just make circles, as opposed to other shapes. In order to make this lens blur to composite better with footage I've shot, I change the Shape value to Decagon, which creates round blooms in the highlights, just what I'm used to from my camera

Figure 4.21 The final image with round (decagonal) highlights. I'll take it.

and lenses. Now my image looks significantly more beautiful than it did initially, the subject just pops of the screen, and the background is all sparkly and beautiful.

The Camera Lens Blur effect also allows you to create blurred areas on a layer based on the grayscale values of another layer (like Compound Blur). But the controls are based on camera terminology (like depth of field). If you are interested in using depth of field to tell your stories (and who isn't?), then you may find the Camera Lens Blur effect the most efficient and flexible way to do that.

I'm going to import the KS103.mov clip from the Artbeats folder in the Media folder in the exercise files.

Figure 4.22 The KS103.mov Artbeats clip.

Next, I'm going to duplicate this layer and double click it to open it in the Layer panel. I'm then going to paint a depth map using grayscale values. I'm going to paint the objects furthest away with black, the kids in the middle with 50% gray, and the part of the image closest to the camera in white. It doesn't have to be pretty or accurate. You'll then need to precompose this layer so that it can be used as a map by the Camera Lens Blur effect. Once you've precomposed this layer, turn off its visibility. As is usually the case with maps, they do not need to be visible to be used as maps, and it's usually preferable that they are not seen.

Now apply the Camera Lens Blur effect to the unpainted layer of the kids in the Artbeats clip. Change the Depth Map Layer drop

Figure 4.23 The depth map I painted in After Effects.

down to the nested comp that you painted the depth map on. The default results don't give us what we want, but you can still see how we've created natural looking depth of field from scratch.

Figure 4.24 After changing the Depth Map Layer to the depth map we painted, we have realistic lens blur.

The Camera Lens Blur effect kept the areas sharp where we painted black, and blurred the bright areas. If you're looking for the opposite results, you can check the Invert Depth Map value in the Effect Controls panel. This will change the way that the map is interpreted, making the bright areas crisp and the dark areas blurry.

Figure 4.25 The result of choosing Invert Depth Map.

These results look spectacular, but this isn't what we're looking for here. This footage is not about grass or trees—it's about kids. Won't someone please think about the children? The way that we shift the focus through this image is by adjusting the Blur Focal Distance parameter. And truthfully, it is the Blur Focal Distance property that really makes this effect so powerful. I deselected the Invert Depth Map option, and took the Blur Focal Distance value to about 0.53. This leaves the children in focus, and blurs the foreground and background.

Figure 4.26 By adjusting the Blur Focal Distance, we can adjust the depth of the area that is in focus.

These results are nothing short of spectacular, especially considering how easy it was to set this project up. But the real power here is in the ability of the Camera Lens Blur effect to animate the Blur Focal Distance property. This can create shifts in the focal plane that are animated, the same way a camera's lens might shift. This effect cannot be created with the Compound Blur effect. The Camera Lens Blur (which, again, is also now found for the most part in the controls of AE cameras) is simply one of the greatest tools in After Effects for creating photorealistic optical blur.

The Channel Blur Effect

The Channel Blur effect is really useful, and for multiple purposes. First, we'll examine how to use it creatively, then we'll use it for a great utilitarian purpose.

Open the Channel Blur.aep project from the Chapter 4 folder. We're going to start out in the Static Logo for AE comp. This comp contains a logo I created in Adobe Illustrator. Apply the Channel Blur effect to the Bkgrd layer. The isolated Bkgrd layer is seen in Figure 4.27.

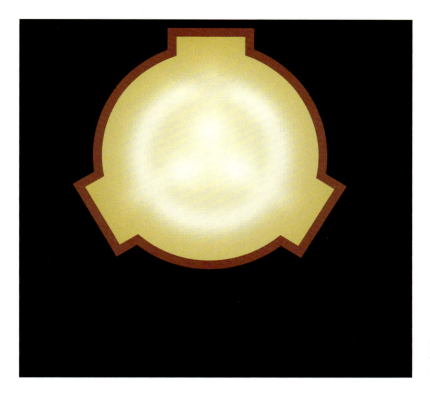

Figure 4.27 The Bkgrd layer in the Static Logo comp. Apply the Channel Blur effect to this layer.

Blurring the Composition Channels

You might have noticed that even though the red in the Background layer was blurred, the red in the text remained crisp. You could blur it by applying the Channel Blur effect to the text layer. Or, you can create an adjustment layer, then apply the Channel Blur effect to the adjustment layer. Then, all of the changes that you make to the effect will adjust the composite color and alpha channels of the entire composition.

The Channel Blur effect is easy to understand, although its practical uses may not be as readily apparent. This effect can individually blur each channel—red, green, blue, and also the alpha channel. Increase the Red Blurriness value, for example, to blur only the red channel. This creates some interesting color variations. In Figure 4.28, I took the Red Blurriness value to 100. This dissipates the red in the image, and seems to add green to the result as more cyan is added on top of the yellow background. Note that in this figure, all of the logo elements have their visibility turned back on, and the blur is only applied to the background layer seen in Figure 4.27.

Figure 4.28 The result of increasing the Red Blurriness value to 100.

Likewise, having a Green Blurriness value of 100 blurs the green, which in effect, adds magenta.

One of the most unique aspects of this effect is that you can also use it to blur the edges of a layer's alpha channel using the Alpha Blurriness property. This creates a soft transparency around the outer edges. In this example, the added transparency creates a dark falloff effect that adds to the feel of the piece.

Figure 4.29 The result of increasing the Green Blurriness value to 100.

Figure 4.30 Increasing the Alpha Blurriness to 100. This reduces opacity, but it only fades the edges of the layer.

I'm going to create a new solid behind the Bkgrd layer and apply the Checkerboard effect (discussed in Chapter 9). Now it might be easier to see the effects of the Alpha Blurriness parameter.

Figure 4.31 After creating a textured background, the results of the Alpha Blurriness property are more clearly visible.

Now that we've seen the Channel Blur in action for creative purposes, let's turn our attention to using the Channel Blur effect for a more practical purpose. Switch over to the paavo balancing comp. This comp contains some green screen footage that has been severely compressed.

Figure 4.32 The footage in the paavo balancing comp.

In the case of most video, noise is stored in the blue channel. To see the various color channels separately, click the lengthily named Show Channel and Color Management Settings drop down at the bottom of the Composition panel. Its icon looks like a little Venn diagram, with three interlocking circles.

Figure 4.33 View channels independently by changing the options here, in the Show Channel and Color Management Settings drop down at the bottom of the Composition panel.

From the Show Channel and Color Management Settings drop down, I'm going to change the value from RGB (which is the default composite view of all color channels with alpha) to Green. This will show us a visual readout of the green light used to make this image. I'm going to also zoom in to about 800% so that we can get a better look at the noise and compression artifacts in this channel.

Figure 4.34 The green channel of the paavo balancing layer.

The green channel looks pretty clean. Now let's change the view to the blue channel and see the difference.

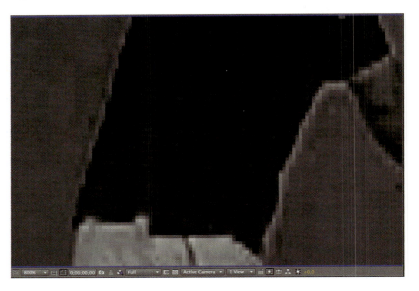

Figure 4.35 The blue channel of the paavo balancing layer. Yuck.

Wow. What a difference in the two channels! The green channel is mostly clean, and the blue channel is extremely noisy. We can use the Channel Blur effect to smooth out the blue channel only, which will result in a cleaner end composite. And as long as we're at least fairly conservative in our channel blurring, the results in the composite should still look sharp.

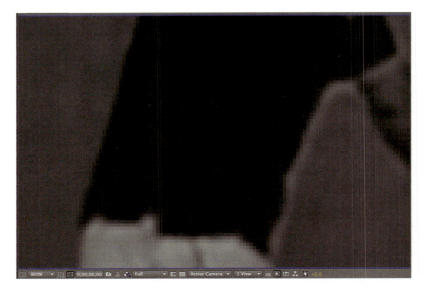

Figure 4.36 The blue channel after being cleaned up by the Channel Blur effect.

Apply the Channel Blur effect to the paavo balancing layer. Take the Blue Blurriness to 2. This will clean up the ugliness in this channel significantly.

At this point, you might be worried about the crispness of our final composite. After all, this was a pretty obvious blur. However, if you're only blurring 1 or 2 channels conservatively, it's enough to remove noise while maintaining quality. Change the value in the Show Channels and Color Management Settings drop down back to RGB to see the composite result of all channels.

Figure 4.37 The final result is still crisp, even after blurring the blue channel. Image shown here at 200%.

The Compound Blur Effect

The Compound Blur effect blurs a layer based on the luminance of another layer. In Chapter 23, we'll look a little closer at using layers as maps to control effect properties. If you're unfamiliar with this concept, the Compound Blur effect is the best place to start.

Open the Compound Blur.aep project from the Chapter 4 folder of the exercise files. The comp we'll be working with here is the Lioness with map comp.

Aside from this lioness photo, this comp also contains two grayscale layers that we'll use as controllers to determine where the lioness layer will be blurred. First we'll look at the layer called blur map. This is a grayscale map that I painted in Photoshop, based on the lioness image. Notice how I painted with white

Figure 4.38 The lioness image in the Lioness with map comp.

where the face of the lioness is, black in the background, and with different shades of gray around the body of the lioness. I realize that it looks really rough, but when using maps to control layer properties, you typically want them soft and free of small details.

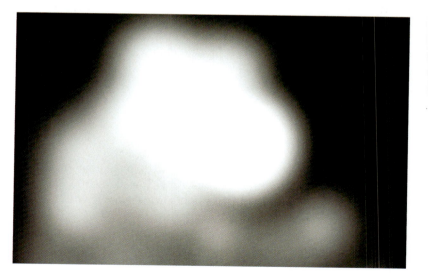

Figure 4.39 The blur map layer that I painted in Photoshop.

Apply the Compound Blur effect to the Lioness layer. The default results resemble a bad Photoshop filter. This is because the Compound Blur effect needs to be controlled by the gray-scale values of a layer in order to work. By default, the effect uses the layer it was applied to as a map to determine how to blur it.

Figure 4.40 The default results of applying the Compound Blur effect.

Change the Blur layer selection to the blur map layer. This will use the luminance values of the blur map layer to control the areas of the Lioness layer that will have blur applied to them. Note that layers used as controllers (i.e., in the Blur layer drop down) do not need to be visible to be used as the Blur layer. In this case, selecting the blur map layer gives us the opposite of the results we were looking for. The face of the Lioness is blurred, and the background remains sharp.

Figure 4.41 Using the blur map layer as the Blur layer in the Compound Blur effect blurs the face of the lioness, but does not blur the background.

The good news is that most effects that use grayscale maps as controllers have a fix for problems like this. Click the Invert Blur checkbox to change the rules. Now, the dark areas on the map will correspond to blurry areas on the Lioness layer. Bright areas will correspond to areas less affected by the blur.

Figure 4.42 After selecting Invert Blur, the blur is inverted.

The results are getting close now that our map is setup properly. However, the default Maximum Blur value of 20 is just too much blur in this case. So, let's complete this look by reducing the Maximum Blur (blur amount) value to 7.

Figure 4.43 Our final results look much better with the Maximum Blur level lowered to 7.

There is another layer in this comp that I want to try out as a Blur layer here. This is a fiery grayscale pattern created with the Fractal Noise effect (discussed in Chapter 11).

Figure 4.44 The Fractal Noise comp layer in the Lioness with map comp.

When we apply this fiery noise layer as the Blur layer, the luminance of the fire pattern is used to control where (and how much) blur is applied to the layer. This creates a more interesting pattern when the Maximum Blur value is increased to 100. Note that this fractal fire pattern animates. Preview this comp to see the blur pattern move around as the fractal fire pattern changes.

Figure 4.45 Applying the Fractal Noise comp as an animated Blur layer, with the Maximum Blur value set to 100.

You could use such maps to create shockwave-type blur effects, or the wavy distortion that appears over flames.

The Directional Blur Effect

Like the horizontal and vertical blurs we looked at earlier in this chapter, the Directional Blur effect allows you to blur pixels at an angle. The difference is that the Directional Blur effect allows you to specify exactly which angle that is. This effect is similar to the Motion Blur effect in Photoshop. This effect is usually used to simulate or suggest motion.

Open the Directional Blur.aep project from the Chapter 4 folder of the exercise files. This project contains a comp with a rocket image I created in 3DS Max.

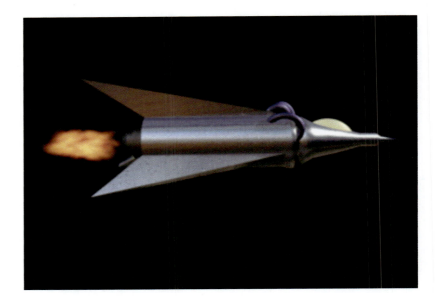

Figure 4.46 The rocket image from the Directional Blur.aep project.

Apply the Directional Blur effect to the ROCKET tiny.tga layer. There are only two properties in this effect. The Blur Length parameter determines the size (distance) of the blur, and the Direction parameter determines the angle of the blur. I'm going to start out taking the Blur Length value to 40. The default Direction value causes a vertical blur.

We can get a similar result from many blur effects. The real power with the Directional Blur effect is that we can specify the exact angle of blur. Take the Direction value to 40 degrees, which is something other blur effects can't do.

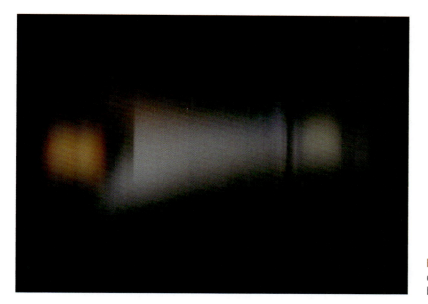

Figure 4.47 With a blur length of 40, we can see the vertical blur here.

Figure 4.48 The Directional Blur options and results. Notice that the notch on the Direction controller displays the angle of the blur.

This effect would look much better if it were underneath a copy of this layer that did not have the effect applied to it (which will only work because the object has an alpha channel that isolates the subject). Most of the time when I use the Directional Blur effect, I use it on copies of a layer that are beneath it in the layer stack in the Timeline panel. So, I'll duplicate this layer by selecting it in the Timeline panel and pressing Ctrl+D(Win)/Cmd+D(Mac). Then, I will remove (delete) the effect from the copy on top. Then, I might change the angle to about 85, so it looks like it's horizontal, but slightly tilted upwards on the right-hand side. Then, I'll move the blurred layer to the left a little bit. Finally, I'll reduce the

Opacity value on the blurred rocket layer to about 60%. All of these steps create the illusion that the rocket is moving.

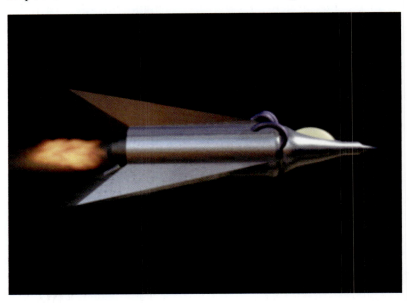

Figure 4.49 The result of duplicating the rocket layer and adjusting the blurry rocket on the bottom.

The effect here is quite subtle. For a more intense, "warping through time" effect, increase the Opacity value of the blurred rocket layer back to 100%, and drag it on top of the rocket without the blur to reorder the layers in the Timeline panel.

Figure 4.50 Placing the blur on top creates a more intense effect.

Even if you're not recreating objects in motion, you can still use the Directional Blur effect to add pizzazz to text, logos, and other graphic elements. Figure 4.51 contains a logo that is similar to something that we'll be creating in Chapter 17.

Figure 4.51 The Directional Blur effect applied to the copies in the background helps to enhance our logo here.

The Fast Blur Effect

The Fast Blur effect is probably the blur effect that I turn to most often. It renders incredibly fast (hence the name), and it is a simple, predictable blur. It's great for everything from softening particles to adding a bit of soft defocus to background elements (although for realistic camera blur, the Camera Lens Blur effect is your best bet, if you have the extra render time for it). As an added bonus, it also functions at 32 bits per channel.

I think (and hope) it's fairly apparent at this point in the chapter what blur does. So, I want to show you how to set up HDR (High Dynamic Range) text that can be blurred with the Fast Blur effect.

Let's start by going to File>New>New Project. Then click the Create a new composition button at the bottom of the Project panel to create a new composition. Use the NTSC DV preset and click OK. Next, press the finger-tangling keyboard shortcut Ctrl+Alt+Shift+T(Win)/Cmd+Opt+Shift+T(Mac) to create a new text layer and place the cursor in the center of the composition. Now type your name. With the text selected (highlighted), increase the size of your text in the Character panel. Also in the Character panel, click the upper left swatch and choose a white color for your text. White is created by using the value 255 for the red, green, and blue channels. You can use the font of your choice. When you've completed your adjustments, accept your changes by selecting the Selection tool in the toolbar, or by pressing Enter on the numeric keypad.

Figure 4.52 My white text thus far.

Next, apply the Fast Blur effect. As you can see, it's another simple effect. We can control the amount of blur with the Blurriness parameter. We can also change the blur dimensions as we talked about earlier in this chapter. Taking the Blurriness value to about 20, we see the expected results.

Figure 4.53 Our text, blurred with the Fast Blur effect.

Now we want to turn this into HDR text. To do that, we must be working in a project that operates at 32 bits per channel. To change my project over, I'm going to go to the bottom of the Project panel. In the area that displays 8 bpc, Alt(Win)/Opt(Mac) click this twice, until it displays 32 bpc.

This puts our project into 32 bits per channel mode, which allows for HDR color. HDR color allows us to create whites that are whiter than white and blacks that are blacker than black. With our project in 32 bpc mode, go back to the Character panel. Click the Fill Color swatch in the Character panel to open the Text Color dialog. In 32 bpc mode, white is created by a value of 1 for the red, green, and blue channels.

Figure 4.54 Alt/Opt click this display at the bottom of the Project panel until it displays 32 bpc.

Note that you're able to change the way colors are displayed throughout After Effects by going to the flyout menu of the Info panel and choosing a different color display format. Many colorists and compositors choose to change this option in the Info panel flyout to Decimal, even when working in 8 bpc mode. So then, you'll only have this "0-1" color model working for you if Auto Color Display or Decimal is chosen as the color display format from the Info panel flyout menu.

Figure 4.55 In 32 bpc mode, white is created by a value of 1, instead of 255.

The magic of this HDR stuff is that we can now take these values above white; whiter than white. You will see the value of this momentarily. For now, take the Red value to 3, leave the Green value at 1, and take the Blue value to 2. This is like adding more intense white light from the red and blue channels. Because the Fast Blur effect processes in 32 bits per channel, it responds to this extra light, and blurs accordingly. The results behave more like light does in the real world.

Figure 4.56 Blurring our HDR text with Fast Blur creates a realistic lighting effect.

The Repeat Edge Pixels Option

Earlier in this chapter, we looked at the Blur Dimensions property that several blur effects have. Many blur effects in After Effects also have a Repeat Edge Pixels option, which is also quite helpful.

When blurring layers, the edges will also blur, which creates transparency in the edges. I'm going to import the beautiful baby. tif file from the Images folder in the Media folder of the exercise files.

When I blur this image with Fast Blur, the edges become blurred and transparent, showing through to the layers beneath.

Figure 4.57 The beautiful baby .tif image.

Figure 4.58 shows the result of blurring the beautiful baby image with the Fast Blur effect. I placed a checkerboard pattern behind the image so you can see where the transparency is created.

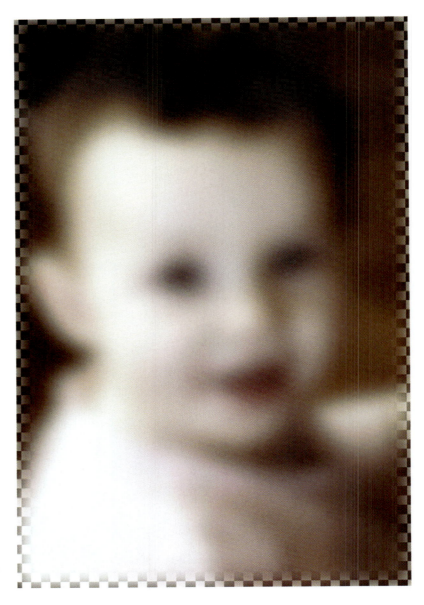

Figure 4.58 When an entire layer is blurred, the edges are usually blurred as well, creating transparency.

If we select the Repeat Edge Pixels option, the pixels on the edge will be allowed to be blurry, but not transparent. However, it should be noted that enabling this option does prevent the blur from going outside of the layer boundaries, which could cause obvious, hard edges.

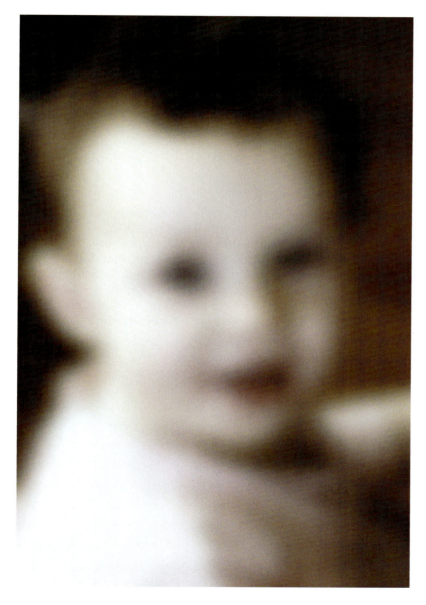

Figure 4.59 With the Repeat Edge Pixels option selected, the edges of the layer are duplicated so that there is no transparency at the edges.

The Gaussian Blur Effect

Those of you familiar with Photoshop probably have a special reverence in your heart for the Gaussian Blur filter. For many years, it was the only way to control how much blur you added to a layer. Because of this, After Effects users that started out as

Photoshop users often come first to the Gaussian Blur effect. However, in After Effects, the Gaussian Blur effect is exactly the same thing as the Fast Blur effect, except for one major difference. The Gaussian Blur effect does not have the Repeat Edge Pixels option that we just looked at. I hate to break your heart (and loyalties) Photoshop users, but the Fast Blur effect makes the Gaussian Blur effect obsolete—in After Effects, anyway. It also seems like the Fast Blur effect renders a bit faster (with the same level of quality) on top of that.

The Radial Blur Effect

The Radial Blur effect is one of my favorites. It can take boring textures and make them spring to life. This effect also functions similarly to the filter of the same name in Photoshop.

The Radial Blur effect has two very distinct blur modes: Spin and Zoom. Let's look first at the default Spin blur. Open up the Radial Blur.aep project from the Chapter 4 folder. This project contains a pattern I created using Fractal Noise (from Chapter 11), the Levels effect (from Chapter 6), and Glow (from Chapter 17).

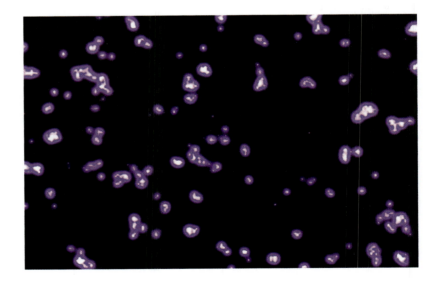

Figure 4.60 The texture from the Radial Blur.aep project.

Apply the Radial Blur effect. The default settings apply a spin blur. This creates a circular (i.e., radial) blur around the edges. It reminds me of what a freeze frame from video of this texture in a dryer might look like.

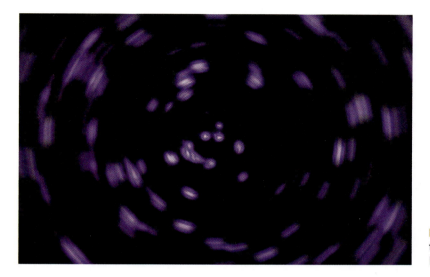

Figure 4.61 The Fractal Noise texture after applying Radial Blur at the default settings.

The first change I'd like to make here is to change the Antialiasing setting at the bottom of the effect in the Effect Controls panel. Change it from its default Low to High. This will help smooth out a little of the nasty little bits of noise that we often get with this effect.

Other than the blur type and the Antialiasing settings, there are really only two parameters here: Amount (as in blur amount) and Center. We haven't seen a Center value in any other blur effect. This allows you to move the blur around, because both

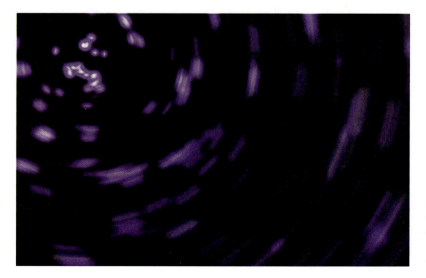

Figure 4.62 Moving the Center value of the effect changes where the center of the blur occurs. Here the Center is moved to the upper left hand corner.

spinning and zooming need a center point. If you wanted to create a quick sun effect, this would be idea.

Now let's look at zoom blur. Hit the Reset button at the top of the Radial Blur effect in the Effect Controls panel to start over again. Now change the Antialiasing back to High again, and change the Type drop down from Spin to Zoom. This creates the jump to warp speed look.

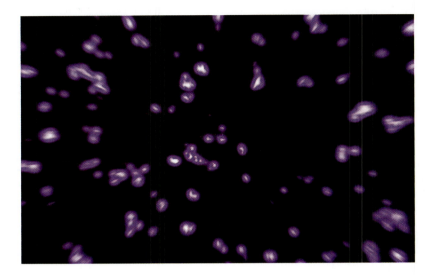

Figure 4.63 The Radial Blur effect with the Type set to Zoom.

I probably use Zoom far more often than Spin because I love how Zoom makes things so much more intense. Zoom blur creates the illusion that things are flying towards you, which is great in a variety of motion graphics settings. However, the default Amount value is far too small for my taste when using zoom blur. I'm going to increase this value to about 80.

I absolutely love what this zoom blur is trying to do. Hey, I'm a nerd to the core. This effect brings out my inner Hans Solo and my inner Captain Kirk at the same time. But this effect is severely limited by all of the ugly noise introduced when you crank up that Amount value. Here's a solution that might work in some cases. Try keeping a lower Amount value (low enough to avoid the ugly, aliased noise), and then selecting the effect in the Effect Controls panel, and then pressing Ctrl+D(Win)/Cmd+D(Mac) to duplicate the effect several times. The results are similar in intensity, but usually look much better.

We'll be coming back to the Radial Blur effect occasionally throughout this book. For example, there's another great trick using the Radial Blur effect in Chapter 7, when we look at the Polar Coordinates effect. The Radial Blur effect really is a

Figure 4.64 The result of taking the amount of blur to 80.

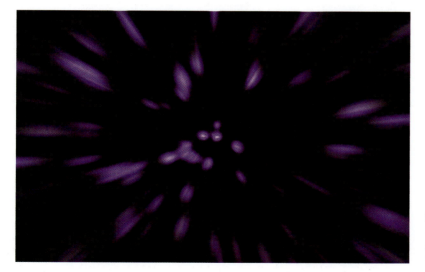

Figure 4.65 The results are much cleaner when using an Amount value of 20, and duplicating the effect multiple times.

great way to breathe life into a texture. If you have the Cycore set of plugins that have shipped with the recent versions of After Effects, you can also try the CC Radial Fast Blur effect, which renders faster, and looks cleaner in many cases.

The Reduce Interlace Flicker Effect

Interlace flicker is often caused by horizontal stripes appearing in interlaced footage. The result is an undesirable moire pattern that appears to flicker on video. The Reduce

Interlace Flicker effect attempts to right such wrongs by adding a slight blur to striped patterns.

To test this effect, open up the Flicker.aep project from the Chapter 4 folder. This project contains the type of high-contrast horizontal stripes pattern that you really want to avoid when creating interlaced video.

Figure 4.66 The interlace nightmare pattern.

Apply the Reduce Interlace Flicker effect to the interlace nightmare layer. The only property you can adjust here is Softness. Increasing the Softness value will add a slight blur that will reduce the contrast between the lines, which will in turn reduce flickering when interlaced and broadcast.

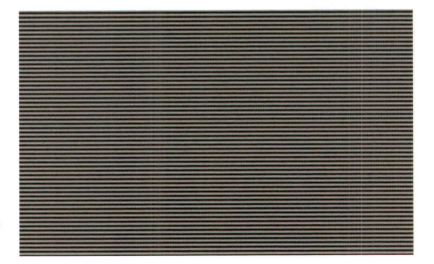

Figure 4.67 Taking the Softness value to 3 reduces contrast by adding a slight blur.

The Sharpen Effect

The Sharpen effect is the first non-blur effect we've looked at in this chapter. While the blur effects in this chapter remove details, sharpen effects enhance them. Sharpen effects are essentially the opposite of blur effects. The Sharpen effect is the most simple way to sharpen a layer, but Unsharp Mask is definitely a more powerful choice for sharpening.

Let's open up the Sharpen.aep project from the Chapter 4 folder of the exercise files. This comp contains a simple video clip.

Figure 4.68 The Sharpen.aep project.

This footage has a good amount of clarity, but we can enhance it further with the Sharpen effect. Apply Sharpen to the Ventura Fountain layer. Sharpening effects usually work their mojo by detecting edges, and then lightening the light side and darkening the dark side. But sharpening is like an addiction: you often get in over your head before you even realize that you have a problem.

In Figure 4.69, I took the Sharpen Amount value to 50. This is an excessively high value that probably should not be used in most cases. I used such a high value here so that you could see the result of the effect, but also so that you could see the artifacts that excess sharpening can create. These artifacts ("halos" as they're called) are to be avoided at all costs. While the Sharpen effect does enhance details, it doesn't give you the control that the Unsharp Mask effect does to avoid such problems. Also remember that as you enhance good details with sharpening (such as the cool brick texture in the background here), you also enhance bad details, such as noise and compression artifacts.

Figure 4.69 The result of increasing the Sharpen Amount value to 50. It's too much, folks.

The Smart Blur Effect

The Smart Blur effect is a lot like the Bilateral Blur effect introduced in After Effects CS4. I actually prefer the look of Bilateral Blur, but the Smart Blur effect is similar and renders much faster. Depending on your hardware and deadlines, you may prefer one to the other.

Both effects attempt to keep edges intact while blurring surfaces. I think it also works well as an effect to stylize a layer like a cartoon or a painting.

Let's open up the Smart Blur.aep project from the Chapter 4 folder. This project has a composition (called Smart Blur) that contains a nested composition with a few layers (a vector logo on top of an Artbeats video clip). It's important to note that this is all on one layer.

Apply the Smart Blur effect to Pre-comp 1 layer here. The default results blur some of the windows and surfaces of the buildings, but the hard edges of the logo have not been affected by this intelligent blur in the slightest.

As with Bilateral Blur, we have a Radius value to determine the amount of the blur. We also have the Threshold value that specifies what constitutes an edge. If I take the Threshold value up to 100 for example, I get a result that only vaguely resembles the original buildings. And still, the edges of the logo are razor sharp.

Figure 4.70 The Smart Blur.aep project. Remember that all this stuff is on one layer.

Figure 4.71 Increasing the Threshold value to its maximum value (100) allows Smart Blur to blur more edges.

One of the things that I don't quite get about this effect is the Mode drop down. You can change it to Edge Only to create a black image with white edges. I suppose that this could be useful in analyzing how the Smart Blur is calculating the edges, based on the Threshold value. The Overlay Edge Mode leaves the colors intact, but adds a white overlay of the edges.

Figure 4.72 The results of using the Edge Only Mode.

Figure 4.73 The results of using the Overlay Edge Mode.

As I mentioned, this effect can also be great to create an artistic, stylized look. Importing the fountain video that we looked at with the Sharpen effect, I applied the Smart Blur filter with the default settings. The results seem to create a painting out of this video.

Figure 4.74 Applying the Smart Blur effect can create painterly effects.

The Unsharp Mask Effect

Out of the two sharpening effects in After Effects (Sharpen and Unsharp Mask), Unsharp Mask is definitely the more powerful of the two. Unsharp Mask is more powerful because it has more controls. It has the same parameters that the Unsharp Mask filter in Photoshop does. If you don't have a Photoshop background, you might be surprised to know that After Effects' best sharpening effect is actually called "unsharp." Long story.

To give the Unsharp Mask effect a test drive, open up the Sharpen.aep project again. Apply the Unsharp Mask effect to this layer. As opposed to the Sharpen effect, the default results make a subtle but noticeable difference.

I'm going to increase the Amount value to 100 so that the results are more obvious on the printed page. I'm also going to duplicate this layer and apply a Linear Wipe transition so that you can see the sharpened version and unsharpened version side by side.

The effect is a subtle one, mostly noticeable in the brick pattern and shrubbery. But that's kinda the point with the Unsharp Mask effect. We want to enhance details, but we don't want that enhancement obvious.

You can increase the intensity of the sharpening the Radius effect, with the disclaimer that it's usually a bad idea to take this value above 2. If the results are too intense, you can lessen the sharpening by increasing the Threshold value.

Figure 4.75 The left half of the image shows sharpening with the Unsharp Mask effect. The right side shows the original image.

Again, I prefer this effect to the Sharpen effect because of the extra parameters (Radius and Threshold). But not only that, the Amount value (that controls the amount of blur in the Unsharpen Mask effect) produces more refined results than the Sharpen Amount property in the Sharpen effect does. It's also far easier to get those ugly sharpening artifacts with the Sharpen effect, while the Unsharp Mask effect generally produces more subtle enhancements.

5

THE CHANNEL EFFECTS

The Channel effects category is difficult to define. All of the effects here deal with the channels in a layer—red, green, blur, and alpha. All of the effects here allow you to change or blend levels together, often with the channels of other layers. This is an effects category filled with both advanced and obsolete effects, and the practical usage of them is not always obvious. I mostly use them to extract data from another layer in the same comp to use as a matte (alpha, luma, a color channel, or some other attribute). Sometimes, I use them for reflections, and every once in a blue moon, I will come up against a problem that only the Channel effects seem to be able to solve. So, even though their use is a little more abstract, it still pays to be familiar with these tools. As a prerequisite to this chapter, I strongly recommend being very familiar with channels, color relationships, and blend modes.

The Arithmetic Effect

The Arithmetic effect allows you to combine channels of a layer with itself using blend modes. Hopefully that definition makes at least some sense. It's probably better than Adobe's own definition of the Arithmetic effect, which you can find by clicking the effect's About button at the top of the effect in the Effect Controls panel.

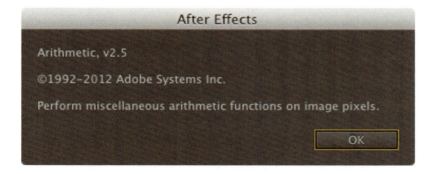

Figure 5.1 Oh, thanks. Now I get it.

Open the Arithmetic.aep project in the Chapter 5 folder of the exercise files. Apply the Arithmetic effect to the orb layer.

Figure 5.2 The Arithmetic.aep project.

In the Arithmetic effect, we have three color parameters, one for each color channel. We can increase the amount of color from any of the three channels, and blend that effect back onto our layer using one of the modes in the Operator drop down. For example, I'll increase the Red Value property to 100, and take

Figure 5.3 The result of increasing the Red Value with the Add operator.

the Operator to Add. This will add red color using an Add blend mode, producing a brighter result.

If we kept the Red Value the same, but changed the operator to Subtract, we get a completely different result. The result is cyan, because the Red Value now specifies how much red to subtract from the final result.

Figure 5.4 The result of subtracting red.

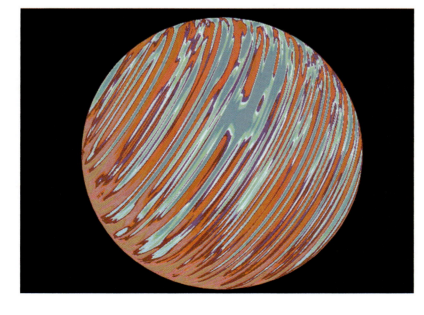

Figure 5.5 The results of increasing the color on all channels and using the Xor operator.

Unless you have a specific purpose in using the Arithmetic effect, the results of your experimentation will most likely seem psychedelic. In this case, I'll increase the green and blue values a little and take the Operator value back to its default value of Xor (short for "eXclusive or," a mathematical formula). The results are just plain weird.

The Blend Effect

The Blend effect is like a really weak version of the layer blend modes in the Timeline panel. There are only five of them here, and one of them is Crossfade, which basically blends two layers together using opacity. There are two benefits with this effect. The first is that you can animate the change of blend mode. It doesn't smoothly interpolate from one to another, as it can only create Hold keyframes. But it's possible to animate them with the Blend effect, while it isn't possible in the Timeline panel (although you could also split the layer and change the blend mode to create the illusion of animated blend modes). The other benefit is that you can use the Blend effect to blend together any two layers in the Timeline panel, even if they aren't next to each other in terms of layer stacking order.

Apply the effect and chose the layer to blend with from the Blend With Layer drop down. Then choose the blend mode from the Mode drop down. To see your results, you will need to reduce the Blend With Original value.

Figure 5.6 The blend modes offered in the Blend effect.

The Calculations effect (coming up next) is much more powerful, and does both of these blend mode tricks, but it does them much better. We'll save our look at these features for our upcoming coverage of the Calculations effect. For all intents and purposes, you probably should be using the Calculations effect instead of the Blend effect anyway.

The Calculations Effect

The Calculations effect is another effect from Photoshop, and it's perhaps the most powerful effect in this chapter. It basically allows you to blend a channel (or the entire composite) of the layer you've applied it to with a channel (or the entire composite) of any other layer in the same composition. You can also composite them using any of After Effects' blend modes, and can animate the changes between them.

Open the Calculations.aep project from the Chapter 5 folder of the exercise files. It's important to note that the comp in this project contains three layers—two Artbeats video clips and some more medieval art from my friend, Will Kindrick. Take special note that the two Artbeats clips are separated by the knight layer.

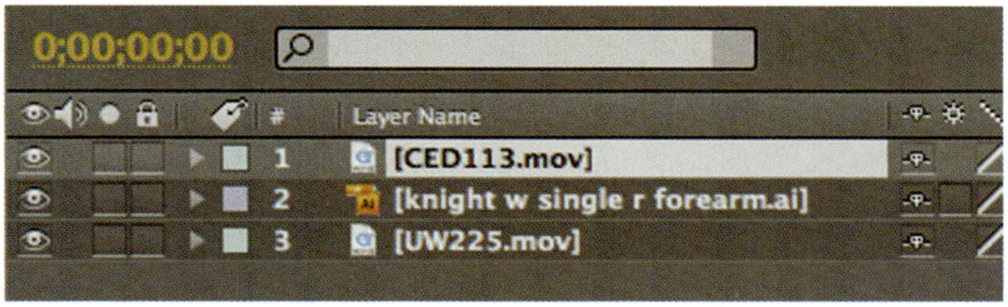

Figure 5.7 The layer stack in the Timeline panel in the Calculations.aep project.

Figure 5.8 The CED113.mov layer.

Figure 5.9 The knight layer.

Figure 5.10 The UW225.mov layer.

Select the layer CED113.mov and apply the Calculations effect to it. At first, these options may seem a little baffling. But they're actually organized very well, and make sense once you understand what this effect is trying to do.

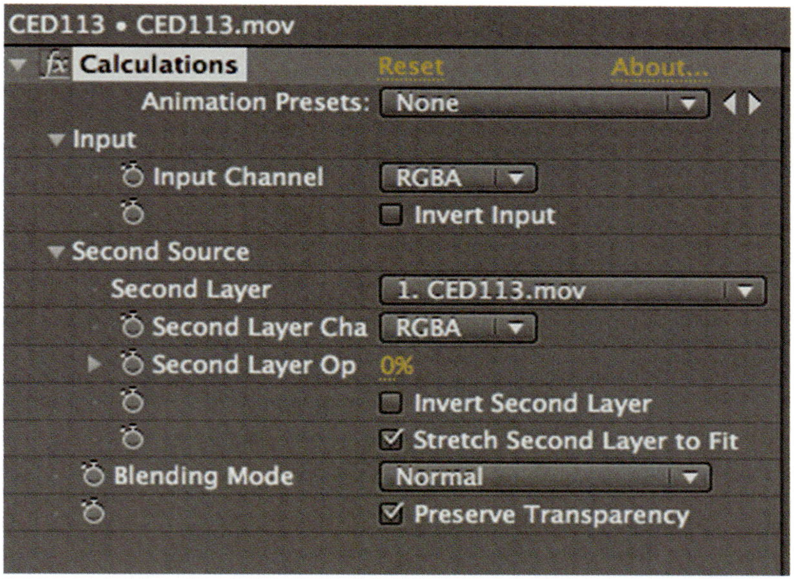

Figure 5.11 The options for the Calculations effect.

The section at the top—Input—is for defining how the current layer will be affected. Basically here, you specify which part of the current layer (CED113.mov) will be used in the final blend. The default setting uses all of the channels, including the alpha.

The next set of options are the Second Source options. Here you define the other layer that will blend with the current layer, and how they will blend together. Choose another layer from the Second Layer drop down in the Second Source area. Herein is one of the great benefits of this effect. Any layer in the comp can be used for the final blend, regardless of where it is in the layer stack.

To keep things simple at first, let's choose the current layer (CED113.mov) as the Second Layer. For now, we'll also leave the Second Layer Channel value set to RGBA, to blend the layer with the full version of itself. Increase the Second Layer Opacity value all the way up to 100%. All that's left now is to specify how this layer should blend together with itself. Let's pick the standard blend mode for self-blending—Overlay. This creates the same results as duplicating the layer and changing the blend mode of the duplicate, but we've kept our Timeline cleaner.

Figure 5.12 The result of using the Calculations effect to blend this layer into itself.

Another difference between this and blending with layers is that we can selectively choose which channel to blend. Take the Second Layer Channel value to Red to blend this layer with its own red channel in the Overlay blend mode.

Figure 5.13 The result of blending the city video with its own red channel in Overlay mode.

Now let's take this up to the next level. In the Second Layer drop down, select the UW225.mov layer. This is the other Artbeats video clip of slow motion water splashing. Note that this layer is not next to the current layer in the layer stack, and yet the Calculations effect still allows us to blend them together. Change the Second Layer Channel back to RGBA, and leave the Blending Mode value at Overlay. These two layers are now blended together using the Overlay blend mode.

Figure 5.14 The blending of the current layer and the UW225 .mov layer using the Overlay blend mode.

The Calculations effect can also be good for reflections of other layers. I'm going to change the Second Layer drop down to the knight layer. I'm then going to take down the Second Layer Opacity value to 50%, and then change the Blending Mode to Add. By default, the second layer is stretched to fill the boundaries of the layer. You can offset this behavior by deselecting the Stretch Second Layer to Fit, but I like the skewed results here, so I'm leaving it selected. We now have something that is starting to look a little like a reflection. I'm also going to drag the actual knight layer on top of the current layer, and turn on its visibility. This will help create the illusion that the knight is casting a reflection on the buildings behind him.

Figure 5.15 Using the Add Blending mode and reducing the Second Layer Opacity can create reflective looks.

The Channel Combiner Effect

The Channel Combiner effect is like Arithmetic and Calculations, in that it performs these really abstract channel calculations. But we can use the Channel Combiner effect to create some extreme color and luminance changes that might be difficult—or even impossible—without it.

If you'd like to follow along with me here, open the Channel Combiner.aep project from the Chapter 5 folder of the exercise files. There are several comps already setup for you here. Let's start in the Channel Combiner Start comp. This contains the 3D garage scene we've been using in this book. Apply the Channel Combiner effect to this image.

Figure 5.16 The 3D garage scene in the Channel Combiner Start comp.

The default results are usually garish beyond description. This is because the default settings convert the current layer's RGB values to HLS values.

Figure 5.17 The default results of the Channel Combiner effect.

This effect allows you to remap colors from one channel or aspect of the layer to another. In the From drop down, you'll see a list of all of the source attributes that you can use. Right below that, the To parameter specifies how the From attribute will be mapped to the current layer. The top five settings here already contain the attribute that they're going to remap to. So, when one of these top five options is selected, the To parameter is grayed out and unavailable.

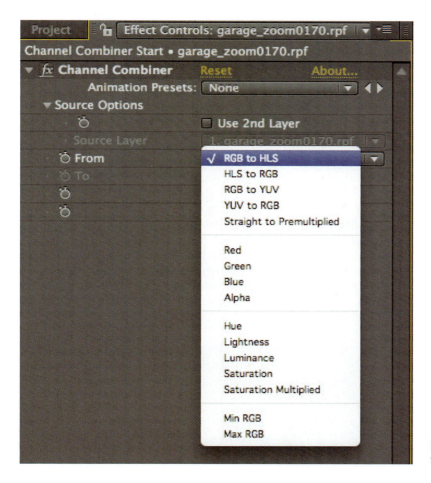

Figure 5.18 The From options in the Channel Combiner effect.

Take the From value to Red to unlock the To property. This is where it starts getting a little abstract, but stay with me here, folks. This is (potentially) good stuff. By default, the To value is set to Lightness. So then, our results now map the red channel to the lightness channel. Huh? To understand this, let's take a look at only the red channel of the original layer.

Figure 5.19 The red channel of the original layer.

By remapping the red channel to the lightness channel, we're telling After Effects to control the lightness of this image using these grayscale values (in the red channel). You can even use the attributes of a second layer by enabling the Use 2nd Layer option, and selecting a layer from the Source Layer drop down.

So what cool stuff can you do with this? To see some more practical examples of this, hop on over to the Darken/Change Color comp. It basically contains another instance of the same comp, with the 3D garage scene and the Channel Combiner effect. But the effect has already been setup for us here. In this case the From value is set to the blue values in this image, and the To value is again set to the lightness values. This is far more interesting because yellow and blue are opposites. That means that the car is very dark in the blue channel because not much blue light is needed to make a yellow car. So, when we use the

Figure 5.20 Mapping the blue channel to the lightness values creates a very dark car.

blue channel to control the lightness of the image, we get a very dark car. Turn on the visibility of the Channel Combiner effect in the Darken/Change color comp to see the results.

This is a very unique result. It would be very challenging to recreate this with a luminance adjusting effect, like Levels or Curves, because of all the intricate highlights, reflections, and other details on this car. But they have not been dimmed at all in this case because it took a lot of blue light to make those bright highlights as well, so they remain bright when the lightness is remapped.

Very little changed much besides the car, which is another impressive aspect of this result. Areas that had lots of blue to begin with (like the blue sky background, or the teal-colored post on the right), are brightened, and areas with warm tones (like the table in the foreground) were darkened a little. But overall, the scene is relatively unchanged.

Let's look at one more example. Switch over to the Intense Reflections comp. Let's say that we wanted to isolate this car to use in a movie poster. In the garage scene, the car looks realistic. But on a movie poster, it would seem to plain and dull. Even isolated by itself, the car seems lonely and in need of some enhancement.

Figure 5.21 The Intense Reflections comp.

Now turn on the Channel Combiner effect here, which is mapping the saturation values to the lightness values. This creates a much more intense car.

Figure 5.22 The result of remapping saturation to lightness.

The results have much more punch and flash (and other Hollywood-esque adjectives) to them than the original. But if this is really for Hollywood, we can't let this alone without adding yet more intensity. The top layer is already in the Overlay blend mode in the Timeline panel. Turn on the duplicate layer underneath it to combine these two layers in the Overlay blend mode, making a very flashy final product. Now the car is ready for Mr. DeMille's proverbial close-up.

Figure 5.23 The final result with the Channel Combiner effect.

The Compound Arithmetic Effect

The Compound Arithmetic effect is exactly like a watered down version of the Calculations effect. It allows you to combine different attributes from two different layers.

▼ *fx* **Compound Arithmetic**	Reset	About...	
Animation Presets:	None	▼	◄ ►
Second Source Layer	1. bird.tif	▼	
⏱ Operator	Copy	▼	
⏱ Operate on Channels	RGB	▼	
⏱ Overflow Behavior	Clip	▼	
⏱	☑ Stretch Second Source to Fit		
▶ ⏱ Blend With Original	0%		

Figure 5.24 The options in the Compound Arithmetic effect follow the same basic structure as the Calculations effect does.

Use the Second Source Layer drop down to select a second layer to blend with the current layer. Choose a blend operation with the Operator drop down, and a few other self-explanatory properties. For more control, use the Calculations effect.

The Invert Effect

In Photoshop, there is an Invert adjustment. For this adjustment, there are no options. You simply apply it, it inverts the colors of your layer and you're done. Boom. End of story. The Invert effect in After Effects is much more exciting because it allows you to invert all kinds of stuff, not just the composite colors. However, if a simple inversion is what you're looking for, then just apply it and walk away.

For this look at the Invert effect, open up the Invert.aep project in the Chapter 5 folder of the exercise files. This project contains a logo I created in Adobe Illustrator.

Figure 5.25 The Invert.aep project.

Apply the Invert effect to this, and instantly the colors of the logo are inverted. If you're looking for the standard Photoshop Invert adjustment, there you go.

Figure 5.26 The default results of applying the Invert effect.

The great thing about this effect is that taking it to the next level is very simple. Other than the ubiquitous Blend With Original setting (basically the opacity of the effect), there is only one setting here—Channel. In the Channel drop down, you specify which attribute of the current layer gets inverted. And that's all there is to it.

Let's take the green channel, for instance. Change the Channel value to Green. This inverts the green channel, and the green channel only. Because there is no green light used to make black, all black areas become 100% green. So, the red and blue channels remain as they were, and all that is inverted is the green channel. I'm not sure of a practical use for this, but creatively, it's great to see some completely different color variations of a layer.

You could also get a little more adventurous than just inverting a single color channel. I'm going to change the Channel drop down to Hue. This will invert the hues of the image, but will maintain the same saturation and lightness values. Note the dif-

ferences between this and the default result. The default result inverts everything (black becomes white, and so forth). This result only adjusts the hue.

The Minimax Effect

The Minimax effect might be the Channel effect used most often. From a technical aspect, the Minimax effect looks at each pixel and forces it to become either the minimum or maximum value of the pixels in a specified radius. In layman's terms, the Minimax effect is typically used to expand or contract the edges of a layer. This can be helpful in polishing up keyed footage, removing strokes, cleaning up noisy edges, and other such purposes.

Open the Minimax.aep project up from the Chapter 5 folder of the exercise files. We'll start in the Creepy Stranger comp. This contains a simple Illustrator graphic with a thin stroke around its edges.

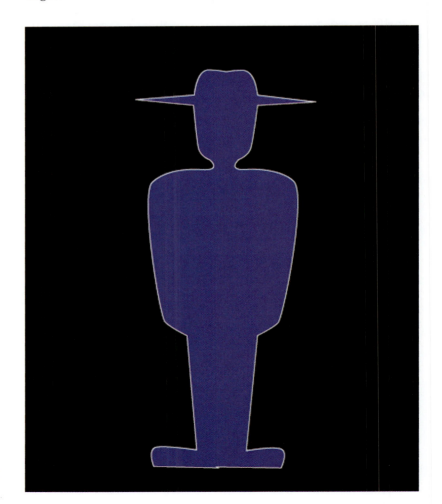

Figure 5.29 The Creepy Stranger comp in the Minimax .aep project.

Apply the Minimax effect to the Creepy Stranger graphic. The Operation drop down at the top is really the key here. The two main behaviors are Minimum and Maximum. Let's first look at the default value—Maximum. To see what this value does, increase the Radius value. I used a value of about 20.

Figure 5.30 Increasing the Radius value to 20 increases the size of the stroke.

Let's examine this a little bit. Remember that this effect looks at neighboring pixels (within a 20 pixel radius, according to our Radius value). It then causes them all to be the maximum value in that search area (because of the Operation setting of Maximum). Because the value with the highest RGB values is white, the 20 pixel area all becomes white. If the stroke were black, then it would have been completely replaced by blue, because blue has the greater of the RGB values.

If we take the Operation to Minimum, then it replaces those same 20 pixels with blue, because blue has the minimum RGB values here. For practical purposes, we could have used this setting to remove the white stroke. The edges are clean, and no one would have ever suspected that this layer ever had a white stroke.

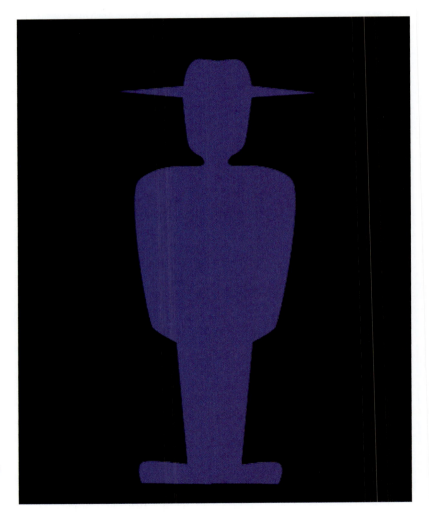

Figure 5.31 Taking the Operation value to Minimum fills the 20 pixels with blue because it has the smallest RGB values (of the two colors here—blue and white).

You can also use a couple settings in the Operation drop down that perform both Minimum and Maximum calculations in order. For example, The Maximum Then Minimum setting performs the Minimax calculations with the Maximum value and then the Minimum value. The results are quite different from what we've seen so far.

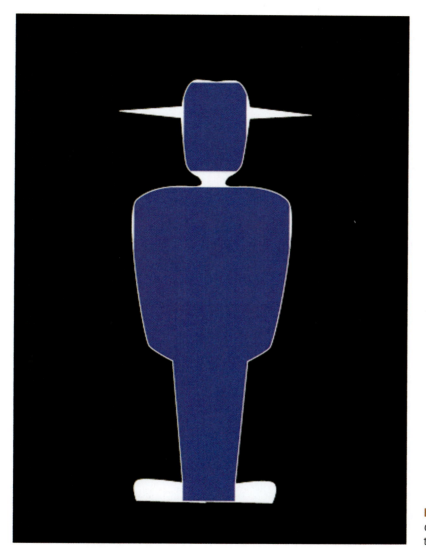

Figure 5.32 The results of changing the Operation value to Maximum then Minimum.

Click the Reset button at the top of the Minimax effect in the Effect Controls panel. We're now going to look at the Channel drop down. So far, we've been looking at obtaining the minimum and maximum color values. But we can change this setting to process individual color channels, or the alpha channel. Change the Channel value to Alpha. Now, when you increase the Radius value with the Operation value set to Maximum, the alpha channel expands.

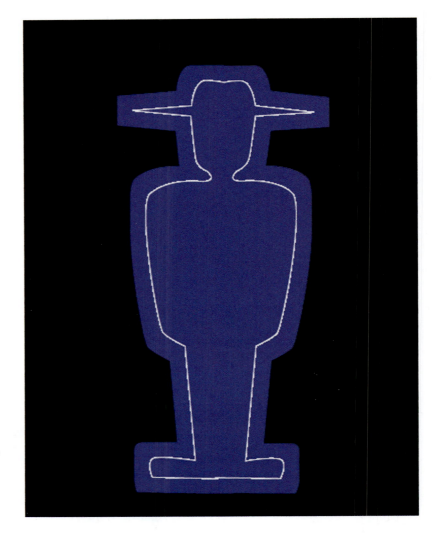

Figure 5.33 The boundaries of the object expand when the Channel value is set to Alpha, and the Operation value is set to Maximum.

Likewise, changing the Operation setting to Minimum will shrink the alpha channel. This can be helpful for removing aliased edges, or edges that didn't quite key out properly when working with blue and green screen footage.

That covers what you need to know about using the Minimax effect for practical purposes. But some people also use Minimax for creative effect, in the same way that you might use an effect in the Stylize category. It can be used to enhance the size of reflections or specular highlights using the Maximum operation. Or it can be used to create a painterly effect.

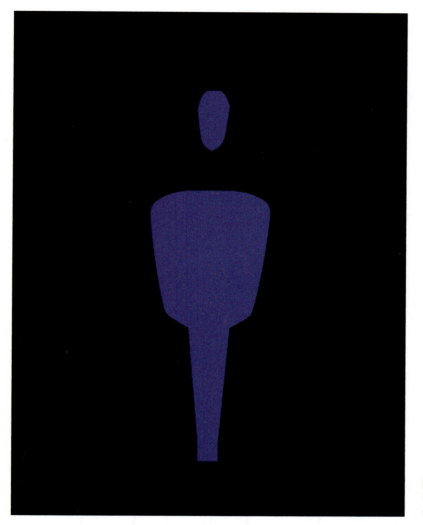

Figure 5.34 Changing the Operation value to Minimum now shrinks the alpha channel.

Switch over to the self-portrait comp. This is a self-portrait painting I did in Corel Painter. Apply the Minimax effect to this layer.

Increasing the Radius value with the Operation set to Maximum will thin the black lines and create dreamlike highlights.

We can also thicken the black lines and create thicker lines in general by changing the operation to Minimum. To demonstrate the effects of the Minimum operation on this image, I've used a Radius value of 2.

Figure 5.35 The self-portrait comp.

Figure 5.36 The result of applying the Minimax effect and increasing the Radius value to 4.

Figure 5.37 The result of using Minimum as the Operation drop down value.

With these results, the edges start getting eroded, as if we had applied a blur effect. To restore the edges, select the Don't Shrink Edges option at the bottom of the Minimax effect in the Effect Controls panel.

The Remove Color Matting Effect

The Remove Color Matting effect basically does the same thing that After Effects does when using the Premultiplied option when interpreting an alpha channel. This is probably best done in the Interpretation Settings dialog in the Project panel. Regardless, let's look at how color matting works, and how the Remove Color Matting effect can remove it.

Open the Matting.aep project in the Chapter 5 folder of the exercise files. This project contains a plant image that I rendered from 3DS Max. When I created this file, I rendered it out using a premultiplied alpha channel, which means that there is some residual background color in the alpha channel. Then, when I imported this image into After Effects, I falsely labeled the alpha interpretation as Straight. This leaves stray pixels around the edges of the object. I'm going to magnify this layer to 200%, so that we can see them more clearly.

Figure 5.38 The plant pre-multiplied alpha comp in the Matting.aep project.

If you want to see this image without its alpha channel, you can change the Show Channel and Color Management Settings option at the bottom of the Composition panel to RGB Straight. Hopefully now, it will be easier to see the fringe blue pixels in Figure 5.47.

Figure 5.39 The original plant image without the alpha.

If you haven't done so already, switch the Show Channel and Color Management Settings option to RGB, so that we can see our alpha here. Apply the Remove Color Matting effect to this layer. At first the results look bad because the default color it's trying to remove is black. That default doesn't work for us here, but black is perhaps the most common background color in premultiplied alphas, and it's usually the most offensive when left uncorrected.

Figure 5.40 The default results of the Remove Color Matting effect.

We need to change the Background Color value to the same blue background on this plant layer. That will tell the Remove Color Matting effect which fringe edge pixels need to be removed. You can do this in a few different ways. You can change the viewed channels back to RGB Straight and click the background color with the eyedropper. Or, you can click the Background Color swatch and enter the RGB values 90, 197, 255. This will then remove all of the speckles of color along the edges of this plant. Remember that you could have also achieved the same results by interpreting the alpha channel as Premultiplied.

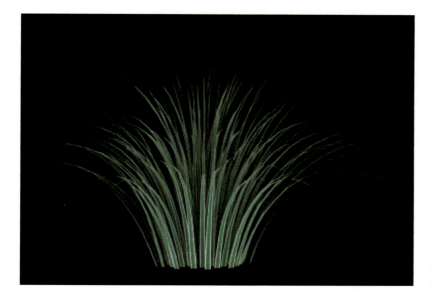

Figure 5.41 The end result, with the color matting removed.

The Set Channels Effect

The Set Channels effect is perhaps the most esoteric effect in this category. Honestly, I haven't found a practical use for this one yet. It basically allows you to recreate a layer using attributes from other layers. This sounds similar, but is very different from say, the Calculations effect. The Calculations effect (and others we've looked at so far in this chapter) blend other attributes into the current layer. The Set Channels effects just completely replaces the current attributes.

Open the Set Channels.aep project from the Chapter 5 folder of the exercise files. This project contains three of the Artbeats video clips we'll be looking at in this book.

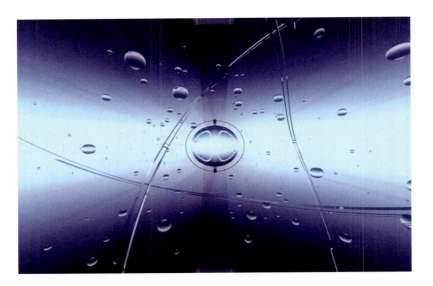

Figure 5.42 The CJ121.mov Artbeats clip.

Figure 5.43 The CED113.mov Artbeats clip.

Select the CJ121.mov layer, and apply the Set Channels effect to it. Basically, this effect allows us to rebuild this layer based on the attributes of other layers. We can select which layer to use for the red channel, for example, and then which attribute of that layer to use to create the red channel.

Figure 5.44 The UM230.mov Artbeats clip.

In the Source Layer 1 drop down, change the layer to the CED113.mov layer (the one that shows city buildings). In the Set Red to Source drop down, you can specify which attribute of the city video that you'd like to use to make the red layer. I chose the blue channel. In the results shows in Figure 5.45, the green and blue channels are taken from the original layer, but the red values are created from the blue channel of the CED113.mov layer.

Figure 5.45 Using the CED113 .mov layer as the source for the red channel.

As you can see, the effect is an interesting blend of the two layers. However, when we start using more layers for additional channels, things get out of hand. In the Source Layer 2 drop down, change the value to the UM230.mov layer (the layer with the falling leaves in front of a green screen). Change the Set Green to Source drop down to Blue to use the blue channel of the leaves layer to create the green channel of the current layer.

Figure 5.46 The result of using an additional layer to create the green channel.

If at this point you're scratching your head, wondering how this could ever come in handy, I'm right there with you. It's an interesting ability, but I only see it being helpful in creating weird blends of layers.

I should point out that you can use the current layer as the source layer, which means that you can also mix and match channels. This essentially turns the Set Channels effect into the Shift Channels effect. There is an interesting example using the Shift Channels effect later in this chapter that you may want to see.

The Set Matte Effect

The Set Matte effect is similar to the Set Channels effect, only that the Set Matte effect allows you to use the alpha channel of another layer as the alpha channel of the current layer. The After Effects help documentation suggest that this effect is obsolete; replaced by the alpha and track matte options in the Timeline panel. However, I think this effect is viable for two reasons. First, it allows you to use any layer in the composition as a matte, as opposed to mattes in the Timeline panel, which require that matte layers be adjacent to the layer they're masking. This effect is also viable because it allows you to use other attributes from another layer—not just the alpha channel. If you do a lot of work with luma or alpha mattes, this effect can open up all new doors of possibility for you.

Open the Set Matte.aep project in the Chapter 5 folder of the exercise files. Our project here consists of one composition with three layers. Our main layer here will be some computer generated lava.

Figure 5.47 The lava layer in the Set Matte.aep project.

There are also two other layers that we'll be using to control the transparency of the lava layer—a layer of lightning and a layer of fractal fire.

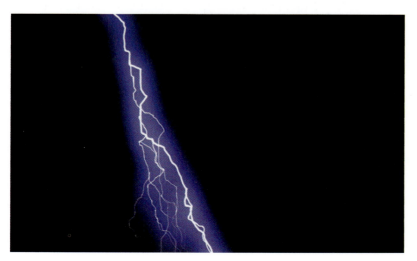

Figure 5.48 The lightning layer.

Figure 5.49 The fractal fire layer.

Apply the Set Matte effect to the lava layer. In the Take Matte From Layer drop down, choose the lightning layer. By default, the alpha channel of the lightning layer now becomes the alpha channel of the lava layer. This is basically the same results that we would have achieved had we used this lightning to create an alpha matte. The problem is that the glow around the lightning creates an ugly halo.

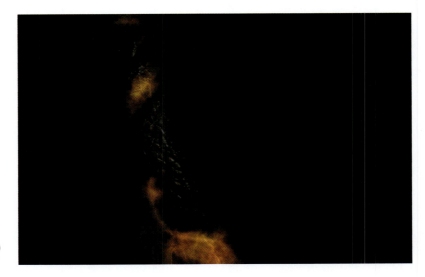

Figure 5.50 The results of choosing the lightning layer in the Take Matte From Layer drop down.

However, with the power of the Set Matte effect, we don't have to be stuck only using the alpha channel of the lightning. Change the Use For Matte drop down to Red Channel. This will use the grayscale values of the red channel only to create transparency. The result is that there is much less of the glow around the lightning used here, which creates a tighter matte.

Figure 5.51 The result of using the red channel to control the matte.

If you selected the Invert Matte checkbox, then the lightning would cut a transparent hole in the lava layer. This lightning has already been animated. If you preview this comp, you'll see that this inverted matte is actually a traveling matte.

Figure 5.52 Selecting the Invert Matte checkbox creates a lighting-shaped area of transparency in the lava layer.

Now let's adjust the Take Matte From Layer drop down to select the fractal fire layer. Change the Use For Matte drop down to use the luminance of the fractal fire to create the alpha channel (matte) of the current layer.

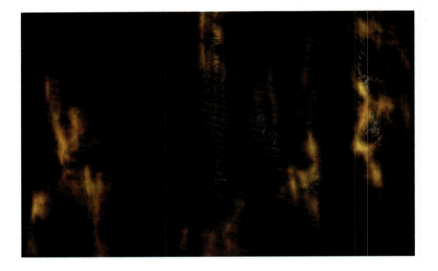

Figure 5.53 Using the luminance of the fractal fire layer as the alpha channel of the lava layer.

The results seen in Figure 5.53 resemble what would be created by making a luma matte with these two layers. Notice that these layers are not next to each other in the layer stacking order in the Timeline panel. And it doesn't have to end here. We could use the green channel, or the saturation, or a whole host of properties from our second layer to create a matte on the current layer. Remember that if you're going to use effects to control the alpha channel with the Set Matte effect (as I've done here with the Advanced Lightning and Fractal Noise effects), then you'll need to precompose the layers that they are applied to first.

The Shift Channels Effect

The Shift Channels effect seems like another weird channel effect without any usefulness. But I actually have an interesting example, using one of the 3D Channel effects that we looked at back in Chapter 2. The purpose of the Shift Channels effect is to take channel data from a layer and use it in other channels on the same layer. This is similar to the Set Channels effect, except we're only allowed to use the attributes of the current layer.

Creating Black and White Images

Note that you can also use the Shift Channels to create a black and white version of layers. To do this, set every color channel drop down in the Shift Channels options to the same color channel. You can use this to see which color channel looks better as a black and white image, and choose that version.

Open the Shift Channels.aep project. This contains the familiar 3D garage scene we've been using as an example in this book. We're going to be relighting the scene using the Shift Channels effect. Note that we're not going to be lightening the scene, as with an effect like Levels, but we're actually going to be changing the current lighting, as if we had this image back in its original 3D rendering application.

Figure 5.54 The Shift Channels .aep project.

The first step is actually to apply the 3D Channel Extract effect to this garage scene. Then, change the 3D Channel value in the 3D Channel Extract options to Surface Normals. I realize that this creates a weird looking result, but just go with me on this one.

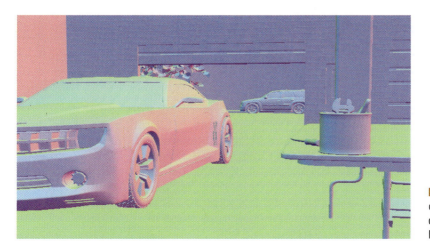

Figure 5.55 The result of changing the 3D Channel drop down value to Surface Normals.

This display of surface normals is showing us which direction each polygon is facing. Notice that the red areas tend to be facing right, green areas tend to be pointing upwards, and blue areas tend to be facing the camera. Areas that face a direction between them have blended colors.

Here's the magic, folks. Because the polygons facing upwards are green, if we can extract that green data and remap it, we can relight the scene. And that's exactly what we're going to do.

Duplicate this layer and delete the 3D Channel Extract effect from the bottom copy only. On the top copy of this garage scene, apply the Shift Channels effect. In the Shift Channels effect, change the Take Red From, Take Green From, and Take Blue From values to Green. This will create a grayscale result that displays the amount of green light in the surface normals in this scene. Note that the areas with the most green light are white.

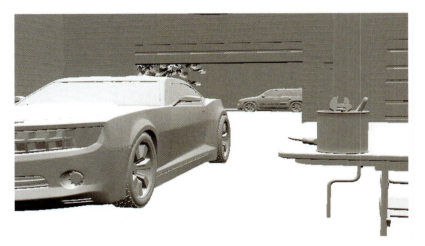

Figure 5.56 The Shift Channels effect can create a grayscale map that represents the amount of green light in the surface normals.

Then, in the Timeline panel, place the top copy of the garage layer into the Overlay blend mode. This will remove the gray areas of the image, and brighten the areas that are white on the top copy, which adds more light to the scene.

To really see the power of what just happened, I'm going to zoom in closer to the car, and do a split screen. What we did here couldn't be accomplished by another luminance adjusting effect, because we just increased the lightness of the objects pointing upwards. This isn't possible without 3D data. Even the crevasses

Figure 5.57 After relighting the scene with the 3D Channel Extract effect and the Shift Channels effect.

Figure 5.58 A close up of our relighting job. The lower left side shows the original pixels and the upper right side shows the result of our alterations.

of the hubcaps that are pointing upwards have been relit in a very natural way.

Notice in Figure 5.58 that only the pixels that are facing upwards were relighted. The side of the car has very little change to it. But the hood of the car and the shop floor are brightened considerably.

The Shift Channels effect is a key ingredient in this recipe. Using the Shift Channels effect, we turned the multicolored surface normals display into a grayscale map of the green channel that we could blend with other layers.

The Solid Composite Effect

We finish out this chapter with a simple effect—the Solid Composite effect. The purpose of this effect is to save you the step of creating a solid layer to blend with another layer. You can create an area of color and blend it into the current layer. Let's see how this works.

Figure 5.59 The Solid Composite.aep project.

Open the Solid Composite.aep project from the Chapter 5 folder of the exercise files. The project contains a photo of a little girl interacting with a llama. Apply the Solid Composite effect to this layer.

The controls here are simple. Just change the Color value to essentially create a new solid. I'm going to select a vibrant blue color. This is a little confusing initially, because you don't see anything different. But what's happening is that this effect has created a virtual solid "layer" beneath your footage. You can then see this blue color by lowering the Source Opacity value, which lowers the opacity of the Source Layer. Be aware that the Opacity value adjusts the opacity of the color, but only after it is made visible by lowering the Source Opacity value, or by changing the Blending Mode. Note that the Blending Mode value blends the source footage and the virtual solid together by treating the source layer as the top layer, so to speak.

Figure 5.60 Solid Composite using the Overlay blend mode to blend the footage into the virtual solid.

Figure 5.61 Using the Hard Light blend mode in the Solid Composite effect.

Try taking the blend mode to Hard Light, which creates a blend result that is less dependent on layer stacking order.

At the end of the day, the Solid Composite effect is a quick and easy way to blend source material into a solid color.

6

THE COLOR CORRECTION EFFECTS

The Color Correction effect category contains more effects than any other single category in all of After Effects—29 now, to be exact. While that isn't really an indicator of importance, it just so happens that these effects might be the most important in After Effects. I say that because all workflows use color, and therefore can utilize color tools. The compositor might never need The Fractal Noise effect. The text animator may never find a use for the Color Difference Key effect. But they both still use color, and will more than likely need to use tools for adjusting color often. The effects in this category change colors, remove colors, isolate colors, colorize footage, bring colors into compliance with a video standard, and almost any other color-related task you can think of.

You might be wondering—why are there so many color adjustment effects? Are there really 29 different things you can do with color? That's a valid question. And actually, many of these color correction effects perform very similar functions, with different ways to do things. If you had footage of a fire that looked red, and you wanted to make it more orange, you could use Hue/Saturation, or Color Balance, Colorama, or even Levels or Curves. All of these effects are very powerful and would do a comparable job. The difference is mostly in the way that they are used. The task is to find color correction tools that allow you to adjust colors in ways that make sense to you.

One of the great benefits of this category of effects, is that you'll see many familiar friends here, if you're familiar with Photoshop. Color and luminance adjustment tools like Color Balance, Channel Mixer, Levels, Curves, Shadow/Highlight, Hue/Saturation, and several more, are in both Photoshop and After Effects. For the most part, these are powerful, intuitive tools, and they are one of the big reasons that Photoshop users find it so easy to learn After Effects.

What's in This Chapter

Before we jump into these effects, I want to give you an idea of what's coming up. Many of you might not want to read such a large chapter straight through. You may be somewhat new to After Effects or color adjusting, and may want to know which color effects perform simple tasks quickly. Or you may be more experienced with After Effects, and you might want to know the most powerful tools to use here. In this little intro section, we'll also look at which effects are mostly worthless in my opinion.

The Simple and the Complex

The first effects in this category all begin with the term "auto," which means that they make corrections for you. For high end projects, these effects might not cut it. But if you're facing intense deadlines, or if you're just looking for something quick and easy, the auto color correction effects are a lifesaver. If you're looking for a quick way to edit shadows and highlights, the Shadow/ Highlight effect is simple and works well and also has some auto settings. If you're looking for the utmost power when it comes to correcting brightness issues, Levels and Curves are the most common, fairly easy to use, and produce some great results.

What about colorizing? The Tint effect is the simplest tool for the job, and the Tritone effect is a little more powerful and very similar. The Colorama effect is the most complex and powerful tool in this chapter by far, and it is also the most advanced tool for colorizing footage in After Effects. I also frequently turn to Hue/Saturation and Color Balance to add or shift colors.

The (Nearly) Worthless Effects

When it comes to the effects in After Effects, I'm fully aware that beauty is in the eye of the beholder. I've heard After Effects instructors or authors say an effect is useless, when I couldn't live without it. I've also been guilty of saying an effect was worthless, until a colleague pointed out an innovative way to use it that I had never thought of.

So, with that disclaimer, I'm going to share with you some of the effects in this chapter that I haven't found innovative ways to use yet; effects that you might be able to live without.

The Color Balance effects is one of my all-time favorite effects. But in this section, there is also an effect called Color Balance (HLS), which I think is worthless when you have the 32 bit Hue/ Saturation at your convenience. I'm also not a big fan of the

Gamma/Pedestal/Gain effect, which is typically a great tool for colorists, but is almost completely useless here (in my opinion) without scopes of any kind. One of the effects that you should probably avoid at all costs is the Brightness & Contrast effect, which does terrible things to your footage. Don't be tempted to use it because of its simplicity, unless using it for a specific purpose as we'll discuss in a moment. Perhaps the most worthless effect here is the PS Arbitrary Map effect.

The purpose of this book is to cover all effects, and that's precisely what we'll do, for the sake of completeness. We'll pass quickly through effects that I consider worthless. And who knows, you may find an innovative way to use them after all.

The Auto Color Effect

The Auto Color and Auto Contrast effects are quite similar. They both attempt to automatically fix color and contrast, respectively. They also work on all of the luminance values of an image, as opposed to individual channels like the Auto Levels effect. Because they don't process each color channel individually, they don't have the potential of introducing a color cast into the footage.

A color cast is when the entire layer has a slight tint towards a particular color. Open the Auto.aep project from the Chapter 6 folder of the exercise files. This is a little project that I created for use with the "auto effects": Auto Color, Auto Contrast, and Auto Levels. This project contains a comp called beluga, which has an image of a beluga whale.

Figure 6.1 The beluga image from the Auto.aep project.

This comp contains the beluga image duplicated twice. The bottom layer is the untouched duplicate. The top copy has a transition effect applied so that when you apply color correction effects, you can more easily see the difference from the original. Sometimes subtle color changes are difficult to see in separate images in print.

Beluga whales are white, but you couldn't really tell from this image. It is too dark, and has an aqua-colored tint from the water and glass. Apply the Auto Color effect to the top layer, beluga EFFECT. This will lighten the image, restore much of the true color of the beluga whale. Remember that there is also a transition effect here, which allows you to see the before (left) and after (right).

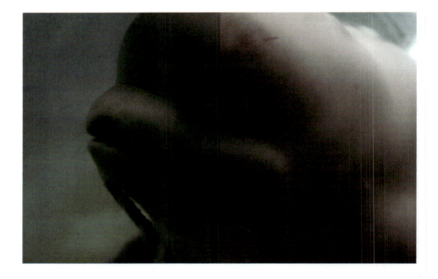

Figure 6.2 The Auto Color effect brightens the image and removes the color cast.

The Additional Auto Effect Properties

In the Photoshop versions of these auto effects, there are no settings to adjust. Note that in these auto effects in After Effects, you also have the ability to adjust a few properties. You can increase Temporal Smoothing if you need to smooth the results over time. The default value for Temporal Smoothing is 0, which means that each frame is processed independently. That means that the changing composition of the shot might cause the auto effects to produce wildly different results from frame to frame. The Temporal Smoothing setting determines how many seconds that the effect will use to smooth the results. So, if this value is at 1, the Auto Color effect will look at one second's worth of frames and smooth the results over those frames so that there are not luminance jitters.

The auto effects also allow you to manually adjust the Black Clip and White Clip for a layer. These properties control how much of the shadows are forced to pure black, and how much of the highlights are forced to pure white, respectively.

The Auto Contrast Effect

The Auto Contrast effect is similar to the Auto Color effect, except that it doesn't do much in the way of shifting colors. Its primary purpose is to adjust brightness values, which it does fairly well. If you're continuing along with the Auto.aep project, choose File>Revert to reset the project to its default status. Or you can open this project from the Chapter 6 folder of the exercise files. Apply the Auto Contrast effect to the beluga EFFECT layer. Notice how the image on the right (the adjusted part of the image) is lighter, but the colors are still similar. Our beluga whale still doesn't appear white.

Figure 6.3 The results of the Auto Contrast effect, right, with the original on the left.

The Auto Levels Effect

The Auto Levels effect is unique from the other auto effects we've already looked at in this chapter. The other auto effects process the entire image, while the Auto Levels effect processes each color channel independently. Because of how this effect works, there is a possibility of it introducing a color cast into the image. Imagine if you had an image that didn't have a full range of highlights in the Red Channel. The Auto Levels effect would increase the red highlights, which could create a reddish tint (cast) in the image.

Open the Auto.aep project from the Chapter 6 folder and apply the Auto Levels effect to the beluga EFFECT layer. Notice how the results are similar to what we saw with the Auto Color effect—the image is brightened, and the color cast is neutralized.

Figure 6.4 The original (left) and the layer with Auto Levels applied (right).

Although these results look similar to what we saw with Auto Color, there is a difference worth mentioning. The Auto Levels effect actually did a better job at removing the color cast than Auto Color did.

To compare all three results, duplicate the beluga EFFECT layer. On the new duplicate (beluga EFFECT 2), delete the Auto Levels effect, and apply the Auto Color effect in its stead. Finally, take the Transition Completion value of the Linear Wipe effect on the beluga EFFECT 2 layer to 75%.

Hopefully, you can see the subtle different in print, but if not, try this on your own. There is a subtle but real difference between the Auto Levels and Auto Color effects. The center portion of Figure 6.5 has the most neutral beluga whale tones, because of the Auto Levels effect.

The Black & White Effect

Seen also in Photoshop, the Black & White effect is perhaps the best way to convert footage to black and white, and even to footage tinted with one color such as sepia tinted footage for that vintage look.

Figure 6.5 The final results, with the original image on the left, the Auto Levels result in the center, and the Auto Color results on the right. It's nearly impossible to see in this screenshot, so try the results on your own with the provided exercise file, or another file of your own.

The Black & White effect converts footage to black and white as soon as it's applied. But then it gives you control over how bright or dark you want specific areas of color. Let's look at an example. Open up the Black and White.aep project from the Chapter 6 folder of the exercise files. I like this clip, and I love how the turquoise hat of the actress just pops. It was designed to make her stand out from the rest of the scene, which has mostly warm tones.

Figure 6.6 The original image. Note the color of her hat.

Now apply the Black & White effect to this layer (called Footage). It instantly makes our image black and white, which is convenient. But now that this is converted to black and white, I don't like the way her hat looks anymore. I loved the color contrast of the cool hat against a warm environment. It made her appear as both the most innocent thing in the scene, but also the focus of the scene. But without the color contrast, the hat is just distracting.

Figure 6.7 After applying the Black & White effect, everything is black and white, but certain objects didn't convert well, like her hat.

In the Black & White effect controls, you'll see that we have controls over various color families. A positive value will brighten that color family, and a negative value will darken it. So not only does this effect just desaturate an image, it gives us control over the transformation from black to white.

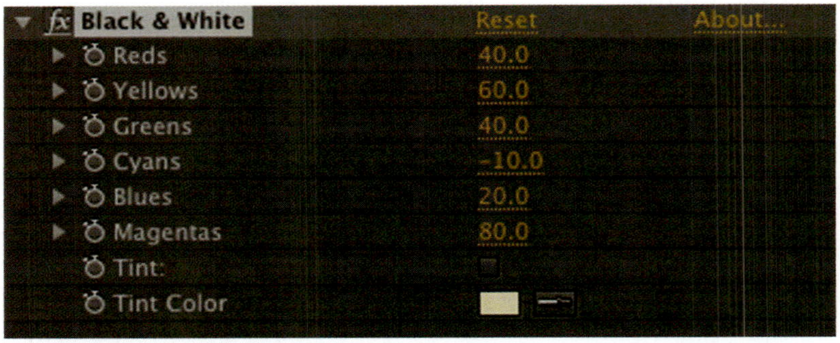

Figure 6.8 The Black & White parameters in the Effects Control panel.

The hat was originally in the cyan family, more or less. So I'm going to take the Cyans value to negative 10 (–10.0), which darkens color values that were originally cyan, hence the hat darkens considerably. Now it blends much better into the rest of the scene.

Another benefit of this effect is that you can also use it to add a single color tint. This isn't that much different from the Tint effect or similar functionality in the Hue/Saturation effect. However, those other effects don't give you control over the black and white conversion like the Black & White effect does. So,

Figure 6.9 With the Cyans value reduced, the hat is darker, while the rest of the scene is unchanged.

to give something a vintage sepia tone, simply enable the Tint option in the Black & White effect controls. The default Tint Color is a little strong, so I clicked the swatch to lighten a bit. Note that you can change this to any color—it doesn't have to be that vintage yellowish tint.

Figure 6.10 After enabling the Tint option, we have a vintage style black and white image.

For this particular scene, I actually don't want to go all the way gray. But there's not a Blend with Original function in this effect, as you might find in a lot of other color correction effects in After Effects. So instead, I cut this effect using Edit>Cut, and then created an adjustment layer placed above the Footage layer. Then chose Edit>Paste to paste the Black & White effect to the adjustment layer. This gives me a lot more control and flexibility. So, I reduced the opacity of the adjustment layer (and, since the Black & White effect is the only thing on the adjustment layer, this is essentially just reducing the opacity of the Black & White effect) to 60%. This gives me the best of both worlds: I have a strong vintage color tint going on, but I also retain some of the original coloring. Note that if I'm blending these two together like this, that I might want to go back and adjust what we just did to the cyans. But for now, I'm happy.

Figure 6.11 After applying Black & White to an adjustment layer and then dialing back the opacity, we have a nice blend between the two.

The Brightness & Contrast Effect

The Brightness & Contrast effect is another effect that is also seen in Photoshop. The difference is that Adobe revamped the Brightness/Contrast adjustment for Photoshop CS3. Unfortunately, the After Effects version of Brightness & Contrast is still the old, terrible version, at least when it comes to lightening images. Even though I recommend eschewing this effect when it comes to lightening footage, it can still have some other useful purposes. And knowing why this effect can be destructive can help you understand why effects like Levels and Curves are so powerful.

The Brightness & Contrast effect only has two properties: Brightness and Contrast. Many users of Photoshop and After Effects turn to a Brightness & Contrast adjustment to quickly brighten an image without the steep learning curve of, say, Levels or Curves. But there is a great problem here. The Brightness & Contrast effect universally lightens or darkens every pixel on a layer. Let's see this in action.

Import the KS103.mov clip from the Artbeats folder in the Media folder of the exercise files. This stock footage clip from Artbeats contains some children playing. Notice the depth of the shadows in the trees behind the kids on the right side of the image.

Figure 6.12 The KS103.mov clip from Artbeats.

In the Project panel, drag this piece of footage down to the Create a new Composition button at the bottom of the Project panel. This will create a new composition with the same specs (e.g., size, pixel aspect ratio, duration, frame rate) as the footage. Then apply the Brightness & Contrast effect to the KS103.mov layer in the newly created comp. Take the Brightness value to 50.

Figure 6.13 The footage after applying Brightness & Contrast and taking the Brightness value to 50. Every pixel is lightened.

Now look in the shadow areas by the trees. They've been lightened, too! That's bad news, folks. When you brighten an image, you want to keep shadow areas dark. So, this is not the way to go.

You could use the Contrast part of Brightness & Contrast, but there are many other ways to increase image contrast that are much better. Another valid use for the Brightness & Contrast effect is to use it on grayscale patterns or maps to control effects. Because it operates at 32 bits per channel, you could also use this effect on HDR footage.

Personally, I just hate the Brightness & Contrast effect. Does that make me a bad person? You may disagree, but there so many other ways to adjust brightness and/or contrast, that you really shouldn't need to use this effect.

The Broadcast Colors Effect

The Broadcast Colors effect probably belongs in the Utility category, and is unique among effects in this category. The Broadcast Colors effect forces colors into compliance with video standards, such as NTSC and PAL. One of the purposes of these video standards is to specify the limits of allowable color and brightness. Sometimes, if you stay up late enough, you'll see badly produced infomercials and local TV programs that have colors that are beyond the limits of what is allowed. The results are that those pixels look too intense; almost glowing, as if only those pixels had just come out of a nuclear experience. The Broadcast Colors effect makes sure that all colors and brightness levels are broadcast safe so that this never happens.

Open the Broadcast Colors.aep project in the Chapter 6 folder of the exercise files. This project contains an image of one of the cutest kids you've probably ever seen in your life. She must have an extremely attractive father, whoever that lucky fellow might be. But with all the beauty of this image, it's far too saturated and intense for video. Apply the Broadcast Colors effect to the hanging out layer in the hanging out comp.

As soon as you apply the effect, you'll notice it springing into action, ridding your layer of any renegade colors that will look bad on video. You'll first want to select a Broadcast Locale, which will be either NTSC or PAL, depending on the country your video will be watched in. I'm in North America, so I'm going to leave this value set to NTSC. Unfortunately in this example image, the results of applying Broadcast Colors look terrible.

The results don't quite look up to par here because the default method of making the colors comply with video standards is to reduce the luminance of the offending pixels. That doesn't work out well in this case because of the textures in her jacket and in the background (which is actually a Lego replica of the Titanic). So, we need to adjust the How to Make Color

Figure 6.14 The hanging out image.

Figure 6.15 The results of applying the Broadcast Colors effect with the default settings.

Safe drop down. Change the value of this drop down to Reduce Saturation to make After Effects reduce the saturation (instead of the luminance) of offending pixels. In this case, the results look a little better.

Also in the How to Make Color Safe drop down, you'll find a couple of settings that don't really make too much sense. But they allow you view the problem areas in your footage. You can completely remove all pixels that are out of compliance by choosing Key Out Unsafe. Or, you can view only unsafe pixels by choosing

Figure 6.16 The results of Broadcast Colors with the How to Make Color Safe value changed to Reduce Saturation.

Figure 6.17 Selecting Key Out Safe from the How to Make Color Safe drop down will show you all pixels that are out of compliance with video standards.

Key Out Safe. After seeing which pixels are out of compliance, you may choose to use another color adjustment effect to adjust those values so that you have more control over how their color is corrected.

The last value at the bottom of the effect in the Effect Controls panel is Maximum Signal Amplitude (IRE), which monitors the brightness of footage. IRE is a unit of measurement, used to measure brightness in a video signal. This value sets the maximum allowable value of brightness in your footage. You can create a higher maximum brightness by increasing this value, but that also increases the chances of creating unsafe colors when viewed on some monitors.

Usually, when using this effect, I don't apply it to individual layers. In my final composition, I will create an adjustment layer and put it at the top of the layer stack in the Timeline panel. Then I will apply the Broadcast Colors effect to the adjustment layer so that all of the layers in the composition have broadcast safe color.

The Change Color Effect

The Change Color effect and the Change to Color effect (that we'll look at next) have annoyingly similar names, and identical purposes—to change a color in footage from its original color to another color. This is helpful for a wide variety of circumstances. Let's say that you had a shot of a large crowd, and an extra in the shot was wearing a shirt of a color that was distracting. You could use these color changing effects to choose a more suitable color.

From my experience, the Change to Color effect works a little better on average, but again here, it ends up as a matter of personal preference. For the sake of comparison, let's look at the Change Color effect.

Open the project Color Change.aep project from the Chapter 6 folder of the exercise files. We'll be using this simple project to compare the Change Color and Change to Color effects. With both effects, we'll be trying to change the color of the dot on the bird's face. Apply the Change Color effect to the bird layer in the bird comp.

Figure 6.18 The bird comp in the Color Change.aep project.

First off, we need to tell the Change Color effect the color we'd like to change. Click the eyedropper next to the Color To Change property, then click the orangish-red spot on the bird's face in the Composition panel. If you did it correctly, there should not be any visible change in the Composition panel, but the color swatch next to the Color To Change property should be should be the rust color of the spot on the bird's face.

Now that we've told the Change Color effect what color to change, we need to tell it how to change it. Use the Hue Transform, Lightness Transform, and Saturation Transform properties to adjust the hue, lightness, and saturation to choose a new color that the rust color in the bird's face will be changed to. Keep in mind that all of these properties can go to negative values to give you a wider range of choices.

In Figure 6.19, I used a Hue Transform value of 39, a Lightness Transform value of 10, and a Saturation Transform value of –50. This makes the red circle change color to blend in more with the rest of the bird's face.

Figure 6.19 The color of the spot on the bird's face changed with the Change Color effect.

In Figure 6.19, you can still see a little orange edge around the part of the bird's face that we tried to adjust. If you find that the Change Color effect isn't affecting as many pixels as you'd like (or if it is affecting too many pixels), then you can adjust the Matching Tolerance and Matching Softness values. Increasing them will select more pixels, decreasing them will limit the number of affected pixels. I found that the default values of 15% for Matching Tolerance and 0% for Matching Softness worked well in this example.

If you're not getting the results you're looking for, you can also change the Match Colors value to use the hue or the chroma of colors to match them. You can also select the option Invert Color Correction Mask to preserve the Color To Change color and adjust all other colors.

Figure 6.20 Selecting Invert Color Correction Mask protects the color we chose for the Color To Change value, and affects the other colors in the image.

The Change to Color Effect

The Change to Color effect is very similar to the Change Color effect. The difference is that the Change to Color effect allows you to select the specific color you'd like to change the other color to. This can be great for compositing two elements together in a scene. Maybe one clip has a different white balance, or some other color that is prominent. You can use the Change to Color effect to match the colors (almost) exactly.

Open up (or Revert) the Color Change.aep project from the Chapter 6 folder. Apply the Change to Color effect to the bird layer in the bird comp. In the Effect Controls panel, there are two color swatches here. The From swatch is the original color (what we are changing the color from), and the To color swatch is the color we want the From color swatch to become (what we are changing the color to). Click the eyedropper next to the From swatch, then click on the rust colored spot on the bird's face. To make sure you're getting the color you want, you can check the Info panel as move your cursor around. The Info panel displays the color of the pixel that your mouse happens to be over.

Figure 6.21 The Info panel displays the color of the pixel under your cursor, and can be used as a guide when selecting colors with eyedroppers.

Making Yourself Sick

Note that there is a stopwatch next to the To property. That means that you can animate a certain color changing to another color. If you wanted to animate yourself (or someone else) getting sick, you could select your skin tone in the From swatch, and then select the same color in the To swatch. Then animate that to change over time to a sickly pale green color. Disgusting.

Now that we've selected a From color, click the eyedropper next to the To color swatch, and then click on the yellow of the bird's face, next to the red spot. The results do need a little more work before they look decent.

One of the advantages of the Change to Color effect over the Change Color effect, is that we have three separate Tolerance controls for Hue, Lightness, Saturation. In the Change Color effect, there is only one Tolerance parameter. Having three values to help you select the exact color range to adjust is very helpful. The Change drop down allows you to select which of the properties you want to change with the effect, which determines which Tolerance controls get used to select color. Be aware that by default, only Hue is selected, which means that only the

Figure 6.22 After changing the From and To colors, the results aren't that great (yet).

Tolerance>Hue property will do much of anything until the Change drop down is altered.

In this case, all we really need to do is to increase the Tolerance>Hue value in the Effect Controls panel to about 17% to get a fairly believable result. We have a much smoother transition from the spot of new color to the rest of the bird's face.

Figure 6.23 After increasing the Hue value, we have a pretty decent removal of the rust-colored spot on the bird's face.

You might notice in Figure 6.23 (or in the project you're working on) that we have some colored noise in this image caused by the high ISO value I used when taking this photo. The problem is that some of that noise is a rusty red color—the same color we're trying to remove here. Because of this, the noisy red pixels are also turned yellow, which doesn't look all that great. And, realistically, if it's not noise, there will probably be something else in your footage that has a similar color to the color you're trying to change.

If you find that, like in this case, there are pixels of the From color that you don't want to change, you can duplicate the layer and create a mask on the duplicate (top) layer. You don't have to create a mask that is tight around the object that you want to change the color of. I used a simple elliptical mask around the bird's head, loosely and quickly created. That gives us a lot more flexibility, and a much improved result. Particularly, notice how much cleaner the black bar is in the background, as well as the bird's body.

Figure 6.24 The result of duplicating the layer, creating a sloppy mask around the bird's head, and changing the color of the spot on the bird's face with the Change to Color effect.

The Channel Mixer Effect

The Channel Mixer is great if you really know a lot about how colors work, and very challenging and unintuitive if you don't. The Channel Mixer effect allows you to blend channels together, which alters the colors of footage. This is great for making precise color adjustments, or for color grading.

Before we get into a practical application of this effect, we're going to take a step back and see exactly what this effect is doing. That way, we'll know what we're doing when using the Channel Mixer effect to adjust the colors of real footage.

Open the Channel Mixer.aep project from the Chapter 6 folder of the exercise files. In the Channel Mixer comp, you'll find two layers—a simple shape layer, and an Artbeats video clip. We'll first look at the shape layer, which already has the Channel Mixer effect applied for you. This shape layer contains three stars—one pure red, one pure green, and one that is pure blue.

The options for the Channel Mixer effect are a challenge to figure out without some help. With parameters like Red-Red, Red-Blue, and Green-Const, the Channel Mixer can certainly be a brain teaser. Even if you know this effect from the similar Photoshop adjustment, the interface is initially less user-friendly here.

Here's the way this works. The name of the color on the left refers to the input color (before applying the effect), and the name of the color on the right refers to the output color (after applying the effect).

Figure 6.25 The shape layer in the Channel Mixer comp in the Channel Mixer.aep project.

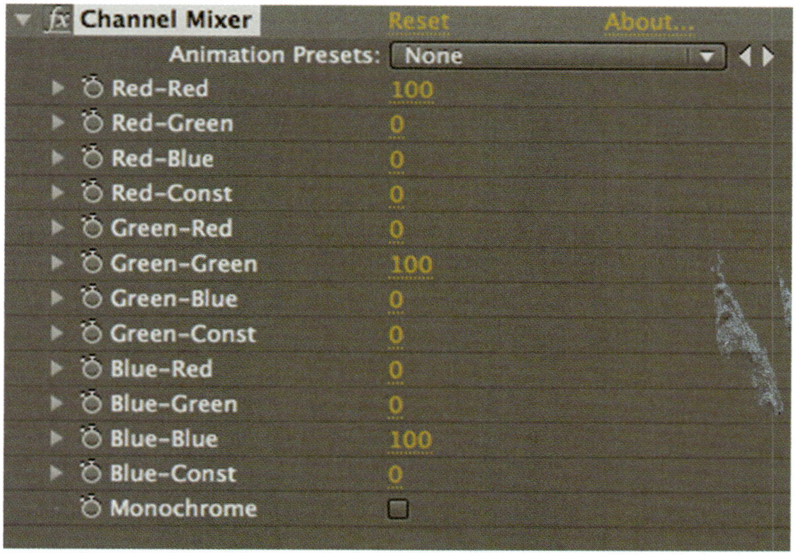

Figure 6.26 The esoteric Channel Mixer settings in the Effect Controls panel.

Let's take for example the Red-Green property. By default, it's set to 0, which means that there is no red (input) in the green channel (output). But if we took this value to 100, then it would add red to the green channel. When we add red to pure green (as seen in the green star in this comp), it becomes yellow.

You'll notice in the Effect Controls panel that the properties that are duplicates (e.g., Red-Red, Green-Green, Blue-Blue) are set at 100 by default. This just means that there is a full amount

Figure 6.27 After taking the Red-Green value to 100, red is mixed into the green channel, which turns the green star yellow.

of red in the red channel, green in the green channel, and so on. If we took the Red-Red value to 50, it would mean that there is half of the amount of red in the red channel. Because the red star only consists of pure red, when we take the Red-Red value down halfway, in effect we reduce the intensity of the red in the red star by half. Notice that the yellow (formerly green) star isn't affected, even though it has red in it. The Red-Red adjustment does not affect the red in the green star because it didn't start out having red, it was added by the effect.

Figure 6.28 With the Red-Red value at 50, the intensity of pure red is reduced.

You can also use this effect to create a great black and white result by selecting the Monochrome option at the bottom of the Effect Controls panel. With Monochrome selected, you can still control how colors are converted to black and white (i.e., their brightness) by using the color sliders in the Channel Mixer's effect options in the Effect Controls panel.

Each channel also has a Const value, which is short for constant. This property basically decides how much a particular color channel is in all color channels. So, if I increase the Blue-Const value to 50, you will notice blue mixed in to every other color.

Figure 6.29 Increasing the Blue-Const value makes all pixels more blue.

Now that we understand what's going on with the Channel Mixer effect, let's turn off the visibility of the shape layer, and turn on the visibility of the Artbeats clip to see how this effect can help you in the real world. The Channel Mixer effect has already been applied to this clip for you.

This Artbeats clip has a slight bluish tint to it. Blue tones—such as those seen in this clip—often suggest a relaxed feel, or a professional tone. But I want to color correct this clip so that it looks like the Los Angeles inner city—hot, rough, dead, and abrasive. To get this look, I want add a yellowish tint, but with a little orange as well. How are we to do this, seeing that there aren't any yellow controls? This is where it pays to know a little color theory. The opposite of blue is yellow, so we can actually add yellow by subtracting blue. Add just a touch of red to create orange.

Figure 6.30 The CED113.mov Artbeats video clip.

To achieve the desired results, I took Red-Green to 45, Red-Blue to 10, Blue-Green to −30, and Blue-Blue down to 85. Basically, we added a little bit of red, and even more yellow by subtracting blue. The results look fantastic.

Figure 6.31 The Artbeats clip after color grading with the Channel Mixer effect.

I'm satisfied with the results as they are, but we can also take this a step further. I added Hue/Saturation to desaturate the cityscape a little, then added a Curves effect with a typical S curve adjustment (both effects discussed later in this chapter). I also applied a mask and the Fast Blur effect to create a slight depth of field effect.

Figure 6.32 We get a slightly more cinematic feel by adding a few finishing touches.

The Color Balance Effect

The Color Balance effect is one of the effects that I use most often. It is very similar to the Channel Mixer effect, but it gives you control over the color in each channel in the shadows, midtones, and highlights. Note that this effect is far superior to the Color Balance (HLS) effect, which actually has nothing whatsoever in common with this effect. And, as with the Channel Mixer effect, it really pays to know about color relationships when working with the Color Balance effect.

Import the UW225.mov clip from the Artbeats folder in the Media folder in the exercise files. This is some beautiful footage of water splashing around. Make a new composition that is the size of this clip, and add it to the comp. Apply the Color Balance effect to this clip.

As seen in the Effect Controls panel, you can adjust the color balance for each color channel in the shadows, midtones, and highlights.

What we we're going to do is to add some more blue to this water. Increase the Shadow Blue Balance, the Midtone Blue Balance, and the Hilight Blue Balance to get blue water. Just a little adjustment will work here, especially if you're increasing shadows, midtones, and highlights. I used a value of about 50 for each.

But let's say now that we wanted to add a slight cyan tint here. We can accomplish that in a couple different ways. We could add cyan by reducing the amount of red. We can also add cyan by increasing green (because there is extra blue here). I'm going to take

Figure 6.33 The Artbeats video clip we'll be using for this section on the Color Balance effect.

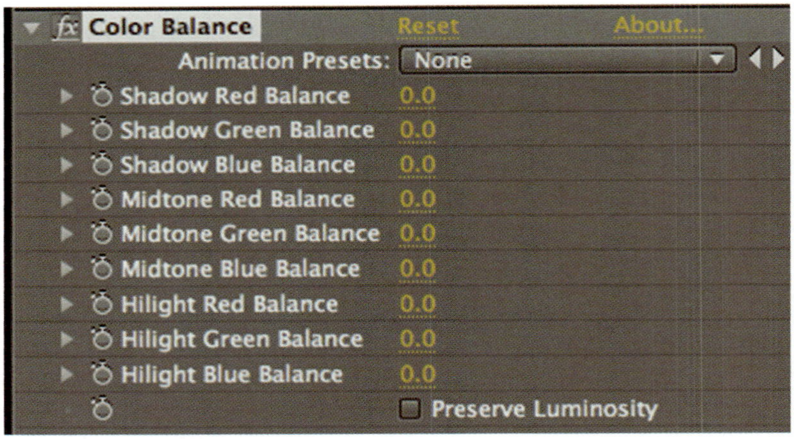

Figure 6.34 The options for the Color Balance effect in the Effect Controls panel.

the Hilight Blue Balance value down to about 25, and then increase the Hilight Green Balance to 50. We could add more green in the shadows and midtones, but the results here look pretty good as is.

When using the Color Balance effect in this example, you might have noticed how the luminance changed in addition to the colors. As we add more light (by increasing the amount of red, green, or blue in the image), things naturally get brighter. The opposite is also true. If we were to subtract blue to add a yellow tint, the image would become darker because we are removing light. If you're worried about that shift in brightness, you can click the Preserve Luminosity checkbox at the bottom of this effect in the Effect Controls panel. In this case, the results become much more intense with added contrast.

Figure 6.35 After increasing the blues in the shadows, midtones, and highlights.

Figure 6.36 The image with an added cyan tint, created by adding a lot of blue and a little green.

Colorizing with Color Balance

The Color Balance effect is not really intended to be used to colorize black and white footage. As a matter of fact, if your layer is pure black and/or pure white, Color Balance will have no effect whatsoever. But if your layer has shades of gray, such as in patterns created by the Fractal Noise effect, then the Color Balance effect can be used to subtly introduce color. Again, it might not be the best tool for the job. I love the Color Balance effect and its results, so I often use it wherever I can. But that's just me.

Figure 6.37 The results of selecting Preserve Luminosity.

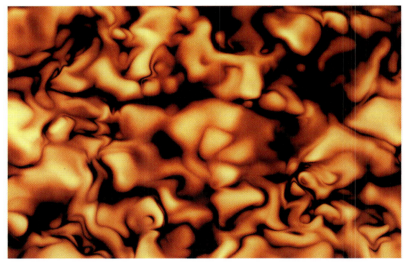

Figure 6.38 The Color Balance effect used to colorize a grayscale pattern made with Fractal Noise. To get this amount of color, I had to use extreme values (e.g., over 70 for positive red values and less than –50 for negative green and blue values).

The Color Balance (HLS) Effect

Contrary to what the name might suggest, the Color Balance (HLS) effect is nothing like the Color Balance effect we just looked at. Instead, it gives you but three parameters: Hue, Lightness, and Saturation. For the life of me, I can't think of any reason to use this effect when you have the Hue/Saturation effect available, and even the After Effects help documentation says that this effect is included only for compatibility with older projects. The Hue/Saturation effect has the exact same controls (but with visual aids), and many others as well. Hue/Saturation also operates at 32 bits per channel, while Color Balance (HLS) operates at only 16 bits per channel.

The only real benefit to this effect is that the Color Balance (HLS) effect is keyframable. Whereas the only way to keyframe Hue/Saturation is to colorize the source layer.

The Color Link Effect

Like Broadcast Colors, the Color Link effect is one that I think would fit better in the Utility category of effects. Its main purpose is to convert an entire layer to the color of another layer. You can have Color Link discover and use the average pixel value of any layer in the current comp, or the brightest or darkest pixel, or the median pixel color, or it can perform such analysis on the alpha channel. This is helpful for quickly creating a layer that is the color of the background color of another layer. One of the best potential uses for the Color Link effect is for color correction with other effects. That's what I thought this effect could be used for. Unfortunately, the Color Link effect is unaffected by other applied effects unless first precomposing the layer, so it's not as helpful as it could be as a reference for color correction.

Figure 6.39 The Sample drop down in the Color Link effect. These options allow you to choose how the Color Link effect will analyze the source layer.

When you apply the Color Link effect, you first specify which layer will be analyzed by the effect in the Source Layer drop down. Then, in the Sample drop down, determine how the Color

Link will find the color it returns. Selecting Average, for example, will cause the Color Link effect to examine the layer chosen in the Source Layer drop down, and fill the layer with the color that represents the average pixel value. You can also then blend this color into the source layer using opacity or blend modes.

So, all in all, Color Link is a valuable effect for analyzing the makeup of a layer, color-wise. This information can then be used for other purposes. But the effect itself is not really a color correction effect.

The Color Stabilizer Effect

The Color Stabilizer effect attempts to stabilize the luminance of video that varies from frame to frame. This is especially helpful for those doing stop motion video, or time lapse photography. Both types of shooting are often plagued by wild variations in luminance from frame to frame because of the difference in time between the capture of each frame. Luminance randomization might also happen because of the inability of a video camera's white point correction to establish a consistent white point. If you'd like to practice stabilizing color, import the shaky luminance.mp4 file from the Video folder in the Media folder of the exercise files.

While it is next to impossible to demonstrate luminance variation over time in a book, it's not difficult to describe the steps to fix this problem with the Color Stabilizer effect. First, let's take a look at the options in the Color Stabilizer effect.

Figure 6.40 The options in the Color Stabilizer effect in the Effect Controls panel.

This effect stabilizes color by analyzing colors from a sample frame to determine how to conform the luminance across all frames. Move the current time indicator to a frame that has the appropriate luminance levels. The click the Set Frame text (button) at the very top of the effect in the Effect Controls panel, next to the Reset and About buttons. If your colors completely freaked out when you first applied Color Stabilizer, clicking Set Frame should also return the look of the layer back to normal.

Before we set Black and White Point locations, we need to adjust the Stabilize drop down. There are three options here: Brightness, Levels, and Curves. If you choose Brightness, the White Point value will be grayed out and you will only be able to specify a Black Point value for luminance stability. Selecting the default value of Levels gives you both a Black Point and a White Point. Selecting Curves allows you to use the Black Point, White Point, and Mid Point values. The default value of Levels is usually what I prefer to use.

Next, put the Black Point effect control point in a dark area of the image, and the White Point effect control point in a light area of the image. Note that it doesn't need to be in pure black or pure white. As a matter of fact, I put my Black Point in the water, and the White Point in the sky, and both of these spots are distinctly blue. The most important aspect of the Black and White Point locations is that the areas must have areas of colors that are easy to track. They must also be in areas where it will be easy to spot changes in brightness. The Black Point and White Point areas also need to be in areas that should have consistent luminance (so, don't put them on a strobe light). Finally, the Black Point area and the White Point area must contrast significantly from each other.

Figure 6.41 The Black Point is in the water on the left, and the White Point is in the sky at the top center.

In our case, particularly with the Black Point in the water, we want to make sure that our stabilization isn't thrown off by whitecaps and shadows. We just want it to take an average of the surrounding pixels. You can increase (or decrease) the size of the area used by the Black Point and White Point by increasing (or decreasing) the Sample Size value.

Be sure that as you use this effect, your effect control points never come into contact with any object that has a different luminance value than its initial spot. Remember that you can animate these points, if needed, to avoid obstacles that might interfere with their ability to consistently track and correct the luminance of the layer. The results here are not perfect, but they are an impressive improvement over the original.

The Colorama Effect

The Colorama effect is one of the most powerful and complicated effects in all of After Effects. It is an effect used to recolor layers, and it's probably the most powerful tool for this purpose that I have ever seen. Even though this effect is so complex and powerful, it also has some quick and easy presets to use if you don't feel like tackling the steep learning curve here. Colorama was created by After Effects genius and legend Brian Maffitt, who also created such great effects as Shatter and Radio Waves, so you know it's good.

Because of the complexities involved with the Colorama effect and the sheer volume of properties here, I strongly recommend following along with this section by opening up the Colorama. aep project you'll find in the Chapter 6 folder of the exercise files. We'll start in the Colorama START comp. Apply the Colorama effect to the Rad Rockets layer in this comp.

Many people are initially scared away from the Colorama effect because the default settings create a garish rainbow effect. To make matters worse, the parameters for the Colorama effect are quite numerous and not always intuitive.

Figure 6.42 The default results of applying the Colorama effect to the Rad Rockets layer in the Colorama START composition.

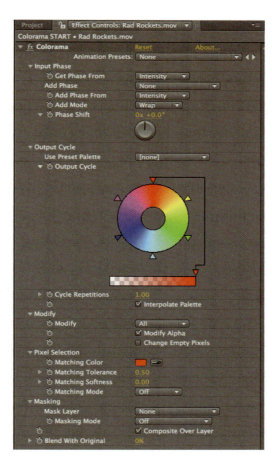

Figure 6.43 The properties of the Colorama effect with the categories expanded.

Colorama Overview

Before we make any changes to Colorama, we need to understand what it is doing. First, Colorama converts the image to grayscale. Unless otherwise specified, this only happens behind the scenes. Colorama then takes those grayscale values and remaps them to a different color scheme. In the case of Figure 6.42, for example, we're not seeing the grayscale values, we're only seeing the result of the color remapping.

Using the controls in the Input Phase area, you can specify which pixels are affected. In the Output Cycle controls, you choose what the colors will be remapped to. The Output Cycle area gives you very precise manual control using a color wheel, or fast and easy control using a host of presets in the Use Preset Palette drop down.

Using the controls in the Modify, Pixel Selection, and Masking areas, you can further customize exactly which pixels are altered with the Colorama effect.

Using the Output Cycle

Let's now get a little more familiar with the Output Cycle properties. No matter how deep or shallow you wish to go in your knowledge of Colorama, you'll want to know at least the basic features of this area. The Output Cycle controls specify the color being output from Colorama. This is also the area that I referenced earlier that contains a wealth of pre-made presets to use.

Go to the Mt. Rainer comp. This comp contains a nested composition of a solid with the Ramp effect applied. I had to precompose it so that Colorama would recognize the gradient. Apply Colorama to this linear gradient.

Figure 6.44 The Ramp precomp in the Mt Rainier layer.

After applying Colorama, you'll see the now familiar over-the-top rainbow colors applied to it. In the Effect Controls panel, open the Output Cycle controls area to see the actual Output Cycle . If you're just reading this book and don't have After Effects in front of you, you can refer back to Figure 6.43 to see the colorful Output Cycle .

The triangles on the Output Cycle are like color stops on a gradient. This gradient is then mapped to the values in the layer. The top of the Output Cycle (red in this case) is currently mapped to red. And then, following the cycle around clockwise, shadow areas are remapped to orange, and 50% gray (the shade of gray exactly between pure white and pure black) is at the bottom of the Output Cycle (cyan in this case). Highlights are remapped to magenta, until you get back to the top of the gradient, which is also where white is remapped to. That is why the black to white gradient seen in Figure 6.44 was remapped to red at both the top (black) and the bottom (white) of the layer in Figure 6.45.

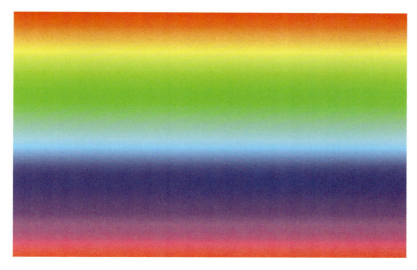

Figure 6.45 The Ramp precomp
with Colorama applied at its
default settings.

The triangles on this Output Cycle wheel can be moved around to remap colors to different parts of an image. You can click in a blank spot around the outer edge of the wheel to launch a floating window with your operating system's color picker to create a new color stop. Also, if you Ctrl(Win)/Cmd(Mac)+click and drag on an existing color triangle, it will create a copy of it. To remove color triangles, simply click and drag it away from the wheel. You can have up to 64 different colors on an Output Cycle color wheel.

I moved around some of these triangles to create a different look with this simple gradient. I moved the magenta triangle closer to the blue one, and the yellow triangle closer to the green one, and completely removed the cyan triangle. Can you see why the results turned out the way they did? Notice that, just like in regular

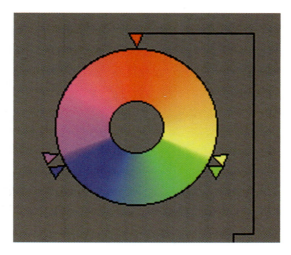

Figure 6.46 The changes I
made to the Output Cycle .

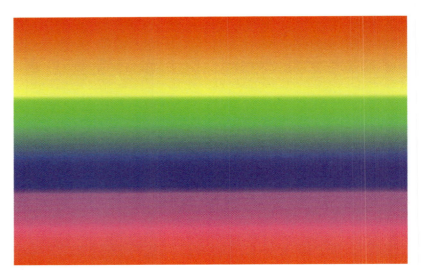

Figure 6.47 The results of my Output Cycle changes on my gradient.

gradients, when you pull two colors close together, the transition between them becomes much sharper and less gradual.

You also might have noticed that when a color triangle is selected, it has a line that goes down to another gradient bar below the Output Cycle . This is for determining the transparency of a particular color. Select a color triangle on the color wheel, then drag the corresponding triangle on the transparency gradient to the left to reduce its transparency. Note that this only reduces the transparency of this color in the Colorama effect. The transparency of the layer itself is unaffected.

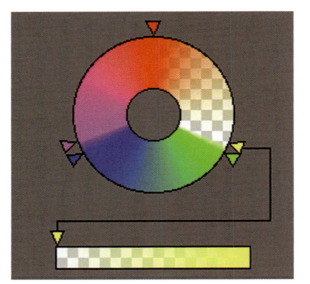

Figure 6.48 The transparency of a color stop is adjusted.

The colors on the color wheel blend smoothly together, or interpolate. If you wanted hard edges between colors instead of a soft transition, you could deselect the Interpolate Palette option in the Output Cycle area. Notice how this also removes the smooth gradations in the Output Cycle color wheel.

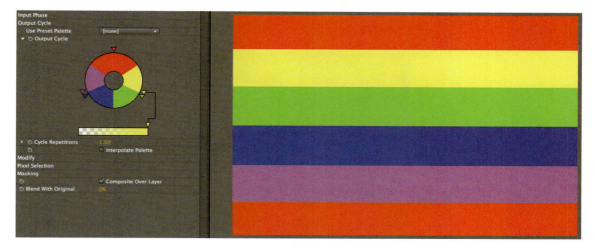

Figure 6.49 The results of deselecting the Interpolate Palette option.

Before we cover the presets that ship with Colorama, be aware that you can also repeat the entire gradient by increasing the Cycle Repetitions value. Let's say you were using Colorama to create a cloudy background. You can manually make a color wheel that has blue and white alternating all around it. That would take a while to create. Instead, you could simply make a color wheel that had one instance of blue and white (or, one cloud), and then increase the Cycle Repetitions value to taste.

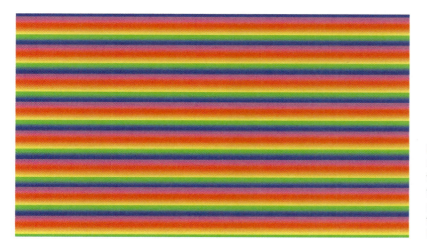

Figure 6.50 Increasing the Cycle Repetitions value causes the same pattern to repeat. In this example, I used the same gradient from Figure 6.47 with the Cycle Repetitions value increased to 9.

Using Output Cycle Presets

Now we come to the easy part of the Colorama effect—the presets. At the top of the Output Cycle area in the Effect Controls panel, you'll see the Use Preset Palette drop down. These contain a wide array of useful presets that you can use as is, or as a starting point for your own color cycles. The top half of the list is for utilitarian purposes, and the presets on the bottom are for creative, colorful uses.

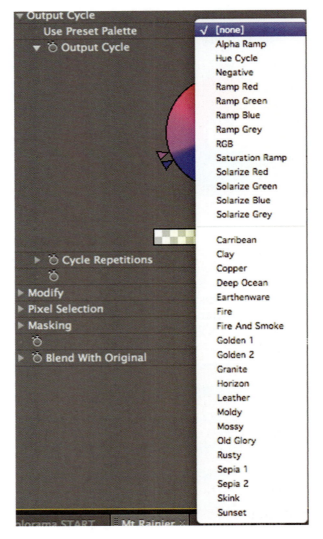

Figure 6.51 The list of Output Cycle presets.

I'm going to hop on over to the Turbulent Noise composition. This contains a grayscale pattern created with the Turbulent Noise effect. Many effects, such as Fractal Noise, Cell Pattern, and

Wave World, only create grayscale patterns like Turbulent Noise does. Using these Colorama presets is the fastest way (and often the best way) to add color to them.

Figure 6.52 The fiery grayscale pattern, created with the Turbulent Noise effect.

This pattern looks a little like fire, but without color, probably no one would make the connection. So, I'm going to select the Fire preset from the Use Preset Palette drop down. This preset contains a rather detailed fiery gradient that adds just the right touch to make my fire more believable.

Figure 6.53 The gradient created from the Fire preset and its results when applied to the Turbulent Noise pattern.

Using the Input Phase Controls

We're now going to back up a step and look at some of the Input Phase controls. The Input Phase controls allow you to determine which color attribute (e.g., intensity, saturation, and so on) will be included in the Colorama calculations. You can, of course, choose color attributes from the current layer, but you can also choose color attributes from another layer.

I'm going to go back to the Ramp precomp layer in the Mt. Rainier comp, and I'll apply the Deep Ocean preset from the Use Preset Palette drop down in the Output Cycle area.

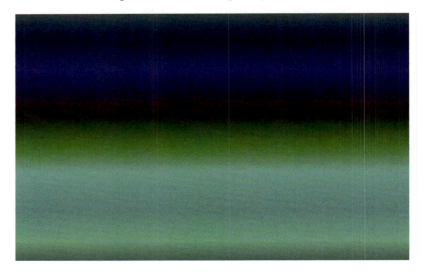

Figure 6.54 The Ramp layer with the Deep Ocean Colorama preset applied.

The layer underneath this Ramp layer is a video clip of Mt. Rainier. The Mt. Rainier layer is currently off, but you can see what this clip looks like in Figure 6.55.

We'll come back to this Mt. Rainier clip in just a moment. First, let's look at the top of the Input Phase controls. The first option is the Get Phase From drop down, which determines what attributes of the current layer are used in Colorama. The next option, Add Phase, allows you to add the phase (or set of color attributes) to the results on this layer. From the Add Phase drop down, I'm going to choose the Mt. Rainier layer. Instantly, the results update, and we see the image of Mt. Rainier in the current result. From the Add Phase From drop down, you can specify the color attributes to use from the Add Phase layer. Think of Add Phase From as being exactly like Get Phase From, but for the other layer.

To use only the phase from the Mt. Rainier layer, change the Get Phase From value to Zero. This will completely ignore the gradient ramp on this layer.

Figure 6.55 The Mt. Rainier layer.

Figure 6.56 The results of using the phase from the Mt Rainier layer.

You can also use the Phase Shift property to cycle the Output Cycle colors through your image.

Fine Tuning Selections

As mentioned, the Modify, Pixel Selection, and Masking properties can be used to fine tune the areas or components of your footage you want adjusted.

The Modify area allows you to control what attribute of your layer you want changed. You can actually use Colorama to

Figure 6.57 The same results as Figure 6.51, with the Get Phase From drop down set to zero.

perform subtle color adjustments by setting the Modify drop down to the same color attribute that you selected in the Get Phase From drop down in the Input Phase controls.

Pixel Selection allows you to choose a specific color to adjust. In order for the other Pixel Selection properties to work, you'll first need to change the Matching Mode drop down to anything but None. Then, select a color using the Matching Color eyedropper (or color swatch) and refine it using Matching Tolerance and Matching Softness.

The Masking section allows you to use another layer as a matte, to control which areas of your layer are affected. The Masking Mode value determines how the matte from the other layer affects the current layer.

Colorama and Luma Mattes

I find these days that I'm using Colorama a lot to help with creating luma mattes, especially for sky replacement, which is what we're going to take a look at now. I own a Canon 7D DSLR camera, and that poor little guy has such a hard time with highlights. Sometimes it feels like it has a two stop dynamic range. So I'm always needing to replace blown out skies, and Colorama is a great help with that. Let's look at an example. For this, I've created a separate project. Open Luma Matte.aep from the Chapter 6 folder of the exercise files. This contains a shot that was intended to go at the end of a movie that features a bunch of children in it. This gloomy, blown out sky just doesn't fit.

Figure 6.58 The original footage.

So, what we need to do is to apply Colorama to the footage layer (an image sequence called jib). Open the Output Cycle area and from the Use Preset Palette drop down, choose Ramp Gray. This basically maps all colors to a black and white gradient. Nothing special here ... YET. The Output Cycle color wheel shows us the gradient that the image is being mapped to. What we need to do is fiddle with this until the sky is white and the foreground is black, with gray edges. That is the ideal because it will make the best luma matte. However, that might be a challenge in some cases, and might need to be supplemented with additional masks, especially if there are highlights in the foreground. That might be a bit of a challenge in this case because the footage is DSLR footage and is highly compressed, and the tress in the background are not sharp.

To try and accomplish this, we're going to try to crush the shadows and dark midtones to black, and blast the highlights and bright midtones to white. So, I'm going to click at a couple places on the Output Cycle to add extra white and black color stops, as shown in Figure 6.59.

With this as my setting, I get a good edge (which is really the key to getting a good luma matte—pun intended). The sky is mostly white, the edges have gray (which will create semi-transparency), and the foreground is mostly black. Of course the highlights in the foreground (such as those found in the window sills) just won't go away, so we will probably need to mask those out.

Now select the jib layer (NOT the Colorama effect—you may need to press F2 or click in a blank spot in the Timeline panel to deselect the effect and the layer, and then click the layer to

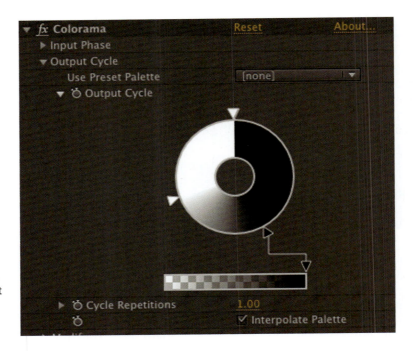

Figure 6.59 My Output Cycle. I manually created the extra white and black color triangles by simply clicking on the Output Cycle in those places and choosing white/black from the color picker.

Figure 6.60 The final luma matte created by adjusting the Colorama Output Cycle.

ensure that the entire layer is selected), and then press Ctrl+D(Win)/Cmd+D(Mac) to duplicate the layer. Then, on the bottom layer (the original layer) go to the Modes column in the Timeline panel, and from the TrkMat drop down, choose Luma Inverted Matte. This uses our grayscale image from Colorama (on the top layer) to create transparency on the bottom layer, which pretty much removes the sky. I've created a simple sky gradient layer beneath this, so you get a feel for what we're going for here. Although on your own, you may want to get an actual footage element with noise and clouds and so forth. Be aware that if you were to do that, at least in this case, you'd also need to track the shot so that the sky would fit. With this simple gradient, that's not really necessary.

Figure 6.61 The initial results of using our Colorama luma matte.

With a sky replacement job, the results most likely aren't going to be perfect. In this case for example, the scene is much more bright and happy, but now the shadows don't match. In a scene with bright sunlight, the shadows would be strong—dark with sharp edges. Here, they are clearly soft and diffuse, and it would be a ridiculous amount of work to try to fix that. But we can do a few things to improve other aspects of this image. We can balance the sky by adjusting the Opacity value of the Gradient Overlay on the sky layer to blend it more into the white solid it's applied to in order to brighten the sky.

This image will also benefit from some color correction so that the foreground matches the new sky. I've already created a couple adjustments for you as a starting point, so just enable the visibility of the Curves and Levels effects on the jib layer. With these adjustments, I increased the contrast (because the shadows would be darker on a brighter day), and I also added some blue to the original layer.

Again, as mentioned, there are things that we can do to improve this further, and it's not perfect, but it's a fairly decent (and quick) sky replacement, especially considering the source material.

Figure 6.62 The final sky replacement composite after adjusting some colors.

Colorama Mini-Project

Simply as food for thought, I've created a small project using Colorama that is included in the Colorama.aep project from the Chapter 6 folder. I've created this using techniques and concepts that we've already covered, so I won't go into detail here. I was going for an edgy look (as the soundtrack layer will attest). I used the footage of Mt. Rainier as the start layer. Then I used some green screen footage of my friend and master unicyclist, Paavo, for the Add Phase layer. I then got rid of most of the background and composited them together. And all of this with one instance of the Colorama effect and with only one layer visible. I then added Color Balance to add color to the end result.

Figure 6.63 My Colorama project from the Finished Project comp.

The Curves Effect

The Curves effect, also found in Photoshop, is another one of my go to effects, and is generally one of the more common effects out there. The most popular use for Curves is to adjust luminance, but you can also adjust the values of each color channel independently if you wanted to use Curves as a color adjustment tool.

Curves is often compared to another luminance correcting Photoshop favorite—the Levels effect. We'll talk in detail about Levels a little later in this chapter. For now, all you need to know is the difference between Levels and Curves. Basically, Levels allows you to adjust three components—shadows, midtones, and highlights. Curves, on the other hand, gives you individual control of up to 256 different tones. As you can imagine, with all of that extra control also comes an extra degree of challenge when learning this effect. But once you understand what's going on, you'll find yourself turning to Curves all the time.

I've created a project that we'll use for both Levels and Curves so that you can use them both on the same files to get a better idea of how to create the same results with both effects. Open the Levels and Curves.aep project from the Chapter 6 folder of the exercise files. First, we'll start with the fireworks comp, which is in desperate need of some Curves love.

Figure 6.64 The fireworks comp in the Levels and Curves project. This image appears courtesy of Angela McInroe.

In this otherwise cool photo, the fireworks aren't quite bright enough as this shot was taken when it wasn't late enough at night. Additionally, as a result of the time of the shot, the night sky isn't quite dark enough. Apply the Curves effect to this layer. In the Effect Controls panel, you'll see the baffling Curves interface.

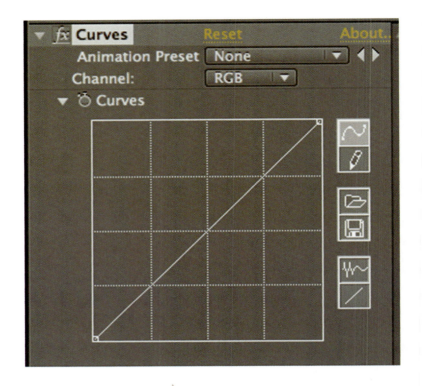

Figure 6.65 The Curves effect in the Effect Controls panel.

This diagonal line represents how the luminance values of this image are mapped. The bottom edge of this graph represents the current luminance values, from black (left) to white (right). The left edge represents how the colors will be remapped, from black (bottom) to white (top). That is why this line is a diagonal line, because by default, black is mapped to black, white is mapped to white, 50% gray is mapped to 50% gray, and so on. But if we were to click 50% gray (the point in the center of the graph), and drag it upwards slightly, it would make the midtones lighter.

Remember that the left edge represents the new (output) luminance, from the dark tones at the bottom to the bright tones at the top. So, when we move a point up, we brighten those values, and when we drag a point down, we darken those values.

I'm going to click the Reset button at the top of the effect to get our curve back to the way it was. What I really want to do to this image is to darken the shadow areas and brighten the highlights. In doing so, we will use such a common method that it has its own name—the S curve. The name comes from the way the curve looks when we're done editing it. To create the S curve, click on the line over the input shadow area (on the left hand side of the curve), and drag downwards. This will darken the shadows. Next, click on

Figure 6.66 Dragging the point that represents 50% gray upwards lightens the midtones.

the line over the input highlights area (on the right hand side of the curve) and drag upwards. This will brighten the highlights. The results in the Effect Controls panel now look like an S curve, and the contrast has been increased dramatically in our image.

Figure 6.67 The result of applying an S curve adjustment.

The real benefit of Curves is that we have this entire curve to adjust, not just three points. If there was a precise shade of gray that you wanted to adjust, you could make it brighter or darker without adjusting other shades. This is much more control than you could get with the Levels effect. On the other hand, this may be too much control in some instances.

Another feature that you'll find in both Levels and Curves is the ability to adjust individual color channels. This is almost like having a built in Color Balance effect. I like the result we achieved with the fireworks image. But it's a little too red for my taste. Let's fix that by going to the Channel drop down, and changing this value from the default RGB, to Red. This gives you a brand new Curves adjustment (a fresh diagonal line), just for the red color channel. To reduce the amount of red in this image, I'm going to click in the center of the curve and drag down slightly. Now our image looks a little more balanced. Taking away red light, also made the image a little darker, which actually works in our favor here. If you take the Channel drop down back to RGB, you'll see that our curve is still here, and was left untouched by what we did to the red channel.

Watch Out for Curves!

One of the things that you should probably avoid for realistic color adjustment is having a point on the left higher on the graph than a point on the right. That would make shadow areas brighter than areas of the image that were originally brighter than the shadows. This usually creates weird, posterized effects. Great for aliens and special effects, but not the best thing for realistic color correction.

Figure 6.68 The results of reducing the amount of red light in this image.

Now open up the sea lions comp in this project. This contains a layer with a photo I took of some sea lions. The photo was taken from a large distance with a budget quality lens, while these sea lions were being covered in the mist from crashing ocean waves. All of these things combined do not a well balanced image make. Apply the Curves effect this image in the sea lions comp.

Figure 6.69 The sea lions layer in the sea lions comp.

Obviously, we need to darken this layer quite a bit. But, if you try the previous method of darkening (i.e., grabbing the curve and pulling downwards), you'll notice that you can't quite get it as dark as it needs to be.

Figure 6.70 The result of darkening the curve by dragging the center of the curve downwards.

The solution here is to do something we haven't yet attempted. We need to darken the black point. In other words, we need to darken the darkest part of the image. So far, we've adjusted the curve itself, but the lower left and upper right corners of the curve represent the darkest and brightest parts of the image, respectively. To darken the black point, drag the lower left corner point of the curve to the right, along the bottom edge of the graph. I stopped at about 40% of the way. If you're wondering how I knew to take it to that particular spot, I used the Info panel as a guide. Thankfully, the Info panel gives you the live update of the color value of the pixel that your mouse is currently over, *after* all applied effects. After darkening the darkest point, I then made a slight S curve in the small, remaining part of the curve to boost the contrast. The results look much better.

Figure 6.71 The final curve and result.

Curves' Two Export File Types

A little known secret about Curves is that it can actually export curve files for reuse later. If you click the little disk icon on the side of the Curves effect in the Effect Controls panel, you'll be prompted to save an ACV file. However, you can also create curves by clicking the pencil icon, and then drawing the curve by hand. Then, when you save the file with the pencil tool selected, you'll save an AMP file. This AMP file can be used with the PS Arbitrary Map effect, discussed later in this chapter. Both ACV and AMP files can be loaded back into the Curves effect (in either Photoshop or After Effects) by clicking the open file icon that looks like an open folder on the right side of the Curves effect in the Effect Controls panel.

The Equalize Effect

If there were a luminance-based communist movement, the Equalize effect would be its leader. The purpose of the Equalize effect is to redistribute luminance values across an image, so that there is a greater balance among all pixels.

Open the Equalize.aep project from the Chapter 6 folder if you'd like to follow along. This project contains a shot of the Space Needle in Seattle, Washington.

Figure 6.72 The space needle comp in the Equalize.aep project.

This image is out of balance, as it was taken as part of an HDR sequence. Because of this, it has a lowered aperture value (f-stop), which eliminates the highlights. However, we need to call in a favor from another tool to really see what's going on with the luminance in this image. Apply the Levels effect to see a histogram, which gives us a readout of the luminance values in our image.

We'll obviously talk much more about this when we cover the Levels effect, coming up later in this chapter. For now, just know that the left side of this chart shows us shadows and the right side shows us the highlights. The height of the graph indicates the amount of that particular luminance value. This histogram is telling us that there are no highlights, loads of middle range values, and a little bit of the darkest shadow areas.

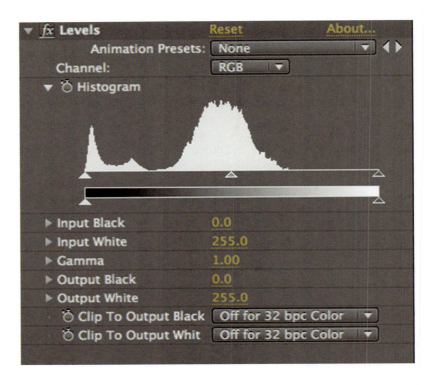

Figure 6.73 The histogram in the Levels effect tells us about the luminance values in our footage.

Now, delete the Levels effect and instead apply the Equalize effect. You can instantly see a significant difference in the tonal balance.

The results look much better as the luminance values are redistributed, or equalized, across the entire spectrum. But in all fairness, you should be aware that the Equalize effect is not always the instant improvement that it was here. What we really wanted to do was to create more tonal balance. If you apply another instance of the Levels effect after Equalize (below it in the Effect Controls panel), you'll see that the luminance values are now more balanced, and there is a little bit of each brightness value.

There are only two options here—the Equalize drop down and the Amount to Equalize value. Amount to Equalize is basically like the Blend with Original property we see in other effects. Really, it's reducing the amount of equalization, but it acts similar to an opacity property for this effect. The Equalize drop down allows you to choose from three different equalizing methods. Photoshop Style and RGB are very similar, as they

Figure 6.74 The result of applying the Equalize effect to this image.

Figure 6.75 The histogram in the Levels effect after applying Equalize.

both attempt to equalize your layer, while still keeping the basic shape of your histogram intact. The other setting, Brightness, tries to make a literal equalization, making most luminance values exactly equal.

Figure 6.76 The histogram and results of changing the Equalize drop down to Brightness.

The Exposure Effect

The Exposure effect is another luminance correcting effect, like Curves or Levels. And although you can use the Exposure effect in projects that are 8 or 16 bits per channel, it was created for the purpose of adjusting the exposure of footage that is 32 bits per channel.

If you'd like to follow along, I've created the Exposure.aep project in the Chapter 6 folder of the exercise files. This contains a camera raw image that is 16 bits per channel (you can tell this from selecting the image in the Project panel and seeing Trillions of Colors at the top), in a project that is 16 bits per channel. That might seem like useless information now, but it will be important soon, so just remember this.

Apply the Exposure effect to this image. There are two ways to adjust an image with this effect—by adjusting the luminance of the entire image, or by adjusting the luminance of each color channel individually. You choose what type of adjustments you'd like to make by choosing either Master or Individual Channels from the Channels drop down at the top of the Exposure effect in the Effect Controls panel. When Master is selected, you can adjust the properties in the Master area, but the individual color channel controls are not adjustable. Selecting Individual Channels

Figure 6.77 The Camera Raw Image comp in the Exposure aep project.

as the Channels value will allow you to adjust the Red, Green, and Blue values, but it will gray out the controls in the Master area.

I usually leave the Channels value set to its default of Master. This is because the Exposure effect attempts to use camera terminology and behavior to adjust luminance, and the Master controls are more fitting for this.

The After Effects help documentation suggests viewing the Exposure property as f-stops on a camera. Accordingly, increasing the Exposure value will brighten an image, and decreasing it will darken an image. The results are pretty good, and we can get these results by just adjusting one property.

The Gamma Correction property can make images lighter or darker by respectively increasing or decreasing its value. The Gamma Correction default value of 1 has no effect. We can use the Offset property to adjust (darken or brighten) shadows and midtones while leaving highlights largely unaffected. However, if I decide to reduce the Offset value (by even −0.06!), you can see that things fall apart very fast.

The reason why this looks terrible is because we're editing in 16 bits per channel. Technically, this effect also works at 8 and 16 bits. Realistically, however, it doesn't work all that great unless you're in 32 bits per channel. So, let's fix this. We

Figure 6.78 The result of increasing the Exposure value to 1 (the equivalent of one full f-stop). The results are quite natural.

Figure 6.79 Taking the Offset value to even −0.06 produces terrible results.

can't put this layer or even this comp into 32 bits per channel mode. Bit depth is a function of the entire After Effects project. So, go back to the Project panel, and Alt(Win)/Opt(Mac)+click the

Figure 6.80 The project bit depth display at the bottom of the Project panel. Alt/Opt+click this display to change the bit depth of the project to 32 bpc.

project color depth display at the bottom of the panel until it displays 32 bpc.

As soon as the bit depth of the project is changed to 32 bits per channel, the results are instantly corrected. This is because there are more colors available in 32 bits per channel mode, so there is more editing room.

Figure 6.81 After the bit depth of the project is expanded, the ugly colors fix themselves.

The Gamma/Pedestal/Gain Effect

The Gamma/Pedestal/Gain effect is an effect that I rarely use. It's yet another luminance correcting effect, like Levels or Curves, but without a graphic interface. The downside of this is that it's a little more challenging to learn and use. One benefit of this effect, is that you can use these controls to power expressions. Of course, if that was your reason for choosing this effect, you'd probably be better off going with the Levels (Individual Controls) effect. Regardless, I think you should still go through this section. It always helps to know as many ways to color correct a layer as possible. This way, if your pet color correction effect doesn't work, you've got some alternatives.

If you'd like some practice with this effect, you can open up the GPG.aep project from the Chapter 6 folder of the exercise files.

Figure 6.82 The GPG.aep project.

The Gamma/Pedestal/Gain effect actually works much like the Curves effect does, except that you don't have any control over the master luminance values, only individual color channels. The Gamma/Pedestal/Gain (GPG) effect gives you a gamma, pedestal, and gain control for each channel. The Gamma settings would be like adjusting the center (midtones) of the luminance curve in Curves.

The Pedestal values control the darkest point of the channel, which is the equivalent of the lower left corner point in Curves.

The Gain values control the highlights in the channel, which is the equivalent of the upper right hand corner point in Curves.

The value at the top of the GPG effect in the Effect Controls panel is Black Stretch. This property might as well be called shadow brightness or some such. Increasing the Black Stretch value will increase lighting and details in shadow areas, although from my experience, it seems to leave pure black alone.

Figure 6.83 The image with the Blue Gamma value set to 2.

Figure 6.84 The image with the Blue Pedestal set to 1. Notice how the shadows are primarily affected.

Figure 6.85 The image with the Blue Gain set to 2. Notice how the highlights are affected, and the shadow areas are largely untouched.

Figure 6.86 The image with the Black Stretch value at 3, which brings out more detail in the shadow areas, while still leaving pure black in the image.

The Hue/Saturation Effect

The Hue/Saturation effect is one of the most useful and intuitive effects in this chapter. The Hue/Saturation effect is a favorite in After Effects like it is in Photoshop. And, unlike other Photoshop transports (such as Channel Mixer and Color Balance), Hue/Saturation in After Effects works very much like it does in Photoshop. It's a great effect for universally shifting all colors, or for globally changing the saturation of an entire image. You can also use it to colorize an image, which turns the image grayscale and then adds a color tint. Finally, you can also use it to selectively choose which color groups to adjust independently. So, if you wanted to desaturate only yellow tones, you could with the Hue/Saturation effect.

For demonstrating this effect, I'm going to use the colorful Artbeats video clip, KS103.mov that you'll find in the Artbeats folder in the Media folder of the exercise files. Import it and add it to a composition. Add the Hue/Saturation effect to this clip.

Figure 6.87 The KS103.mov clip before any adjustments.

First, let's look at how Hue/Saturation deals with global changes, or in other words, changes that affect the entire image. If we adjust the Master Hue property, it will cycle all colors in the image around the color wheel. This usually creates a psychedelic effect that I still haven't found a practical use for. This hue parameter will prove to be very useful a little later, though, so don't judge this book by its proverbial cover.

Figure 6.88 Adjusting the Hue property for the entire image will shift the colors through the color spectrum, creating weird results. Here, the Master Hue value was taken to about 200 degrees.

We can also adjust the Master Saturation property to manipulate the saturation for the entire image. This is much more helpful than Master Hue, in my experience. In Figure 6.89, I reduced the Master Saturation amount by about half (50), which creates a nostalgic feel.

Figure 6.89 The result of reducing the Master Saturation value.

Going down the list in the Effect Controls panel, the next property we come to is Master Lightness. Don't ever ever use this on images. This property is the equivalent of the Brightness slider in the Brightness & Contrast effect. It universally lightens or darkens every pixel, which results in bad images. See the Brightness &

Contrast effect earlier in this chapter for an example of the kind of havoc wreaked by this kind of image edit. Only use this property if you are adjusting unrealistic subjects (such as with vector art), or if you have changed the Channel Control value and you're adjusting a specific color set. For most images and video, you want to keep darks dark and brights bright.

If you want to colorize an image, simply select the Colorize checkbox at the bottom of the Hue/Saturation effect in the Effect Controls panel. This will convert the image to grayscale, and then tint it with a color you select with the colorize properties. After selecting the Colorize checkbox, the colorize properties at the bottom of the effect become available to use. Adjust Colorize Hue and Colorize Saturation to tint this image in the exact color you're looking for. Note that Colorize Lightness is a bad idea to use, just like Master Lightness is a bad idea to use.

Figure 6.90 After selecting the Colorize checkbox, you can adjust the colorize properties to created an image tinted with a single color.

I'm going to hit the Reset button at the top of the Hue/Saturation effect in the Effect Controls panel to start over with the Hue/Saturation effect. The real power in this effect in my opinion, is in the Channel Control drop down. By default, this is set to Master, which means that the hue, saturation, and lightness properties that we've been adjusting apply to all colors universally.

Let's take the Channel Control drop down to Blues. This will restrict our changes to only the blues. Note that this is not specifically referring to the blue channel, but instead just to blues in general. You can tweak the lines in the Channel Range area to hone in on the exact color that you're looking to adjust. I took the Blue Hue value to about +100. Because the only blue objects in this shot are the sky and the shorts of the girl on the right, only those colors were adjusted.

Figure 6.91 By selecting Blues in the Channel Control drop down, only the blue colors in this footage are altered when we adjust the hue.

We can also perform more practical adjustments. I'm going to change the Channel Control value to Yellows, which will allow me to adjust the field that the girls are running on. It looks like it should be green, but it's kinda dying, yellow, and dry. Remember the opposite of yellow? It's blue. So here's a little trick—if you want to make grass and other greenery seem more alive and rich, add a little blue. With the Channel Control value at Yellows, take the Yellow Hue value to 40 degrees to add some life to this dying grass.

Figure 6.92 The grass looks much more alive once we selectively adjust the yellows and shift their hues a little.

For what it's worth, I use the Hue/Saturation effect frequently. It's very simple to use, and you can do a lot with the few parameters here. It also does a pretty good job of selecting colors to isolate for editing.

The Leave Color Effect

The Leave Color effect allows you to select a color to leave behind, while you desaturate other colors. This can create a really cool effect, like that seen in the movie *Schindler's List*. And I'm not sure exactly why, but this effect seems to do a much better job at selecting color than other color-selecting effects, like the Change to Color effect. It also seems to do a better job of ignoring the large amount of noise in images.

For this example, I'm going to import the bird.tif image from the Images folder in the Media folder of the exercise files. Add this image to a comp and apply the Leave Color effect. This is the same image we looked at earlier in this chapter with the Change Color and Change to Color effects.

Figure 6.93 The bird.tif image.

The first thing we want to do here is to select the Color to Leave. This is the color that will remain when all other colors are desaturated. I'm going to click the eyedropper next to the Color to Leave property, and then click in the blue background in the bird layer in the Composition panel. Then increase the Amount to Decolor property to determine how much other colors (besides the Color to Leave color) will be desaturated. A value of 100% will completely desaturate the other colors in the image.

The other properties, which are similar to what we saw with the Change Color and Change to Color effect, can help you to tweak the results if needed.

Figure 6.94 The final results with the Leave Color effect.

The Levels Effect

And now we come to what is perhaps the most commonly used luminance adjusting effect. The Levels effect is quick and easy, and it also has a histogram, which gives us information about the luminance values in our footage. Although the Curves effect gives us more control when color correcting, the ease of use and histogram that the Levels effect offers makes it one of the standard go to effects in After Effects.

To follow along, open the Levels and Curves.aep project from the Chapter 6 folder. This is the same project that we used earlier in this chapter when we looked at the Curves effect. We'll be using the same project for both effects so that you can more clearly see which tasks are easier to do with which effect. We'll start in the sea lions comp. This is a perfect candidate for the Levels effect because it's lacking pure white and pure black, as well as any shadow data. Apply the Levels effect to the sea lions layer.

After applying the Levels effect to the sea lions layer, look at the chart, called a histogram, in the Effect Controls panel. From left to right, this chart represents the dark to light colors in the image. As a reference, you can use the gradient bar immediately beneath the histogram. Note that you might need to expand the Effect Controls panel to see all of the histogram

Figure 6.95 The sea lions comp without applied effects.

and gradient, as they're rather wide. The height of the graph represents the amount of that particular tone in the image. As you can see in Figure 6.96, the left side of the histogram is completely flat, which means that there are no black (or even dark gray) pixels at all.

The key to fixing this image is in the three little triangles at the bottom of the histogram. These represent (from left to right)

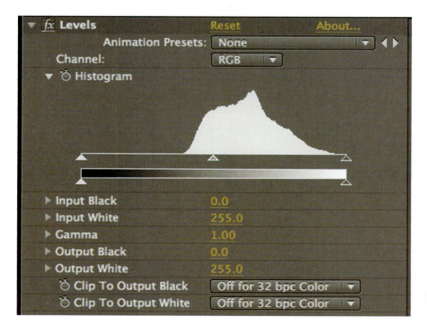

Figure 6.96 The histogram and gradient in the Levels effect.

the black point, midtone, and white point. If there are no black pixels, we need to click and drag the black point triangle slider to the right until it is under the darkest pixel in the image. This will force that pixel to black, and reshuffle the other luminance values accordingly. Be sure that you stop dragging the black point slider to the right once you've gotten to the first pixel. If you go any farther, you'll lose details in the shadow areas. You can also fix the highlights in your image by dragging the white point to the left to the first pixel (bump on the graph) that you come to.

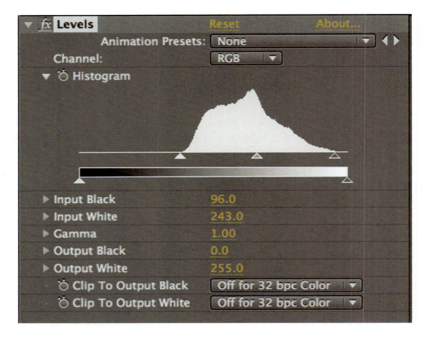

Figure 6.97 Drag the black point slider to the right to the first pixel to get perfect shadow areas, and drag the white point slider to the left to the first pixel to get perfect highlight areas.

Our sea lion image is now starting to look much better. The contrast particularly has had a major improvement. The highlights are a little brighter, and there are now dark portions of our image as well. But even though the highlights and shadows look good, overall the image is too light for my taste.

We can adjust the midtones of this image by using the middle triangle slider underneath the histogram. Remember that dragging to the left increases brightness, and dragging to the right reduces brightness. Drag the center triangle to the right to darken the midtones to taste. This is like clicking in the center of the curve and dragging downwards in the Curve effect. The results are a big improvement over the initial image.

Another trick when using the Levels effect (or any other color correction effect for that matter) is to apply another

Figure 6.98 The image looks much better, but the midtones are still too bright.

Figure 6.99 The final results with Levels applied to the sea lions layer.

instance of the Levels effect on top of all of the other effects that you've added. This extra copy of the effect is not to make adjustments, but to use its histogram to get a readout of the new luminance values.

Next, let's switch gears and go over to the fireworks comp. This comp contains an image of fireworks, taken while it was still dusk. So, the fireworks aren't quite so bright, and the sky isn't quite dark enough.

Apply the Levels effect to these fireworks. As before, check the histogram to see the exact problem with this image. Notice that

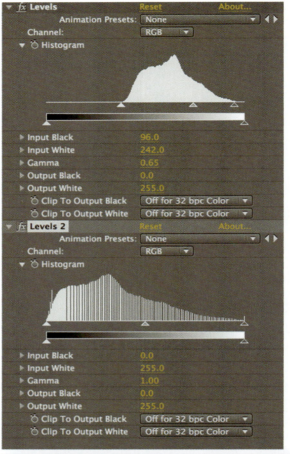

Figure 6.100 Use another instance of the Levels effect to see a histogram that displays the luminance values of your corrected footage. In this case, we see that have far more shadow areas than highlight areas.

Figure 6.101 The fireworks comp.

even though we want this image to be darker, there is still pure black already here. And we're also missing pure white and almost all highlights.

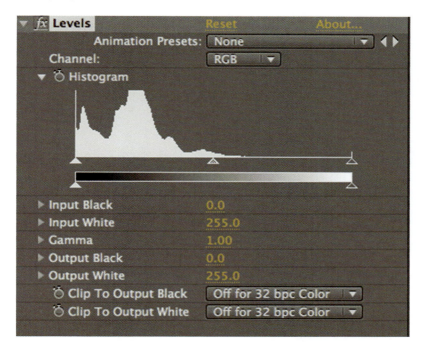

Figure 6.102 The histogram for the fireworks image.

So, as before, drag the white point slider in to the first pixel, and drag the midtone slider to the right to darken the midtones to taste.

As with this example in Curves, the results are too red for my taste. We can fix this by going to the Channel drop down at the top of the effect in the Effect Controls panel, and changing the value from RGB to Red. When looking at the histogram for the red channel, drag the midtones slider to the right to remove red light from this result. The final is a little more balanced.

Note that you can also change the Channel drop down to work on the alpha channel of a layer. While it's not super common to use Levels like this (that I know of), I find that it helps often to fix holes or remove specks in an alpha channel. Because of this functionality in the Levels effect, the Alpha Levels effect has been removed from After Effects. They basically did the same thing.

Finally, you may be wondering about the sliders underneath the gradient below the histogram. The three sliders below the histogram—from left to right—correspond to the Input Black, Gamma, and Input White properties. The two sliders below the gradient bar—from left to right—correspond to the Output Black and Output White values. These properties determine

Figure 6.103 The adjusted histogram and result.

Figure 6.104 The final result, after dragging the midtones slider of the red channel to the right a little.

the final output intensity of black and white. If you wanted to reduce the amount of white in an image (say from 255 to 240), then you would reduce the Output White value, or drag the slider underneath white in the gradient bar to the left. Or, perhaps, the black values in your image are too dark, you could drag that to the right to lighten them up. I use these often when compositing to get layers to have the same levels of luminance.

The Levels effect is so quick, easy, and ubiquitous, that we'll be using it all over the place throughout this book.

The Levels (Individual Controls) Effect

The Levels (Individual Controls) effect is exactly like the regular old Levels effect we just looked at. The problem with the standard Levels effect is that it's not really meant to be animated, or used with expressions. And in an animation powerhouse like After Effects, you kinda need that functionality. So, they created the Levels (Individual Controls) effect, which allows you to adjust all color channels and the composite at the same time. The real advantage to this is that you can connect these properties with expressions.

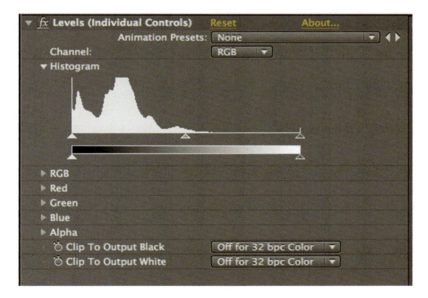

Figure 6.105 The controls for the Levels (Individual Controls) effect.

The Photo Filter Effect

The Photo Filter effect is another effect that has its roots in Photoshop. The effect mimics the physical filters that are put on the end of camera lenses to give a tint to photos. Typically these tints come in the form of warm tints (orange) or cool tints (blue), but they can be in any color. For all intents and purposes, the Photo Filter effect simply applies a color tint to an image.

Open the Photo Filter.aep project from the Chapter 6 folder of the exercise files if you'd like to follow along with me. This project contains a photo I took of a lioness, and it's a little on the warm side, meaning that it is tinted in warm colors like yellow, orange, or red.

Figure 6.106 The image in the Photo Filter.aep project.

Apply the Photo Filter effect to this image. The default results are so subtle that they're almost imperceptible. I think this is Adobe's way of hinting that we should use this effect to create subtle changes. I couldn't agree more. But just so we can see the difference in the screenshots here in this book, let's increase the Density value, which is somewhat like the opacity value for this effect. Increasing the value to a relatively high 75%, the results make this footage look like a photo taken in the 70's.

I'm going to take the Density back down to its default value of 25%. One of the advantages of this effect is that it offers a quick way to remove color casts. We already had a warm tint going into this, so we can apply a cooling filter to counter act the warm tint. In the Filter drop down list, select the Cooling Filter (80). In case you were wondering, the numbers in parentheses can be thought of as the intensity of the filter. Thus, the Cooling Filter (80) creates a more subtle cooling effect than the Cooling Filter (82). This is just the right amount of coolness to balance out the warm cast that was on this image.

Remember that there are also other colors of filters to use. Typically, these photo filters are used to give an emotional tone to an image. If you wanted to create a formal, professional tone, you might use a cooling filter. If you were taking photos of a wedding or some other sentimental occasion, you might try shooting with a warm filter.

Figure 6.107 The Photo Filter effect with the Density value at 75%.

Figure 6.108 With the Cooling Filter (80) selected, the image is brought back into balance as the warm tones are neutralized by the cool tones of the filter.

The PS Arbitrary Map Effect

The PS Arbitrary Map effect is essentially worthless, although it is a really interesting effect. It is an old effect that is mostly kept around just to provide compatibility with older After Effects projects. It's basically like the Curves effect, but the only way to get it to work is to click the Options button at the top of the effect in the Effect Controls panel. This action will open the Open dialog box, at which point you will need to navigate to an AMP (arbitrary map) file. This is a file created by the Curves effect (in After

Effects or in Photoshop), and saved from the Curves effect while the pencil tool is selected. For more information on how to create these files, refer back to the section on the Curves effect from earlier in this chapter. Note that this effect can't even use the ACV files from the default style of Curves.

Once these AMP files are imported, that exact luminance adjustment curve will be applied to the current layer. The Phase property allows you to shift the curve through the layer. While it is a fascinating intellectual curiosity, the PS Arbitrary Map effect is better fodder for nerdy museums and history books than for practical application in the modern age.

The Selective Color Effect

Another Photoshop transplant, the Selective Color effect allows you to really play with the mixing of colors. To be honest, I used this all the time when I worked in the print industry, as it really helped to get all of the color out of the blacks. I don't use it as much in After Effects. But I can see how it would be helpful. It's almost like a more specific version of the color range selection tools in Hue/Saturation, except that you have less control over the range selection, but more control over what you do with the colors in that range.

We have some footage here to play with. This is a 16-bit raw clip, so we've got a lot of room to play with colors (which room might not be available with all formats). Right now, the forest is darker than the sky, and the whole thing is kinda washed in cyan. It's a little over the top, but I like it.

Figure 6.109 The original image.

As mentioned, the Selective Color effect allows us to work on specific color ranges. So, we're going to create more separation between sky and trees. First, take the Colors drop down to Greens. As you can see here, we can add more cyan (with positive

Subtractive Color and You

Note that Selective Color deals with CMYK, which is a subtractive color model. Subtractive color models are typically reserved for ink and printing applications, so it might throw you off a bit.

Subtractive color means that as you subtract cyan (for example), the image will get brighter (as if you removed cyan "ink"). This is the opposite of what happens with light, where an image gets brighter as you add color to it. So when you add color using Selective Color, you're actually darkening your image a bit. Just be aware that your luminance will be indirectly affected by Selective Color, and in a way opposite of what you might expect.

values) to the greens or take out cyan (with negative values). You can also do the same for magenta, yellow, or black.

In this case, we want to make the greens more green. There's no "green" slider here, but we know that green is the opposite of magenta. So, take the Magenta value down to −100%. We've now essentially added green to only our forest, leaving the sky the way it was. Note that because this selection is color-based, we can just set this up once, and barring any major lighting changes, no tracking, rotoscoping, or keyframing is necessary to maintain this adjustment throughout a shot.

Figure 6.110 Removing magenta from the greens adds more green to only green areas (the forest, in this case).

Next, let's work on the sky. There is a "Cyan" option from the Colors drop down, and that's probably the closest color to the sky. However, this is too close in color to the forest, and any adjustment would affect the entire image. And again, we don't have the flexibility to alter what "cyan" is, so we need to choose another color family to work on. I'm going to choose Blues from the Colors drop down.

I want to make this more blue, and like with green, there's no blue value to adjust. But since blue is the opposite of yellow, we can add more blue by subtracting yellow. So take the Yellow value to −100%. This is looking good, but to provide a more equal balance between sky and forest, increase the Black value to 100% to darken the blues. And there you go.

Figure 6.111 The final image after adding more blue to the sky, more green to the forest, and balancing their luminance a little bit.

The Shadow/Highlight Effect

The Shadow/Highlight effect is akin to the auto effects that we looked at in the beginning of this chapter. It attempts to restore details from shadow areas that are too dark, or highlight areas that are too bright. If you are new to image correction, this is a great effect. If you know your way around Levels or Curves, I recommend sticking to those effects as they will usually produce far better results.

For this effect, open the Shadow Highlight.aep project from the Chapter 6 folder. This contains a photo that I took that has some cliffs that are a little dark.

Figure 6.112 The Shadow Highlight.aep project.

Apply the Shadow/Highlight effect to this layer. The effects are instant, but not necessarily fantastic. The results are overblown and noisy, even though this photo was shot with an ISO setting of 100, which typically creates an image with relatively low noise.

Figure 6.113 The result of applying the Shadow/Highlight effect.

To fine tune this effect, you can open the More Options section, and adjust those settings. You can also uncheck the Auto Amounts checkbox to get access to the Shadow Amount and Highlight Amount properties. This allows you to customize (read:reduce) the effect of the insanely intense defaults.

Figure 6.114 The results of customizing and lowering the Shadow Amount.

I got some pretty good results by deselecting the Auto Amounts option, and then taking the Shadow Amount value down to 20 (from its ridiculously high default of 50). But I would still prefer to be using Levels or Curves.

The Tint Effect

The Tint effect (and the Tritone effect coming up next) is used to recolor footage by remapping all of the color values. In the case of the Tint effect, all color values are remapped to two values— one that specifies what black is remapped to, and one that specifies what white is remapped to. This effect can be used to remap the colors in already-colored footage, or it can be used to add color where there is only grayscale values, such as with patterns created with the Fractal Noise effect.

For practicing with the Tint and Tritone effects, I've created a project called Tinting.aep that you'll find in the Chapter 6 folder of the exercise files. This project has two compositions. The grayscale pattern comp contains a watery pattern created with the Fractal Noise effect that is in desperate need of color.

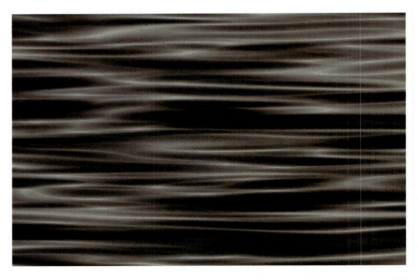

Figure 6.115 The Fractal Noise pattern in the grayscale pattern comp.

The other comp contains a cool Artbeats video of some CG elements spinning around.

Let's start with the grayscale pattern comp. Apply the Tint effect to the layer here. When the Tint effect is first applied, it remaps the darkest tones to black and the brightest tones to white, turning it grayscale. When applied to grayscale footage, there is no visible change.

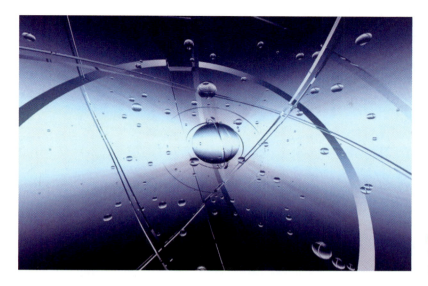

Figure 6.116 The Artbeats video clip in the Tinting.aep project.

The task now is to click the color swatches for the Map Black To and Map White To values to reassign these tones to other colors. For the Map Black To value, I'm going to click the color swatch and select a dark blue color. For the Map White To value, I'm going to click the color swatch and select a really bright blue. Although you can fade the tinting by using the Amount to Tint property, I'm going to leave this at the default 100% to get the tint in its full strength. The end results look much more like water.

Figure 6.117 The result of remapping the black and white points with the Tint effect.

Remember that effects often work better when used in conjunction with other effects. Sometimes when using colors other than black and white with the Tint effect, you can lose contrast. In this case, I added contrast with the Levels effect.

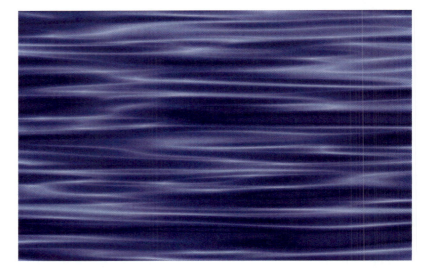

Figure 6.118 After adjusting the black and white points and midtone contrast in the Levels effect.

Now let's see what the Tint effect looks like applied to video. Switch over to the other comp with the Artbeats video footage in it. Apply the Tint effect. As previously mentioned, when you first apply this effect to footage, it is completely stripped of color.

Figure 6.119 When applying the Tint effect, the colors in the footage are turned to grayscale.

In the case of this video clip, I want a totally different look. As seen in Figure 6.120, the whole footage is tinted in cool tones. So, I'm going to choose a deep dark red for the Map Black To value, and a pale orangish-yellow for the Map White To value. The results are very different, but not a "me in high school" kind of different. Good different.

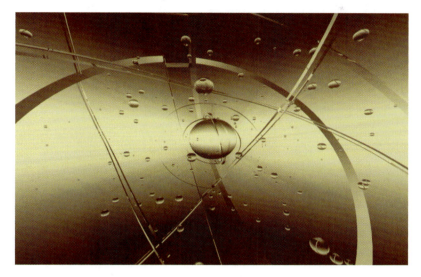

Figure 6.120 The results of remapping shadows to dark red and highlights to bright yellow.

If the grayscale pattern comp got to use extra effects to create a better result, then it's only fair that we add some extra effects to this video clip as well. I added the Curves effect to deepen the shadows and brighten the highlights, and the Glow effect to make it look, well, glowy.

Figure 6.121 The final result of tinting this video clip with the Tint effect, and then adding finishing touches with the Curves and Glow effects.

The Tritone Effect

The Tritone effect is exactly the same as the Tint effect, only that it has three adjustable color values, instead of the two you find in the Tint effect. The Tritone effect allows you to remap highlights, midtones, and shadows.

Open (or Revert) the Tinting.aep project from the Chapter 6 folder if it's not open already. First, apply the Tritone effect to the fractal water pattern in the grayscale pattern comp. Because of the default brown tone of the Midtones value, the default settings turn layers brown.

Figure 6.122 The default settings of the Tritone effect turn this layer into a layer of fractal chocolatey goodness.

I changed the Highlights color swatch to a light pale green, the Midtones value to light blue, and the Shadows to dark blue. Since there isn't much pure white in this pattern, we don't see as much of the highlight color. The obvious advantage of the Tritone effect over the Tint effect is that it has an additional color property that you can control. But one of the disadvantages of this is that it becomes more difficult to balance these three color values in your image. The Tritone effect doesn't really give you a way to adjust the way colors are mapped, which would be a handy feature when you have more than two colors. If you need control over the mapping of colors, you can apply a luminance adjustment effect (such as Levels or Curves) before the Tritone effect in the Effect Controls panel.

Let's go over to the comp with the video clip in it, and apply the Tritone effect to this footage. I changed the highlights color to a light pale yellow, the Midtones to a vibrant orange, and the Shadows to a dark rich purple. Remember that we can also enhance these results with additional effects.

Figure 6.123 After changing the Tritone colors to more watery colors.

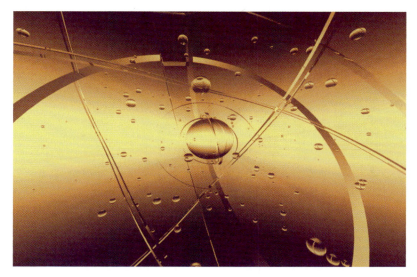

Figure 6.124 The result of adjusting the Tritone colors applied to the Artbeats footage.

The Vibrance Effect

Oh boy, do I love me some Vibrance effect! On the surface, Vibrance seems just like a regular old saturation effect. And in fact, it does indeed saturate stuff. However, Vibrance is significantly better.

To understand the magic of the Vibrance effect, let's look at what regular saturation does. We have this image of my lovely wife. Although she looks pretty and is still very sexually attracted to me, this image is a little washed out and could benefit from some saturation.

Figure 6.125 The original image of my wife.

So, I'm going to apply the Vibrance effect because it has a regular old saturation slider on it. But you can increase saturation in a number of ways (Hue/Saturation, etc.). I'm going to take the Saturation value to 70. Uh-oh. That's not good. Although it does boost the color, it turns her a hideous, Jersey Shore orange.

Figure 6.126 My beautiful wife is an Oompa Loompa! Oh well. We had a good run.

Wouldn't it be awesome if there was some tool that would allow me to increase saturation but take it easy on skin tones? And that, ladies and gentlemen is where Vibrance comes in. Vibrance does exactly that: it saturates an image with extra care towards skin tones so that they saturate much more slowly than other colors. This allows us to make really beautiful cinematic imagery. Take the Saturation value down to 0, and now take Vibrance all the way up to 100. It's a very high value, but as you can see from Figure 6.127, it can handle it.

Figure 6.127 Ah yes. Thank you, Vibrance.

The background and her pink hair are an almost cartoony level of vibrance, but her skin tone still looks normal. We'd probably want to dial this back a little bit, but I wanted to show you just how far you can push Vibrance before skin tones start to suffer.

7

THE DISTORT EFFECTS

The Distort effects all bend, warp, and otherwise disfigure pixels. What's not to love? The Distort effects can be used to distort characters for things like facial expressions, or even body movements. Some of my favorite Distort effects for character animation are Displacement Map, Liquify, and Puppet.

They can also be used to distort objects like clothes, flags, the surface of water, or chimney smoke to simulate movement, like being blown in the wind, for example. Distorting objects like these can be great for bringing matte paintings to life. Often times, in order to make a matte painting look like video, all you need are some slight movements, such as rippling water or smoke coming out of a chimney. If your matte painter (or you, if you are the matte painter) separated these objects on to separate Photoshop layers, it would only take a moment with one of these Distort effects to bring that object to life in a realistic way. If you want to experiment with some of them, try Turbulent Displace, Ripple, and Wave Warp.

Distort effects can also be used on simple, geometric objects to bring them to life, so that they can be used as motion graphic elements. For example, all you would need to create a beautiful spiral is a rectangular solid and the Twirl effect. You can also use effects like Bulge and Polar Coordinates to create beautiful graphics from simple objects.

Because of the diversity of purposes that the Distort effects can be used for (and also because I love them so much, actually), we'll be looking at a couple different examples for most of these effects. That way you can see them in action in a variety of ways. I've created a project called Distort.aep that you'll find in the Chapter 7 folder that we'll be using here and there throughout this chapter. This project contains a comp with motion graphics elements with a gradient background, and another comp that contains a funnel of fractal smoke. There's also an HDR comp with a glowing bar for those Distort effects (like Twirl) that operate at 32 bits per channel. Before we jump into the effects, let's take a look at Figures 7.1–7.4 to see what these objects look like without effects applied to them.

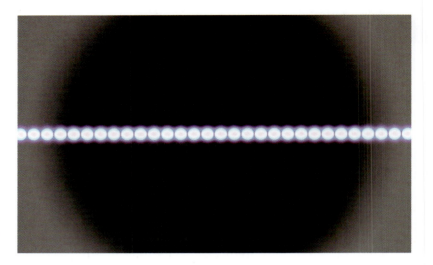

Figure 7.1 The dotted line layer in the Motion Graphics comp in the Distort.aep project.

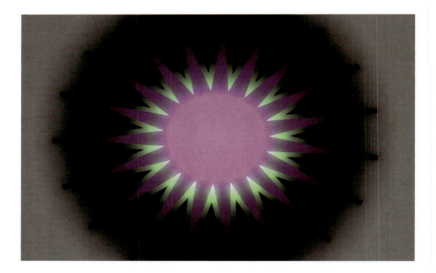

Figure 7.2 The star layer in the Motion Graphics comp.

As you work with these exercises, imagine your own assets in their place. Or, better yet, try these effects with objects that you've created. This is one chapter where it really pays to be familiar with all of the effects, because you never know when they will come in handy.

Figure 7.3 The fractal smoke in the Smoke comp.

Figure 7.4 The HDR shape layer in the HDR comp.

The Bezier Warp Effect

The Bezier Warp effect might also be called the Corner Warp effect. It gives you three bezier warp points at every corner—one for the corner itself, and two others to control the sides around the corner. The effect refers to the corner point as the vertex, and the two other points as tangents. And, other than a Quality property, this effect only consists of these 12 warp points. Keep in mind that all of these points can be animated. Because this effect creates smooth distortions around its edges, it's great for warping virtual paper. The regular Distort.aep project isn't the best to demonstrate this effect, so for this example, we're going to be using the Bezier Warp.aep project in the Chapter 7 folder of the exercise files.

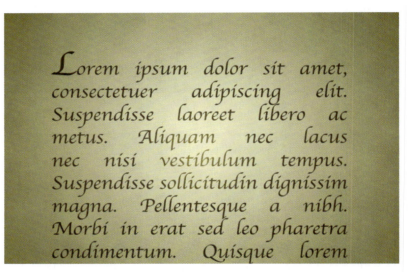

Figure 7.5 The Bezier Warp.aep project in its default state.

Apply the Bezier Warp effect to the PAPER precomp layer. Adjust the vertices and tangents as desired. When you're done, you should have very organic, paperlike distortions, such as those seen in Figure 7.6. Notice that the upper right corner is even folded over. I did this purposely to show you what this looks like. There's a little sliver of transparency that also folds over, causing a small hole in your layer. You'll also notice some blocky, aliased pixels on corners that have been folded over. These little problems might not make the effect worthwhile if you're looking for bended corners, so it's something to be aware of.

I suppose the moral of the story is that the Bezier Warp effect is not good for folding objects on top of themselves. But for easily warping the corners of objects (and even animating that warping) the Bezier Warp effect does a pretty good job.

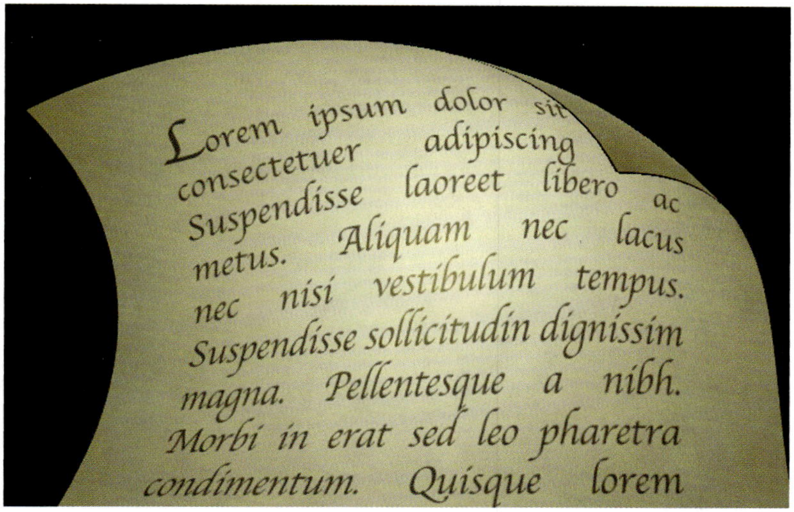

Figure 7.6 The paper looks more realistic after being distorted (and animated) with the Bezier Warp effect.

The Bulge Effect

The Bulge effect is very similar to the Spherize effect. Both effects attempt to create a round, bulging distortion on a layer. If you're looking for a quick and simple effect, go for Spherize. If you're looking for more control over your bulging, use the Bulge effect.

There are a lot of uses for bulge distortions. You can apply Bulge to an elastic wall or a painting to make it look like there is something trying to break out. You can apply Bulge to the belly of a large cartoon character to animate his belly jiggling while he is laughing. You can animate the Bulge effect as it's applied to the chest of a character, to simulate their heart beating.

Let's actually experiment with a few more examples. We can create these from the Distort.aep project from the Chapter 7 folder. First, let's apply Bulge to the dotted line layer in the Motion Graphics comp. When you apply the effect, you'll see a circle with four points around its "corners." This circle determines the area on your layer that will be distorted with the Bulge effect. Instead of using the sliders in the Effect Controls panel, you can move the points on this circle around in the Composition panel. Moving these points left and right will adjust the Horizontal Radius value, and moving them up and down will adjust the Vertical Radius value. You can move the entire bulge distortion area with the Bulge Center property or by dragging the effect control point at the center of the circle. Bulge Height determines the strength of the bulge distortion. Keep this value small for a more subtle effect. Or you can take it to a negative value to create an indentation instead of a bump. The Taper Radius parameter helps blend the bulged pixels in with the regular pixels. If you want to create the illusion that there is a ball under the surface, for example, you would want to keep this value low because there would be a stark transition between the ball and the area that isn't distorted.

In Figure 7.7, you can see the result of the Bulge effect on my dotted lines. If we were to animate the stroke of this line, the Bulge effect would create the illusion that the dotted lines were zooming towards you. Almost like the magnification of the dock icons on the Mac OS. Here, my settings are 340 for Horizontal Radius, 90 for Vertical Radius, 1.5 for Bulge Height, and 114 for the Taper Radius.

I also usually keep my Antialiasing value at High. This effect renders quick enough on any machine that meets After Effects' minimum software requirements, that it shouldn't slow you down keeping this effect at high quality.

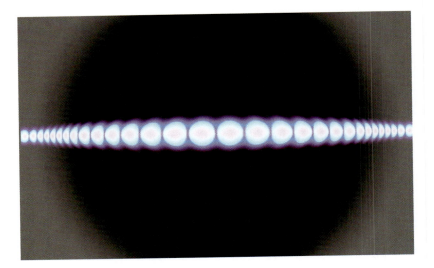

Figure 7.7 The Bulge effect applied to the dotted line layer.

Note that at high Bulge Height levels, the pixels on this layer start getting distorted and pixelated. In a moment, we'll look at Bulge applied to a vector-based shape layer, and there will not be any pixelation.

You can use the Horizontal Radius and Vertical Radius values to create a bulge shape that is more elliptical than circular. In this way, you can create non-uniform squishes and bulges.

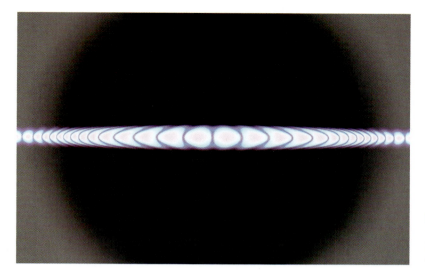

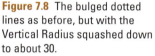

Figure 7.8 The bulged dotted lines as before, but with the Vertical Radius squashed down to about 30.

Let's now try applying the Bulge effect to the star layer. Be sure to also turn off the visibility of the dotted line layer. For the bulging of the star layer, I'm going to use the same basic settings I used for bulging the dotted lines. Notice the absence of pixelation in distorted areas, due to the vector nature of the shape layer star. The Bulge effect seems to almost create an eye shape out of our star.

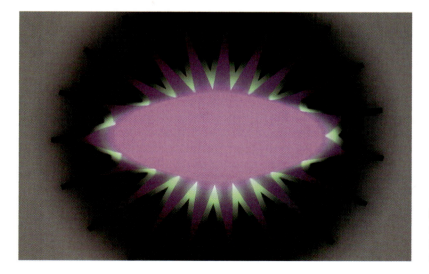

Figure 7.9 The Bulge effect applied to the star layer, using another elliptical-shaped distortion area.

Now, let's hop on over to the Smoke comp, and apply the Bulge effect to the smoke layer. I made the Horizontal Radius and Vertical Radius values very large. I then moved the Bulge Center off to the side. This created the effect of a blowing wind, coming from the left of the smoke. You see, the Bulge effect (and other Distort effects) don't have to directly distort an object. Sometimes, they can be used as forces that act upon an object, from wind to a karate kick.

Figure 7.10 The Bulge effect applied on the smoke layer, to the side of the actual smoke. This creates the appearance of a slight breeze.

The Corner Pin Effect

If you've only played with a handful of the effects in After Effects, chances are that one of them was the Corner Pin effect. As one of the most popular and prolific effects in After Effects, the Corner Pin effect comes in handy often. The Corner Pin effect is almost identical to the Bezier Warp effect, except that here, there are no extra tangents. All that we can adjust with the Corner Pin effect are the 4 corner points. And that's all there is to the entire effect. But because of its simplicity, it's quite easy to use.

Most of the time, when people use the Corner Pin effect, it is to use another image to replace a billboard, a window, or some other rectangular object. Because of the way that Corner Pin distorts a layer, it can be used to distort layers to look like they exist in 3D space. Why not just use a 3D layer? Personally speaking, I prefer Corner Pin for many tasks because it's much easier to adjust the 4 pins of the Corner Pin effect than to get a 3D layer to animate in 3D space exactly the way you want it to.

We're going to use the Corner Pin.aep project for this effect. In the Monitor comp, we'll use the Corner Pin effect to recreate another common Corner Pin task—using another layer to replace the screen of a computer monitor.

Figure 7.11 The Monitor layer. We're going to replace this screen with another layer.

We want to apply the Corner Pin effect, but not to the Monitor layer. We don't want the monitor to distort at all. Turn on the visibility of the adobe-pumpkin layer. This is an embarrassing photo of me (yet another one), with a pumpkin I carved for Halloween. No, this image was not faked in Photoshop. I really am nerdy enough to hand carve the Adobe logo into a pumpkin, on a day when everyone else is out eating candy and going to parties.

Apply the Corner Pin effect to the adobe-pumpkin layer. As with other effects, when the effect is selected in the Effect Controls panel, you can see its effect control points in the Composition panel. These control points are especially helpful with the Corner Pin effect.

Figure 7.12 The adobe-pumpkin layer.

Using the corner pins, drag the corners of the adobe-pumpkin layer until they precisely match the corresponding corners of the monitor in the Monitor layer. You will probably want to zoom in closely for the most accurate matching. When you're all done, it should look like the adobe-pumpkin layer is the screen saver of the monitor.

Figure 7.13 The adobe-pumpkin layer distorted to appear as the screen of the computer monitor.

As far as the Corner Pin effect goes, we're done with this example. But I just can't leave this project alone without adding a couple of finishing touches.

The first offense (and it's a bad one) is that this result composites terribly. The adobe-pumpkin photo is very dark, but images on the computer screen are created with light. It should be much brighter. Also, the room where the monitor was photographed is very bright, and all that ambient light would definitely lighten the monitor screen. So, I'm going to apply the Curves effect to the adobe-pumpkin layer. In the Curves effect, I'm going to lighten black (typically a no-no), and then generally increase the brightness of the layer. Figure 7.14 shows the curve I used to create the result seen in Figure 7.15.

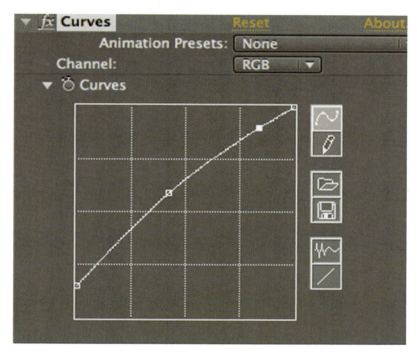

Figure 7.14 The settings I used in Curves to lighten the adobe-pumpkin image.

The next thing we need to do is adjust the color of the adobe-pumpkin layer to match the color of the monitor layer. If you look closely, you'll notice that the monitor is an apple monitor. In real life, these are gray aluminum. In this image, the monitor appears very yellow. We need to adjust the adobe-pumpkin layer to also look more yellow. So, I'm going to apply the Color Balance effect, and slightly reduce the blue values (to add yellow). You also might want to warm things up by adding magenta. You can add magenta by slightly reducing the green values.

Figure 7.15 The Corner Pin result, lightened with Curves.

Figure 7.16 The Corner Pin result, after Curves and Color Balance.

We could, of course, spend much more time getting this to look perfect. But we've got bigger fish to fry, so we'll end this by just adding a couple of layer styles. I'm going to apply the Inner Shadow layer style (which you can access by right clicking on the adobe-pumpkin layer and choosing Layer Styles>Inner Shadow). This is to recreate the tiny shadow that is caused by the protrusion of the monitor's edge over the actual screen. I also added a Gradient Overlay layer style, reversed it (so that black was on bottom and white was on top), and drastically reduced the Opacity of the Gradient Overlay (to about 30%). This helps to simulate the glare from the lights in the room. While it's not perfect, the results are significantly more believable than they were before. If you'd like to deconstruct what I've done here, I've included my work in a project called Corner Pin FINISH.aep in the Chapter 7 folder of the exercise files.

Figure 7.17 The final results of my compositing.

References and Compositing

It's always a good idea to use reference material when compositing. In the case of this computer monitor scene, I was constantly going back to the original screen for clues as to how to composite the adobe-pumpkin layer. In other instances, you may need to do a Google image search or go out and take your own pictures. You'll be surprised at how much better your compositing is for having used reference images.

Corner Pin and Star Wars Text

Another very common use of the Corner Pin effect is to create text that mimics the "scrolling into outerspace" look on the text introductions at the beginning of the Star Wars movies. Switch over to the Star Text comp in the Corner Pin.aep project. Here, we have a big block of static text.

Apply the Corner Pin effect to the text layer in the Star Text comp. Next, take the top two corner points down (about 150 pixels from the top of the comp), and in towards the middle of the comp. If desired, you can also move the bottom points away from each other along the X axis. This distortion creates the illusion that our text is receding into the far reaches of the galaxy. In Figure 7.19, I've also added a background layer of Fractal Noise applied to a solid. To create the starfield, I increased the Contrast to about 600, decreased Brightness

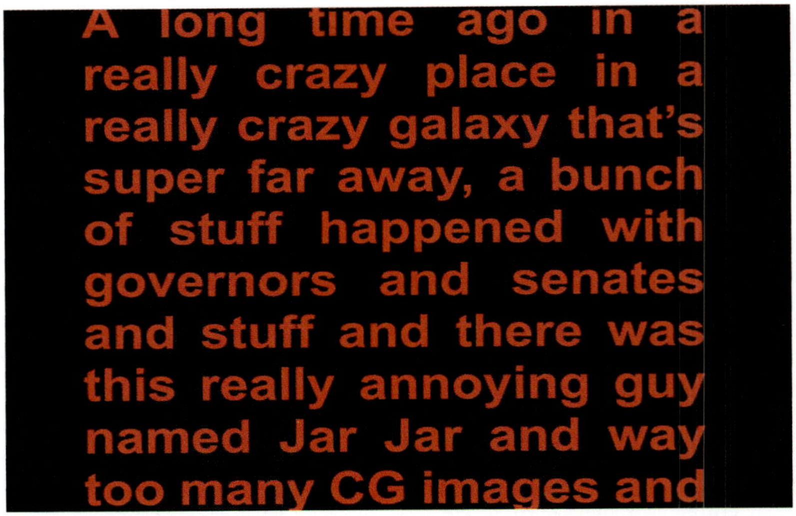

Figure 7.18 The text layer in the Star Text comp.

Figure 7.19 The final Star Wars text with the Corner Pin distortion and the added fractal starfield background.

to about -230, and reduced Scale (in the Transform area) to about 3. Now, all we need is to apply a text animator to create scrolling text.

The Displacement Map Effect

The Displacement Map effect is a little challenging to get the hang of, especially if you're not acquainted with using grayscale maps as effect controllers. If you need some more help with that topic, you can quickly jump ahead to Chapter 23 and come back. The Displacement Map effect is essentially worthless without maps as controllers.

The Displacement Map effect is similar to (but works far better than) the Displace effect in Photoshop. It uses maps as references to displace—or move—pixels around. The Displacement Map effect can use the lightness, red channel, green channel, blue channel, saturation, and other image properties in controller layers. That makes this a very versatile effect.

So, what is this effect used for? Sometimes, you just want to disrupt pixels. Let's say you've got some footage of people on the beach, and the director wants you to change that shot into a day-for-night shot, and also wants you to create a bonfire next to the people. We covered day-for-night shots in Chapter 6, and we'll cover how to create fire from scratch in Chapter 11. But what about the distortions that are created in the air above a fire? In this case, you could use the Displacement Map effect to create those distortions.

I have a trick that I like to use Displacement Map for. You can take a photo, paint a quick and rough displacement map, and then use that to bring the photo to life—rotating the subject a few degrees. This is great for quick cuts of photos. Years ago, Ken Burns revolutionized documentary filmmaking by moving the camera around photos, making them come alive. Years later, filmmakers started putting the subjects of old photos on separate layers in Photoshop and panning around them with virtual cameras. Using Displacement Map however, you can add seemingly 3D twists and turns.

To see this in action, open the Displacement Map.aep project in the Chapter 7 folder. Go to the Chad displaced comp. There is another comp in this project, called displacement wave. This comp will not be shown in the book because the effect is difficult to detect with still images. But you can use this for more practice with the Displacement Map effect.

I've set this comp up already for you, for your ease of use. But it's very important to set up Displacement Map jobs correctly, or else the effect might not work properly. So, let's warp on over to Photoshop, where I created the map we'll be using to displace a photo.

First, I started with a photo of myself.

Figure 7.20 The photo of myself in Photoshop.

Next, I duplicated the layer, which you can do by using the keyboard shortcut Ctrl+J(Win)/Cmd+J(Mac). Then, I reduced the Opacity value for the top layer to about 30%, and locked it by pressing the padlock icon at the top of the Layers panel. We're going to paint a displacement mask, and I want to use the top layer as a reference, but I don't want to accidentally paint on it. Then, on the bottom layer, I paint with black and white according to the depth of the image, or its proximity to the camera. For example, my nose is the object that is closest to the camera, so it is pure white. The green background is the object farthest from the camera, so it is pure black. All of the other depths painted accordingly. Notice how, in Figure 7.21, my eyes are darker than my cheeks, because they are farther away from the camera than my cheeks are.

You might also notice in my displacement map—as seen in Figure 7.21—that this is a terrible rendition of me. You might be wondering "why didn't you just convert it to grayscale, moron?" That's a great question. But we really do want the map soft like this, or else there will be tearing when the layer is displaced. The map looks awful by itself, but trust me on this one folks—it will work great as a displacement map.

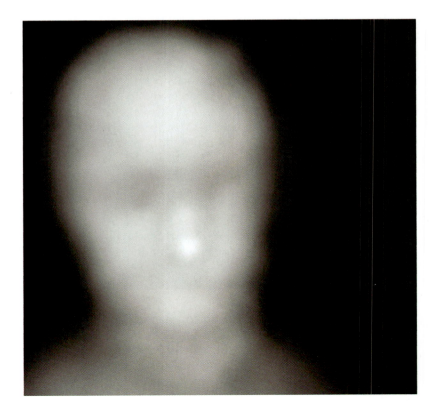

Figure 7.21 The displacement map that I painted.

Next, comes the import into After Effects. If you want your displacements to be precise (such as in our case with this photo), it is absolutely critical that your displacement map and your photo be the exact same size. The best way to ensure that is to import the PSD file as a Composition (NOT Composition—Cropped Layers), so that your layers and their accompanying displacement maps are imported at the size of the document.

Now let's play Dr. Frankenstein and bring this photo to life. Back in After Effects, apply the Displacement Map effect to the Chad layer in the Chad displaced comp. Initially, the results look bad. This is because the effect uses the layer it was applied to as the displacement map. So, the first thing we want to do is to change the Displacement Map Layer drop down to the chad DIS layer. The chad DIS layer is our displacement map.

You can use the Displacement Map effect to displace a layer horizontally or vertically. In this case, we'll be displacing my face horizontally and ignoring the vertical settings. But for future reference, vertical displacement is helpful for things that are moving upwards, such as our earlier example of fire on the beach. In that case, horizontal displacement would not be very useful. I've also used horizontal and vertical displacement together for a soda ad that needed the bottle to rotate, but all I had access to was a photo of the bottle at a diagonal angle. I used both horizontal and vertical displacement to make the bottle rotate diagonally.

Speaking of vertical displacement, we need to turn it completely off. Take the Use For Vertical Displacement drop down list to Off. Then take the Max Vertical Displacement value to 0. And yes, you do need to do both.

Now, take the Use For Horizontal Displacement drop down to Lightness, as we'll be using the brightness of our displacement map to control this effect. Using subtle changes to the Max Horizontal Displacement property, we can now animate the displacement. To get the most out of this effect, I usually animate this property from a small negative number, to a small positive number. Figures 7.22 and 7.23 show the extremes of the animation. I've actually exaggerated these values a little so that the changes are obvious. This exaggeration has caused some ugly distortion on the edges of my head. But I personally allow a little bit of ugliness at the extremes (the lowest negative and highest positive max displacement values) because the ugliness will only be visible for one frame, but it will allow for a wider range of movement.

If the edges start to pull away from the sides, you can select the Wrap Pixels Around option, which will copy the pixels from the other side to fill in the gap. The results of this option aren't always great (depending on the similarity of your edges), but they often look better than not having it on.

Fixing Displacement Maps

Often, when you create displacement maps, you'll realize after animating them that they are "off" a little. Remember that you can re-edit these Photoshop files to update the paint on them, and you don't need to adjust your After Effects project at all. Simply open up the folder containing the original Photoshop files (this will not work with compositions, even if they are created from PSD files), right click on one of the original Photoshop layer of the updated document, and select Reload Footage.

Figure 7.22 The Displacement Map effect, with the Max Horizontal Displacement value at –9.0.

Figure 7.23 The Displacement Map effect, with the Max Horizontal Displacement value at 9.0.

Grayscale Effects as Maps

Many effects in After Effects—such as Fractal Noise, Cell Pattern, and Wave World—generate grayscale patterns. Several other effects—such as Displacement Map, Shatter, and Caustics—can use patterns like this. So, even though we've used a custom hand drawn map for use with Displacement Map in this chapter, don't forget about all of the countless ways After Effects provides for you to create additional controller maps from scratch.

The results here are fairly realistic and creepy. We've essentially brought some life to this photo, and it didn't take long at all. Through the skillful painting of our displacement map, we avoided having to even make a selection, let alone cut up any layers!

The Liquify Effect

The Liquify effect is one of my favorites, and it acts very similarly to the Photoshop plugin of the same name. It has great practical application, and it's the ultimate cure for boredom. Think of the Liquify effect as turning a layer into clay. In the Liquify effect controls, you are given access to tools that allow you to sculpt a layer as digital clay. As you can imagine, this is great for a million and one reasons. You can diminish unattractive features. You can also exaggerate facial features—like eyes—to create a creepy look. Or, as we'll see, you can use it as the ultimate science-fiction/fantasy character creation tool.

Figure 7.24 The baby layer in the Liquify.aep project. This photo appears courtesy of Angela McInroe.

Figure 7.25 The tools in the Liquify effect.

Let's see how this works. Open the Liquify.aep project from the Chapter 7 folder of the exercise files. Apply the Liquify effect to the baby layer in the Liquify comp.

In the Liquify effect's controls in the Effect Controls panel, you'll find a set of tools to use on your layer.

The default tool is the Warp tool (its icon looks like a finger), which allows you to push pixels around as you might with your finger. Just click and drag to pull pixels as you please. If you want to change the size of your brush, open the Warp Tool Options area in the Effect Controls panel and change settings like Brush Size or Brush Pressure. Note that some keyboard shortcuts for painting work here as well, such as holding the Ctrl(Win)/Cmd(Mac) key while dragging your cursor in the Composition panel to dynamically resize your paintbrush.

Figure 7.26 I used the Warp tool in the Liquify to readjust the pixels in the baby's mouth. Why so serious?

Immediately below the Warp tool, you'll find the Bloat tool, which is like a mini-Bulge effect. It puffs up areas of pixels, making them appear bloated.

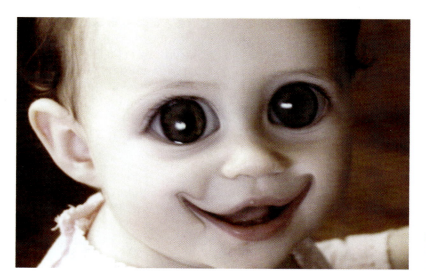

Figure 7.27 After using the Bloat tool on the eyes of the baby.

The tool in the top right spot of the tools area is the Pucker tool, which does the opposite of the Bloat tool. The Pucker tool acts as a vacuum, sucking in and pinching surrounding pixels.

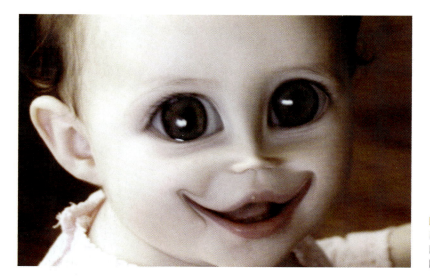

Figure 7.28 After using the Pucker tool on the nose of the baby. Now this is starting to look crazy.

The other tools are less important and more self-explanatory. The only other tool that it's crucial to be aware of is the Reconstruction tool. It's the tool located directly below the Pucker tool, and it looks like a paint brush with some dots under it. When you paint with this tool, it removes all applied distortions, returning the painted pixels to their regular state.

The way that the Liquify works its magic behind the scenes is that it creates an invisible mesh around the object, and then distorts the layer as the mesh is distorted. You can click the stopwatch for the Distortion Mesh property to animate your changes to the mesh. Or, you can animate all changes at once with the Distortion Percentage value. I can take this value to 50%, which will reduce the amount of all distortions by half.

Figure 7.29 With the Distortion Percentage value at 50%, all of my distortions are still here, but are now less intense.

What might not be as obvious is that you can actually take this value above 100%, which will further exaggerate the applied distortions.

Figure 7.30 The same image with my Distortion Percentage value at 150%.

Because of the flexibility of this value, you can create some very interesting results by applying a Wiggle expression to it. If you wanted to make a surface boil, or have other random distortions, this might be the fastest way to do it.

The Magnify Effect

The purpose of the Magnify effect is to make a portion of an area larger, without the spherical distortion that we see in the Bulge and Spherize effects. This effect is used to zoom in to a particular area, which is great for demonstrating products in marketing ads, or for the medical/biological field, where things often need to have a closer look.

If you'd like to follow along, I'll be using the Magnify.aep project in the Chapter 9 folder of the exercise files. In the example here, I've created a magnifying glass (out of two shape layers and some layer styles), and we also have an Artbeats video clip of a city flyover on another layer.

Using Freeze Area Masks

When using the Liquify effect, there might be some pixels that you absolutely don't want to change in any way. In that case, create a mask around them. Then, in the Warp Tool Options area of the Liquify effect in the Effect Controls panel, choose the mask you created from the Freeze Area Mask drop down.

Figure 7.31 The Magnify.aep project.

We're going to use the Magnify effect to magnify the Artbeats city footage. We're going to create the illusion that we're doing some spy-esque reconnaissance work on some of the people in these buildings. We'll match up the size of the magnified area to the glass in the magnifying glass. Then we'll connect them using expressions, so that we can just move the magnifying glass around (or animate it doing so) to see different parts of our footage magnified.

Apply the Magnify effect to the Artbeats footage on the CED113.mov layer. Before we play around with the magnifying glass, let's turn off the magnifying glass layer to just see what the

Magnify effect looks like on its own. It's a little difficult to see the results with this footage until we change the settings.

Figure 7.32 The Magnify effect applied to the CED113.mov layer.

In the Effect Controls panel, you can change the shape from Circle to Square. You can move the magnified area around with the Center property. You can intensify or reduce the amount of zoom with the Magnification parameter. After increasing the Magnification and moving the center of the Magnify effect, the

Figure 7.33 The Magnify effect is more obvious in this example when the Center value is adjusted, and the Magnification value is increased. Here, the Magnification value is over 400.

effect results become easier to see. Note that if you want a layer to magnify beyond its boundaries, you'll need to select the Resize Layer checkbox at the bottom of the effect.

The Link drop down contains interesting options. If you change this value from the default to Size to Magnification, it will link these two properties. Size still acts independently, but when you adjust Magnification, the size of the magnified area also increases. This drop down will also allow you to link Size & Feather to Magnification.

One other property that deserves coverage is the Scaling drop down. If you increase the Magnification property a lot, it can become pixelated. You can change the Scaling value to Soft to smooth out the results. You can also change it to Scatter, which creates a grainy result.

Figure 7.34 Magnify applied to other footage, with a Magnification value of 450, and the Scaling value set to Standard.

Usually, I don't mention the Blending Mode drop down, because it's obvious what it does. But with this effect, realize that this drop down can help you create a distinct look for your magnified area. You might use the Magnify effect to create a POV shot through a rifle scope, for example. You may want to use a different blend mode to make the scope view stand out more from its background.

Figure 7.35 After changing the Scaling value to Soft, the ugly noise and pixelation is considerably improved.

Figure 7.36 Changing the Scaling value to Scatter creates a grainy effect.

Figure 7.37 The Magnify effect, using the Difference blend mode.

Or, if the scope view is what you're going for, you could also just change the Blending Mode from Normal to None, to isolate the magnified area.

Figure 7.38 Changing the Blending Mode in the Magnify effect's controls to None will hide all non-magnified pixels.

Linking Magnify to the Magnifying Glass

Now it's time to turn the Magnifying Glass layer back on. We'll now link the Magnify effect on the CED113.mov layer to the position of the magnifying glass so that wherever we move the magnifying glass, it magnifies pixels, acting like a real magnifying glass.

Hit the Reset button on the Magnify effect at the top of the Effect Controls panel. Either that, or apply a new instance of the Magnify effect to the CED113.mov layer. Then take the Size value to 89, which will match the size of the glass in the magnifying glass. In the Timeline panel, open the disclosure triangles to reveal the Position property of the Magnifying Glass layer. Then, in the Effect Controls panel, Alt(Win)/Opt(Mac) click the stopwatch for the Center property. Then, go down to the Timeline panel and click and drag the pickwhip that just showed up to the Position property of the Magnifying Glass layer.

Figure 7.39 Link the Center value to the Position of the Magnifying Glass layer using the expression pickwhip.

Figure 7.40 The Magnify effect on the CED113.mov layer is linked to the position of the Magnifying Glass layer.

Once you've done this step, the magnified area will follow the magnifying glass wherever it goes. Note that in order to make this work simply as it does here, you'll need to make sure that the layer with the Magnify effect is the same size as the comp, and that it is also centered in the composition.

The Mesh Warp Effect

The Mesh Warp effect is almost like the Liquify effect discussed earlier in this chapter. Both effects create a distortion mesh that is used to control the pixels of a layer, so that they can be distorted. Both effects create fairly organic distortions when used temperately. The difference is that in the Mesh Warp effect, you don't have any extra tools. Instead, you edit the mesh directly.

Open the Distort.aep project from the Chapter 7 folder of the exercise files. Apply the Mesh Warp effect to the dotted line layer in the Motion Graphics comp. As soon as you apply the effect, you will see the distortion mesh.

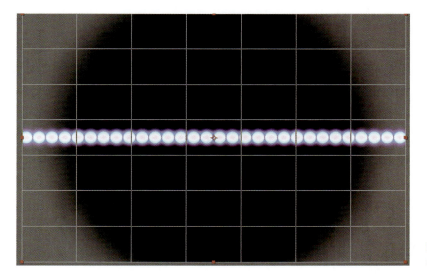

Figure 7.41 The distortion mesh of the Mesh Warp effect.

Note that as you're distorting the mesh in this effect, that there are several ways to distort the mesh. When you click on a grid intersection (a corner), you can move that corner around to distort the layer. This is the most simple and flexible way to adjust the mesh. Also, when you have a corner point selected, you'll notice four bezier handles coming off of the corner point, which you can also pull and adjust to fine tune the distortion.

The parameters of this effect in the Effect Controls panel are very simple and straightforward. First, you control the resolution of the mesh by adjusting the Rows and Columns properties. Having a mesh with high resolution (i.e., high Rows and Columns values) will result in smoother distortions. However, having a low resolution mesh is much easier to adjust and correct.

You can also adjust the Quality although again, I don't usually notice any difference in performance by adjusting this property. So, I usually keep my Quality value at 10 (the maximum amount).

As with other mesh-based distortion effects, you can animate the distortions you make to the mesh in the Mesh Warp effect by clicking the stopwatch for Distortion Mesh.

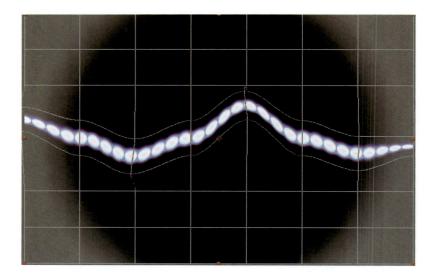

Figure 7.42 After adjusting the mesh, the dotted lines distort accordingly. I left the distortion

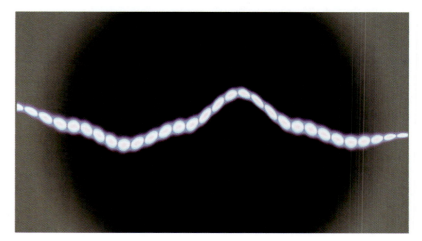

Figure 7.43 The same distortion applied to the dotted line layer, with the distortion mesh deselected to hide the mesh.

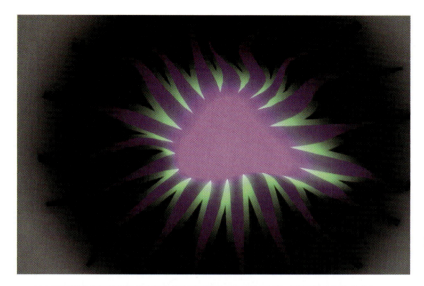

Figure 7.44 After warping the star layer with the Mesh Warp effect.

Figure 7.45 After warping the smoke in the Smoke comp with the Mesh Warp effect.

Which Distortion Effect Should I Use?

At this point, you may be wondering, "Which distortion effect should I use for what occasion?" Unfortunately, there isn't a list of when to use what effect. And actually, I don't have an extra list for you, either. For most character animation, the Puppet tools usually handle every task I need them to. But as far as regular warping goes, I find that sometimes I prefer one effect, and sometimes that same effect just doesn't work quite right. So, it's not only a matter of personal preference, it's a matter of personal preference for each project and job that you do. Hopefully, seeing effects at work in several different scenarios will give you a better idea of what effects will work for the work that you do.

The Mirror Effect

The Mirror effect is a simple effect that creates a mirrored reflection of your layer. The main feature of this effect is that it hides any portion of the layer that intersects with its reflection. This is is great for creating reflections from a literal mirror, and it can also produce some really cool kaleidoscope effects by applying multiple copies of the effect, each with its own Reflection Angle and Reflection Center values. You might be wondering if the Mirror effect can create those cool iTunes-like reflections that you see everywhere nowadays. Unfortunately, it can't. The Mirror effect doesn't give you any control over the masking—or even the opacity—of the reflected object.

Open the Distort.aep project and apply the Mirror effect to the dotted lines layer. There are only two properties in this effect. Reflection Center determines the center point of the virtual mirror. The Reflection Angle value allows you to rotate the reflection around the Reflection Center. Note that the default settings appear to make nothing happen because the Reflection Center is on the right edge of the layer by default, and the default Reflection Angle is vertical.

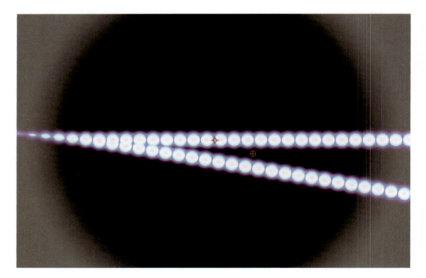

Figure 7.46 The Mirror effect applied to the dotted line layer. I left the effect selected here so that you can see the Reflection Center (the effect control point).

All in all, the Mirror effect is definitely not the best way to create a reflection, as you might infer from the name. But it's not called the Reflection effect, it's called Mirror. And mirroring is something that this effect actually does quite well. If you wanted

Figure 7.47 The Mirror effect applied to the star layer.

Figure 7.48 The Mirror effect applied to the smoke layer in the Smoke comp.

a simple mirrored look, it might be challenging getting the pivot points spot on. But this is a task that is very easy with the Mirror effect.

If you do need to create an iTunes-like reflection that has faded opacity and a falloff to boot, you can get the same effect by duplicating the layer, and then applying the Mirror effect to the duplicate layer. Then, precompose the duplicate with the Move All Attributes option selected. Next, in the new precomp layer, mask out the original portion of the layer, isolating the reflection. You are then free to lower its opacity and apply another mask that has feathering to create the transparency falloff.

Another common motion graphics trick that Mirror really helps with, is when you're creating a "bundle" of stuff, as seen in Figure 7.49. This is a screen shot of a project I did, and Is used the Mirror effect to duplicate the dragon(s), the treble clef(s), the robot(s), and the guitar(s). Often, you'll want objects to be symmetrical on each side of said bundle like this. The Mirror effect is great for this as well.

Figure 7.49 The Mirror effect is great for motion graphics projects that are structured like this.

The Offset Effect

The Offset effect is another simple effect. It just allows you to tile an object by offsetting it. It differs from simple position because it repeats the layer like a tile, as demonstrated in Figure 7.50. We'll be continuing on in this effect with the Distort.aep project.

Keep in mind that if you like what you see with the Offset effect, you really might want to check out the Cycore effect, CC Tiler, which has the same parameters as the Offset effect does, but it also allows you to scale the tiles, which creates the illusion of a sea of duplicate clips that all play back at the same time. The CC Tiler effect also renders quickly, even when rendering many scaled-down, virtual copies of the same layer.

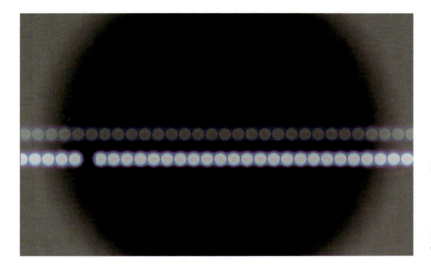

Figure 7.50 The Offset effect applied to the dotted line layer in the Motion Graphics comp. Here, the offset copy is shifted down and to the right of the original dotted line, and the Blend With Original value is at 30%.

There is also an interesting feature that allows you to see the original layer—Blend With Original. As you increase this value, it becomes like an opacity value for the original, and also indicates how much transparency is removed from the Offset copy. An example of this is seen in Figure 7.50.

The Offset effect is obviously great for things that need to tile. If you were going to create a news ticker at the bottom of the screen that you wanted to keep playing over and over, you could just make one instance of the ticker, and cycle it with the Offset effect. This same trick could be used in a similar way with cars on a freeway, passing stars in the sky, the numbers on an odometer, and so on.

But because of this little Blend With Original value, we can also use the Offset effect to quickly create multiple copies of an object by duplicating it. By lowering the Blend With Original value, your layer seemingly becomes two layers. With every duplicate of the Offset effect, you create another instance of the composite result of all previous applications of the Offset effect. So, as you duplicate the Offset effect, the number of instances of your original layer increases exponentially. I wish my checking account had an Offset effect.

The Offset effect can also be helpful if you're looking for some simple symmetry. In Figure 7.52, I applied the Offset effect to the star layer, and offset it on the Y axis. That's it. No copies of the effect, and no adjustment of the Blend With Original value.

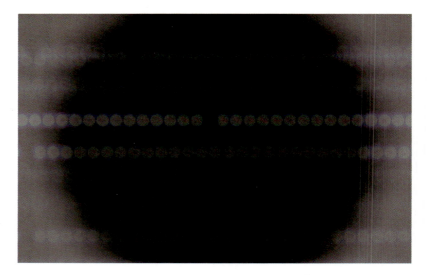

Figure 7.51 The dotted line layer with 4 instances of the Offset effect. Notice the highlights created by overlapping copies with lowered opacity.

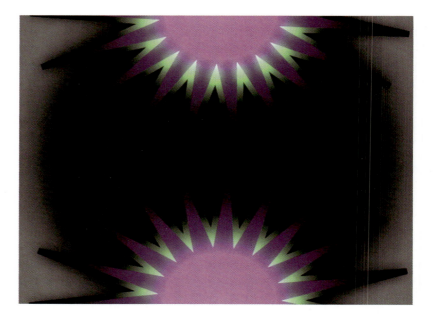

Figure 7.52 The Offset effect applied to the star layer, and the stay layer offset along the Y axis.

In the Smoke comp, I've applied two instances of the Offset effect to the smoke layer. I've also used Blend With Original to create a larger wall of smoke. You could get this same effect by duplicating the layer several times. But remember that with the Offset effect, we can control multiple instances of the smoke at once.

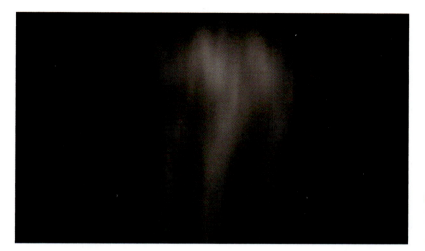

Figure 7.53 The smoke layer in the Smoke comp with two instances of the Offset effect applied.

The Optics Compensation Effect

The Optics Compensation effect is a unique effect in this category. Most Distort effects distort a layer for visual effect. The Optics Compensation effect fixes the distortion at the corners of footage, caused by certain camera lenses. So, Optics Compensation is a distortion effect that fixes a distortion problem. I guess in this case, two wrongs do make a right.

Open up the Optics Compensation.aep project from the Chapter 7 folder if you'd like to follow along. This footage is a still shot I took with a fisheye lens over Snoqualmie Falls in Washington State. As you can plainly see, the fisheye lens has caused a lot of distortion in this image.

Figure 7.54 The original Fisheye layer.

The Optics Compensation effect can be used in two ways. It can add lens distortion, or it can remove it. If I increase the Field Of View (FOV) value to about 106, you can see the added distortion it creates. This even shrinks the corners of the layer, and creates a pincushion effect.

Figure 7.55 Increase the Field Of View (FOV) setting only, and lens distortion is added to the layer.

This extra distortion might be a cool trick for another day, but right now, we need to get rid of this lens distortion, not add to it. The way to get the Optics Compensation effect to remove our lens distortion is to select the Reverse Lens Distortion checkbox. Selecting this option and changing the FOV value to about 70 gets

Figure 7.56 The fisheye lens distortion is gone when we take the FOV value to 70 and select the Reverse Lens Distortion checkbox.

this image so straight that it looks like it just graduated from a military academy. Either that or it saw a chiropractor.

All joking aside, the real purpose of this effect is to aid in compositing. If we did have to composite a character—or some other object—into this scene, we would have a difficult time making a believable composite because of the lens distortion. That is the reason that this effect can add lens distortion or remove it. Of course, the example I have here is exaggerated so that you can see the results. But even a subtle inconsistency in field of view can cause a composite to look artificial.

The Polar Coordinates Effect

I love graphics that feel like they're zooming towards you, and that's why I love the Polar Coordinates effect. What Polar Coordinates actually does, is allow you to fold your layer such that the left and right side meet at the top. Picture those plastic, glow-in-the-dark necklaces and bracelets kids sometimes wear. When you purchase them, they are straight, but you wrap the two ends around to connect them, making a circle. Polar Coordinates does the same thing with layers. As we'll see, when you do this with certain layers, the effect makes all sorts of cool vortexes and other graphics that give the illusion that they are coming towards you.

Let's open the Polar Coordinates.aep project from the Chapter 7 folder of the exercise files. This project is identical to the Distort.aep project we've been looking at in this chapter, but it also contains another comp developed specifically for this effect called Anime Background. Later in this section, we're going to use Fractal Noise and Polar Coordinates to create an anime cartoon-style background.

First, let's start with the basics. Open the Motion Graphics comp, and apply the Polar Coordinates effect to the dotted line layer. There are only two settings here—Interpolation and Type of Conversion. Before we look at what these do, we need to understand two terms—rectangular and polar. Rectangular basically means left to right, and polar basically means around in a circle. Another way to describe this is to think of this effect converting X and Y (rectangular) coordinates to radius and angle (polar) coordinates. The Polar Coordinates effect takes a layer of one type (rectangular or polar) and converts it to the other type. Type of Conversion property determines whether you are taking a rectangular layer and wrapping it around itself (polar), or vice versa. The Interpolation parameter controls how much a layer is converted.

In the effect controls of the Polar Coordinates effect, change the Type of Conversion to Rect to Polar, and increase the Interpolation value to 100%. This will create a circle out of the dotted line. You'll also see the great downfall of Polar Coordinates, in that it almost always degrades the quality of the layer. This happens even when the pixels aren't stretched very much. In cases like this, I usually avoid those effects like the Plague. But, the distortion created by Polar Coordinates is so unique, that I still use it frequently. I usually just use Fast Blur, or start with a layer twice as large and then scale it down, or I use some other method to cover up the pixelation caused by this effect.

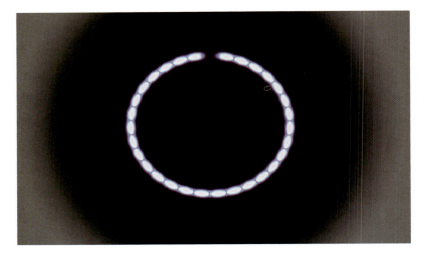

Figure 7.57 The Polar Coordinates effect applied to the dotted line layer creates a circle out of this normally straight layer.

Note that we can also get interesting results by using Interpolation values other than 100%. Figure 7.58 shows the same example as 7.57, but with the Interpolation value at 33%.

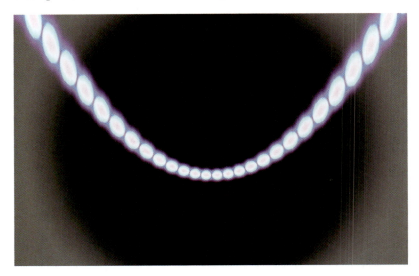

Figure 7.58 The Interpolation value in the Polar Coordinates effect shown at 33%.

Now that we know what it does, it's pretty easy to imagine what the results of applying Polar Coordinates will be on simple lines. But what about when we apply it to the star layer? The results aren't so predictable.

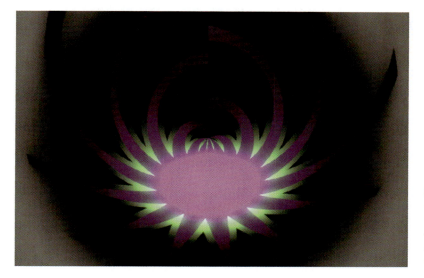

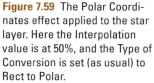

Figure 7.59 The Polar Coordinates effect applied to the star layer. Here the Interpolation value is at 50%, and the Type of Conversion is set (as usual) to Rect to Polar.

Usually, I set the Type of Conversion drop down to Rect to Polar. But this star is somewhat radial (circular) in nature. Let's unwrap this circular object and make it rectangular by changing the Type of Conversion drop down to Polar to Rect. As you can see from Figure 7.60, this is a great (and quick) way to create icicles, and other spiky surfaces.

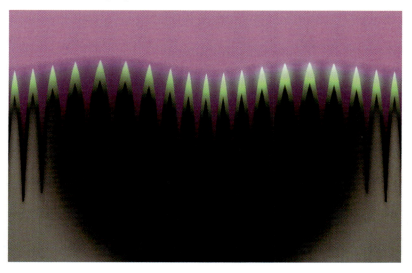

Figure 7.60 Taking the Type of Conversion value to Polar to Rect will cause the spikes of the star to be arranged linearly. Here, the Interpolation value is at 100%.

As I previously mentioned, I usually keep my Type of Conversion setting to Rect to Polar. I almost never use the Polar to Rect setting because the results are unpredictable when used with most objects. However, if you're looking for a simple, artsy background, "unpredictable" may be just what you're looking for.

Figure 7.61 By leaving the Type of Conversion value at Polar to Rect, and taking the Interpolation value down to 50%, we get some pretty interesting (and beautiful) results.

When I applied the Polar Coordinates effect at the standard settings (Interpolation at 100% and Type of Conversion set to Rect to Polar) to the smoke layer in the Smoke comp, it created the illusion of a puff of gas being emitted with force from a small opening. Insert your own lowbrow joke here.

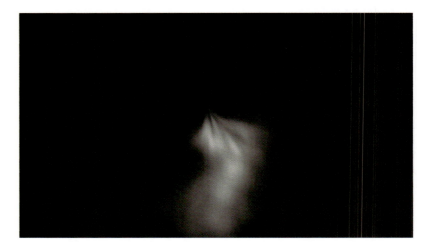

Figure 7.62 The Polar Coordinates effect applied to the smoke in the Smoke comp.

Remember that the Polar Coordinates effect, along with several others in the Distort category, operate at 32 bpc. I've included a comp in this project called HDR, if you'd like to experiment with it.

Let's move on to our project to create an anime background. Open the Anime Background comp in this project to see the Fractal Noise we've applied here.

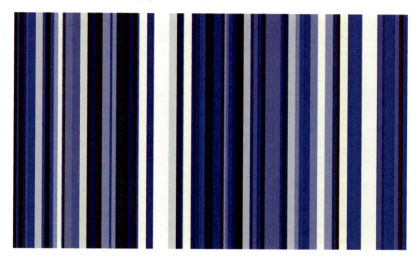

Figure 7.63 The Anime Background comp.

Apply the Polar Coordinates effect to the fractal layer, and as usual, take the Interpolation setting to 100%, and the Type of Conversion to Rect to Polar. This creates a cool anime-style background. It also shows how easy it is to create motion graphics that feel like they're rushing towards the viewer.

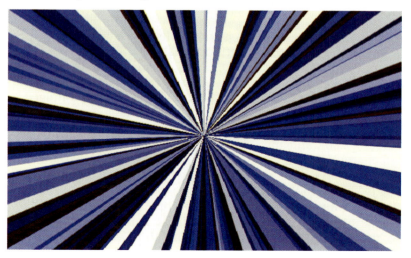

Figure 7.64 The anime background is created by applying Polar Coordinates to the fractal layer.

Creating "Techy" Circles

You can also use the Polar Coordinates effect to create those concentric, techy circles that were often seen on technical websites, or on high tech electronics interfaces in movies and TV shows. You can create them by making a series of short, wide rectangles, and then applying the Polar Coordinates effect with Interpolation at 100%, and Type of Conversion set to Rect to Polar.

Unfortunately, the pixelated ugliness caused by the Polar Coordinates effect is more than I can tolerate in this example. Because of the nature of this example, we can turn these edges razor sharp by (ironically) applying a blur effect. Apply the Radial Blur effect to the fractal layer, increase the Amount value to about 95, and then change the Type to Zoom. Because this effect blurs pixels in the same directions as these lines, the pixelated edges are smoothed, and we have a beautiful result. Using blurs to enhance edges? Yep. Don't forget that the key with effects is to know what they do, so that you can use them for unconventional purposes.

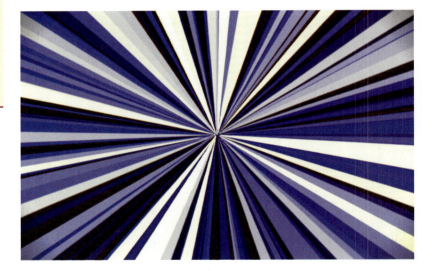

Figure 7.65 Using Radial Blur, we can smooth and tighten the edges of these lines.

Combining these effects is so fun, that I just can't help myself. I should be focused on writing this book instead of playing around with After Effects, but adding effects is like an addiction, and I just can't stop once I've started. Family members tried to stage an intervention, but I'm beyond hope. So, I've indulged in my visual arts addiction by applying the Bilateral Blur effect (with Colorize checked, the Radius value set to 10, and the Threshold value at 200), and then duplicated it. Then, I applied the Glow effect and adjusted to taste. I then capped it all off with the proverbial cherry—the Levels effect, which I used to darken the shadows and midtones.

Remember that this texture is still "live," meaning that I can bring this vortex of light to life by going all the way back to the Fractal Noise and animating the Evolution value, or

Using Multiple Effects

In Chapter 22, we'll look exclusively at the topic of using multiple effects to achieve the end result. But until then, remember that most effects only reach their true potential when combined with other effects. For example, you could use the Offset effect to create a loop of the dotted lines, and then apply Polar Coordinates to create objects rotating around in a circle. The anime background that we created was a great example of this as well. Remove any of the ingredients in that recipe, and the results would be dramatically different. The Polar Coordinates effect is great to use when combining multiple effects. Try making a pattern with any other effect, and then topping it off with Polar Coordinates. In many cases, you'll create significantly more interesting patterns by experimenting with this effect.

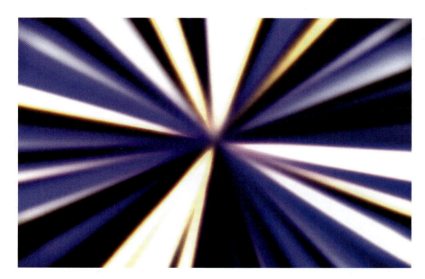

Figure 7.66 The result of my multiple effects binge.

other properties. I've included my final results in a project called Polar Coordinates FINAL.aep that you'll find in the Chapter 7 folder.

The Reshape Effect

The Reshape effect allows you to distort a layer into another shape. This is done by creating one mask (the Source mask) that defines the boundaries of the current layer, and another mask (the Destination mask) determines what shape the layer will become when it is reshaped.

The Reshape effect is most commonly used, perhaps, as a morphing tool. It's not necessarily a *good* morphing tool in most cases, though. You'll never use the Reshape effect to recreate the morph seen in the movie *Lord of the Rings: The Two Towers* when Theoden breaks the spell of Saruman and returns to normal. But as we'll see, it is capable of matching edges well, and even allows you some manual control in this department.

You can also use the Reshape effect in character animation. For instance, you can reshape the layer of a character's mouth to form certain phonemes. The Reshape effect also allows you to use a third mask as a Boundary mask, if you so choose. The Boundary mask restricts the reshaping to a certain area of the layer. So if your character's mouth and face are on the same layer, you're not out of luck because you can use a Boundary mask to isolate the distortion to just the mouth.

Open up the Reshape.aep project from the Chapter 7 folder. This project contains a few comps. We'll mostly be working with the Reshape comp because I've done a lot of the setup for you. If you wanted to start from scratch, I've also created a comp called Reshape Start from Scratch.

In the Reshape comp, we have two layers. The Creepy Stranger layer contains the glowing silhouette of a shady looking character.

Figure 7.67 The Creepy Stranger layer in the Reshape comp.

The Ghost layer contains an old school ghost I drew in Illustrator. We're going to morph the Creepy Stranger layer into this Ghost layer, as if the creepy stranger is really a ghost. Hey, it could happen.

Figure 7.68 The Ghost layer in the Reshape comp.

Critical to this trick working out correctly, we need a mask of each layer, on each layer. In other words, on the Creepy Stranger layer, we need a mask of the creepy stranger and a mask of the ghost. And, we need both of those masks on the ghost layer as well. This is because we're going to morph the stranger into the shape of the ghost. But at that point, it will still look like the stranger, just in a different shape. So, we're going to morph the stranger into the ghost shape, and the ghost *from* the stranger shape, back into the normal ghost shape. Then, we'll cross dissolve them together, and hopefully create the illusion that the stranger is becoming the ghost.

Figure 7.69 Each layer should have a mask that goes around its boundaries, and then another mask that goes around the boundaries of the other layer.

Note that if you need to make a mask of an outline of a layer, you can use the Layer>Auto-trace command. You can also copy the mask of one layer's outline—by selecting the mask in the Timeline panel and pressing Ctrl+C(Win)/Cmd+C(Mac)—and then paste it (Ctrl+V(Win)/Cmd+V(Mac)) to apply it to the other layer. Also, be sure that the Mask Mode value in the Timeline panel for each mask is set to None, so that the masks don't remove any portions of the layers that they are applied to. In the Reshape comp here, I've already created and copied the masks for you, so you're all ready to go. The Creepy Stranger layer mask is called guy mask, and the Ghost layer mask is called ghost mask.

Next, you need to apply the Reshape effect to both the Creepy Stranger layer and the Ghost layer. Set the Source Mask drop down to guy mask for both layers because they will both start in the shape of the stranger. For the Destination Mask, we need to set both to ghost mask because both layers will morph into the ghost shape at the end.

To get the layer to distort from its Source Mask shape to its Destination Mask shape, animate the Percent value. Elasticity determines how smooth the movement is. The default value is Stiff, and gets more smooth as you go down the list, until you come to Super Fluid. And let me tell you, there is a huge hit on render time every time you go up any degree in smoothness. With Stiff selected as the Elasticity value, my Mac Book Pro renders this simple example at almost 3 frames per second. When I use Super Fluid Elasticity, it takes almost 8 seconds to render one frame. You can imagine how much that would multiply with other objects animating, a standard amount of layers, anything in the background, HD video, and so forth.

Another important aspect of the Reshape effect is correspondence points. A correspondence point is a point on one mask that corresponds to a point on the other mask. This tells the Reshape effect where a certain part of a mask be when it's done reshaping. If the stranger's hat were to morph off to the right and become the arm of the ghost, it would not be a good distortion in this example. So, we would create a correspondence point connecting the top of the stranger mask to the top of the ghost mask to tell the Reshape effect where that point should go.

We don't have to create correspondence points for every spot on the masks. We only need to create them where there are problems, and in many cases, Reshape will correctly guess how to morph the layer. You can create as many points as you want, but each pair of points will slow down render time.

To create correspondence points, Alt(Win)/Opt(Mac) click somewhere on a mask, then Alt/Opt click the corresponding point on the other mask. Once you've created a correspondence point, you can click and drag on it to move it along the mask. The Correspondence Points area in the Effect Controls panel shows you how many pairs of correspondence points you have. Note that you can only see correspondence points when the Reshape effect is selected in the Effect Controls panel.

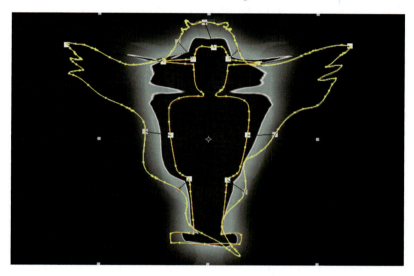

Figure 7.70 The dots and lines that connect the masks are correspondence points. Notice that there aren't any down at the bottom of the masks. This is because I didn't need them because the effect properly guessed how to morph this area.

The final step is to animate the fading out of the Creepy Stranger layer, and the fading in of the Ghost layer. This produces a cross dissolve, and if performed correctly, can help us create the appearance that the stranger is becoming the ghost.

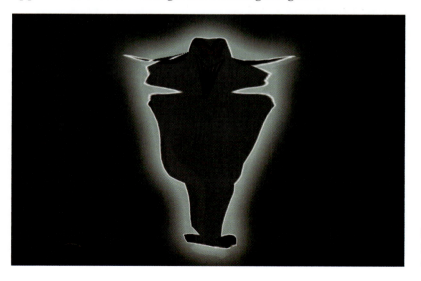

Figure 7.71 The reshaping layers must be crossfaded to create the morph.

Reshape and Interpolation

Interpolation plays a role in the quality of the results of the Reshape effect. First of all, there is the Interpolation Method drop down in the Effect Controls panel. Use Linear for masks with flat edges, Smooth for masks with curved edges, and Discrete for automatic, high quality interpolation. You can also Shift+click individual points to change their interpolation as well. Changing the interpolation of one point automatically changes the interpolation of its corresponding point. After doing so, the correspondence points will change shape in the Composition panel (square is linear; circle is smooth), but there will not be any indication of this in the Effect Controls panel.

The Ripple Effect

The Ripple effect creates an (almost) auto-animated ripple-type distortion. If you had a photo of still water and wanted to make it look like the surface of the water was rippling because someone threw an object into it, you would only have to apply the Ripple effect, increase the Radius value, and render. That's it. The Ripple effect creates its distortions by creating concentric rings of distortion that emanate from center, called the Center of Ripple in this effect.

To see the results of this effect, I'm going to apply the chads water—glistening pool.ffx animating preset to a solid layer. You can find this preset in the Animation Presets folder in the exercise files. This animation preset creates somewhat still water, which will be great for distorting with the Ripple effect.

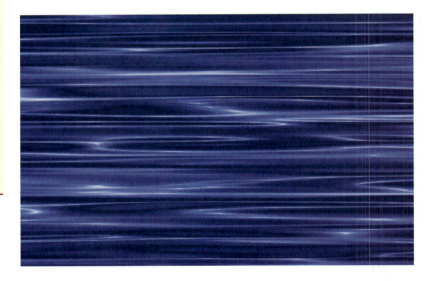

Figure 7.72 The glistening pool animation preset.

Before we apply the Ripple effect to the solid that this animation preset was applied to, we first have to precompose the white solid layer so that the Ripple effect can be seen in the fractal water. After precomposing, apply the Ripple effect to the precomp of the water. Increase the Radius value to about 50 to start seeing results. The Radius value specifies how big the rippled area is.

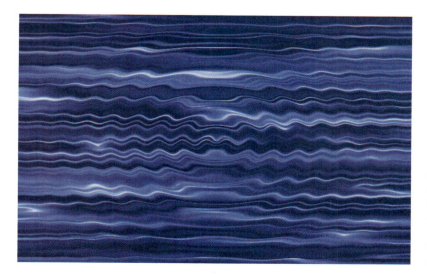

Figure 7.73 After precomposing the fractal water and applying the Ripple effect, increasing the Radius value will allow you create ripples in the water. In this figure, the Radius value is set to 50.

You can change the Center of Ripple value to create a different place that the ripples emanate from.

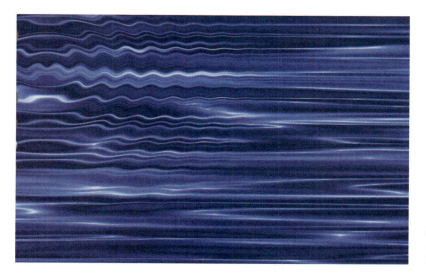

Figure 7.74 With the Center of Ripple in the upper left area instead of the center.

Since this effect essentially auto-animates, you can control the speed with the Wave Speed property. Control the size of the ripples with the Wave Width value. Control the depth (intensity) of the ripples with the Wave Height value.

Figure 7.75 The results of the Ripple effect, with the Wave Width value at 60, and the Wave Height value at 70.

The Ripple Phase value is like an offset for the wave distortion, in case you'd like the wave to look differently at a particular frame without changing any of the other settings.

The Rolling Shutter Repair Effect

The Rolling Shutter Repair grew out of the Warp Stabilizer effect (covered later in this chapter), but it has more power for correcting this issue than Warp Stabilizer does. Its purpose is to correct the rolling shutter distortion common in cameras with CMOS sensors. As these cameras move too quickly, the footage appears to wave and bend. This wavy distortion is colloquially referred to as "jello cam" because of the way the footage appears to wobble like jello. This affects cameras from the iPhone video camera to Canon DSLR's to the venerable RED One.

In the Rolling Shutter Repair.aep project in the Chapter 7 folder of the exercise files, you'll find an example of this. It's kind of hard to show in a book because subtle, fixable examples don't show up well as a still. And extreme examples can't be repaired by this effect. But if you try this effect with this project (or your own footage), you'll see a difference. In this original footage, I was panning while shooting video with my iPhone handheld. So the "jello" in this shot is fairly strong. In Figure 7.76, you can see this effect most noticeably in the trees, which are slanted towards the right. The house in the background and the target/post thingy in the foreground are also leaning similarly.

Figure 7.76 The original image. It looks like the world is in italics.

Apply the Rolling Shutter Repair effect to this layer. You'll notice an instant correction. But the default Rolling Shutter Rate value of 50% is best for less rolling shutter than we have. Typically, 50–70% is ideal for rolling shutter from DSLR cameras. But for the iPhone, Adobe recommends punching this value all the way up to 100%. Once we do that, our trees straighten out quite a bit, and our shot looks much better, especially when played back.

Figure 7.77 The completed shot. I love you Mr. Cosby, but there's no room for jello here.

Note that there are some choices if you're not getting the results that you're looking for (which is pretty common with bad rolling shutter shots). You can enable the Detailed Analysis button if you're using Warp as your Method. You can also try Pixel Motion for the Method value.

Additionally, if you have a shot that your camera was turned sideways, you might want to look at the Scan Direction option. Almost all sensors go from top to bottom, so the default value of Top→ Bottom is great. But if you rotate the sensor while recording (which is especially common with phone cameras), you can adjust this value accordingly.

The Smear Effect

The Smear effect is very similar to the Reshape effect, except that the Smear effect is not intended to morph a shape into another shape. The purpose of the Smear effect is to simply warp and smear pixels around. The controls are much easier to understand and use than those in the Reshape effect. As with the Reshape effect, we need to create masks to tell the Smear effect how to do its job. We create a source mask to tell the Smear effect which part of the layer will be distorted. We also create a boundary mask to set a limit as to how much that portion of the layer can be distorted.

Open up the Smear.aep project from the Chapter 7 folder. This contains a comp with a rocket image. We'll be using Smear to distort the trail of fire coming out of the exhaust of the rocket. I've already created two masks for you on this layer—an elliptical mask that will be the source mask, and a rectangular mask that we'll use as a Boundary Mask.

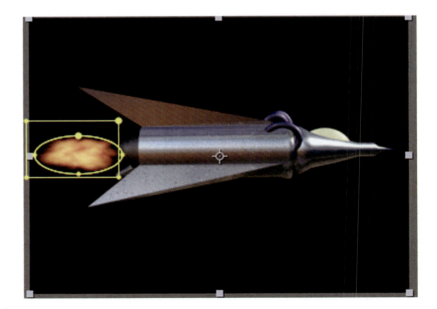

Figure 7.78 The two masks on the Rocket layer in the Rocket comp.

Next apply the Smear effect. Before you worry about what's going on, first change the Source Mask value to Mask 1, and the Boundary Mask value to Mask 2.

The Smear effect allows you to deform the portion of the layer inside the source mask in three basic ways: moving, scaling, and rotating. When you first apply the Smear effect, you might have noticed an additional shape that matches the shape of the source mask. This area is like a smear controller, as the pixels in the source mask will be pulled towards the pixels in the smear controller. The position of this smear controller can be adjusted by the Mask Offset property.

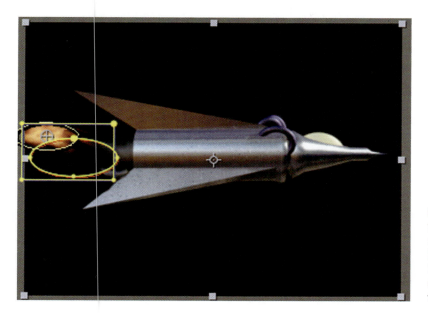

Figure 7.79 The extra ellipse with the effect control point is created by the Smear effect to be used as a controller of sorts. Notice how the pixels in the source mask are being pulled towards it.

Use Mask Offset to move the pixels in the source mask. Use Mask Rotation to rotate the pixels in the source mask. And use Mask Scale to adjust the scale of the pixels in the source mask. Notice, however, that these properties only work to the degree that you've increased the Percent value. Think of the Percent value as the master distortion control in this effect. The Elasticity and Interpolation Method parameters (which we covered in the Reshape effect, earlier in this chapter) are also here to help you customize your distortions.

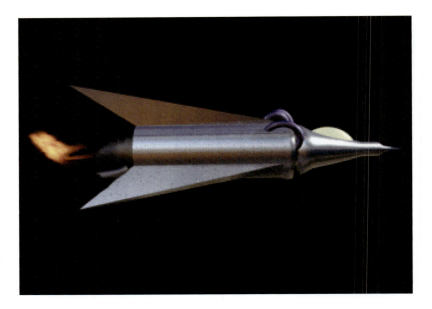

Figure 7.80 The tail fire of the rocket distorted with the Smear effect. Here, we see it scaled down, moved, and rotated.

The Spherize Effect

The Spherize effect is the much simpler version of the Bulge effect. Both effects create a bulging, round distortion around a specified center. The Spherize effect only allows you to control the size of the spherical distortion (with the Radius property), and its location (with the Center of Sphere property). So, use the Bulge effect if you need more control. Use the Spherize effect if you need a quick and simple bulging effect.

The results of using the Spherize effect are essentially the same as the results of using Bulge. To see these results, see the Bulge effect earlier in this chapter.

The Transform Effect

The Transform effect contains the five basic transforms that we have for layers: Anchor Point, Position, Scale, Rotation, and Opacity. It also adds the ability to adjust Skew, Skew Axis, and the ability to adjust and animate the Shutter Angle, which controls the amount of motion blur. All of these properties (including Shutter Angle) operate independently from the other corresponding settings in the layer and composition.

You might be wondering why anyone would need another set of layer transforms. There are actually a few good reasons. One is that it is often advantageous to have two sets of the same property. Let's say you had a layer with a light bulb, and you wanted it to flicker while fading out. You could use the layer's Opacity property to flicker the light, and then apply the Transform effect to have another Opacity value, which you could then use to fade out the layer.

Another great benefit of this effect is that it can sometimes substitute for precomposing. Let's say that you had several layers of graphic elements that you wanted to resize (or, perhaps, move or scale). If you didn't want to precompose those layers, you could create an adjustment layer above the graphic elements layers, and then apply the Transform effect to the adjustment layer. Any adjustments to the Transform effect on the adjustment layer will affect all layers below it.

Along those lines, you could also use the Transform effect to defy the render order. Typically, transforms (from the layer) are rendered after effects. By using the Transform effect, you could place the Transform effect before (i.e., on top of in the stack of effects in the Effect Controls panel) other effects, thereby changing the render order.

Finally, you could also use the Transform effect as a last resort helper when you've run into animation troubles. I'm ashamed to admit that on more than one occasion, I've botched an animation because I animated Anchor Point and Position, and the results were terrible. Using Transform, you can add an additional set of animation controls, which can often bail you out of such sticky circumstances.

As previously mentioned, one of the unique components of this effect is the ability to adjust Skew and Skew Axis. Skew is like the object equivalent of italics. It gives an object a slanted distortion. The Skew Axis property determines where the center of the skew is.

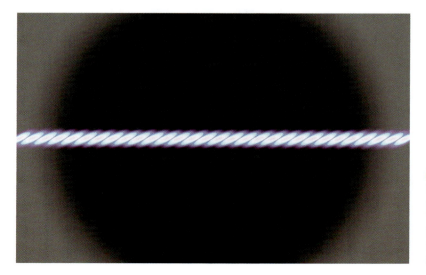

Figure 7.81 The dotted line layer in the Distort.aep project with skewing from the Transform effect. To make a layer skew from left to right, change the Skew Axis value to 90 degrees.

The Turbulent Displace Effect

The intent of the Turbulent Displace effect is to create organic distortions using a fractal noise pattern. Because of this, you'll notice many similarities to the pattern powerhouse, Fractal Noise that we'll look at in Chapter 11. Turbulent Displace is almost like the Displacement Map effect that's only using the Fractal Noise effect to create the displacement map, and you can't see the Fractal Noise itself, only its effects.

Perhaps the most common way to use the Turbulent Displace effect is creating waving flags out of flat layers. We'll look at how to do that, as well as what this effect looks like with some of the other examples we've looked at in this chapter already. There are some cool examples here, so hopefully you'll find something you can use in your workflow.

First, open the Turbulent Displace.aep project from the Chapter 7 folder. Let's start in the Flag comp. This comp consists of a solid with the Checkerboard effect applied. We'll look more at the Checkerboard effect in Chapter 9, but just know for now that it made this checkerboard from scratch instantly. Also notice that the solid that this effect has been applied to is slightly smaller than the comp. This will be important later.

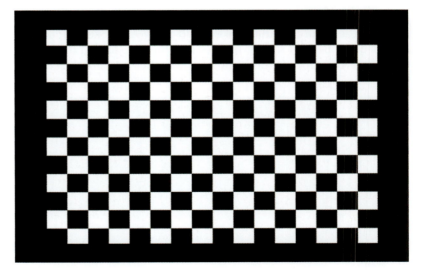

Figure 7.82 The Flag comp in the Turbulent Displace.aep project contains a solid with the Checkerboard effect applied.

Apply the Turbulent Displace effect to the Flag layer in the Flag comp. Right away, even without making further adjustments, you can see the effect of the distortion on this layer.

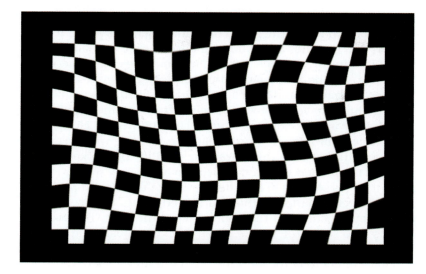

Figure 7.83 The Flag layer after applying the Turbulent Displace effect. The default settings for the Turbulent Displace effect are shown here.

The first setting I want to address here is the Pinning property. By default, this value is set to Pin All, which basically means that the corners and edges remain undisplaced. Does that mean they're just "placed"? Ha! You can see in Figure 7.83 how the center of the flag is distorted, but the corners and edges remain flat. This is a really helpful setting in some instances, but this makes our flag look really fake. Instead, take this value to None, which allows the entire flag to be distorted. The Pinning value allows you to determine a part of the layer to be frozen, as if it were anchored down on a pole or if someone were holding it in place.

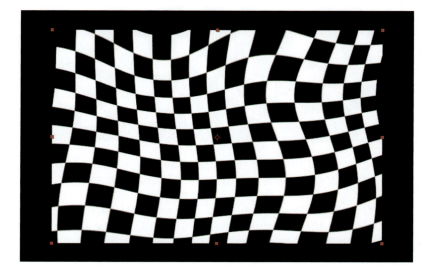

Figure 7.84 With Pinning set to None, the entire layer is distorted, but the edges are still flat.

You'll notice that in the Pinning drop down, there are basically two sets of options—the group of Pinning settings at the top are regular and the ones at the bottom have Locked at the end. Let's take Pin Top for example. When Pin Top is selected, the entire top edge will be restricted from warping. However, it will be allowed to shift left and right a little bit. This would be good if you were going to have an object dangling from another object that might sway a little, such as clothes hanging from a clothesline. But if this were hanging from a flagpole, the flag wouldn't move so much. In that case, you'd want to use Pin Top Locked, which restricts the pinned side from moving at all.

Our flag is starting to look better. One of the biggest problems in the current example is that our flag edges are flat because the flag is getting cut off at the boundaries of the layer. The solution to this is to select the Resize Layer checkbox, below the Pinning parameter. This allows the distortions from the Turbulent Displace effect to go beyond the regular boundaries of the layer. Now this is starting to look like a flag. And actually, if you wanted to animate this like a flag on a flag pole, you'd probably want to take the Pinning value to Pin Left Locked.

Figure 7.85 fter selecting Resize layer, the edges look more realistic, because they are permitted to go beyond the layer's boundaries. Notice the visible edges of the selected layer here.

Now, let's start from the top of the effect in the Effect Controls panel and look at some of the most important settings here. In the Displacement drop down list, you'll notice that there are different methods here that you can use to distort your layer. Instead of displacing it with turbulence, for example, you can make it bulge or twist. I usually find the default value of Turbulent to be the best setting for most jobs.

The Amount value determines the intensity of the displacement. I find that the default value of 50 is a little high most of the time. For animating this flag, I took this down to about 35 for a softer wave. You can also take this value ridiculously high to create some interesting art.

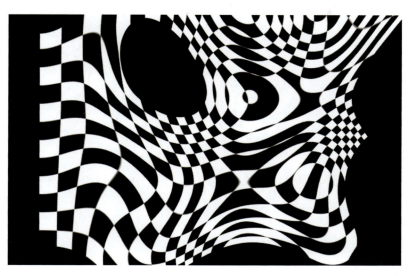

Figure 7.86 The flag project with the Amount value set to 350.

The Size value is a little abstract. This refers to the size of the fractal noise working behind the scenes to distort the flag. Take this value down really small (to about 5) if you want to create many tiny ridges, as if you were animating something underneath turbulent water. Use large values for large, sweeping waves of distortion.

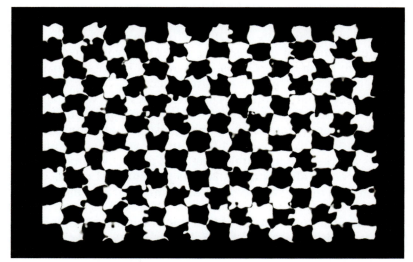

Figure 7.87 With the Amount value at 150 and the Size value at 5.

You can create more intricate edges by increasing the Complexity value. This refers to the complexity of the fractal noise making the displacement.

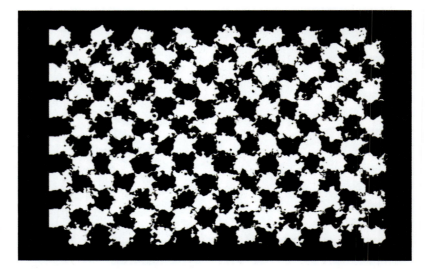

Figure 7.88 Using the same settings as those seen in Figure 7.87, but with a Complexity value of 3.

All that's left now is to bring this effect to life. You can do that with the Evolution parameter, which causes the noise to just move around. It might as well be called the "Spring to Life" property. In the case of our flag, animating this value will cause the flag to wave. You can also use the Cycle Evolution parameter (which we will cover in the Cell Pattern effect in Chapter 9) to create a seamless loop of distortion.

You can also animate the Offset (Turbulence) property to create the illusion that wind is blowing through your layer, or that flames are rising upwards. Just animate the X or Y dimension of this parameter to achieve the desired effect.

Let's see what Turbulent Displace looks like when applied to the other objects that we were using previously from the Distort.aep project. Note that these are also included in the Turbulent Displace effect for your convenience. I think the results are particularly interesting with the fractal smoke. Note that this effect also works in 32 bits per channel mode, which is great for creating a fiery look with our HDR star in the HDR comp.

These examples are saved in the Turbulent Displace.aep project, if you'd like a closer look at what I've done in these figures.

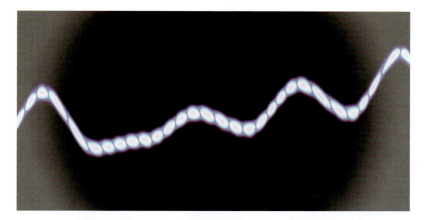

Figure 7.89 The Turbulent Displace effect applied to the dotted lines layer in the Motion Graphics comp.

Figure 7.90 Turbulent Displace applied to the star layer in the Motion Graphics comp. Here, Twist is used at the Displacement type.

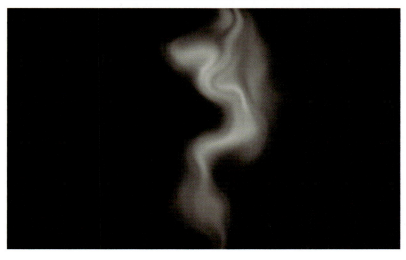

Figure 7.91 The Turbulent Displace applied to the smoke creates an increased degree of realism because of the randomness and smoothness of the distortion.

Figure 7.92 Applying Turbulent Displace to the shape layer in the HDR comp can create a fiery look. I achieved this by increasing the Amount value (to 300) and the Complexity value (to 2), and decreasing the Size value significantly (to 3).

The Twirl Effect

The Twirl effect is one of the more simple effects in this category. It creates a distortion that looks like someone grabbed your layer and twisted part of it.

If you'd like to follow along, open up the Distort.aep project from the Chapter 7 folder of the exercise files, and apply the Twirl effect to the various layers here. There are three parameters: Angle, Twirl Radius, and Twirl Center. It might seem weird to you (as it did to me) that there isn't a Twirl Amount property. This is because the effect is brought to life by increasing the Angle value. Then, you can use the Twirl Radius value to increase the size of the twirl, and the Twirl Center value to determine where the center of the twirl is.

Let's first apply Twirl to the dotted line layer in the Motion Graphics comp. We'll start simple. Take the Angle value to 90, and leave all other properties at their defaults.

You'll notice in Figure 7.93 that the edges of the dotted line are unaffected. This is due to the Twirl Radius setting. To have the entire layer join the twirl party, increase the Twirl Radius. Anything over 42 does the trick in this case.

Also note that Twirl can also process in 32 bits per channel. So let's apply Twirl to the shape layer in the HDR comp. When you do so, increase the Twirl parameter above 360 degrees. When dealing with rotation, one full revolution usually looks the same as no rotation at all. With the Angle value in the Twirl effect, it

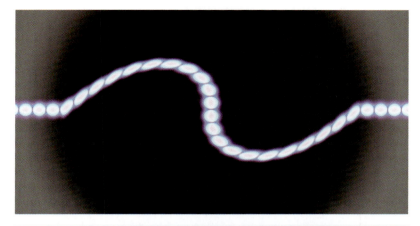

Figure 7.93 Twirl applied to the dotted line layer.

Figure 7.94 The Twirl effect applied to the star layer.

Figure 7.95 The Twirl effect applied to the smoke layer in the Smoke comp. Here I lowered the Twirl Radius value, and moved the Twirl Center to the bottom, so that only the bottom of the smoke would be twisted.

doesn't work like that. The more you increase the Angle value, the more the layer spins around itself, creating a tighter wind. Figure 7.96 shows the result of taking the Angle value to 4× +99 degrees, the Twirl Radius to 90, and moving the center of the twirl down and to the right a bit.

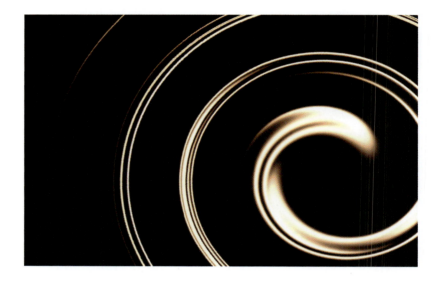

Figure 7.96 The result of applying the Twirl effect to our HDR star.

The Warp Effect

If you've used the text warping features in Adobe Photoshop or Adobe Illustrator, then you already know how to use the Warp effect. It basically allows you to warp a layer in one of several preset warp styles. Personally, I prefer to use the other distort effects because they give you more control over specific warp styles. If I apply the Bulge preset in the Warp effect, I don't get any Bulge-specific controls. If I apply the Bulge effect, I get all sorts of controls that are specific to bulging. That's the way I roll. But that's just my preference.

Again open the Distort.aep project. Apply the Warp effect to the dotted line layer in the Motion Graphics comp. The default settings for the Warp effect create an arc distortion.

I'm not going to go into what each different Warp Style setting does, because they are fairly self-explanatory. It is important to know that the Warp Axis parameter specifies whether the distortion is oriented horizontally or vertically. The default setting is Horizontal, which basically means that it creates a horizontal arc. Taking this value to Vertical makes a vertical arc distortion;

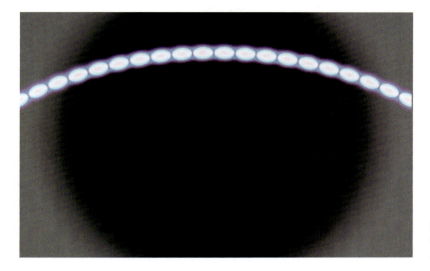

Figure 7.97 The results of applying the Warp effect to the dotted line layer.

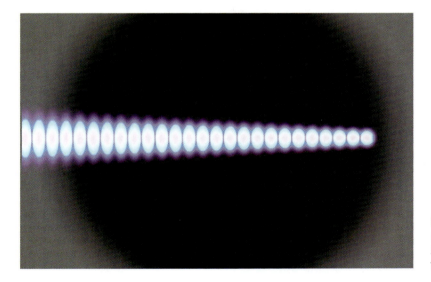

Figure 7.98 We achieve vastly different results from the Warp Axis property when we change the axis to Vertical.

a completely different result. The Bend property corresponds to the amount of warping applied.

Next, I'm going to switch over to the star layer and apply the Warp effect to that. I'm going to change the Warp Style to Flag. This Warp Style distorts a layer in a wave shape, like a waving flag. Note that this is not a good idea to use for actually animating a flag.

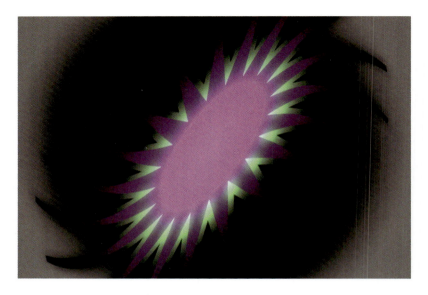

Figure 7.99 The star layer with the Warp effect applied, with the Flag Warp Style.

The other properties that we haven't discussed are the Horizontal Distortion and Vertical Distortion properties. These properties determine how distorted or pinched objects are on one side. For example, taking the Horizontal Distortion value to 100 will pinch the left side and enlarge the right side of the layer. Take the value to negative 100 to create the opposite effect. Taking the Vertical Distortion property to a positive number will pinch the top and bloat the bottom, while a negative Vertical Distortion value will bloat the top and pinch the bottom.

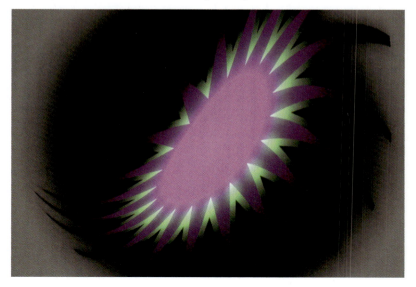

Figure 7.100 Using the same settings as Figure 7.99, but with the Horizontal Distortion value at 100.

I also applied the Warp effect to the fractal smoke in the Smoke comp, and used the Wave Style, and set the Warp Axis to Vertical to create curved, wispy smoke.

Figure 7.101 The Warp effect applied to fractal smoke.

The Warp Stabilizer Effect

The Warp Stabilizer effect is not just a good effect, it's one of the best reasons to use After Effects. The technology behind this stabilizing plugin is so magical that if it were invented in New England in the seventeenth century, Adobe would have been accused of being a witch. I literally can't count how many shots that were otherwise unusable that Warp Stabilizer has completely saved.

This is no ordinary stabilization tool. Most stabilizing tools choose a point and then stabilize that point. That's still helpful in some situations. But what the Warp Stabilizer does is actually LOOK at your footage and it examines what should be stabilized. Typically, in a shot with great depth, a regular stabilizer wouldn't be of much help because as you shake a handheld shot, the parallax shifts. In some amazing way, After Effects puts all of those shaken up pieces back together. You can have some motion in the footage, and After Effects won't stop that motion (unless you want it to), it will just enhance and smooth what's there. It's seriously incredible. But just like a light saber, it can really mess you up if you don't know how to wield it.

For our first example, I'm going to use a clip that I actually used in a critical scene in a short film that I just made called GODLIZZA. This short film was an experiment to see if I could make a film without any crew at all, and with the only cast being my children. The film won the Grand Prize in a short film competition at the Seattle International Film Festival in 2012, so Warp Stabilizer must've done something right!

Open the Warp Stabilizer.aep project from the Chapter 7 folder of the exercise files, and go to the GODLIZZA shot composition. In this shot, we've just entered a baby's dream world, and we see this imaginary city for the first time. It's supposed to look like a flyover, but in reality it was me holding my heavy camera between my legs while I walked forwards. And the shot looks like it was held between someone's legs (it's really shaky). Just apply the Warp Stabilizer effect and wait. When it's done analyzing the footage, it's going to be as smooth as if I didn't walk with it between my legs.

Figure 7.102 The shot we're going to stabilize (which, incidentally looks exactly the same in a screenshot when it's been stabilized—so just imagine this shot being really smooth).

Now, in all fairness, it's shots like this (i.e., with a shaky moving camera) that the Warp Stabilizer was designed for, so the default settings work perfectly. But sometimes it doesn't always do what you want it to do. If your shot is supposed to be locked off (without any camera motion), then you'll want to change the Result value in the Effect Controls panel from Smooth Motion to No Motion.

Warp Stabilizer also has a cool, lesser known trick. By default, the Framing value in the Borders section is set to Stabilize, Crop, Auto-scale, which indicates the procedures that the effect is going to perform on your footage. Once footage is stabilized, the edges go crazy and look terrible. So the default solution here is to just slightly scale up the footage. You can add more scale with the Additional Scale parameter, or you can choose one of the other Stabilize/Crop options in the Framing drop down, and choose your own scaling value.

But there's another option that is quite interesting—Stabilize, Synthesize Edges. What this option will do, is try to keep your scaling at 100%, and then when the edges don't quite meet up, it will try to guess what the edges should be, and fills them in. Sounds like a disaster waiting to happen, right? Sometimes. But sometimes, as in this case, it actually works pretty well. Figures 7.103 and 7.104 show the before and after of an edge that Warp Stabilizer had to synthesize and how it did. I'm impressed.

Figure 7.103 The original edge of the image after stabilization, but without scaling.

Figure 7.104 The same frame after Warp Stabilizer synthesized the edges. It's not perfect—you can still see a tiny patch in the bottom right corner that it failed to synthesize for some reason. But all in all, quite impressive.

There is a big gotcha to the Warp Stabilizer effect that I ran up against on a very important shot. Because it was important, I had to make a workaround, and I'd like to share that with you, in case it might save you some headaches.

In the other comp in this project, princess in bed, you'll find a shot that I used for an iPad app I've been working on called The Princess and the Paintbrush. The camera pushes in on this shot, and it's a little shaky because I used a crappy slider.

Figure 7.105 The sad princess on the shaky bed.

You would think that the Warp Stabilizer would fix this up quick, right? Yeah, that's what I thought, too. But it actually freaks out half-way through the clip because it's trying to analyze the movement of the princess as she rolls over in the bed. The secret here is to pre-compose the layer, and make a mask in the precomp that doesn't have the princess in it, as demonstrated in Figure 7.106. Then apply Warp Stabilizer to the nested precomp layer in the parent comp. Without that distraction, it will totally work! After it has stabilized everything successfully, you can go back to the nested comp and remove or disable the mask, and your shot will still be stabilized in the parent comp! Ha HA! Fooled you, Warp Stabilizer!

Figure 7.106 I only used this much of the shot for stabilizing, and masked out the rest. The camera move is still detectable in this little sliver, so it works.

The Wave Warp Effect

Finally in this chapter, we come to the Wave Warp effect (not to be confused with the Wave World effect in the Simulation category). I really like this effect. The Wave Warp effect applies different types of wavy distortions to a layer. This effect also auto-animates. Another aspect of this effect that I like is that there are many different types of wave shapes that you can use, and they are all very different. The results are fairly high quality, and you also have control over the Pinning. For creating interesting motion graphics, the Wave Warp effect is a terrific asset.

Let's take one last gander at the Distort.aep project from the Chapter 7 folder of the exercise files. Apply the Wave Warp effect to the dotted line layer in the Motion Graphics comp. Instantly the line is distorted and will animate when played back. All of the settings here are similar to what we've seen in other effects in this chapter (such as the Ripple effect), so we don't need to cover those again here. But what I do want to do, is to show you how different the various wave types are. Before we do that, I'm going to increase my Wave Height value to 70 to make the wave distortion more prominent.

Normally, I wouldn't take the time to show you what every single option of a particular property does. But the Wave Type effect changes the results so radically, that it may be a great undiscovered tool for creating motion graphics. Let's say you wanted to create a series of slashes, or half circles, or waves of noise, or small bars. You might not think of it that way, but the Wave Warp effect is capable of creating all of these patterns and more. Just create a simple line with a masked solid or a shape layer, use a blend mode if desired, and apply the Wave Warp effect and one of these presets to create instant animated textures.

Cut Off Edges

When using the Wave Warp effect, it's common to have the distortion wave your layer outside of its own boundaries, causing cut off edges. This kind of this is what the Grow Bounds effect (covered in Chapter 20) was created for. Just apply the effect BEFORE the Wave Warp effect (or drag Grow Bounds above it in the Effect Controls panel) and increase the Pixels value until your layer is no longer getting cut off.

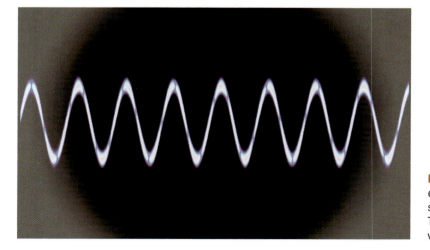

Figure 7.107 The Wave Warp effect, with the Wave Height setting at 70, and the Wave Type set to the default value—Sine.

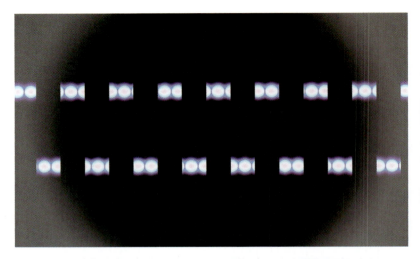

Figure 7.108 Using the same settings, but with the Square Wave Type. Use the Wave Height property to increase the vertical spread between these bars.

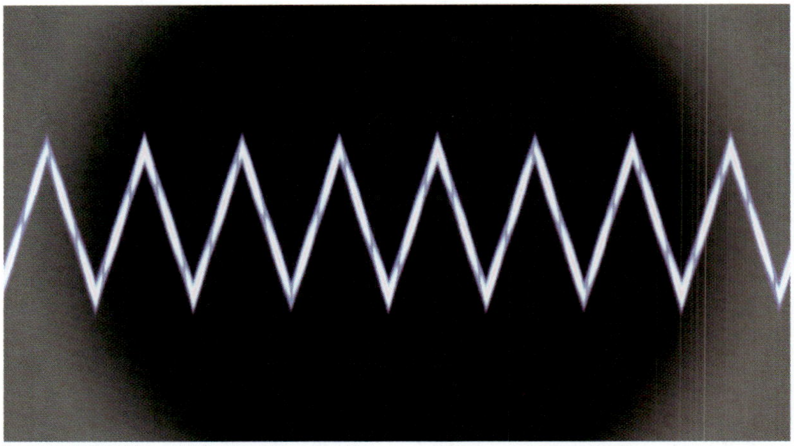

Figure 7.109 With Wave Type set to Triangle.

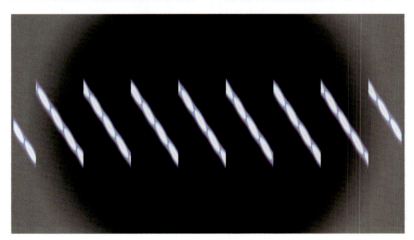

Figure 7.110 With Wave Type set to Sawtooth. This is a cool texture even without animation. To stop this layer from moving, take the Wave Speed value to 0. To move it in the opposite direction, take the Wave Speed value to a negative number.

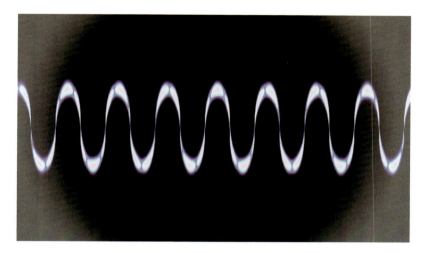

Figure 7.111 With Wave Type set to Circle.

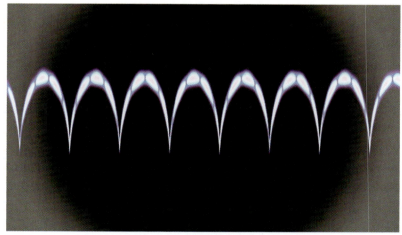

Figure 7.112 With Wave Type set to Semicircle.

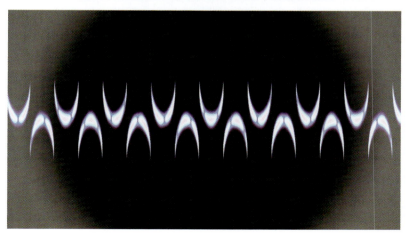

Figure 7.113 With Wave Type set to Uncircle.

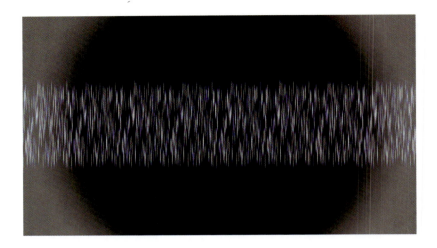

Figure 7.114 With Wave Type set to Noise.

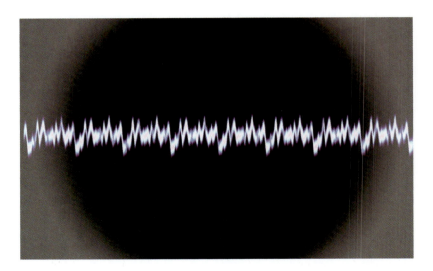

Figure 7.115 With Wave Type set to Smooth Noise. This is interesting. There are several other ways to create art that looks like a music wave (such as with the Audio Waveform or Audio Spectrum effects). But none of them allow you to create those waveforms and shapes out of an existing layer, which is what we did here.

8

THE EXPRESSION CONTROLS EFFECTS

The Expression Controls category of effects contains what is perhaps the most odd group of effects. Other than the effects in the Audio category, most effects make some kind of visual change. The Expression Controls effects are used to control expressions, which are used to control the values of layer properties. In effect, they control the controllers.

One of the big limitations of expressions is that they cannot be animated. Let's say you wanted to simulate an earthquake by applying a Wiggle expression to the Point of Interest value on your camera layer. Once you applied the expression, the wiggling would last for the entire duration of the layer (or, the composition, whichever ended first). Enter the Expression Controls effects, which can be used in conjunction with expressions to create animations. In this case, we could create a null layer and apply the camera controlling expression control effect to the null. As we'll also see, these Expression Control effects can also used simply as a visual controller for expressions, to make them easier to work with.

Because all of the Expression Controls effects are applied and function in a similar manner, let's take a look at how expressions can be controlled with them. Then we'll look briefly at what each Expression Controls effect can be used for.

Create a new After Effects project, then a new composition at the NSTC DV size. Then create a new solid (any color) at the comp size. Go to the Animation menu at the top of the interface and select Apply Animation Preset. Navigate to the Animation Presets folder in the exercise files that came with this book, and select the chads fire—campfire.ffx preset. This is a simple fire pattern created with the Fractal Noise effect (Chapter 12) and colored with Colorama (Chapter 6).

In the Timeline panel, select the solid layer and press UU (that's the letter U two times fast). This will reveal all of the properties that have been altered from their default settings.

Figure 8.1 The chads fire—campfire animation preset.

Look for the Effects>Fractal Noise>Brightness property. Hold the Alt(Win)/Opt(Mac) key and click the stopwatch for the Brightness property. A text field will open up in the Timeline panel for you to type in an expression. Completely replacing all existing text in this area, type wiggle(5,10). This will create random brightness values within 10 units of the existing value for the Brightness property 5 times every second. This will create an organic flicker of brightness.

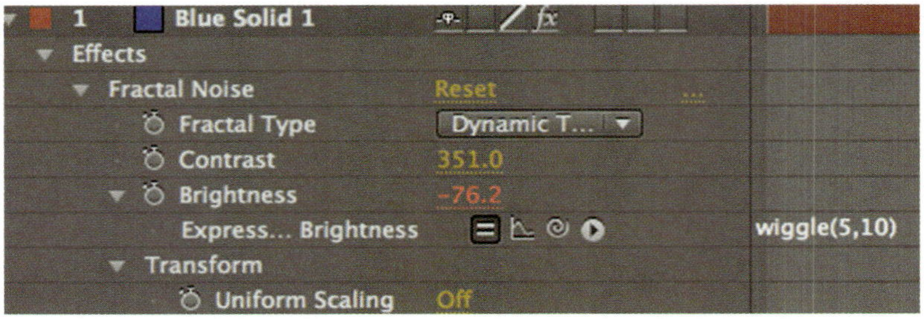

Figure 8.2 The wiggle expression applied to the Brightness property.

So, the results look great, but what if we wanted to increase the intensity of the flicker over time? For this, we must turn to expression controls.

Apply the Slider Control effect (in the Expression Controls area) to this solid layer. Click in your expression once again to make the text editable. Then, as if in a text editing application like Microsoft Word, click and drag to highlight (select) the second number, 10.

Figure 8.3 Select the number 10, the second number in the wiggle expression.

With the number 10 selected, click and drag the pickwhip in the Timeline panel to the Slider property of the Slider Control in the Effect Controls panel, and release the mouse.

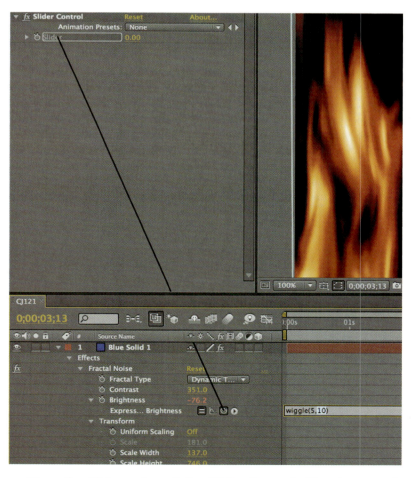

Figure 8.4 With the number selected, click and drag the pickwhip to the Slider property in the Effect Controls panel.

Now, the Slider value of the Slider Control effect is controlling the amount of variation in the brightness wiggle. We can

Naming Effects

If you plan on using Expression Control effects, it's a really good idea to rename the effect so you can instantly discern which property it is controlling.

set keyframes (or even other expressions!) to control the Wiggle expression, because of the Expression Controller effect we've added here.

As you can probably tell, there's really nothing special about this Slider Control effect. It's just a slider that does nothing. It really doesn't serve any other purpose, other than to control other behaviors in After Effects.

This example demonstrated a simple effect with one simple Slider parameter. But what if you wanted to control the Evolution property in Fractal Noise, or rotation, or some other property that uses revolutions and degrees? A simple slider wouldn't be the best controller in that case. For that purpose, you'd need a controller that used revolutions and degrees. And this is why there are several effects in the Expression Controls category. Let's take a glance at the nature and purpose of each controller, as well as a few examples of them in action in real world projects.

The Angle Control Effect

The Angle Control effect is for controlling properties with angle controls. It has degrees, and can keep track of the number of complete revolutions.

Figure 8.5 The angle control effect.

The Checkbox Control Effect

The Checkbox Control effect is for controlling effects with an on/off switch, such as Invert.

Figure 8.6 The checkbox control effect

I recently used this on a really fun project—a tutorial for Red Giant TV (which can be found for free at redgiantsoftware .com/videos). The tutorial was actually about 3D in After Effects, but I created this theme of a vintage *Twilight Zone* show opening as my design motif.

Figure 8.7 An end frame of my Red Giant TV tutorial.

At the end of the tutorial, I showed the final text, but I also wanted creepy, sudden flashes of cracked text to interrupt the calm final text display.

Figure 8.8 A figure of the cracked "interruption" text.

So, I created an adjustment layer with the Checkbox Control effect applied. Then animated the Checkbox property to be mostly off, then occasionally turn on. Then (and here's the key), on the Opacity property of the shattered version of the logo, I applied this expression:

```
    if (thisComp.layer("Controller").effect("Checkbox
Control")("Checkbox") == 0 ) Opacity = 0;
    if (thisComp.layer("Controller").effect("Check
box Control")("Checkbox") == 1 ) Opacity = 100
```

In more simple terms, this expression says that if the Checkbox is off (0), then the opacity of the shattered text is 0% (which is off, essentially). The next line says that if the Checkbox is on (1), then the opacity of that layer is 100%. On the regular text layer, I simply reversed this, telling it be be 100% opaque when the Checkbox is set to 0 and completely transparent when it's set to 1.

That basically turned the Checkbox slider into an on/off switch (and an off/on switch) for these two layers. And this is the power of expression controls in a nutshell. We can control all kinds of stuff with just one checkbox or slider or what have you.

Another detail here is that I also created an Adjustment layer at the top of the layer stack here, and applied a Glow effect, a Levels correction, and a Transform effect with a Wiggle expression on the Position property. I applied the same expression as above to its Opacity value as well. So, once I clicked the Checkbox on, not only did the shattered version of the logo turn on, but it also was brighter, had glow, and shook a bit.

The Color Control Effect

The Color Control effect allows you to select and animate the color change of a color swatch. This can be used to control the change the color of multiple properties at once.

Figure 8.9 The Color Control effect.

The Layer Control Effect

The Layer Control effect is a unique effect in a group of unique effects. The Layer Control effect only gives you the option to select a layer. That's it. It's the only Expression Control effect that doesn't animate.

Because it doesn't have the capacity to animate, the Layer Control effect can't be used as the "standard" expression controller. Use the Layer Control effect when you need to swap several layer-controlled parameters at once. Let's say that you're using the powerful Caustics effect which has many parameters that are controlled by other layers. Additionally, you may add to this other effects (such as Colorama) which can also be controlled by other layers. If you change one of the map values, you may want all of the other properties that use this map to change as well. You could use the Layer Control effect to make the change so that all properties connected to this controller change to the new layer as well. It's not something that your viewing audience will ever see, but it can help you work more efficiently.

Figure 8.10 The Layer Control effect.

The Point Control Effect

The Point Control effect is for controlling properties with an effect point control. These are usually properties with X and Y position values.

Figure 8.11 The Point Control effect.

The Slider Control Effect

The Slider Control effect is perhaps the most useful of the Expression Control effects, probably because most properties in After Effects work like the Slider effect works. It simply adjusts (and allows you to animate) from one value to another. But, as noted in the example earlier in this chapter, it is extremely helpful in its simplicity.

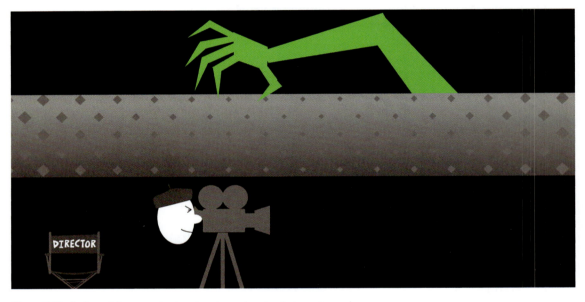

Figure 8.12 The Slider Control effect.

Let's take a look at this effect in use in a real project. I recently created this monster arm for use in a promotional intro for tutorials on my blog, Movies & Computers (moviesand computers.com).

Figure 8.13 A shot of the monster hand and arm (made of shape layers).

Moments later in the animation, this monster hand swoops down and grabs the camera away from the unsuspecting director.

I knew that I wanted this animation, but I also wanted the flexibility to control this complex rig easily. There are, after all, 13 different shape layers here, and once things are animated, it would be a complete and total mess trying to change things. So, to help me keep from pulling my hair out on this project, I created a "rig" of this arm and hand. I used a Slider effect to control everything, and it actually makes this fun to play with.

In the Slider.aep project in the Chapter 8 folder of the exercise files, you'll find the Rigged Arm START comp. This contains the 13 pieces used to make the monster arm. I've gone ahead

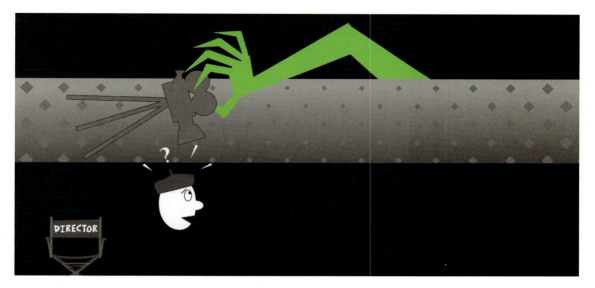

Figure 8.14 YOINK!

and parented them all up for you. But even with these parenting relationships, it would still be a bother to animate.

So, let's set this up RIGHT. Create a new adjustment layer and name it ARM CONTROLLER (or whatever you want). Apply the Slider effect to the adjustment layer, and in the Timeline panel, expose the Slider value of the Slider effect.

Then, on each of the visible layers (except for palm, forearm, and upper arm), (AltWin)/Opt(Mac)+click on the stopwatch for the Rotation property, and then drag the newly created pickwhip to the Slider property of the Slider effect on the ARM CONTROLLER adjustment layer. That creates a simple expression that allows the Slider value to control the rotation property of each of these layers. Figure 8.15 shows this process in action.

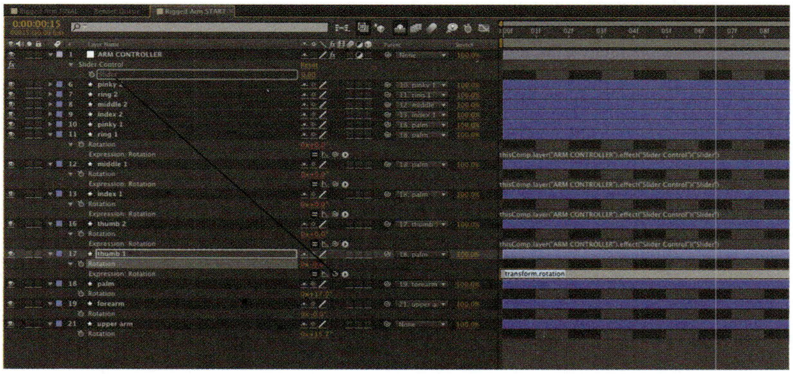

Figure 8.15 This process in action.

With that done, the Slider control now rotates all of these layers at once. Take the Slider value to 20 for example, and all of the fingers move!

Figure 8.16 The fingers move in the same direction, controlled by the expression control.

This is cool, but we don't want them all to rotate in the same direction. What about opposable thumbs? How could Darth Vader air-strangle people without those? So, we need to modify some of these expressions slightly. On the thumb layers (called "thumb 1" and "thumb 2"), click in the expression in the Timeline panel and add *–1 to the end of the expression. This will multiply the Slider value by negative 1, making the thumb layers rotate in the opposite direction as the rest of the fingers.

Figure 8.17 After correcting the expressions on the thumb components, the thumbs are opposable, allowing you to grab as desired. Shown here with a Slider value of –31.

If you want to, you can also add another couple slider controls to the adjustment layer and link each with an expression to the forearm and upper arm rotation values. You can then click the name of the Slider effect and press the Enter/Return key to create new names for these Slider effects (e.g., grip control, elbow control, etc.). This took a couple minutes to set up, but it's now so flexible and easy to adjust, not to mention loads of fun.

9

THE GENERATE EFFECTS

As one of the most densely populated effects categories, the Generate effects contain a multitude of creativity. The common theme of the Generate effects is creating from scratch. That's what makes these effects so fun to me. They represent the starting point of experimentation in many cases. If you need to create motion graphics elements or textures from scratch in your workflow, then it really pays to be familiar with the Generate effects.

The 4-Color Gradient Effect

As the name implies, the 4-Color Gradient effect creates a four-color gradient. Although, the effect doesn't quite behave as you might assume it does. It essentially creates four individual color points that blend together. In almost every other Adobe application (and elsewhere in After Effects itself), colors in a gradient blend together in a line (linear gradients), or in concentric color rings (radial gradients).

The main components of the 4-Color Gradient effect are the four color spots, which each have their own color swatch and effect control point. By default, the colors are a little wild so that you can clearly see each area of color.

Gradient Alternatives

If you're looking to create a multi-colored linear or radial gradient that behaves like traditional multi-color gradients in other Adobe programs, create a rectangular shape layer that fills the screen, and fill it with a gradient (linear or radial). The gradient editor for shape layer fills is more traditional. You can also create gradients with the Gradient Overlay layer style, or the Ramp effect, discussed later in this chapter. You can then use blend modes to composite the gradient into the layers below.

Figure 9.1 The 4-Color Gradient at its default settings, with the effect control points for the four colors visible.

The Blend value determines how well the colors blend together. Increasing the value causes them to blend together more, like drops of food coloring in water. Decreasing the Blend value makes each color more distinct. The Jitter value adds a small amount of noise in the gradient. There are also opacity and blend mode settings as well, so that you can blend these colors into the source layer the effect was applied to.

My biggest problem with the 4-Color Gradient effect is that I can't create a spot that doesn't have gradient color. Otherwise, this effect would be great for creating a quick and easily adjustable vignette. As it stands, the 4-Color Gradient effect can still be used to create animated lights, like lights at a party. It can also be used to shift focus on photos during documentary pieces by making two of the colors dark, and two of them light, and using the Overlay blend mode, and then animating the effect control points appropriately.

When I wrote the first edition of this book, I really hardly ever used this effect. However, I've changed a little bit. I often find that I like to use gradients on layers with flat areas of color, like text or some graphics from Illustrator. I'll often use these gradients to add depth by adding highlights or shadows. While Ramp is quick and a good old standby, its lack of blending options (other than Blend With Original) doesn't help in these cases as much I'd like it to.

So then I turned to the Gradient Overlay available through Layer Styles. But that doesn't give me any kind of controls over exactly where the gradient stops go on the object. Additionally, there are some issues with 3D intersection when you deal with Layer Styles.

And thus I find that I'm continually turning to the 4-Color Gradient effect. Having four gradient control points, with no ability to have more or less colors, is honestly kind of annoying. But when I'm adding shading to an object, it is really cool to be able to manually place my fake highlights and shadows. And being able to blend my highlights and shadows onto my source layer by using the Overlay and Soft Light blend modes is another great advantage in this instance as well.

The Advanced Lightning Effect

The Advanced Lightning effect is one of the greatest powerhouses in all of After Effects. It creates very realistic lightning, but it's also great for sparks and other electrical demonstrations. One of the impressive features in this effect that may not be readily apparent is its ability to work around alpha information. So, you can have lightning wrap around a logo or some other object, and the effect is spectacular.

Let's first look at how to apply the effect in a basic way, and go from there. First, let's open the file Advanced Lightning.aep from the Chapter 9 folder of the exercise files. In the haunted house comp, all layers should be shy except for the subtly named !!LIGHTNING!! layer. Select that layer and apply the Advanced Lightning effect to it. As soon as you do, you'll notice that the black solid has been completely hidden, as it has been completely replaced by the lightning. This newfound transparency allows the background layers to show through.

We're having a difficult time seeing our lightning because the default location for the lightning in this effect is in the middle of our comp. Normally, that's all fine and good, but in this case, our house is covering up the lightning. So we need to change its position. We can adjust the position of lightning by moving the Origin and Direction points. These are both effect control points. The top effect control point is the Origin point; where the lightning originates. The bottom effect control point is the Direction point; where the lightning ends up at the end of the strike. So, I moved my Origin and Direction points over to the right a little (ending up at approximately [516,–20] and [630,446], respectively). Now, we can properly see the entire lightning bolt. Note that unlike the regular Lightning effect (found in the Obsolete category), the Advanced Lightning effect does not auto-animate. We'll look later at how to get this lightning to animate.

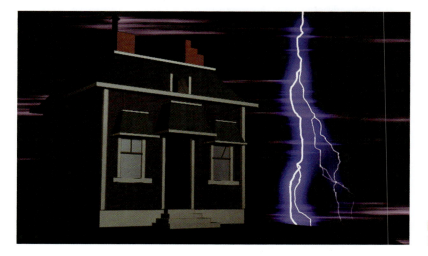

Figure 9.2 The Advanced Lighting effect.

Adjusting Lightning Type

Above the Origin and Direction values, we have the Lightning Type drop down. This controls the type of lightning, or rather the behavior of the lightning strike. Most of these settings are fairly similar, but I wanted to point out a few special ones that might be helpful when using this effect to create something besides lighting.

Options like Strike and Breaking are just variations of lighting, with some alterations to forking, which we'll look at in a moment. Changing the Lightning Type drop down to Bouncey, however, yields very different results. Bouncey is extremely random. Sometimes it creates plain strikes of lightning, and sometimes it creates these huge balls of sparks. As far as I can discern, there's no method to the madness that is the Bouncey lightning type. This setting is great for creating nerdy wizard fights, where someone might conjure a big fury of sparks in their hands before shooting lightning bolts at an enemy sorcerer.

Figure 9.3 The Advanced Lightning effect, with the Lightning Type value set to Bouncey. I left my layer controls on in this image so you can see where my effect control points (for Origin and Direction) are.

With some Lightning Type options, the Direction point will change to an Outer Radius value. Such is the case with the Omni lightning type. Omni shoots out sparks in random directions. This setting is great for creating sparks emanating from something like a Tesla coil, or one of those magic orbs from Radio Shack that charges you with static electricity. Since the direction of such random electricity cannot be controlled, the Direction value changes to Outer Radius. Outer Radius allows you to control how far away from the Origin point that the lightning is allowed to go.

Another interesting lightning type is Two-Way Strike. This creates lightning that strikes from the Origin point to the Direction point, but it also strikes back from the Direction point to the Origin point. This is good if you wanted to create lightning going back and forth between two poles, two hands, or two other objects.

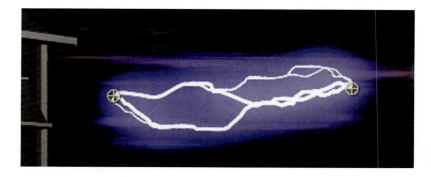

Figure 9.4 The Two-Way Strike lightning type.

What the Fork?

The concept of "forking" is important when getting a grasp of the Advanced Lightning effect. Forking is the amount of lightning branches that splinter off from the main bolt, or core, of lightning. There's even a Forking value that you can increase if you want more or less forking.

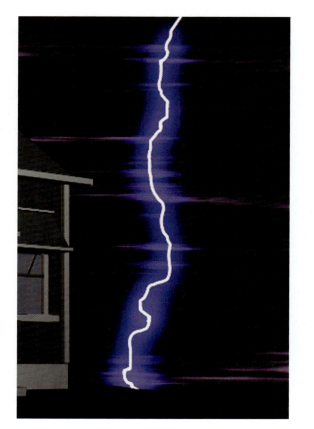

Figure 9.5 Lightning with the Forking value at 0%.

Forking Genius

If you need even more control over forking, as well as other advanced properties, open the Expert Settings area at the bottom of the effect in the Effect Controls panel. Most users will be happy with this effect without these additional controls, but it's good to know about them in case you need to make fine tuned adjustments to your lightning.

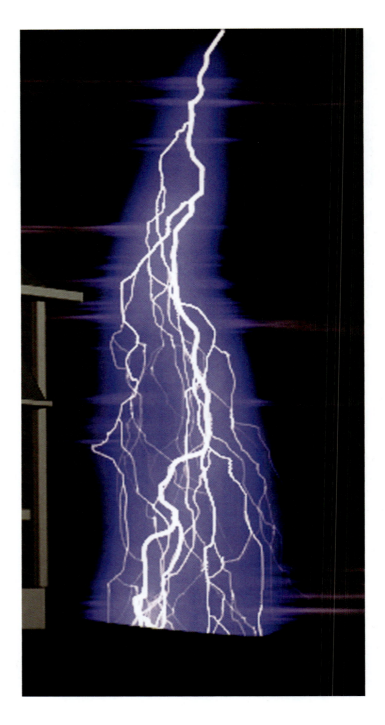

Figure 9.6 Lightning with the Forking value at 100%.

Animating Advanced Lightning

After playing around a bit with Advanced Lightning, you may notice that this effect does not auto-animate. So, what property brings this effect to life? In most cases, you can animate the Conductivity State value to add life to the lightning created with this effect. Any value will work, as there isn't smooth interpolation between Conductivity State values. However, large Conductivity State values cause extremely jumpy animation. Use smaller values for standard lightning effects. A Wiggle expression with a small amplitude value would also work well here.

Even though Conductivity State is the standard way to animate Advanced Lightning, you can also use other properties. If you're going to have your lightning move, you might not want to animate much besides the Origin or Direction points. Movement of these points will cause enough randomization to create animated lightning. Animating both direction points and Conductivity State can create too much random movement in many cases.

What about creating a lightning strike, where the lightning appears to strike, and then retracts or quickly flashes away? There are a couple options here. Perhaps the simplest and most controlled way to create a lightning strike is to use the Strike option for the Lightning Type. That way, you can animate the Direction point and have the lightning strike an object, or strike and then go away.

For other Lightning Types, you can animate an increase in the Decay parameter, making sure that the Decay Main Core option is checked. Alternatively, you could also use the Strobe Light effect (covered in Chapter 16) to cause lightning to just flash on and off.

Advanced Lightning as a Design Element

In the Advanced Lightning.aep project, you'll find a composition called Design Element. This contains a couple of solid layers, with the top one containing some lightning from this effect, and the bottom containing a simple texture. As I've been stressing throughout this book, it's important to be aware of alternate uses of effects. Because Advanced Lightning doesn't animate on its own, we can use it to create sketchy lines or cracks when creating grungy textures.

Figure 9.7 The Advanced Lightning effect, used as a design element.

3D Scratches

For these scratches, I've reduced the Turbulence value to smooth the lines a little, and reduced the Core Radius value in the Core Settings area in the Effect Controls panel. I've also opened up the Glow Settings area and removed the glow by taking the Glow Radius value to 1.0 (its minimum value), and the Glow Opacity value to 0%. Because these lines are so thin, they hold up well when animated in 3D space.

Using Alpha Channels with Advanced Lightning

You can use alpha channels with the Advanced Lightning effect to contain lightning within a layer, or to exclude the lightning and have the lightning strike around the alpha. This is one of the most powerful features of the Advanced Lighting effect. If you wish to follow along, open the comp Logo Lightning-Start. This contains a logo I created in Adobe Illustrator. Apply the Advanced Lightning effect to the Arrows layer.

When you first apply the effect, the Arrows layer disappears. To make it visible with the lightning, select Composite on Original. What we're going to do here is to fill the Arrows layer with lightning, but only where there are already pixels. To make our lightning more visible, I'm going to take the Lightning Type value to Bouncey.

And then, all you have to do is adjust the Alpha Obstacle value. That's it! Take the Alpha Obstacle value to a negative number to force the lightning to stay within the confines of the arrows. You'll also want to make sure that the Origin point is located on one of the arrows, for best results. To get mine looking

Figure 9.8 The Logo Lightning-Start comp.

Figure 9.9 Reducing the Alpha Obstacle value forces the lightning to be contained within the opaque pixels of the layer.

Figure 9.10 When the Alpha Obstacle value has a positive number, the lightning stays in the transparent pixels on the layer.

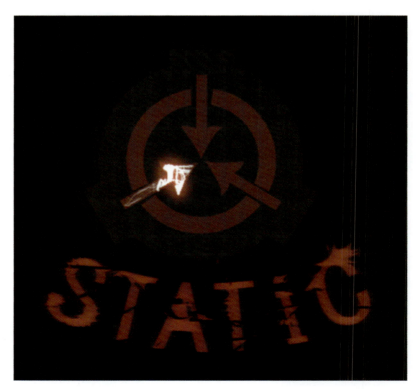

Figure 9.11 The Logo Lightning-End comp.

correctly, I had to reduce the Glow Radius a bit. I also reduced the Core Radius and Forking values a little.

If you take the Alpha Obstacle value to a positive number, then the lightning will wrap around the alpha channel of the layer it's applied to.

The Logo Lightning-End comp contains a finished project, where I've animated a blur on the text and some flickering lighting effects. There are also a couple layers in this comp that are not currently visible. These layers contain an additional lightning effect on the text as another creative option here. I've left them off because they need to be animated to look decent, but I encourage you to turn them on and experiment with them.

The Audio Spectrum Effect

The Audio Spectrum effect generates visual patterns based on the amplitude of an audio layer. Personally, I find that these patterns are very interesting, but it's difficult to use them as they are without having them look tacky. In many cases, it might take a blend mode, or a severe opacity change to blend in well with other art.

You can open the Audio Spectrum.aep project from the Chapter 9 folder for practice. There is only one comp here: Audio Spectrum. In that comp, there are two layers, a solid layer for application of the Audio Spectrum effect, and an audio layer to control the visual properties of the effect. Both ingredients are necessary to get this effect to work. Apply the Audio Spectrum effect to the solid layer.

The Audio Spectrum effect auto-animates—kind of. At its default settings, it's impossible to get this effect to do anything, let alone animate. What you need to do is change the top property, Audio Layer, to a layer that contains audio. In our example here, change the Audio Layer to the Totally 80s Groovathon audio layer. As soon as you do, you'll notice this effect spring into action. From left to right, this line represents the EQ bands of the audio track from the low bass tones to the high treble tones.

Figure 9.12 The Audio Spectrum effect, powered by an audio layer. The spikes in the bands on the left indicate loud bass tones.

Custom Spectrum Shapes

 If the standard line gets boring, you can use your own custom shape or path with the Audio Spectrum effect. This will cause the spectrum to wrap around a path of your choosing. Just create a mask on the layer, and select it from the Path drop down in the Audio Spectrum effect settings in the Effect Controls panel.

One of the things that I usually do when first playing with this effect is to increase the Maximum Height value. That way, I can see what this effect is doing a little better. Sometimes, you can also get more action across the entire band by reducing the End Frequency value. You can move the spectrum by adjusting the Start Point value (the left edge of the spectrum), or the End Point value (the right side of the spectrum). You can alter the number of points along the path by adjusting the Frequency bands property. Or, make them larger or smaller by adjusting the Thickness property.

Color and Audio Spectrum

The Audio Spectrum effect allows for a lot of control over the colors used to make the spectrum. There is an Inside Color value, which controls the color of the core of the bands, and an Outside Color value, which controls the color of the glow on the outside of the bands. The Softness property controls the amount of feathering between the Inside and Outside Color values. You can also adjust the Hue Interpolation property to cycle other colors through the spectrum. Figure 9.13 shows the result of adjusting these color properties. Also in this figure, you'll see the result of enabling the Use Polar Path option at the top of the Effect Controls panel, which wraps the spectrum around itself. This causes the spectrum to emanate radially from the Start Point.

Audio Spectrum and Adobe Flash

There are only a few things in After Effects that will remain vector when output to the SWF file format. Text layers that are not in 3D and do not have blur applied can remain vector. Solids with unfeathered vector masks and Illustrator files that don't have gradients can as well, if they don't have any effects applied to them. But that's just about it when it comes to outputting vectors into the SWF file format. Even shape layers cannot be output to vectors when output to SWF. For some reason that I don't understand, the Audio Spectrum and Audio Waveform effect (discussed next) both become vector when output to SWF. Be aware that the file sizes do get quite large, as a new Flash symbol is created for every band on each frame. Also note that the Softness and Outside Color properties in the Audio Spectrum effect are ignored when output to SWF, and only a flat color is used for each band. Not sure why, but add the Audio Spectrum and Audio Waveform effects to the very short list of elements from After Effects that support vector-based output to the SWF file format.

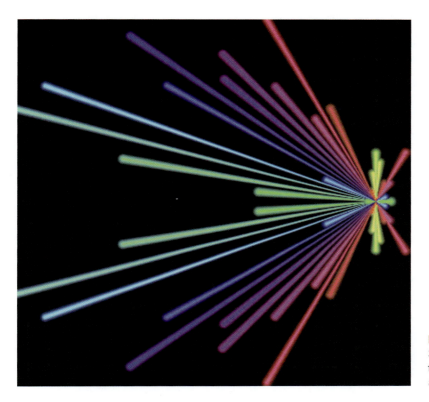

Figure 9.13 The Audio Spectrum effect after selecting the Use Polar Path option and adjusting the colors.

The Audio Waveform Effect

Similar to the Audio Spectrum effect, the Audio Waveform effect also produces visual patterns based on an audio layer. The difference is in the type of pattern it creates. Audio Waveform creates a jagged line that resembles an audio waveform. In effect, this looks like the Audio Spectrum effect with the bands connected.

To practice with the Audio Waveform effect, you can open the Audio Waveform.aep project from the Chapter 9 folder of the exercise files. This is the same project as Audio Spectrum.aep, in case you'd like to delete the Audio Spectrum effect and continue on here. As with Audio Spectrum, select Totally 80s Groovathon as the Audio Layer to see the results. Most of the properties in this effect are identical to the properties we just looked at in Audio Spectrum. The Displayed Samples value is the equivalent to the Frequency bands property in Audio Spectrum, which basically increases the amount of waves here.

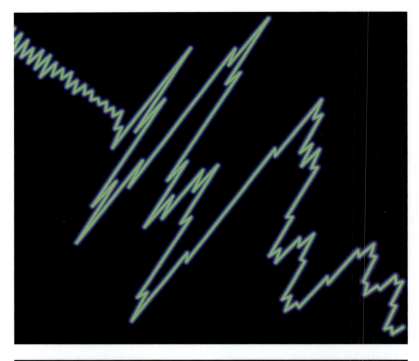

Figure 9.14 The Audio Waveform effect, after adjusting the Start and End Points, and a few of the basic properties.

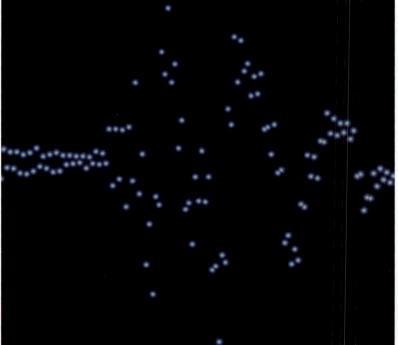

Figure 9.15 The Audio Waveform effect with the Display Options set to Analog Dots.

One of the more interesting and unique properties of the Audio Waveform effect is the Display Options parameter. The default setting is Analog Lines. Changing it to Digital will recreate the waveform using only small vertical lines. The other setting is Analog Dots, which turns the waveform into a series of dots at the top and bottom of each wave. The results are quite interesting when animated. Perhaps adding multiple effects, such as distortions and blurs, could turn this into a type of particle system.

The Beam Effect

The Beam effect is a common favorite for sci-fi fans. It's great for creating shooting laser beams as well as the ever-popular light saber, and it's very easy to use. The Beam effect creates a beam of light that goes between two points. You have control over the length of the beam, as well as its size at each end of the beam. You'll also find similar color controls to what we saw with Audio Spectrum and Audio Waveform (e.g., Inside Color, Outside Color, Softness).

I'm going to open the Beam.aep project from the Chapter 9 folder of the exercise files. The comp in this project contains a video of me having a light saber duel with my friend, Paavo, but you can't really tell because of the black solid covering up this layer. We'll apply the Beam effect to the APPLY BEAM TO ME! layer. Once we apply Beam, the solid will disappear, leaving only the beam.

I'm going to create the light saber effect by clicking the effect control point on the left (the Starting Point value in the Effect Controls panel), and dragging it to the bottom of the fake light saber that I'm holding. Then I'll take the other point on the right (the Ending Point) and drag that to the top of the light saber. I'll then take the Length value to 100%, so that the beam goes all the way from the Starting Point to the Ending Point. Next, I'll reduce the Starting Thickness to about 5, and increase the Ending Thickness to about 9. This will cause the bottom of the light saber to be smaller, and the top of the light saber to be larger. This corresponds to the way the stick looks that I'm holding, because it adds perspective to the beam. Finally, I changed the color of the beam by using a light blue as my Inside Color, and a bright, vibrant blue as my Outside Color, and then I topped it all off by adding the Glow effect.

Figure 9.16 The Beam effect, used as a light saber.

The Cell Pattern Effect

The Cell Pattern effects creates grayscale patterns, many of which resemble biological specimens. In Chapter 12, we'll look at Fractal Noise, which is very similar to Cell Pattern. Here, we'll just look at the big differences between the two effects.

Create a new comp and a new solid at the comp size, and apply the Cell Pattern effect to that solid layer. Even at its default settings, the Cell Pattern effect looks like an abstract biological texture.

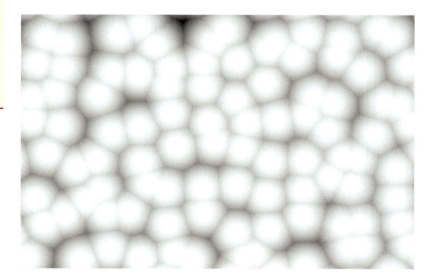

Figure 9.17 The Cell Pattern effect with the default settings.

From my experience, the single most important property in the Cell Pattern effect is the Cell Pattern property (I know that sounds redundant, but that's really what it's called). This changes the type of cellular structure that the pattern is trying to emulate. If we change the settings from the default Bubbles pattern to Tubular, we get another type of cellular pattern.

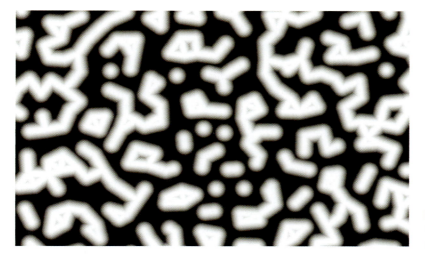

Figure 9.18 The Cell Pattern effect, with the Cell Pattern drop down set to Tubular.

While the Invert, Contrast, and Size parameters are self-explanatory, they really go a long way in changing the appearance of the Cell Pattern effect. Figure 9.19 shows the Cell Pattern type set back to the default Bubbles, with Invert selected, and Contrast and Size adjusted.

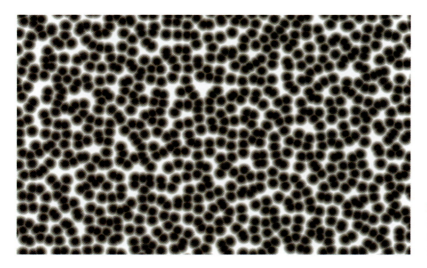

Figure 9.19 The Invert, Contrast, and Size properties make a big difference in the Cell Pattern effect.

Another parameter that allows for some unusual visual results is Overflow. This property controls what happens as the Contrast value is increased so much that values get brighter than white and darker than black. The default value is Clip, which means that brightened highlights will all turn to white, and darkened shadows will flatten to black. Another option is Soft Clamp, which shrinks the entire luminance spectrum, so that nothing gets brighter than white or darker than black. Soft Clamp has a tendency to look washed out. Finally, there is Wrap Back, which creates weird, psychedelic looks. With Wrap Back selected as your Overflow value, white values that are brightened more (by increasing the Contrast value) wrap back to black. See Figures 9.20–9.22 for examples of each Overflow value. Note that all of these figures show the Cell Pattern effect with the Bubbles pattern, the Disperse value (discussed next) reduced all the way, and the Tint effect applied to give it a pink color. All of these figures have the exact same values, except for the change of the Overflow property. These figures are also good examples of the potential of the Cell Pattern effect to create interesting patterns. None of these look much like cellular or biological patterns at all.

The Disperse property controls how much the "cells" are spread apart. Increasing this value will increase the space between cells. Decreasing this value will make the distribution of the cells more uniform. In Figure 9.23, I chose the Tubular Cell Pattern, greatly reduced the Disperse value, and added the Tint effect to tint the cells blue. This creates a Pacman-like maze. A low Disperse setting can also create grids, blocks, and other uniform geometric patterns.

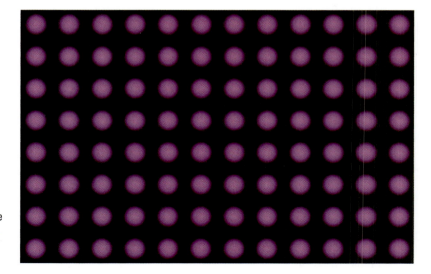

Figure 9.20 After increasing the Contrast value significantly, we get very strong contrast with the Overflow value set to Clip.

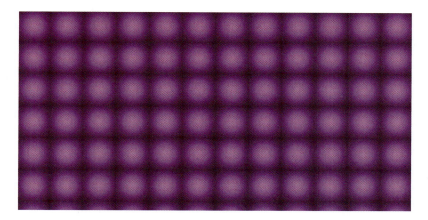

Figure 9.21 Changing the Overflow value to Soft Clamp reduces contrast, and allows you to see the entire range of luminance values. Reminds me of a disco floor.

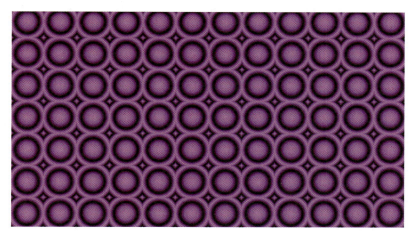

Figure 9.22 The Wrap Back Overflow value causes values that are brighter than white to wrap back around the spectrum to black. This results in layers of light and dark values.

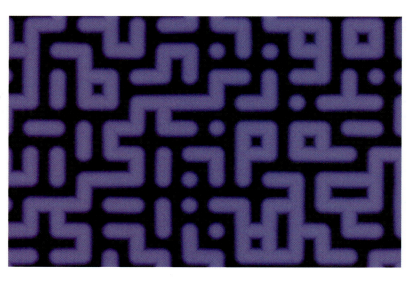

Figure 9.23 Reducing the Disperse value makes the cell distribution more uniform.

Animating Cell Pattern

To bring these cells to life, use the Evolution parameter. It causes the cells to move and wiggle around in very organic ways. The Evolution property works like a layer's Rotation property. There are two values. The value on the right determines the angle of Evolution. The value on the left determines how many complete revolutions of Evolution you are using. Note that the left Evolution value is only useful for animation, or for seeing variations of static patterns.

Although the Evolution property is usually the best way to bring these cells to life, you can also create movement among these cells by animating the Offset property. Offset is almost like a Position property, but for the cells.

Many times when creating patterns with effects like Cell Pattern, you want those patterns to be background textures that repeat over and over again. The problem is that when they repeat, there's a little bit of a jump as the pattern goes back to the first frame of the animation. There's actually a way to get around that and have your cell patterns repeat seamlessly, and it's built into the Cell Pattern effect. What you need to do is open up the Evolution Options by clicking the disclosure triangle next to its name. Then select Cycle Evolution. Now here's the tricky part. You need to make sure that the Cycle value matches the complete number of Evolution revolutions in your animation.

For example, if I animated the Evolution property from 0 degrees at the first frame to three complete revolutions (the Evolution value on the left) at the last frame, then I would take my Cycle value to 3. At this point, you will have a loop, kind of. The first and last frames will be exactly the same, which will cause a one frame pause as the loop repeats. To make this loop literally seamless, drag the second keyframe one frame after the end of the comp. Believe it or not, this is the most simple way to get the pattern to loop. For more information on additional loop options, consult the After Effects Help.

What Good is a Seamless Loop?

Creating a seamless loop helps in a wide variety of places. I've created seamless loops for tradeshows and conferences, where a texture played continuously on monitors in the background. I've used them on DVD menus as seamless video loops in the background. And they're also great time savers for big projects. Just create a small, seamless loop that's a few seconds in duration, then prerender that, and import it back into your project. Then, in the Project panel, you can go the Interpret Footage settings for that file, and specify how many times that piece of footage should loop. It will save you time and processing power!

Cell Pattern Animation Presets

Because of the wide scope of possibilities with the Cell Pattern effect, I've included some animation presets on the disc that accompanies this book. You can use these presets for your personal projects, or just to spark some creativity of what is possible. Figure 9.24 shows a collage of some of the cell pattern animation presets included with this book.

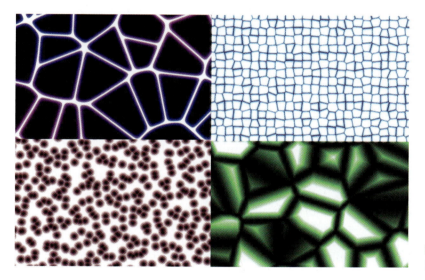

Figure 9.24 A sample of the cell pattern animation presets.

The Checkerboard Effect

The Checkerboard effect simply creates checkerboard patterns. The one thing that is unique about this effect is that it actually is creating a checkerboard pattern in the alpha channel. So, although it appears to create a simple black and white checkerboard, it's actually creating a transparent and white checkerboard. These checkerboards can be stretched and squashed, and the colors of the white squares can be changed to whichever color you'd like.

You can also create an interlaced ribbon looking pattern by using the Feather property. In the Checkerboard effect, the Feather property allows you to feather in two dimensions independently. In Figure 9.25, I've added some feathering in the X dimension (left/right) by increasing the Width value in the Feather area. After changing the Color value to brown, it looks like we've created a basket.

Figure 9.25 The Checkerboard effect with horizontal feathering and a brown color resemble a woven basket.

Creating a Waving Checkered Flag

Some of you may be wondering how to create a waving checkered flag. There are no such distortions available in the Checkerboard effect. Instead, you'll need to apply the Turbulent Displace effect, which was specifically created to create waving flag-type distortions. All you need is a solid layer, the Checkerboard effect, and the Turbulent Displace effect to create a waving checkered flag from scratch!

The Circle Effect

I admit it. The Circle effect (and the Ellipse effect coming up next) sound absolutely worthless, especially considering the powerful addition of shape layers back in After Effects CS3. But I find that they are actually still useful, and for different reasons. When you first apply the Circle effect, it creates a circle, and a really plain circle at that. Even the properties (such as Center, Radius, Color, Opacity, etc.) seem really uninspiring.

The trick to making this effect interesting is the Edge drop down. A value of None keeps this shape a boring old circle. But any of the other options allow you to create a ring. These options basically determine how you create the size of the ring. But the larger benefit is that options other than None allow you to access the Feather Outer Edge and Feather Inner Edge properties. These feather properties can be adjusted independently of each other. This allows you to create things like an eclipse, much easier than you would with shape layers. It's also helpful that Circle generates it's own alpha channel, which allows underlying layers to show through the feathering.

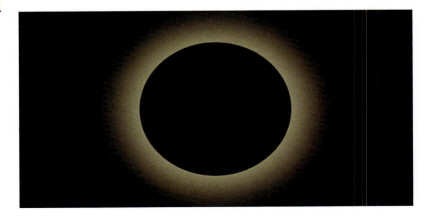

Figure 9.26 The Circle effect with an increased Feather Outer Edge value.

The Ellipse Effect

With default settings, the Ellipse effect creates a circle, similar to the Circle effect. The difference is that Ellipse allows you to adjust the width and height of the shape independently, creating an ellipse instead of a circle if you want. You also have control over the Inside Color and the Outside Color, like we saw with Beam. Unfortunately, although the Ellipse effect does have a Softness (i.e., feathering) parameter, it does not allow us to feather the inside and outside edges independently. Also, the Softness property tops out at 100%, which is not always enough to make this effect look great. This effect typically looks better with a small Thickness value. When the Thickness value is high, you can see flat edges on the outside of the shape, which looks terrible.

Why Ellipse and Circle were ever created as separate effects, and not just one mega "round thing" effect, I will never know. Still, the Ellipse effect can be useful for the quick halo or planetary rings. It's not the best, but it's much faster to create this type of object with the Ellipse effect, than with shape layers.

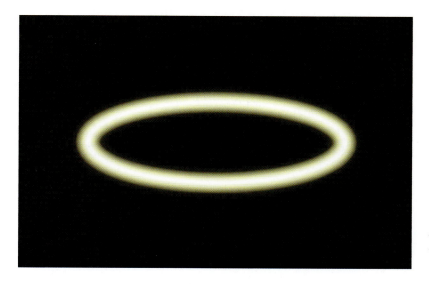

Figure 9.27 A halo created with the Ellipse effect, topped off with a Glow effect for a better result.

The Eyedropper Fill Effect

The Eyedropper Fill effect is like my arch nemesis. For the life of me, I can't think of when I would ever want to use this over another effect (such as the much more powerful Paint Bucket, discussed later in this chapter) for anything. This effect allows you to sample a pixel's color (like the eyedropper in Photoshop), and completely replace the current layer with that color. The problem is that you can't apply colors from another layer. There are very few times when I think to myself "Hey, you know what this video needs? To be completely replaced by a solid color!" Of course you can blend the results with other layers using blend modes. But why not just use a solid layer? Besides, a solid layer, combined with the Fill effect and a sampleImage() expression applied provides a much more powerful way to sample the colors of another layer.

There are a couple features to be aware of should you slip and fall on your computer and accidentally apply this effect. Selecting Maintain Original Alpha will fill the alpha channel of the layer, instead of the layer's boundaries. The Sample Point is where the effect is getting its color from. And Sample Radius determines how many pixels around the Sample Point will be averaged to get the actual color. Reduce the value to select the exact color of the pixel of the Sample Point. Increase the value to take an average color value of a given area.

The Fill Effect

The Fill effect might be more accurately named the Mask Fill and Feather effect. This effect allows you to fill an individual mask with a solid color. It also allows you to apply Horizontal and Vertical Feather to blend the Fill effect color with the edges of the original color. Figure 9.28 shows the Fill comp from the Fill.aep project you'll find in the Chapter 9 folder of the exercise files, if you'd like to follow along. This comp contains a single solid layer, with many elliptical masks on it.

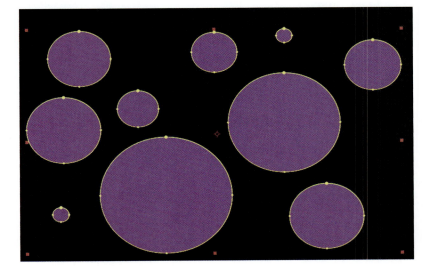

Figure 9.28 The original layer with multiple masks on the same purple solid layer.

Once you apply the Fill effect to this layer, you can choose a mask (or all masks) to apply the new color from the Fill effect to. In my case, I've chosen Mask 7 from the Fill Mask drop down, and I've chose a green for the Color value. To fill the space on the layer that is not occupied by masks, select Invert. To fill other masks on the same layer with different colors, just duplicate the Fill effect by selecting it in the Effect Controls panel and pressing Ctrl+D (Win)/ Cmd+D (Mac). Then, change the Fill Mask on the duplicate(s).

Figure 9.29 After applying the Fill effect, choosing a mask, and filling it with a different color than the solid layer it was applied to.

All in all, the Fill effect gives you a lot more control over coloring and feathering masks than the regular mask tools in After Effects. It's ideal for motion graphics, or any other instance in which masks are used to create areas of flat color. I find that I use this effect often when I'm trying to create silhouettes of an object, especially something I've shot with a green screen or something that has an interesting alpha channel.

The Fractal Effect

First of all, don't get this effect confused with the all-powerful Fractal Noise effect. Their names are similar, but they are two completely different effects. The Fractal effect creates ornate geometric shapes based on complex mathematical formulas. The edges of these fractal patterns are particularly ornate and spectacular. However, this is one effect that is not designed to be intuitive, except for mathematicians. The Set Choice drop down, for instance, reveals such options as "Mandelbrot Inverse over Julia," which is almost as esoteric as the Equation drop down options like "z = z^2 + c." Occasionally, I might use this effect to create luma mattes (you can't even use them for alpha mattes because the fractals are created against a black background, not transparency). But even then, the beauty of this effect is greatly mitigated by the fact that it renders so incredibly slow.

Figure 9.30 The Fractal effect.

The Grid Effect

The Grid effect allows you to create a grid from scratch. It's great for creating simple motion graphics for conservative business clients, or for projects pertaining to technology. We'll see another creative use for the Grid effect a little later. If you'd like to follow along and dissect the grid examples in this chapter, you can open up the Grid.aep file from the Chapter 9 folder of the exercise files.

When you apply the Grid effect, it removes the content of the source layer and creates transparency, and creates a colored grid using the Color parameter in the Effect Controls panel (default = white). One of the properties that's important to get a grasp on quickly with the Grid effect is the Size From drop down. The default setting is Corner Point, which allows you to adjust the size and dimensions of the squares in the grid by adjusting the Anchor and Corner properties. Changing the Size From value to Width Slider, creates a perfectly square grid. You can then use the Width slider to increase the size of the squares in the uniform grid. Perhaps the Size From option that gives you the most control is Width & Height Sliders. With this option selection, you adjust the size and dimensions of the squares in the grid with the Width and Height values. However, you can also move the grid in 2D space by adjusting the Anchor parameter.

The other properties control the visual appearance of the grid. Border determines the thickness of the grid lines. Invert Grid creates a transparent grid on a white background. And Color, Opacity, and Blending Mode are self-explanatory. Figure 9.31 shows a common use of the Grid effect. After applying the Grid effect, it is common to apply an effect like Corner Pin (in the Distort effects category), so that you can reposition the grid in 3D, perhaps as a floor. Don't try to act like this effect doesn't make you want to recreate Tron.

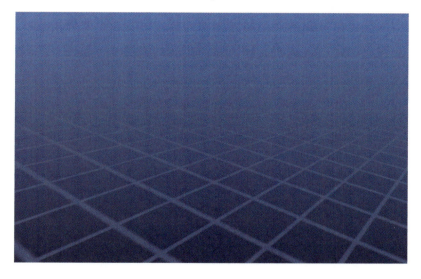

Figure 9.31 After applying Grid, I applied the Corner Pin effect to create the illusion that that the grid is a floor.

Another way to use this effect is to create a picket fence. In Figure 9.32, I adjusted the size of the squares in the grid, then created a jagged mask to create the illusion of the tops of the fence. I finished it all off with a subtle Bevel and Emboss layer style to add some dimension to the fence.

Figure 9.32 Using the Grid effect and a mask to create a white picket fence.

The Lens Flare Effect

The Lens Flare effect emulates the result of a bright light hitting the lens of a camera at just the right angle, producing a flare. The flare typically consists of the main flare, and a few other small extras, such as rings. While lens flares are designed to recreate a camera looking at a bright light for compositing situations (e.g., for camera moves through fake environments), they are also often used for extra highlights for sparks, flashes, explosions, and so forth. Because they create an easy, instant flashy effect, they are often overused, so be sure to use them with restraint, especially if you're just using the default settings. I like to apply the Lens Flare effect on a black solid layer, and then composite it into the rest of my scene using a layer blend mode, such as Add.

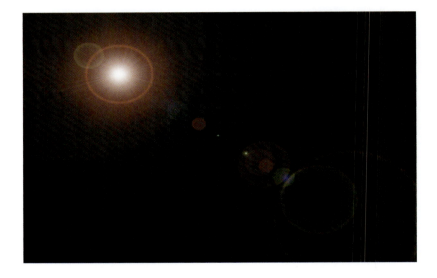

Figure 9.33 The Lens Flare effect on a black solid layer with the default settings.

The parameters for the Lens Flare effect are simple. Flare Center controls where the main area of the flare is located. The rings and other flare appendages move accordingly. Flare Brightness does determine the brightness of the flare, but it also affects the size of the flare as well. Under the Lens Type drop down, there are three main types of lens flares, each based on a different type of camera.

If you'd like to follow along, I've created a Lens Flare.aep project in the Chapter 9 folder of the exercise files. In the Rad Rockets comp, you can see the result of applying the Lens Flare effect as a highlight, instead of an actual lens flare. Using the Flare Center effect control point, I positioned the flare over the fiery exhaust of the rocket in this video. I also used a feathered, elliptical mask to isolate the main area of the flare, and hide the additional rings. In this case, I would also want to animate the center of the flare to follow the rocket. I could also apply a Wiggle expression to the Flare Brightness property to add further realism.

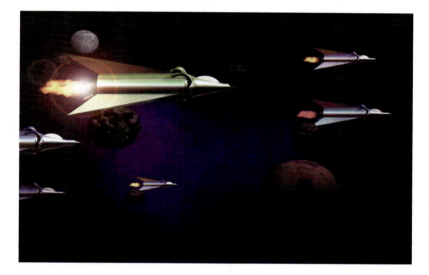

Figure 9.34 The Lens Flare effect, applied as a highlight to give emphasis to the flames being emitted from the main rocket.

The Paint Bucket Effect

In writing a comprehensive book like this, naturally I ran into a few effects that I hadn't gotten familiar with yet. The Paint Bucket effect was one of those. I wasn't very excited about studying it, either, because of other unimpressive fill effects like Eyedropper Fill, and because of the horrible Paint Bucket tool in Photoshop.

Well, I'm happy to report that the Paint Bucket effect was actually one of my favorite discoveries. The Paint Bucket effect allows you to paint different pieces of a layer. It also allows you to add and adjust different types of strokes. It presumably gets its name from the common Paint Bucket tools in Photoshop, and most other drawing and painting applications. In most programs, you click in an area, and that area gets filled with a color. The Paint Bucket effect has a similar end result, but a different means to that end.

You'll probably want to follow along with me to get the hang of this effect. To do that, open the Paint Bucket.aep project from the Chapter 9 folder of the exercise files. We'll start in the Paint Bucket Start comp. Apply the Paint Bucket effect to the Arrows layer. Instantly, the entire layer is filled with red. This happens

Fixing Paint Bucket Edges

If you zoom in to areas filled with the Paint Bucket effect, you might notice that some edges aren't filled in correctly. This is because of the Tolerance value. If you increase the Tolerance value, more pixels will be filled. If the color seems to be spilling out beyond the boundaries of the layer, reduce the Tolerance value to clean up those edges.

for two reasons. First, the Fill Selector drop down is set to Color & Alpha, which means that the entire layer will be filled with a solid color (ala the Eyedropper Fill effect). It also fills the screen because of the nature of our art and the Tolerance value. Just like in Photoshop, the Tolerance value controls how many pixels are allowed to get painted. The default Tolerance value in this case must have been enough to fill the layer. Finally, the Fill Point determines what part of the layer gets filled. As we'll see, the Fill Point value is a very important one here.

To really see what this effect can do, I'm going to put the Fill Point over one of the arrows so it will fill with color. I used the position 197, 127. Next, I'll change the Fill Selector value to Opacity, so that the Paint Bucket effect only fills opaque pixels. Now, we can begin to see what's going on here.

Figure 9.35 The Paint Bucket effect fills one of the pieces of this layer.

If you set the Fill Selector to Transparency, you can fill the transparent pixels on the layer with color. You'll also need to move the Fill Point to a transparent part of the layer. In the case of this logo, the results are a stark difference from the original.

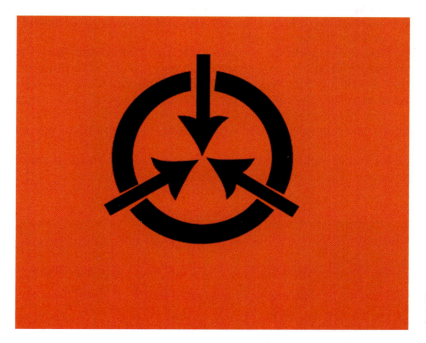

Figure 9.36 The Paint Bucket effect, with Fill Selector set to Transparency.

The Stroke parameter is another source for creative playing with the Paint Bucket effect. Once you change this value to any other value, the property immediately below it becomes adjustable. Set this to Spread to expand the effect beyond the opaque pixels, like increasing the size of its outline. Set the Stroke value to Choke to erode the edges away. Or set it to Stroke to create only a stroke (with no fill).

The Paint Bucket Final comp in this project contains what I did with this project. I applied a wiggle expression to the Fill Point property in the Paint Bucket effect. That way, the Fill Point would only occasionally land on an opaque area of the layer, and fill it with color. The result is a very cool strobelike effect.

The Radio Waves Effect

The Radio Waves effect is a simple particle system. It shoots out a constant stream of concentric shapes. As you might imagine, the purpose of the effect is to simulate radio waves being emitted. But this is a very powerful effect that does much more.

As with most particle systems, the effect auto-animates. We don't control the particles; we only control the system that emits the particles. Now, there are loads of parameters in Radio Waves, and most of them are either self-explanatory or not very useful. So, we'll just hit the highlights here.

From my experience, the two most important parameters are Frequency (in the Wave Motion area), and Producer Point (at the very top of the Effect Controls panel). Increasing the Frequency value increases the rate at which the waves are produced, which in effect creates more waves. You can also animate the Producer Point. In many other effects, animating its position (in effect) wouldn't be such a big deal. But with Radio Waves, it leaves a really cool trail of waves. The coolness of the effect is compounded by animating the Color value (in the Stroke area).

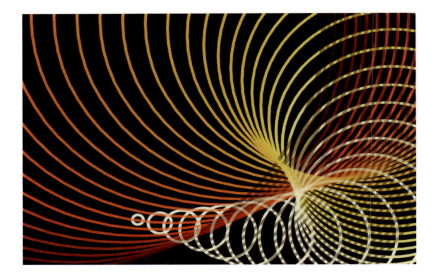

Figure 9.37 The Radio Waves effect, with Frequency increased, and the Producer Point and Color values animated.

Under the Polygon area of the effect, there are some options that give you control over the shape. It's interesting to note that the initial shape of this effect isn't really a circle. It's really a 64-sided polygon. To increase the smoothness of the circles, increase this value. If you reduce this value enough, you will create on object with flat sides. Taking this value to 3, for example, will create triangles. Increasing the Curve Size and Curvyness values to create polygons with rounded edges. Or, you can check the Star checkbox to create concentric stars.

The Wave Motion area contains some useful parameters also. Expansion controls how fast the waves move away from the Producer Point once emitted. Think of the caterpillar from

Alice in Wonderland blowing smoke rings into Alice's face. The smoke came out quickly, traveling a great distance, and then slowed down. To recreate that effect, we would increase the Expansion value. Orientation and Spin are similar, in that both control the rotation of the waves (which is difficult to see when your waves are circular). Orientation determines the angle of the waves when first emitted. To animate spinning waves, animate the Spin property. Velocity controls the speed at which waves are emitted. If the Velocity value is greater than 0, then you can use the Direction property to determine the direction that waves are emitted. The Lifespan property determines—in seconds—how long each wave exists before it disappears.

When a wave's lifespan is complete, it just vanishes. Poof. Gone. To have it die out more gradually, adjust the Fade-out Time property in the Stroke category. This, along with the other properties in the Stroke area determine the visual appearance of the waves. The Fade-in Time property allows you to make waves fade in as they are created. You can also allow the start and end size of the waves' stroke with the Start Width and End Width properties.

In the Stroke area, you'll find a Profile drop down. This affects the profile of the stroke used to create the wave. The default value of Square is the most straightforward, as it is a standard stroke—completely solid. The other options allow you to create a semi-transparent, gradual fade from opacity to transparency.

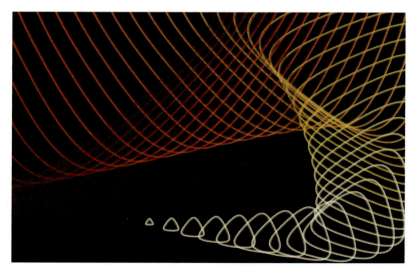

Figure 9.38 Here, the Stroke > Profile value is set to Sawtooth In, which causes the inside edge of the stroke to have a slight feather.

Radio Waves and Water Simulation

Because Radio Waves creates trails of circles, it's a great effect to use when simulating water effects, such as a pond ripple, or someone dragging their finger around on the surface of water. You can use Radio Waves as a displacement map with the Caustics effect (discussed with the Simulation effects in Chapter 16). You can also use the Reflection property (the checkbox at the bottom of the Wave Motion properties) in the Radio Waves effect. The Reflection property creates reflections of waves when waves get close to the edges of a layer. This mimics the way waves work in water, as the forces that create water ripples bounce off of objects at the water's edge.

Using Another Layer as a Wave Shape

Another one of the great features of Radio Waves is that you can either use a mask, or the contours of another layer as the shape of emitted waves. In the Radio Waves.aep project that you'll find in the Chapter 9 folder of the exercise files, you'll find the Radio Waves layer in the Radio Waves comp. This is a solid layer that contains the Radio Waves example I've used in the previous figures. If you turn off that layer, you'll see two other layers: face asleep (an Illustrator drawing of a person's sleeping face), and sheep.psd (a raster outline of a sheep). We're going to use the Radio Waves effect to make this slumbering vector guy counting sheep in his sleep.

Make sure that the visibility of the Radio Waves layer is off, and then turn on the visibility of the face asleep layer. Then create a new solid, place it on top of the face asleep layer in the layer stack in the Timeline panel, and then apply Radio Waves to the new solid. The solid background will be removed, and you will see the waves composited over the top of the sleeping face.

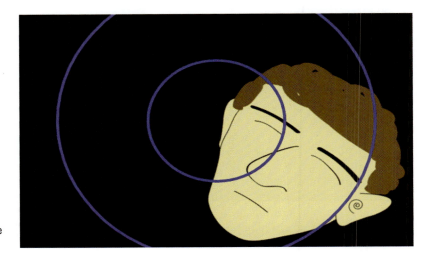

Figure 9.39 The Radio Waves effect on a solid layer above the face asleep layer.

Next, in the Stroke area, I'm going to change the Color value from its default blue, to a sheep-like white, or light gray. Then, change the Wave Type drop down from Polygon to Image Contours. This property tells Radio Waves where to look for the wave shape. By default, it's set to the polygon that it creates. We've changed it to Image Contours because we want to use the outline of the sheep layer as the wave.

Once Image Contours is selected as the Wave Type, the Polygon area is grayed out, and the Image Contour area becomes adjustable. From the Source Layer drop down in the Image Contour area, select the sheep layer. By default, the contours are taken from the Source Layer's alpha channel. But you can change the Value Channel drop down to use the source layer's hue, saturation, red channel, and so on. For now, we'll leave this set to Alpha. Now, all we need to do is to animate and adjust the basic Radio Waves properties we've already looked at, and our little vector friend can fall into deeper sleep as he counts our radio wave sheep.

Figure 9.40 Changing the Wave Type property to Image Contours allows you to use the alpha channel of another layer as the shape emitted by the Radio Waves effect.

The Ramp Effect

The Ramp effect is extremely simple. It creates a two-color gradient. I'm not sure why they're staying away from using the "g" word in this effect, but ramp is a synonym for gradient here. The Start of Ramp property determines the place where the gradient starts, and the Start Color determines what color that should be. The End of Ramp and End Color values determine the position and the color of the last gradient stop, respectively. Increasing the Ramp Scatter value adds noise to the gradient. The Ramp Shape drop down allows you to choose between a Linear Ramp (aka linear gradient), or a Radial Ramp (aka radial gradient).

I hardly ever use the Ramp effect on its own as a decorative element, but it works great when applied with other effects, or used to create a simple luma matte or map for effects, or to add a little bit of shading to break up areas of flat color, as on text. You might use this effect as a map to control other gradients. Or you might use this effect to blend into a textured background to create the illusion of an external light source. As an alternative, you can typically get more colors and control by using the Gradient Overlay layer style. See the coverage of the 4-Color Gradient effect at the beginning of this chapter for more information and comparisons on different ways to create gradients in After Effects.

The Scribble Effect

The Scribble effect is just adorable. It takes areas of flat color, and gives them the appearance that they were created with hand-scribbled lines. This auto-animating effect can create animated, wiggly scribbles. It can create big loopy scribbles. It can create angry, scratchy scribbles. The down side of the Scribble effect is that it can only work with masks, and closed masks (masks that make a complete shape, without any open gaps in its edges) at that.

Figure 9.41 The original ghost graphic.

If you'd like to play with this effect, open the Scribble.aep project found in the Chapter 9 folder of the exercise files. The Ghost Body layer is the body of the ghost, and has already been set up with a mask. If you tried applying the Scribble effect to another layer, such as Ghost Eyes, the layer would completely disappear because it does not contain a mask.

Apply the Scribble effect to the Ghost Body layer. You'll notice a couple of things. First, you'll notice that the contents of the layer (actually, the selected mask) have been completely filled by the Scribble effect. Any details or textures on the layer are replaced. Also, you'll notice the Scribble effect is white by default, regardless of the original color of the layer. And, as mentioned previously, the Scribble effect automatically animates the scribbles that it creates.

The first thing I'm going to do with this effect is turn off its visibility in the Effect Controls panel, and click the eyedropper next to the Color property to sample the original color of the ghost. I want this effect to make the ghost look like he is hand-drawn and alive. And, after turning back on the visibility of the effect, I will deselect the Toggle Mask and Shape Path Visibility button at the bottom of the Composition panel, so that we don't have to look at the yellow outline of our mask here. Also, make sure that Mask

Figure 9.42 The Scribble effect after changing the color of the scribble to match the original color of the ghost.

1 is selected in the Mask drop down. We'll also leave the Fill Type set to Inside, but you could also use this drop down to make a scribbled stroke on a mask. You'll also notice that all of the scribbles tend to follow the same direction. This direction can be controlled with the Angle property. You can also increase or decrease the size of the line with the Stroke Width parameter.

This effect starts getting a lot more interesting once we start playing around with the properties in the Stroke Options area. Increase the Curviness value to make the scribbled lines round and loopy instead of straight and jagged. Increase Curviness Variation to add some randomness to the curves. Increase Spacing to spread the scribbles apart, and increase Spacing Variation to randomize the spacing. Path Overlap allows the scribble to go over the original mask line. A positive Path Overlap value will expand the scribble beyond the mask, while a negative Path Overlap value will contract the scribbles, as if the mask was shrinking. Path Overlap Variation adds some randomization to the way that the scribble overlaps the path. When the Scribble effect is first applied, it looks too synthetic and digital. Using these properties, you can add enough randomness to make this scribble look much more organic and handmade. And, as you can tell from Figure 9.43, this is an excellent effect to use to create digital spaghetti.

Figure 9.43 The Scribble effect, after adjusting many of the Stroke Options properties.

The properties at the bottom of the Scribble effect help bring it to life. You can animate the Start property (or the End property) to animate the scribble being drawn. You can also use the Wiggle Type and Wiggles/Second value to determine how the path wiggles, and how fast it wiggles, respectively.

The Stroke Effect

The Stroke and Vegas effects are very similar. They both create a stroke along an open or closed path. The Stroke effect is the more simple of the two, so we'll explain the basics and some commonalities between them here.

To follow along, open up the Stroke.aep project from the Chapter 9 folder of the exercise files. Let's start in the Stroke Intro comp, with a simple example to get familiar with what this effect does. The blue solid layer in this comp contains a mask. This is a necessary component of working with the Stroke effect. Apply the Stroke effect to the blue solid layer. At first, only the astute observer will notice a difference. The default settings for both the Stroke and Vegas effects create a small white stroke that is only two pixels wide. That is only slightly larger than the size of the mask! So, the first order of business—with both of these effects— is to increase the Brush Size value so that you can actually see what you're doing.

As the name of the Brush Size property indicates, the stroke in this effect is actually created with a series of brush strokes, like brush strokes in Photoshop. Increase the Spacing parameter to spread out the individual brush strokes and see what's going on. As a bonus prize, you will also create a cool dotted line pattern.

> **Keeping Scribble Still**
>
> If you don't want the results of the Scribble effect to move, take the Wiggle/Second value down to 0.

Figure 9.44 The Stroke effect with the Brush Size and Spacing values increased.

If you're interested in animating this stroke, use the Start and End values. These control how far along the path the beginning (Start value) and end (End value) the brush strokes go. So, if you animated the Start value from 100% at the beginning of the comp to 0% at the end of the comp, you would create an animated trail of dots in this case.

The Paint Style drop down can also change the result of the Stroke effect dramatically. By default, the value is set to On Original Image, which just means that the stroke "paints" on top of the original layer. That is why we can still see the blue solid that we applied this effect to. Changing this value to On Transparent will remove the source layer, and show you the effect only. But when we change the value to Reveal Original Image, things start getting interesting. This settings makes the paint strokes reveal the original layer. So, our blue solid background disappears, our Color value becomes irrelevant, and the paint strokes now appear blue because they are revealing the blue solid layer. Used creatively, this can have beautiful results.

If you switch over to the other comp, Stroke Example, we can see a better instance of the Reveal Original Image setting. Note that in this comp, there is only one layer with many masks. You can apply a single instance of the Stroke effect to all masks on a layer by selecting the All Masks checkbox. When you animate the Start or End values, all of the masks will demonstrate the same behavior. If you additionally chose the Stroke Sequentially option, each mask will be entirely stroked before paint is applied to any of the other masks.

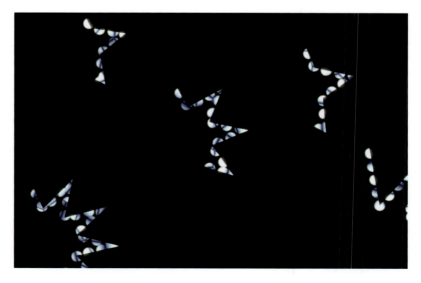

Figure 9.45 The Stroke Example comp. Notice that All Masks are receiving brush strokes simultaneously, and are also revealing the original pattern of the layer (which was created by effects).

The Vegas Effect

The intent of the Vegas effect is to recreate the marquee lights that were often seen on marquees in the old days of Las Vegas. Of course, like most of the effects in this book, it achieves even greater results when used for purposes for which it was never intended. If you'd like to see some examples of Vegas in action and follow along with me in this chapter, open up the Vegas Baby. aep project from the Chapter 9 folder.

Figure 9.46 The Vegas effect, in its native habitat.

The image seen in Figure 9.46 is in the Marquee comp in this project. Let's hop on over to the Vegas, baby! comp to get some experience with this effect. In this comp there is a blue solid with a star-shaped mask applied to it. Apply the Vegas effect to this layer, and take the Stroke value (at the top of the effect in the Effect Controls panel) from Image Contours to Mask/Path. On this solid, we only have one mask, but if you apply Vegas to a layer with multiple masks, you would also need to choose the mask to apply Vegas to from the Path drop down in the Mask/Path area. At this point, as with the Stroke effect, you'll need to increase the size of the stroke to accurately see what's going on. To do that, increase the Width value in the Rendering area. You can then see what Vegas looks like before making any changes. It kind of looks like a bunch of comets having a parade.

Figure 9.47 The Vegas effect, after increasing the Width value.

Let's first look at the appearance of these little dots. The parameters that control the visual appearance of the marquee segments are found in the Rendering area. You can alter the transparency of the dot along the axis of the path by using the Start Opacity, Mid-point Opacity, Mid-point Position, and End Opacity values. You can adjust the transparency on the outside edges of the dots by adjusting the Hardness value. Other properties in this area, such as Blend Mode, Color, and Width are similar to properties we saw in the Stroke effect.

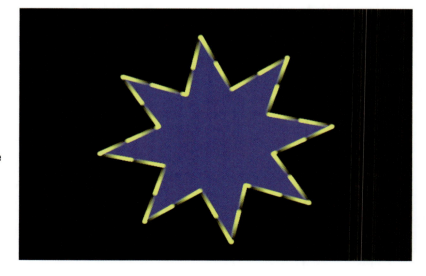

Figure 9.48 After increasing the Hardness value to its maximum (1.000), the outer edge of the dots get a hard edge. The back of the dots are permitted to retain semi-transparency, as Hardness does not affect this part of the dot.

In my mind, the most impressive features of the Vegas effect are in the Segments area. You see, unlike the Stroke effect, Vegas creates a series of strokes, not just one. You can control how many strokes (dots) it creates with the Segments parameter, and control how long those segments are with the Length property. You can then cycle the segments around the path by using the Rotation property. Experimenting with these properties yields results that are much more stimulating than a simple marquee.

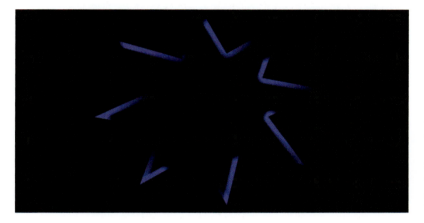

Figure 9.49 The Vegas effect with the number of segments and their length reduced, and the Blend Mode changed to Stencil (the equivalent of selecting Reveal Original Image in the Stroke effect).

One of the things that's fun to do with the Vegas effect is to create a series of wildly odd masks, and apply the Vegas effect to them. Take the Segments value down to 1 or 2, and animate the Color parameter to create flowing streams of light. You can also duplicate the effect or the layer it's applied to and then flip or move the layer. That way, you can create the illusion that there are more whips of light. The Swooshes comp in this project contains a sample of these whips of light.

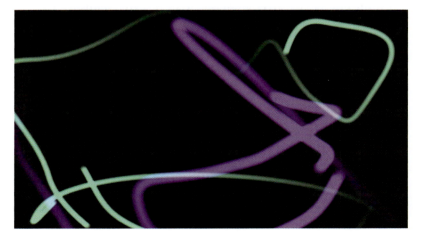

Figure 9.50 The Swooshes comp in the Vegas Baby.aep project.

The last comp in this project, EKG, shows another use of the Vegas effect. Here, I use it to create an EKG, or electrocardiogram. I realize that if you are a physician, this is probably an obvious hoax. But if you're creating a movie, and need to show someone's lifeline in the background, this is a good trick to keep on hand. It's just the Vegas effect with a jagged mask, and only one long segment.

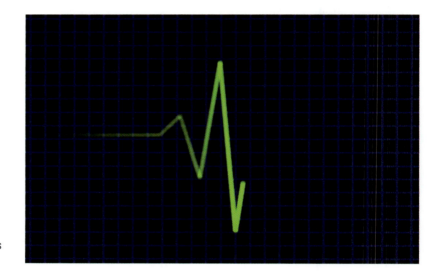

Figure 9.51 The Vegas effect can also create an EKG effect. Notice the special guest appearance by the Grid effect, discussed earlier in this chapter.

The Write-on Effect

The Write-on effect creates animated strokes. The purpose of this effect, more or less, is to create animated signatures. Many users have cast off this effect in favor of the more powerful painting engine in After Effects. However, the painting engine in After Effects does not let you paint to reveal the original layer. This is a significant advantage of the Write-on effect that we'll use to create the ever popular growing vines effect a little later on.

For now, open up the Write-on.aep project from the Chapter 9 folder, and go to the Write-on Start comp. Select the black solid layer and apply the Write-on effect to it. Again, as with Stroke and Vegas, the default Brush Size value of 2 doesn't do us any good (were these effects designed for hobbits?). Bump that up to a value that will allow you to see it. Many of the properties here are identical to what we've seen in other effects in this chapter.

It's when you start animating the Brush Position that you start to see the magic of this effect. As you animate the position of the brush, it maintains a line, allowing you to create an animated signature or other line drawing.

An Easier Way to Animate

If you're going to have the Write-on effect draw something complex, like a signature, it's probably a better idea to use another method than manual animation of the Brush Position property. You could use Motion Sketch to capture complex motion quickly, and then connect the keyframes created by Motion Sketch to the Brush Position property in the Write-on effect with an expression.

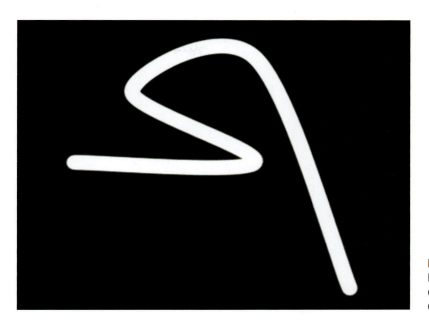

Figure 9.52 Animating the Brush Position of the Write-on effect can create animated drawings.

As mentioned, the real treasure of this effect is its ability to reveal the layer it's applied to. We can use this to create the animated vines look that is so ubiquitous these days. If you go to the Growing Vines FINISH comp, you'll see the complete animation with growing vines. Note that the trick here is to have the vines (or whatever else you want to be gradually revealed) on separate layers. This gives you more control over when to reveal what parts.

Figure 9.53 Animating growing vines like this is all the rage with kids these days.

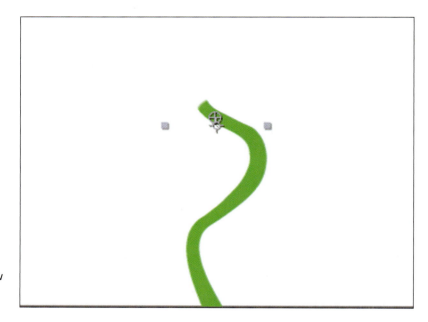

Figure 9.54 Painting objects with the Paint Style set to Reveal Original Image will allow you to paint objects appearing or growing.

In the Growing Vines START comp, you'll find 5 layers of vines to animate revealing. Select the Main Vine layer. You may want to turn off the visibility of the other vines if they get distracting. Apply the Write-on effect to the Main Vine layer. Take the Brush Position control point down to the bottom of the vine, as we'll be revealing it from the bottom up. Increase the Brush Size value until it completely covers the vine. Currently, it's just painting white on the vine. But when we take the Paint Style value to Reveal Original Image, the paint only reveals the vine. So, animate the Brush Position covering the vine, and your vine will appear to grow. It's just that simple. I find it easier to leave the Paint Style on its default setting while I'm painting so that I can see where to animate the Brush Position value to. Also, note that if you animate a property such as Brush Size, it will apply to all brush strokes that have been created, at all times. If you want to animate the brush size getting smaller as you paint more intricate details, and you don't want to affect your original paint strokes, change the Brush Time Properties to the properties that you want to animate. The effect will then honor your keyframed values for Brush Size and/or Brush Hardness.

10

THE KEYING EFFECTS

The term keying is used to describe the process of removing part of a layer to reveal the layers beneath it. This is usually used to refer to the removal of a blue or green screen background for compositing. In case you were curious, blue and green are the colors most often used because they contrast the most with the colors in skin tones, no matter how light or dark the skin. You would think that after all these years of having this workflow, that you could now just click a button and everything blue or green would be gone. Unfortunately, that's not the case. Keying is a craft, sometimes requiring many tools to do the job. Thus, we have many effects in this category, all with the same intention of removing parts of a layer to isolate objects to be composited.

The third-party keying tool Keylight is far and away the most powerful keying tool of the bunch. Unless you're not shooting against a green screen or a blue screen, you should always start with Keylight (covered later in this chapter).

Of course, some of the rest of these effects are more important than others. And not all of them work with blue or green screens. Sometimes, you might want to use keying effects—such as the Luma Key effect—to remove very bright or very dark areas from a layer. Or, you may want to remove a multi-colored background, in which case you might want to check out the powerful Inner/Outer Key effect. Additionally, you can use the very powerful (and automated) Rotobrush tool, which isn't technically a keying effect at all. My point is that while not all workflows require the removal of blue or green screens, most workflows still can benefit from some degree of keying.

Here's an example of a recent project I did using these keying tools. I started with some green screen footage of myself reading a newspaper.

I started by removing the green screen using some of the methods discussed in this chapter. I then composited this footage on top of a 3D model of a subway scene, courtesy of

Figure 10.1 The author recorded in front of a green screen.

Figure 10.2 The green screen footage composited with other elements with the green screen removed.

Kymnbel Bywater of spilledinkanimation.com. Kymnbel created the subway scene with transparency in the window. This allowed me to add a video that my wife took whilst hanging a camera outside of the window of our car on a drive up the Oregon Coast in the background. I also masked out the stool that I was sitting on, added a reflection in the window, and played with the color using the effects we covered back in Chapter 6. As you can imagine, the proper use of keying techniques can allow you to create a plethora of virtual situations.

Universal Keying Concepts

Before we get started into the individual keying effects, I want to cover a few concepts that are important to keep in mind while keying. A few of these concepts are just a good rule of thumb, while others will be issues you will be dealing with on most keying jobs.

About Spill and Spill Suppression

With most keying effects, even after keying out the blue or green screen, you are still left with a halo around your subject that is the color of the blue or green screen. This is caused by the lights in the scene bouncing some of the color of the screen back on to the subject. This extra bit of color on the subject is referred to as spill. Getting rid of spill is referred to as spill suppression. If you have any control over production, you can usually eliminate most spill with the clever placement of lighting on your subject, and by keeping your subject away from the blue or green screen.

And in many studios, this is just impossible. But if you are shooting in a large space and you have some say in the production, you might also want to insist on using daylight-balanced lighting (as opposed to the much warmer tungsten lights). From my experience, daylight-balanced lights really make the green screen pop, whereas tungsten lights shift the screen color more towards skin tones and diminish separation between subject and background. I've even experimented and had great success using green gels on greenscreen lights, but that only works if you have a really deep greenscreen and can put your talent in another zip code (or about 10 feet away). Of course, if a greenscreen shot calls for tungsten lighting, a DP will probably overrule you. But these are just a few extra tips to try out.

Keep a Clean Screen

It's a really good idea to make sure that your blue or green screen is completely uniform. In other words, you want the entire screen to be the exact same shade of blue or green. Oftentimes, these screens are created with hanging pieces of large fabric. Like most fabrics, they wrinkle easily. Wrinkles cause variations in color, causing keying to become a more challenging process. Many green screen studios even use extra material to create rounded corners where the walls and floor meet. This is so that there are no shadows. Shadows and wrinkles (or any variations in color or luminance) in the blue or green screen add a great deal of headaches into any keying job. Uneven lighting can also create a non-uniform color on a background.

Of course, like many rules that pertain to how to shoot on set, you might not have any control over how this is shot. As is also the case with many of these guidelines, they are much easier to say than to do. I'm frank to admit that I've been VFX Supervisor on many sets, and it just wasn't possible (for a variety of reasons) to set things up the proper way. Be prepared in post to be flexible.

Previewing Your Key

When I first started learning about keying in After Effects, I would import footage with a blue or green screen, and then practice removing the screen. The problem was that I usually practiced this without a layer underneath the layer I was keying. Using a black background is usually not the best way to see problems in your key. Instead, use a color that contrasts strongly with the color of the green screen so that you can easily see any problems. You can also enable the transparency grid at the bottom of the Composition panel to check your key. It's a good idea to preview your key against a variety of backgrounds, just in case you missed some stray pixels that don't belong.

Creating a Garbage Matte

Most of the time when keying a subject to remove a background, you don't need the entire layer. So, the typical process is to create a loose mask, called a garbage matte, around the subject. It should be close enough to the subject to remove junk in the frame, such as boom mics and any other equipment in the shot, leaving only the blue or green screen. But it should not be so close that the subject moves outside of the matte at any point in time. Or, if they do move outside of the garbage matte, then you must animate the mask to follow the subject so that it is always completely encompasses the subject.

Let's say that I wanted to key out the background, and isolate myself in the shot seen in Figure 10.3.

Figure 10.3 The shot I want to pull a key from.

My first step would be to create a mask that would get rid of all of the background stuff—the stuff I know that I don't want in the final result. This makes it so much easier for the keying effect to remove the background. Even if the entire background was made up of only the green screen (without extra equipment showing), it still helps the keying process to create a garbage matte.

Figure 10.4 The same footage, with a garbage matte created. As you can see, it doesn't demonstrate the highest level of sophisticated mask making, but it's only supposed to be a rough outline like this.

Using Other Effects

We talked at the beginning of the book about how effects need to be used together to reach their potential, and we have an entire chapter on that very subject at the end of the book. But I just wanted to make a quick note about how especially important that is with the keying effects. With the plethora of controls that these effects have, you may be tempted to think that they stand alone and need no others. But often times, stubborn keys can only be perfected with the help of other effects, such as Channel Blur, the Color Correction effects, or the Matte effects (discussed in the next chapter) for example. You can also use multiple keying effects on the same layer, or duplicates of the same effect on the same layer.

Use the Highest Quality Footage Possible

It kinda goes without saying that you should always use the highest quality footage possible. But this is even more important when it comes to keying. Sometimes, when a video with a blue or green screen is shot perfectly, it can still be difficult—or impossible—to key well if it has been overly compressed. I know that in many cases, you probably don't get to choose how the footage you work with is created. But if you have any say in the process, try to get as little noise, as little compression, and the largest color gamut possible in the creation of blue or green screen footage. And if possible avoid shooting chromakey footage with a DSLR like the plague. DSLR's create beautiful footage, but it's extremely compressed, making it a real challenge (read: annoyance) to pull a good key from.

Layer Your Keys

Humans are complex animals, speaking from a keying perspective. We have hard edges clothes and soft edged hair. We have areas of complete opacity and areas of semi-transparency. Most of the time, you'll never get the "perfect" key by using one pass. No, it's way better in most cases to get a general key where the core/body of the subject looks good, and then make a mask to isolate that. Then, duplicate that layer and invert the mask to focus on the edges of the character, especially if there is something semitransparent there, either with their hair or clothing. Depending on if your subject moves around a lot, you might need to do some rotoscoping, but this is a small price to pay for a great key.

The Color Difference Key Effect

If the concept of keying intimidates you, then you may want to skip ahead and come back later to the Color Difference Key effect. This effect works really well, and can even key out tough jobs (like smoke or wispy hair) better than most. But it can be a little daunting at first.

To follow along with me, open up the Color Difference Key.aep project from the Chapter 10 folder of the exercise files. For this project, we'll be using a photo, rather than a video. This effect does much better with lightly-compressed or non-compressed video. And since those are more challenging to distribute, and we're only using one frame anyway, we're using a photo. Apply the Color Difference Key effect to the Chad Key layer in the Chad Key comp.

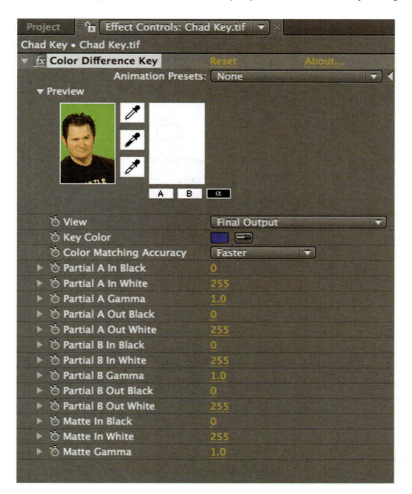

Figure 10.5 The parameters of the Color Difference Key effect.

I realize that these parameters look somewhat intimidating at first glance. They're certainly more intimidating than the parameters of the other keying effects. But they make a lot more sense when you realize what the effect is doing.

Using Figure 10.5 as a guide, you'll see that there are actually three main sets of properties here: Partial A, Partial B, and Matte. The Color Difference Key effect creates two mattes, and then combines them together to create the final alpha. Partial A is the first matte. Partial B is the second matte. And the Matte controls affect the final result (the alpha channel). Essentially, we have controls similar to those seen in the Levels effect for each of the three groups of properties.

To use this effect with this example, we first need to change the Key Color value, which is set to a default blue color. Click the eyedropper next to the Key Color swatch and then click on the green background of the photo. From my experience with this

Figure 10.6 The color difference key results. Notice how the subject is also partially erased, showing the magenta solid beneath it.

effect, the initial results are always terrible. But don't worry about that. We'll get this key near perfect in just a moment.

The next step to perfect our results is to adjust each of the two partial mattes individually. In this effect, you can do this in two ways. You can use the matte selector and eyedropper tools at the top of the effect in the Effect Controls panel, or you can use the regular controls at the bottom of the effect. We need practice at both, so we'll use the controls at the top of the effect to adjust Partial A, and then the controls at the bottom to adjust Partial B.

First, select the A matte by clicking the A button underneath the layer thumbnail in the upper right hand corner of the effect. Now we're going to adjust this matte by using the eyedroppers. The top eyedropper is the equivalent of the Key Color property, which we've already adjusted. The second (black) eyedropper is used to click on the areas of the matte that should be black (completely transparent). Partial A's background looks pretty good, but just to be safe you can select the black eyedropper and click in the area of the image that has the green screen.

Next, you use the bottom (white) eyedropper to select areas that should be completely opaque, like your subject. So, I'm going to select the white eyedropper and click on my face somewhere.

From here, you could select the B underneath this thumbnail to adjust the B matte, or even the greek alpha symbol (looks like a little goldfish to me) to adjust the final alpha. But we're going to go down and adjust the Partial B matte by using the regular slider parameters. Most of the properties in this effect refer to some form of black or white. Before getting into adjusting these properties, remember that black areas will be transparent in the final matte, and white areas will be opaque. So, if you're wanting to remove some left over pixels caused by wrinkles in your green screen, adjust the parameters that refer to black. If you eat away at your subject too much, restore it by using the parameters that refer to white.

In my key, I have too much of the background leftover, and I'm still partially invisible. So, to further remove the background, I'm going to increase the Partial B In Black value. This is like dragging the far left arrow under the histogram in the Levels effect to the right. I then want to restore some of the pixels making up the subject. I can do this by reducing the Partial B In White value. This is the equivalent of dragging the far right arrow under the histogram in the Levels effect to the left.

To double check your final matte, it's always a good idea (in all keying effects and applications) to view the matte in grayscale. This way, you can easily tell exactly how well you did at keying. In most instances, you will want a pure black

Tweaking the Color Difference Key Effect

Here are a couple tips when working with this effect. First, use the View drop down to see the results of individual mattes, or the final matte. Second, I usually get the best (and quickest) results from the Color Difference Key effect by getting a rough key using the thumbnails and eyedroppers at the top, and then by fine tuning my results with the regular parameters at the bottom.

background (which indicates complete transparency), a pure white subject (white indicates full opacity), and gray along the edges (which indicates partial transparency). In our matte here, we can see that we have a little bit of gray on the fringes of my hair, which is great. This will help those fringes of hair composite better into their new background. In the Color Difference Key effect, you can view this grayscale matte by changing the View value to Matte Corrected.

Figure 10.7 The matte corrected option in the view drop down shows us our key as grayscale values. These values indicate the degree of transparency in each pixel.

Things are looking pretty good here, so let's now take the View drop down to Final Output to see the result of our key. You might notice that we're still getting a little bit of green in the feathered areas of my hair. Sometimes, it's just impossible to keep semi-transparent edges (which is usually desirable) from picking up some of the colors of the background. We could adjust the Partial A and Partial B In White values to remove the green screen from these hairs, but that would also create hard edges, which would be bad for compositing. To keep the semi-transparency in the edges and remove the color, use the Spill Suppressor effect, discussed later in this chapter.

Figure 10.8 The final result of our key with the Color Difference Key effect.

The Color Key Effect

The Color Key effect is probably the polar opposite of the Color Difference Key effect. The Color Key effect is extremely simple and straightforward, but the results are usually, well... bad. Even with really clean footage that has subjects with solid edges, the Color Key effect has a tough time.

Figure 10.9 The Artbeats footage of leaves falling.

I'm going to import the Artbeats video clip UM230.mov from the Artbeats folder in the Media folder of the exercise files. This is professionally shot footage of autumn leaves falling. Low noise, good lighting, perfect green screen—the whole bit.

You would think that this would be easy footage to key, right? Well, not for the Color Key effect. Let's see how the results turn out. Click the eyedropper next to the Key Color swatch and click on the green screen in the footage in the Composition panel. Only a handful of pixels are removed, so increase the Color Tolerance value to remove more of the green screen background. Chances are, the results will look awful no matter how much you play with this setting. You can use Edge Feather to soften the edges. You can also use Edge Thin to fix the edges, but be careful here. Increasing the value just a little bit will eat away at the edges of the subject. Taking this to a negative value will expand the edges of the subject. It's best to use this property sparingly, if at all.

All in all, it's almost impossible to pull a good key with this effect. Even if you manage to get a frame looking good, usually after previewing the video, the edges of the subject will "dance" around, looking jittery. I would only use this effect if a client was standing over my shoulder, or in some other instance where I needed an instant key and quality was not important. Even then, I would probably rather choose the Linear Color Key effect, discussed later in this chapter.

Figure 10.10 The Color Key effect usually leaves a little bit of the green screen around the edge of the subject (as shown here), or erodes its edges.

The Color Range Effect

For those of you familiar with Photoshop, the Color Range effect works very much like the Color Range selection feature in Photoshop. The big difference here is that you first have to select a color space from the Color Space drop down—either Lab, YUV, or RGB. If you don't get good results in one color space, you can try pulling a key in a different one. But it's very important to do this first because changing the Color Space will completely alter your key, and you will have to start all over again.

Once you've chosen a color space, click the eyedropper tool at the top of the Color Range effect in the Effect Controls panel, and then click the color you want to key out in the Preview area, or in the Composition panel. Invariably, this will leave large amounts of the key color left behind. So, then select the Plus eyedropper to select additional colors to add to the key. If you accidentally select colors that you don't want to remove, you can click on them with the Minus eyedropper to remove them.

As with Color Range in Photoshop, increasing the Fuzziness value is like increasing a Tolerance value; more colors will be selected. The Fuzziness value usually needs to be increased quite a bit. You can then tweak the levels of individual color channels with the Min and Max properties. Note that the cryptic letters (L, Y, R) refer to the first channel of Lab, YUV, and RGB, respectively. The properties that contain (A, U, G) refer to the second channel of Lab, YUV, and RGB, respectively. After increasing the Fuzziness value, our key of the Artbeats autumn leaves footage is looking pretty good, especially considering the lack of help from other effects. Also note that the edges of these leaves are smooth when played back.

Figure 10.11 After pulling a key with the Color Range effect.

The Difference Matte Effect

The Difference Matte effect is a really great idea—in theory. But in practice, it just doesn't always work out that great. But perhaps you'll have better luck with it than I have. The purpose of the effect is to use two layers that are otherwise identical, and isolate the part(s) of them that are different. Let's say you had a video of a dancer dancing around. And you also had a segment of the video (or perhaps a still camera shot) of the same spot where the dancer was dancing, but without the dancer. In theory, you could use the Difference Matte effect to compare the footage with the dancer, and the footage without the dancer, and then extract the dancer.

Let's look at an example of this effect in action. If you'd like to follow along, open the Difference Matte.aep project in the Chapter 10 folder. I have here some footage of my buddy Paavo from mala-chyte.net doing some crazy unicycle work.

I also have a still (actually an extracted frame from the same video shot), that contains just the benches.

The idea is that we can isolate Paavo using the Difference Matte effect because we have these two pieces of footage. But we'll quickly

Figure 10.12 Paavo doing unicycle tricks.

Figure 10.13 The same shot from Figure 10.12, but without the unicyclist.

see why this effect often falls apart. Apply the Difference Matte effect to the unicycle on bench.mov layer (the top layer in the bench comp). By default, the effect uses the layer it was applied to as the Difference Layer, which completely hides the entire layer. Change the Difference Layer drop down to the Benches alone PRECOMP layer. Selecting more pixels by increasing the Matching Tolerance value. Feather the edges with the Matching Softness value. The problem is that this shot (as with most shots) has a lot of small, moving parts—shadows, moving sunlight, leaves blowing in the wind, and so on. All of these things cause problems in the matte. The final results are less than stellar, but could be used for a cool, stylized effect.

Figure 10.14 The final results of the Difference Matte effect.

The Extract Effect

Before tackling the Extract effect, you might want to brush up on the Levels effect, covered in Chapter 6. The Extract effect works best (works only?) with footage that has extreme light values or extreme dark values to key out. If the luminance of your subject is similar to the luminance of your background, you'll have a difficult time getting the Extract effect to work well. If you'd like to follow along, you can open the Extract.aep project in the Chapter 10 folder.

So, we have here a photo of some fireworks, courtesy of Angela McInroe.

Figure 10.15 The fireworks comp in the Extract.aep project.

Apply the Extract effect to the fireworks layer. There is a histogram with a graphic interface, but I much prefer to use the regular sliders/hot text adjusters with this effect. With the Channel drop down set to Luminance, increasing the Black Point value will remove dark areas of the layer. Increasing the Black Softness value will soften the edges of removed dark pixels. Decreasing the White Point value will get rid of bright values in the layer, while White Softness will soften the edges of removed bright pixels. If you're interested in using the graphic interface (the bar underneath the histogram), the top points represent the Black Point and White Point, while the bottom points indicate the Black Softness and White Softness values.

Note that you can also change the Channel drop down to things like the blue channel or the green channel, but that doesn't help with this effect unless the blue or green screen is exceedingly dark or light.

The results of the Extract effect are similar to what you would get if you simply used a blend mode like Multiply or Screen, but it does allow you more control over what gets removed and softness.

Figure 10.16 After removing the dark pixels of the fireworks layer with the extract effect, you can see the rad rockets. mov layer behind it.

The Inner/Outer Key Effect

Many of the effects in this chapter aren't really helpful all that much. And if they are helpful, they usually aren't very interesting. But the Inner/Outer Key effect is both helpful and interesting, and it's helpful for far more than just blue and green screen work.

You'll probably want to follow along with this one, especially seeing how different it is from the other effects in this chapter.

I'll be using the Inner Outer Key.aep project from the Chapter 10 folder of the exercise files. This project contains a comp that has in it some footage of Seattle. The difference here is that I have created two masks. You see, what we want to do here is to isolate the city by removing the sky and mountains in the background. The Inner/Outer Key effect allows us to use these two masks to help us in this otherwise challenging task.

Figure 10.17 The Seattle footage with two masks applied.

The Inner/Outer Key effect functions similarly to the Extract plugin in Photoshop. You first create two masks on your layer—one to specify areas which should absolutely completely opaque, and then another mask that tells the Inner/Outer Key effect where the border is between the stuff we want and the stuff we don't want. So, in this case, we have one mask around the city, and there's nothing in that mask that we don't want to keep. With the other mask, we encompass everything we want to keep, but we also encompass some of the skyline. This mask covers ALL of the stuff we want (the city), which includes some of the stuff we don't want (the sky and background).

Apply the Inner/Outer Key effect to the Seattle layer. Instantly, it uses the mask of the city (Mask 1) as the Foreground (Inside) mask, and the mask of the city, with its edges and some of the sky (Mask 2) as the Background (Outside) mask. Even the default settings remove the background fairly well. If you were to use another keying effect (such as Extract or Luma Key), the white pyramid in the foreground (which, coincidentally, is actually called the Key Arena) would also have been removed.

More Than Two Masks

The Inner/Outer Key effect actually allows you to use several masks if you need to. The additional masks can be chosen in the Additional Foreground and Additional Background areas. These extra masks can be used to cut holes in the masks, if needed.

Figure 10.18 After applying the Inner/Outer Key effect, the background is instantly removed, even before making adjustments to settings.

There are the standard keying tweaks here, such as Edge Thin, Edge Feather, and Edge Threshold. But there is also an Invert Extraction checkbox. Clicking that checkbox in this instance would remove the city, and keep the background. Remember this as you use this effect in the real world, in case you find an instance where it's easier to mask out a background than a subject.

Figure 10.19 Selecting the Invert Extraction checkbox will mask out the subject, leaving the background. This also allows you to see the imperfections in my initial matte.

Another thing that makes this effect unique is that you can actually use masks to restore lost foreground or remove more background. And it does this by creating a stroke around the mask. I know—weird, right? To show you how this works, I'm going to create yet another mask—a rectangular one this time—on this layer. I'll then take the Mode value for this mask to None in the Timeline panel so that it doesn't affect the layer directly. To restore more of the subject (i.e., foreground), open the Cleanup Foreground area and select Mask 3 from the Path drop down in the Cleanup 1 area.

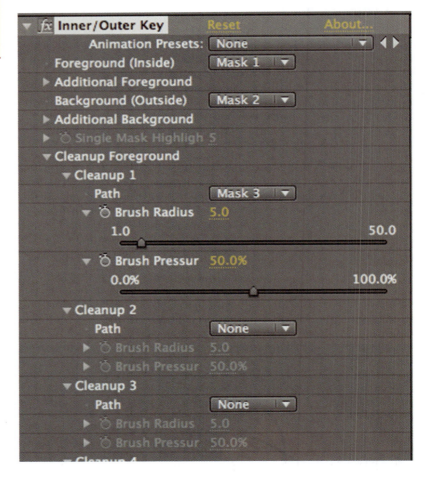

Figure 10.20 Choose the mask that you created (Mask 3, in my case) from cleanup foreground>cleanup 1>path.

Because we chose this mask in the Cleanup Foreground area, it will cleanup, or restore, pixels. Again, this comes in the form of a stroke around the mask. You can control the size of the stroke with the Brush Radius value, or the Hardness of the stroke with the Brush Pressure value.

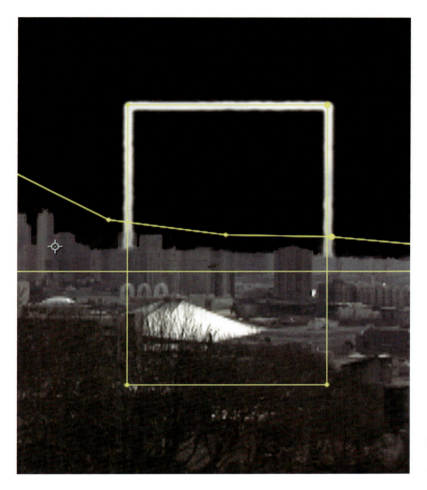

Figure 10.21 Using a mask to cleanup the foreground, or in other words, to restore pixels.

If we wanted to remove more of the pixels in this matte, we would go into the Cleanup Background area, and go through the same process there. Figure 10.22 shows the same mask as seen in Figure 10.21, but used to cleanup the background. The masks have been deactivated in this screenshot so that the removed pixels will be more obvious.

And so, in summary, the Inner/Outer Key effect can seem like Grand Central Station for masks. It allows you to input up to 36 simultaneous masks for various purposes (yes, I counted). But whether you use this effect to its fullest, or on a more simplistic level, the Inner/Outer Key effect can easily extract portions of a layer that other keying tools would have a difficult time with.

Figure 10.22 Using an extra mask to cleanup the background, or in other words, to remove pixels.

The Keylight (1.2) Effect

Keylight is a keying tool created by The Foundry and has been included as a bonus with After Effects for the last several versions. It used to retail for $1000 as a standalone plugin, if that's any gauge of its quality.

Keylight is designed to remove blue and green screen backgrounds, and it also has pretty decent (and automatic) color correction tools that helps footage get all the green or blue off.

Let's look at some of the basic tools in Keylight. I have some footage of a model sneaking some footage with an 8mm camera. I've already created a simple garbage matte.

Figure 10.23 The original layer.

This is 4k raw footage, so it's extremely flat. So, before I apply Keylight, I want to get this footage to a good base level. I also want to make sure that the green screen actually looks green. Keylight really responds to saturation, so it might be a good idea to apply Hue/Saturation, set the Channel Control to Greens and boost as needed/desired.

In the Keylight.aep project in the Chapter 10 folder of the exercise files, you'll find the Keylight START comp. The vintage camera.R3D file is what we're going to be keying. To get us to a good starting point, I've applied Levels and Hue/Saturation already.

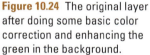

Figure 10.24 The original layer after doing some basic color correction and enhancing the green in the background.

Now apply the Keylight effect to this layer. The very first thing we want to do is to choose the Screen Color, which is the color (or "color" if that's the way you do things) of the background. So click the Screen Color eyedropper and click on the green background of this footage.

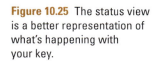

Figure 10.25 The status view is a better representation of what's happening with your key.

Color Picking Tips!

Choosing the best color is absolutely essential to getting good results with Keylight. So, there are a couple of tips here. First, if you hold down Alt(Win)/Opt(Mac) while moving your eyedropper around, Keylight gives you a real time preview of what the initial results of that key will be. You aren't looking for perfection here, just the best results. This is also helpful for avoiding a stray pixel (such as those resulting from noise) and getting a wacky result. Also, if you choose a color and decide it's not the best, do not just select the eyedropper and try to choose another. This won't yield good results for several reasons. What you'll want to do first is to take the View Drop down to Source and then choose a new color. Alternatively, you could also create a new viewer in After Effects that had this footage in the Layer panel, so you always have it around.

When you first select a Screen Color, Keylight jumps into action and creates an initial key, but also tries to do some color correction to remove spill. Because this is such a radical shift, there is a temptation among new users to be satisfied with the initial results. Don't fall into that trap. Change the View drop down from Final Result to Status to see what's really happening here.

The white areas are the areas that are going to be completely opaque. The black areas are completely transparent. The gray areas represent pixels that will be semi-transparent. Our initial results here are actually pretty good (better than usual). But we still have some work to do.

The end goal is to have the core of our subject completely white, the background completely black, and some of the edges and softer details (like hair and reflections) gray.

Let's first start out by making the background black. There are two contorls to do this: Screen Gain (at the top) and Clip Black (inside the Screen Matte group). The Foundry recommends staying away from Screen Gain because overdoing it can ruin the delicate edges of your footage, which is a critical aspect of a good key. However, I've gotten great results by using the Screen Gain parameter that I couldn't get with Clip Black. So use it to taste.

To get rid of the holes in your subject, you'll want to decrease the Clip White value in the Screen Matte section. And you'll want to adjust all of these settings with the intent to preserve a little gray on the edges and the softer portions of the image.

As a general rule, with all of these settings, there's never a formula for getting a good key. Unless you're shooting with the same camera, same lights, and the same talent, in the same position, and in the same studio, don't worry about creating Animation Presets or writing down settings. They'll always be different. And I've found that there are some controls that mess up most of my footage, and then one day, that parameter saves my life when nothing else could. So it's a balancing act, rather than a recipe that we're going for here.

Another general rule is that you only want to use the adjustments in the Keylight effect as much as you absolutely need to. With every adjustment, there is a trade-off in the final quality of the key. So be temperate, and don't push things to white or black (or soften the key or contract the key, etc.) any further than you absolutely have to.

So here are the settings I used in this case. To make the background black, I increased Screen Gain to 108 and Clip Black to 25. I didn't find that I needed any Clip White adjustment, which is actually quite rare. It's great if you can get away with that, but

I find that I usually have to take this value to about 80 to make sure that my subject is intact.

That got my black and white where it needed to be, but when I took the view drop down back to Final Result, the edge is ugly. It's too rough and there's some semi-transparency on the top of her head that doesn't look good.

So let's look at some other settings to help this out. I took the Screen Pre-blur value to 2. This is great for smoothing keys in many cases. Note that this doesn't actually blur anything that you see. This is just a behind-the-scenes blur that Keylight applies to the key before it does its magic. This can help to get rid of noise, which can cause noisy or "sizzling" edges when the footage is played back.

In the Screen Matte section, I also contracted the matte a bit by taking Screen Shrink/Grow to –3.5. That's a lot more than I usually use, but it works in this instance. Note that a positive value here will expand the matte, while a negative value like this will shrink it. This is starting to look good.

At this point, I think I'm going to turn on the background layer (IMG_3452.CR2) to see how our composite is coming along. Looks alright, but her edge is really strong, which is a dead give-away of a composite. So let's soften that. I'm going to take Screen Matte>Screen Softness to 2. Be careful not to take it too much further than that, as an edge that is too soft is just as much of a dead giveaway of fakery as an edge that's too hard.

Figure 10.26 After fiddling with keylight and enabling our background layer, we have a fairly decent composite.

The thing that's missing here is a little extra color correction to our subject. She's a bit too dark and red (and a little too blue) and saturated for this background. The Keylight FINAL comp has my final color correction and composite. I didn't spend too much time with it, but we're more in the ballpark.

Figure 10.27 The final composite in the keylight FINAL comp.

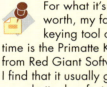

My Favorite Keying Tool(s)

For what it's worth, my favorite keying tool of all time is the Primatte Keyer from Red Giant Software. I find that it usually gets me a better key faster than Keylight, and it's very intuitive. It also comes in a suite of tools called the Keying Suite that has many tools for refining keys and matching background color for better composites. It's an extra purchase, but I wouldn't be able to survive without it.

One other thing about Keylight that I wanted to mention was its automatic color correction. This is usually an amazing feat of wonder and miracles. But sometimes, it causes more problems than it cures. I was once working on a project and couldn't figure out why my footage was so terribly noisy, when it looked great before I brought it into After Effects. The problem was that Keylight was adding tons of noise as a result of its color correction. If this is happening to you, or for whatever other reason, you just want to turn off the Keylight color correction, take the View drop down from Final Result to Intermediate Result.

The Linear Color Key Effect

The Linear Color Key effect is a quick and simple keying tool. It's slightly more complex than the simple Color Key, but the results are usually much better. For this example, I'm going to be using the Linear Color Key.aep project from the Chapter 10 folder. This contains a video clip of me looking like a total doofus in front of a green screen. As much as this footage humiliates me, it's also extremely compressed. If you can pull a good key with this footage, you can probably pull a good key with most footage.

First, let's apply the Linear Color Key effect to the Chad with Hand Dot.mov layer. These settings should look familiar to you if you've been working with the other effects in this chapter, so I won't mention them again here. The two notable differences are that you can choose to match color using RGB, Hue, or Chroma (color—which refers to all attributes of color, not just the hue). You can also choose to adjust the Key Operation value to Key Colors (remove them) or Keep Colors. This property is helpful if the Linear Color Key effect accidentally removes too much of a color in your subject, you can apply another instance of the Linear Color Key effect and keep (or restore) the missing colors.

Click on the Key Color eyedropper and select the green in the green screen that is closest to our subject, as there is some darker vignetting happening in the corners of this shot. I found the best results with this clip with my Match Colors drop down set to Using Chroma. I also used a Matching Tolerance of 5%, and a Matching Softness value of 4%. The results came out pretty good, especially considering how badly this footage is compressed, and the fact that I've only applied this effect once, and I'm not using a Spill Suppressor or any other effect here. Remember that for the best results, it's best to constantly change the view to the grayscale matte so that you know exactly how transparent your pixels are.

Figure 10.28 The quite impressive (and quick) results with the Linear Color Key effect.

The Luma Key Effect

The Luma Key effect is similar to the Extract effect in that it attempts to pull a key by looking at a layer's brightness, and keying out either light or dark values. The Luma Key effect doesn't give you as much control (as the Extract effect also allows you to adjust individual color channels), but it is easier to use, and the results are comparable.

For this look at the Luma Key effect, we'll be using the Luma Key.aep project from the Chapter 10 folder, which is identical to the project we looked at with the Extract effect. That way, you can compare and contrast the results with what we saw of the Extract effect a little earlier.

Apply the Luma Key effect to the fireworks layer. The default Key Type is Key Out Darker, which removes dark pixels. You can change this value to Key Out Brighter to eliminate bright areas. To remove any pixels, you need to increase the Threshold value. The Tolerance parameter functions similarly to Threshold, but only works when Key Out Similar or Key Out Dissimilar is chosen as the Key Type. When Key Out Similar or Key Out Dissimilar is chosen as the Key Type, you can use both the Tolerance and the Threshold properties simultaneously to key out a wider range of tonal values. Key Out Similar is very much like Key Out Darker, and Key Out Dissimilar is very much like Key Out Brighter. The other properties (Edge Thin and Edge Feather) have been covered already in this chapter.

Figure 10.29 The results of keying with the Luma Key effect. These results were achieved with all properties at their default values, except for threshold, which was at 60.

The Spill Suppressor Effect

As we've been playing around with keying effects in this chapter, you might have noticed that some keying effects leave a small trace of green around the edges of the subject. Sometimes, there's just a green reflection from the screen on your subject. The purpose of the Spill Suppressor effect is to remove the colors of the background that are left around the edges of your subject. It is the only effect in this category that doesn't remove pixels; it only desaturates them.

For this example, open the Spill Suppressor.aep project from the Chapter 10 folder. This contains a more realistic use of some of the footage we've been keying. We have two clips from Artbeats—one with falling autumn leaves against a green screen, and the other depicting running children. We're going to composite these leaves over the footage of the children, to make it look like these leaves were actually in the shot with the children.

In this project, I've already keyed out the green screen using the Color Key effect. Because I'm using the Color Key effect, you know that the results aren't going to be spectacular. Notice how the green outline around the leaves makes this look especially fake.

Figure 10.30 The comp in the Spill Suppressor project, with a bad key courtesy of the Color Key effect.

Figure 10.31 The final keying result, after removing the green from the edges with the Spill Suppressor.

Now, add the Spill Suppressor effect to the UM230.mov layer (after the Color Key effect). The first order of business is to inform the Spill Suppressor effect which color needs to be desaturated. You could turn off the visibility of the Color Key effect to see the green screen again, and then select it with the Color to Suppress color swatch eyedropper. Or if you have good aim, you could just click the Color to Suppress color swatch eyedropper, and then click the green Key Color color swatch in the Color Key effect. Then, you don't have to fiddle with effect visibility.

Then, just increase the Suppression value until the green edges of the leaves are gone. For better results, take the Color Accuracy value from Faster to Better. The Spill Suppressor effect will desaturate the color in the Color to Suppress value, making the final result much more believable.

11

THE MATTE EFFECTS

The primary focus of the Matte effects is transparency; or more specifically, the alpha channel of a layer. They are usually used in conjunction with keying or rotoscoping. The Matte effects restore holes in a layer (typically caused by keying), and can also eat away at the edges of a layer.

In the first edition of this book, we looked at the two original effects in this category: Matte Choker and Simple Choker. Since After Effects CS5, we have two new additions—Mocha Shape and Refine Edge. Mocha Shape isn't really a standalone effect—it's designed to be used with Mocha, which is a separate app included with After Effects CS6. So we won't be looking at that here.

But the new gem of this category is the powerhouse Refine Matte effect. This effect contains options that are part of the Rotobrush feature. But these options were so amazing, they were made a separate effect (Refine Matte). And although Matte Choker and Simple Choker still work great, I always go first to Refine Matte. It is almost frighteningly intelligent, and has fixed many problems that I thought impossible to fix.

Here's a simple breakdown of these effects compared. Simple Choker is the fastest to render and easiest to understand. Matte Choker is the hardest to understand but it gives more control than Simple Choker and renders very quickly. Refine Matte gives the best results in most cases and certainly does all kinds of great things the others can't do, but it is by far the slowest to render. And while it's more intuitive than Matte Choker, it's much more annoying to experiment with because everything takes so much longer. Still, Refine Matte is my go-to native effect when working with mattes.

For Matte Choker and Simple Choker, there are some common terms that we should look at before proceeding. The first concept is that of spreading. Spreading is when you increase the size of the alpha channel (matte), usually by filling in holes inside the layer. The other concept we'll use is that of choking. Choking refers to shrinking, or constricting the matte, usually to get rid of a halo of pixels around a subject.

3rd Party Matte Assistance

Since writing the first edition of this book, I've since discovered (and subsequently fallen in love with) the Key Correct tools from Red Giant Software (redgiantsoftware.com). Key Correct is a suite of 15 tools designed purely to help with refining mattes, pulling better keys, and getting a better overall composite. It seems like I use at least one Key Correct effect every single time I do compositing work, and I can't imagine life without them. If you do a lot of this kind of work, I highly suggest taking a look at what Key Correct can offer you.

The Matte Choker Effect

The Matte Choker effect is used to both spread and choke a matte. If you open the Matte Choker.aep project found in the Chapter 11 folder of the exercise files, you'll see a simple project. Here, I've taken a photo of me, your humble author, in front of a green screen and keyed out the background using the Color Key effect. But, as is the case with keying on occasion, we've actually created some holes in our subject.

Figure 11.1 A close up of the subject as seen in the Matte Choker.aep project. The bright blue areas are holes in our layer.

We're going to use the Matte Choker effect to restore these areas back to full opacity, and to fine tune the edge of the matte as well. I've created a bright blue solid and placed it below the subject in the layer stack. This will help us identify and fix problems in our key.

The first thing we need to realize about the Matte Choker effect, is that it is made up of two main sections, each with the same three controls. The three controls are Geometric Softness, Choke, and Gray Level Softness. The first set of these controls will be used to spread (restore) the matte. The second set will be used to shrink (constrict) the matte.

▼ *fx* **Matte Choker**	Reset	About...
Animation Presets:	None	◄ ►
▶ ⎔ Geometric Softness 1	4.0	
▶ ⎔ Choke 1	75	
▶ ⎔ Gray Level Softness 1	10%	
▶ ⎔ Geometric Softness 2	0.00	
▶ ⎔ Choke 2	0	
▶ ⎔ Gray Level Softness 2	100.0%	
▶ ⎔ Iterations	1	

Figure 11.2 The parameters of the Matte Choker effect.

One of the beefs I have with this effect is that the default settings aren't the best defaults, as I see it. No matter what your settings are when using this effect, it's almost guaranteed that they will be very different from the default values.

Let's look first at Geometric Softness 1. Geometric Softness controls how smooth the edges of the matte are, and it also shrinks the matte a little. Take this value to about 3. A higher Geometric Softness might look better here, but taking this value too high will limit our ability to properly choke back the matte later.

Next is the Choke 1 value. A positive Choke value chokes the matte, while a negative Choke value spreads the matte. Since we're spreading the matte with the first group of controls, take the Choke value to –125. This allows the holes in our subject

Checking Your Matte

Often, checking mattes against the default black background is a bad idea. Mattes can be tricky little devils. Many times, you won't be able to see problems with a matte until you either view the alpha channel (using the Show Channels and Color Management Settings button at the bottom of the Composition, Footage, and Layer panels), checking the matte against the transparency grid (also a button at the bottom of the Monitor panel), or by previewing your matte against different color backgrounds. Sometimes, it takes a combination of all of these before I catch a problem.

Figure 11.3 After spreading the matte.

Gray Level Softness 2 Default

The default value for the Gray Level Softness 2 property is set at an almost ridiculous 100%. In many cases, this will prevent you from seeing any changes you make to the second set of properties. If you're just fiddling with the second group of properties, be sure to first reduce the Gray Level Softness parameter so you can see what you're doing.

to become opaque again. Finally we come to the Gray Level Softness 1 value. This controls the softness of the edge of the matte. Take this value to about 7%.

Our results already look much better. And, although I still look cheesy, I don't look swiss cheesy—the holes on my layer have been filled. But in order to make things even better, we need to use the second set of these controls in the Matte Choker effect to choke back the matte.

Essentially, what I did in this case, is to duplicate the values of the first set again, except that the Choke 2 value is set to a positive 125 to choke the matte. This means that Geometric Softness 2 is set to 3, and Gray Level Softness 2 is set to 7%. The iterations value can be increased also, which is like adding another round of spreading and choking.

Figure 11.4 The final result after spreading and choking the matte.

The Refine Matte Effect

The Refine Matte effect was added with the Rotobrush tool back in After Effects CS5. It should be noted that the same tools exist in both. The Refine Matte effect is simply the best matte refinement tool that exists in After Effects. It's almost magical what it can do to a key, including removing a background from a moving subject with motion blur. I don't know of another tool that can do that.

We're going to look at a simple example here. Open the Refine Matte.aep project from the Chapter 11 folder of the exercise files. Go to the Refine Matte START comp, where I have a shot from my short film GODLIZZA. I keyed this footage with Keylight after applying color correction and all that stuff. But it's still just rough. I really don't want to contract the matte anymore because it would eat away too much of the image before it would smooth it out. Most of the problems are around the hair of both kids. I could (and should probably) make a duplicate layer with a separate mask and rotoscope that. But it's just that I'm so lazy.

Figure 11.5 The original material after being color corrected and keyed.

So let's apply the Refine Matte effect to this. Wow. Even the default settings are an improvement over our original. I should point out that a lot of these settings are things that we've seen before—Smooth, Feather, Choke, etc. But the magic here is that they're not sensitive at all, as opposed to these controls in other effects.

I'm going to increase Smooth to 2.5 (Smooth is actually the most sensitive parameter here, and you have to be a bit careful). Let's bump up Feather to 50%, and Choke up to 85% (yep, 85%). You would think that settings that high would destroy our footage. But such is not the case. Refine Matte was made for fine tuning adjustments, just like this.

In our case, we don't need it look for motion blur, so we can just deselect that option. We do have a wee bit of green spill left over. Making sure that Decontaminate Edge Colors is selected, take the Increase Decontamination Radius to 3.0. This increases the area that is decontaminated. Like Smooth, this is another control where a little goes a long way, so be aware of that.

Figure 11.6 The final image after refining the matte.

Also with this effect, be aware that as great and as helpful as it usually is, the Use Motion Blur and Decontaminate Edge Colors options can occasionally ruin this effect. If you're noticing weird artifacts and visual glitches, try turning off these options and see if your problems aren't fixed. But remember that they can be life-savers in some cases also.

The Simple Choker Effect

Although the Simple Choker does, in fact, live up to its name and is quite simple, it can be useful in a variety of circumstances, as we'll see. There is just one parameter here—Choke Matte. Negative Choke Matte values spread the matte, while positive values choke the matte. Obviously there's less control here than with the Matte Choker or Refine Matte effects, but there's also a lot less fuss. Let's open up the Simple Choker.aep project from the Chapter 11 folder.

Here we see the example we looked at previously. What I did here is try to simulate all the work we did with the Matte Choker effect. The Simple Choker appears to round and soften the matte edge slightly already. So, I applied the Simple Choker effect, and took the value to negative 3.6, because negative values spread the matte. This filled in all the holes. Then I selected the effect in the Effect Controls panel, and pressed Ctrl+D(Win)/ Cmd+D(Mac) on my keyboard to duplicate the effect. On the duplicate, I changed the value to a positive 2. This replicates what we did with the Matte Choker effect because it spreads, then chokes.

Figure 11.7 The result of fixing the matte with two copies of the Simple Choker effect.

Next, go over to the 3D edge cleanup composition. This is a file that we looked at in the beginning of the book in our coverage of the 3D effects. You might have noticed then that these 3D files have terrible aliasing on the edges. That's just the nature of 3D files when imported into After Effects this way. The Simple Choker effect can actually help us smooth out those ugly rough edges.

Figure 11.6 shows the result of our 3D file with the ID Matte effect applied, and the car isolated. Even though I've already tried here to smooth the edges of the matte with ID Matte's Feather property, they still look awful.

So what we're going to do is apply the Simple Choker effect. Remember that the Simple Choker effect also smoothes the matte in addition to spreading or choking it. In many cases, that can be a detriment as corners get rounded. But in this instance, a little extra smoothness is just what the doctor ordered. Apply the Simple Choker effect and take the Choke Matte value to a positive 1.5. Even zoomed in at 200%, the results look pretty good.

What else can the Simple Choker effect be used for? I find it handy for those times when I've imported a layered Photoshop file that contains objects I cut out of a background. Sometimes, if I'm working in a hurry in Photoshop, my selections might not be

Figure 11.8 The blocky edges on the isolated car are seemingly impossible to fix. Feathering the edges just makes a bigger mess.

Figure 11.9 The results after applying the Simple Choker effect.

the best. That means that there will probably be some extra pixels on the edges of my imported Photoshop layers. A quick application of the Simple Choker effect can often fix the problem.

I've heard it suggested that the Simple Choker effect can also compensate for an incorrect alpha interpretation. For example, if an object you import has a premultipled alpha channel, and you import it as straight, it will have a halo around it. The suggestion was to remove the halo with the Simple Choker effect. However, I don't recommend this course of action. You will almost always get significantly better results from interpreting the alpha channel correctly in the Interpret Footage dialog box (which now has a nifty shortcut button in the bottom left hand corner of the Project panel in After Effects CS4 and later), rather than by using effects to "interpret" the alpha.

With a lot of these simple tasks, I might still prefer to use the Simple Choker effect, rather than calling on the slow rendering, big guns of Refine Matte.

12

THE NOISE & GRAIN EFFECTS

The Noise & Grain effects all deal with noise in some form or another. Some effects add noise, while others remove it. A couple of these effects—Fractal Noise and Turbulent Noise—are in a class all on their own, as they create grayscale patterns. Let's look at a few important concepts to help you get the most out of this chapter, and to get an overview of what is coming up.

Good Noise

In the video world, noise gets a bad rap. Noise isn't always a bad thing. Often, adding noise is desirable because it creates a sense of grit and realism. Photographs and computer-generated images are notorious for looking too clean and polished. Adding noise can help them look more filmlike. When gradients appear to have banding (posterization), noise can be added to smooth the transitions between colors. Some effects (such as Match Grain) are here to help you create a consistent amount of noise between composited elements. It's one of the great ironies in the visual effects world, but adding dirt or grain can sometimes be what makes your final results so believable.

Noise vs. Grain

There are many effects in this category—11, to be exact. Except for the 2 that generate patterns, they all either remove or add noise. So, it goes without saying that not all Noise & Grain effects are created equal. Thankfully, there is a secret way to identify the best effects here. The key is the word "grain." Effects in this category that have the word grain in their title (e.g., Add Grain, Match Grain, and Remove Grain) are all cut from the same high quality mold. They are more complex, but sometimes even the default results are all you need. If you're looking for quick, simple, and easy effects in this genre, go for the other effects.

The Powerful Pattern Generators

In the Noise & Grain category of effects, there is a large elephant in the room. Actually, since After Effects CS4, it's now two elephants. I'm referring to the Fractal Noise and Turbulent Noise effects. These two effects are unlike any of the others in this category. They generate organic grayscale patterns (so shouldn't they be in the Generate category?). That might not sound interesting, but these effects can create a wealth of different effects. I use the Fractal Noise effect (or the almost identical Turbulent Noise effect) to create seamlessly repeating animated backgrounds, for grayscale maps to control other effects, for creating luma mattes, for generating organic patterns such as fire, water, fog, smoke, clouds, lightning, and much more. The time you will invest in learning Fractal Noise will be time well spent. Trust me on this one.

The Add Grain Effect

Seeing that this effect has the word "grain" in its name, we know it's going to be a good one. The Add Grain effect attempts to make video look more like film by adding grain. To the untrained eye, the noise created by this effect might look similar to the noise created by the Noise effect (also in this Chapter). If that describes you, then by all means, use the Noise effect instead of Add Grain. The Add Grain effect takes a very long time to render. For those with discerning visual palettes, you will appreciate the intelligence of this effect. If you're not an expert in noise and grain patterns, you might get frustrated by the complexity of options and the long render times with the Add Grain effect.

Open the Add Grain.aep project from the Chapter 12 folder. This project contains an image of a 3D character I created in 3DS Max named Herbie the Robot. Here Herbie poses, as if in the movies.

In reality, this image is far too clean to appear like a frame from a movie. Apply the Add Grain effect to this image. The results are obvious once the effect is applied. However, the results only show in a small preview window because of the long render times that this effect can yield. I'm going to zoom in closer (200%) so that the differences are more clear.

You can move the preview area around if you'd like to, or even change its size, color, and width to height ratio. Just open the Preview Region area in the Effect Controls panel to see the available options. When it's time to render, or if you want to see the grain in the entire frame, change the Viewing Mode drop down at

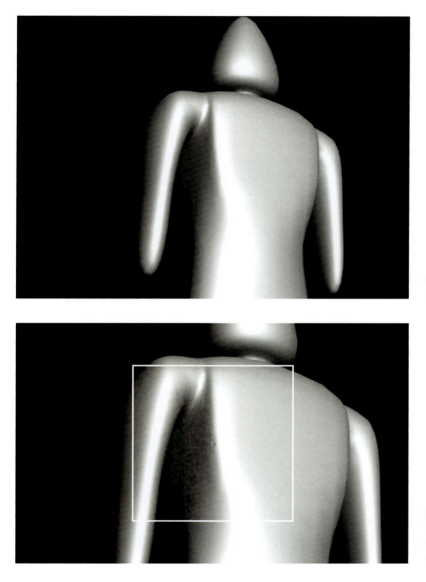

Figure 12.1 The Add Grain.aep project.

Figure 12.2 The default results of applying the Add Grain effect, with the zoom percentage at 200%.

the top of the effect in the Effect Controls panel from Preview to Final Output.

There's a multitude of properties in this effect for fine tuning the grain it creates. You can change everything from the amount of red in the dark bits of grain to how this grain will animate. You can use these properties to create grain that matches other objects in the comp. There are so many options to customize the added grain here, that they don't all fit on my screen at once!

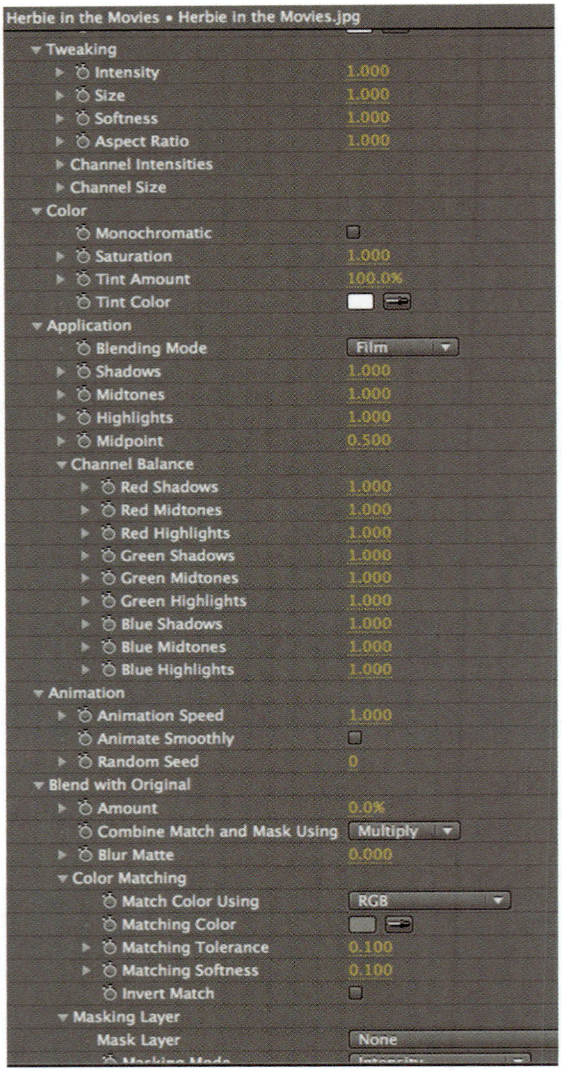

Figure 12.3 The options in the Add Grain effect (well, some of them, anyway).

One of the best shortcuts with this effect is the Preset drop down at the top of the effect. Note that this is not the Animation Presets drop down, which is above the Preset drop down. Note that if this is not showing, you can go to the Effect Controls panel fly out menu and enable the Show Animation Presets option. From this drop down list you can choose from a series of grain patterns that have been modeled after commonly used film stock grain.

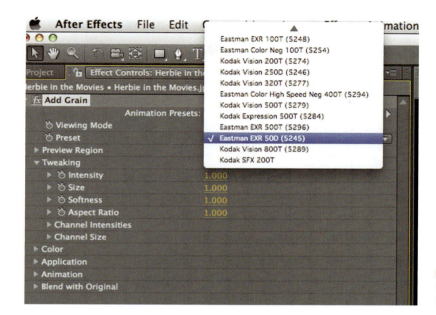

Figure 12.4 The options in the Preset drop down in the Effect Controls panel.

I'm going to use the Eastman EXR 50D (5245) preset. This creates more fine noise than what was returned with the default results. I'm also going to change my Viewing Mode drop down value to Final Output so we can see what this noise looks like when applied to the entire image.

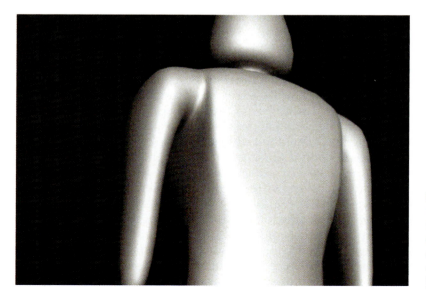

Figure 12.5 The final results create more of a film style look. Changing the Viewing Mode drop down to Final Output allows us to see the results across the entire image, not just the preview region.

The Dust & Scratches Effect

The Dust & Scratches effect attempts to remove the small blemishes that often occur with film. It achieves this by blending visual anomalies into the background. The controls are similar to those found in blur effects.

For this exercise, I'm going to open the Dust Scratches.aep project from the Chapter 12 folder. This contains a shot that I've doctored to look like vintage film, complete with the occasional random film scratch.

Figure 12.6 The scratchy video layer in the Dust Scratches.aep project.

Apply the Dust & Scratches effect to this footage. Even with the default results, the 3 faint scratches on the right side of the image have been removed completely. However, the image has also been blurred just a little in the process.

The Radius value increases the blemish removal effect, but also increases the blurriness in the image. This can be restored to a degree by increasing the Threshold value. Take the Threshold value too high, however, and your dust and scratches will return. The general rule for this effect is to take the Radius value as low as you can, and take the Threshold value as high as you can to achieve your result. In our case here, there's no way to completely remove the thicker line on the left, and still keep the image clean. For my final results, I left the Radius value at 1, and took the Threshold value up to 13. This brought back more details in my image, without bringing back the three lines that we removed. We've still lost some of the highlights and details, such as in the shrubbery. But they were necessary casualties of blemish removal.

Figure 12.7 The default results of the Dust & Scratches effect removed three of the problem lines, but also softened the details in the image a little.

Figure 12.8 The final results of the Dust & Scratches effect.

The Fractal Noise Effect

The Fractal Noise effect is one of the most common tools in After Effects, effects or otherwise. It generates grayscale patterns using virtual layers of Perlin noise. It is in these layers that the Fractal Noise effect finds the core of its power. While this book is not meant to be an effects manual—giving you the technical details of every single property in every effect—we are going to take an unusually exhaustive look at Fractal Noise.

I'll also give you some sample recipes to get started with when creating textures. I'll also show you an example of how I used Fractal Noise to create a body scan effect for a sci-fi show that I worked on.

With the Fractal Noise effect, we don't really need any exercise files. We're starting from scratch. Create a new project (File>New>New Project), then click the Create a new composition button at the bottom of the Project panel to create a new composition. Use the NTSC DV preset and click OK. As is the case with all effects, Fractal Noise must be applied to an existing layer. A solid layer works great for this. Create a new solid of any color, making sure it's the size of the comp. Then apply the Fractal Noise effect.

The default results of the Fractal Noise effect create something akin to the Clouds filter in Photoshop, which is probably why more newbies shy away from this effect.

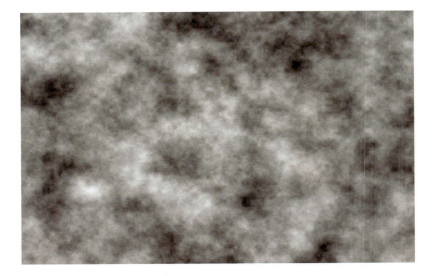

Figure 12.9 The default result of applying the Fractal Noise effect.

As mentioned, the Fractal Noise effect creates grayscale patterns, and that's it. If we want color here, we'll have to use one of the colorizing effects that we looked at back in Chapter 6. We will add color to this a little later, but for now, I want to keep things black and white. Forgive the less-than-spectacular screenshots, but the beauty of color sometimes interferes with what the Fractal Noise effect is really doing.

As we go through this section, be aware that the patterns generated by Fractal Noise are random. Your results might not match mine exactly. And, as a matter of fact, you might find it difficult to reproduce the same pattern twice because of the random nature of this effect.

The option at the top of the Fractal Noise effect is one of the most important: Fractal Type. This drop down contains a series of patterns that will substantially alter the look of this effect.

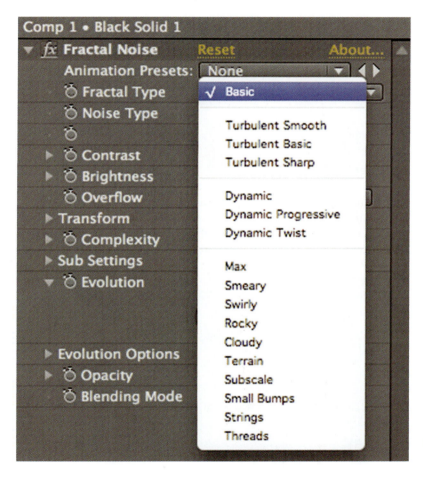

Figure 12.10 The Fractal Type options.

The first thing we're going to do is change the Fractal Type drop down to Turbulent Basic. There's really nothing special about this particular pattern, but it will help us to understand what's going on with this effect.

Next we're going to skip ahead, down to the Complexity parameter. Fractal Noise is so powerful because it creates layers of noise. We can adjust these layers of noise by transforming them, adjusting their opacity and more. We can control how many layers of noise are being created by adjusting the Complexity property. The

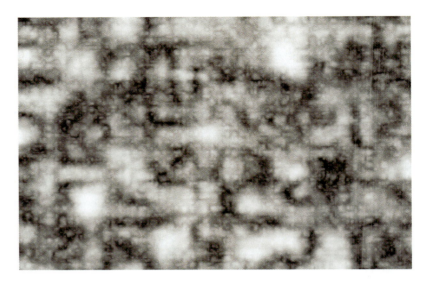

Figure 12.11 The Fractal Noise effect, with the Fractal Type drop down set to Turbulent Basic.

default is 6. As we slowly reduce this value, it may not be apparent what exactly is going on. Take the Complexity value to 1. All that you'll see will be one single layer of noise. This is the equivalent of peering behind the wizard's curtain.

Figure 12.12 Taking the Complexity value down to 1 shows you a single layer of fractal noise.

This one layer of noise isn't much to look at. It could be great as a displacement map or a luma matte, but it's not much on its own. You might not even be able to see the relationship between the two patterns. Take the Complexity value to 2, then to 3, and so on, to add more layers of noise, and restore the original pattern.

Figure 12.13 The image with a Complexity value of 2.

Figure 12.14 The image with a Complexity value of 3.

And so, as we proceed, remember that Fractal Noise is really a series of noise layers. If a texture has too much detail (or not enough), you can usually fix the problem by adjusting the Complexity value.

I'm going to now click the Reset button for the Fractal Noise effect at the top of the effect in the Effect Controls panel. Now, we're ready to add some color. We'll start simple. Apply the Tritone effect after Fractal Noise. Change the Midtones value to a blue color, leaving Highlights at white and Shadows at black.

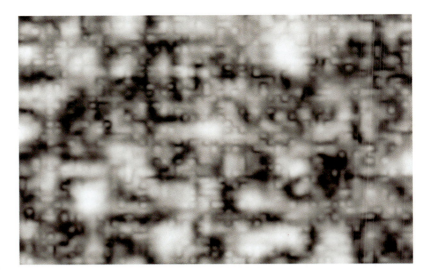

Figure 12.15 The image with a Completely value of 4.

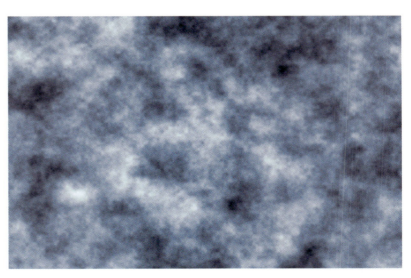

Figure 12.16 The result of applying a simple tint using the Tritone effect.

Next, we're going to look at another important setting in Fractal Noise—Noise Type. At first, this appears to be a quality setting for the noise. It seems like that's the case, but this is actually more of a smoothness setting. Sometimes smoothness is not what you're looking for. Let's start by taking the Fractal Type value to Max. The Noise Type value changes will be more obvious with this fractal type selected.

The default Noise Type value of Soft Linear is almost the smoothest noise type. The only type smoother is Spline. The

Figure 12.17 Fractal Noise with the Max fractal type selected.

Spline noise type can take significantly longer to render, but it also can produce much more organic textures because of its smoothness. It's the Billy Dee Williams of noise types. This noise type, combined with the Max fractal type creates a pattern reminiscent of gurgling water.

Figure 12.18 The Spline noise type is the smoothest of the 4, but it also takes the longest to render.

The Noise Type value that is a little less smooth than the default Soft Linear type is Linear. While the results are much more blocky than even the default Soft Linear value, the pattern created looks like gems. Again, don't mistake the Noise Type property for a quality setting. The quality here is still high, even though the noise type is less smooth.

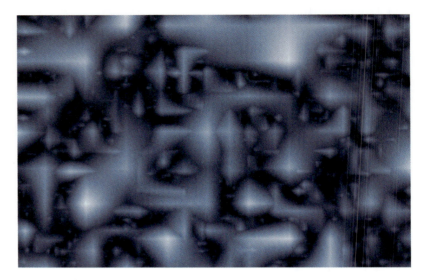

Figure 12.19 The Linear noise type creates a look like sapphires in this case.

The results are even more startling when we take the Noise Type value to Block. Personally, I love the results created from the Block noise type. This is great for creating quick geometric backgrounds. Can you imagine creating all of those little squares, with all of the variations in color, from scratch?

Figure 12.20 The Block noise type creates a series of squares.

Now, what if we wanted these squares to move around? One of my favorite aspects of Fractal Noise is that you bring almost every pattern to life with the Evolution parameter. Whether you've created squares, or fire, or water, or fog—they all spring to life with the Evolution parameter. I can't fully demonstrate the organic animation created with this property in a book. But notice how different the size and colors of these squares are by just increasing the Evolution parameter.

Figure 12.21 Adjusting the Evolution value completely changes the pattern.

What if you wanted to create a pattern like this, but with fewer squares? Easy! Just reduce the Complexity value.

Figure 12.22 Reducing the Complexity value to 1 creates a more simple pattern.

Let's hit that Reset button again to start over. I'm also going to change the Midtones color in the Tritone effect to a deep red color.

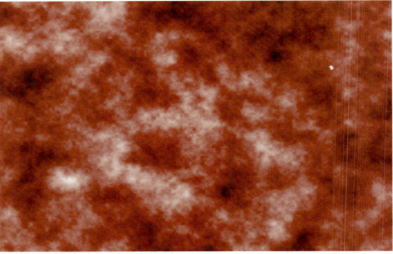

Figure 12.23 Reset Fractal Noise and change the Midtones value in the Tritone effect to red.

We're going to look at the Contrast and Brightness values, and the difference they make. And, we're going to be creating a gory brain-like texture in the process. Take the Fractal Type drop down to Dynamic.

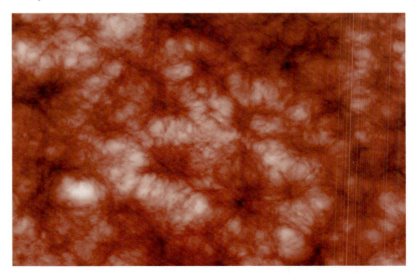

Figure 12.24 The brainy texture with the Dynamic fractal type.

Usually, when effects have a built-in set of brightness or contrast controls (such as Hue/Saturation), I usually steer clear. I prefer to make such luminance adjustments with tools meant for the job, like Curves and Levels. But I make a marked exception with the Brightness and Contrast controls in Fractal Noise.

Now I need to get more intensity into my brain, so I'm going to increase the Contrast value to 200.

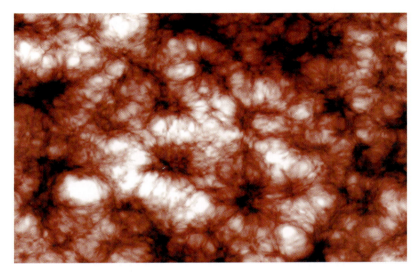

Figure 12.25 Increasing the Contrast value to 200 makes the brainy texture more intense.

Our brain texture looks pretty good. But what if I wanted only subtle hints of the brain? By decreasing the Brightness value, we increase the black areas in the pattern. Don't worry. You won't lose your contrast. If you darken things too much and want to restore some highlights, while maintaining the amount of black areas, increase the Contrast property some more.

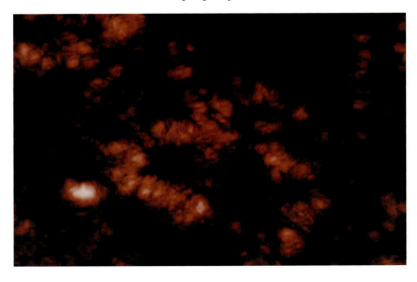

Figure 12.26 Decreasing the Brightness value adds a lot of black to the final result, while still maintaining good contrast.

So, it's safe to say that Brightness didn't act exactly like we thought it might. Another parameter that has a similar surprise up its sleeve is the Invert checkbox (immediately below the Noise Type drop down). You might think that checking Invert would simply flip black and colored areas. Not exactly. As a matter of fact, the results in this case produce a texture that might remind you of neurons, or something in the cosmos.

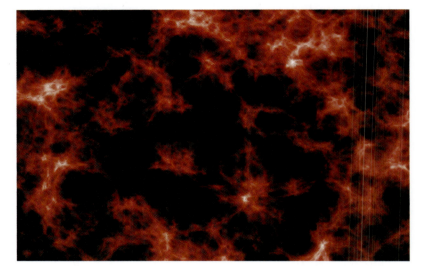

Figure 12.27 Checking the Invert checkbox creates a completely different texture.

Now it's time to look at the Transform options. Fractal Noise allows us to scale, rotate, move, and perform other transformations to our texture. These will come in handy as you try to create

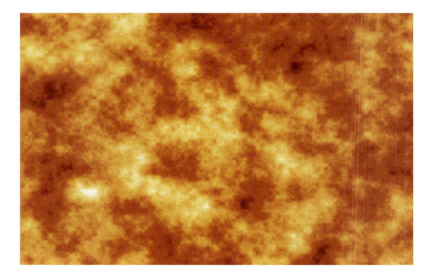

Figure 12.28 The default Fractal Noise settings, with the Colorama effect applied. Kinda looks like a freeze frame from a *Lethal Weapon* movie.

specific looks. We'll use them now to create fire from scratch with the Fractal Noise effect.

Once again, let's start over. Click the Reset button at the top of the Fractal Noise effect in the Effect Controls panel. This time, delete the Tritone effect. In its stead, apply the Colorama effect (covered back in Chapter 6). In the Output Cycle area of the Colorama effect, you'll find a Use Preset Palette drop down. Change the Use Preset Palette value to Fire. This will use fiery colors, which will help make our fire texture more believable.

In the Fractal Noise settings in the Effect Controls panel, change the Fractal Type to Dynamic Twist.

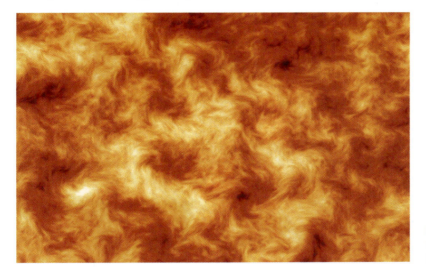

Figure 12.29 The texture with the Fractal Type drop down set to Dynamic Twist.

Next, take the Contrast value up to 250, and the Brightness value down to -40. This creates more black, maintains the contrast in our flames, and makes this texture look like flames instead of a big mass of fiery nothingness.

Transforming the Sub Layers

The properties in the Transform area allow you to transform the entire fractal pattern. However, if you open the Sub Settings area, you'll see another set of transform properties. These refer to the sub layers of noise. The Sub Influence value, for example, refers to the opacity of the sub layers. You can animate these sub layers by using the Sub Offset parameter. Or, you can offset these sub layers in perspective by selecting the Perspective Offset parameter in the Transform category, and then adjusting Offset Turbulence. This creates a parallax effect with the noise layers. This can also allow for animation when you don't want to adjust the texture with the Evolution property. You can also use Offset Turbulence to create the illusion of forces acting on your texture. Animating the Y axis of Offset Turbulence, for example, can create the illusion of the flames rising.

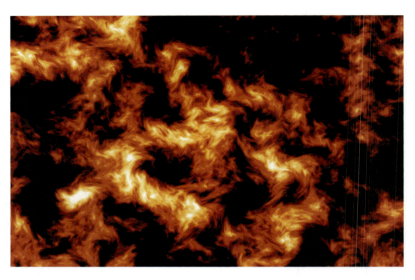

Figure 12.30 The texture after increasing contrast and reducing brightness.

Next, open up the Transform controls and uncheck the Uniform Scaling option. You will then be able to adjust the Scale Width and Scale Height properties (as opposed to just the Scale property, which scales the width and height proportionately. Adjust the Scale Width property down to 80, and the Scale Height property to about 700. This creates narrow, tall fire.

Figure 12.31 After deselecting Uniform Scaling, you can reduce the width and increase the height of the fire.

This is looking pretty good, but there's a little too much texture in the fire for my liking. I'm trying to create a match flame-type fire. How do we reduce texture? That's right. Take down the Complexity value. I'm going to reduce the Complexity value to 4.

Figure 12.32 Reducing the Complexity value to 4 creates smoother flames.

Now that we're in the ballpark here, you can adjust Evolution, Offset Turbulence (the Fractal Noise equivalent of a Position property), Contrast, and Brightness to taste. Once you're done, you can create a mask to isolate a flame if you'd like. Note that if you want to feather the mask with the Colorama effect applied, you'll probably want to precompose the solid layer before creating the mask (using the "Move all attributes ..." option in the Pre-compose dialog).

Figure 12.33 The final flame after precomposing the Solid layer, then applying a feathered mask.

Let's look at one more recipe, this time for fractal water. I want to start from scratch here, so I'm going to create a brand new solid. I'm then going to apply the Fractal Noise effect to this. Since we've got the hang of this by now, I'm going to go a little faster.

Change the Fractal Type to Smeary. Change the Noise Type to Spline. Select the Invert checkbox. Take the Complexity down to 2. We've still got some more adjusting to do, but we've already got something that looks like caustics on the bottom of a pool.

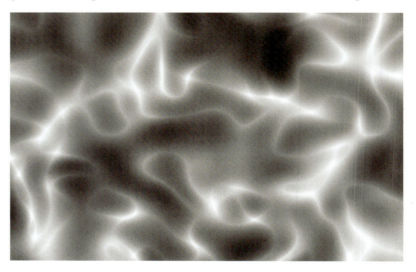

Figure 12.34 The water texture thus far.

Now, we're going to look at the Overflow drop down. This determines what happens to values at the top and bottom of the spectrum (e.g. white and black) when they are lightened or darkened, respectively. Allow HDR Results allows super white and

Figure 12.35 The water texture with Soft Clamp as the value for the Overflow property.

super black values. Clip creates a luminance ceiling, and high-lights that are brightened flatten out to white, and shadows that flatten to black when darkened. Soft Clamp equalizes all luminance values, creating very dull, low contrast textures.

The Overflow value we really want for this water is Wrap Back. This creates interesting patterns. When you have bright textures, and you brighten them further, Wrap Back causes these values to wrap back to black. Changing the Overflow value to Wrap Back won't cause any obvious change. To see what it does, I'm going to temporarily increase the Contrast value to an astronomical 1100.

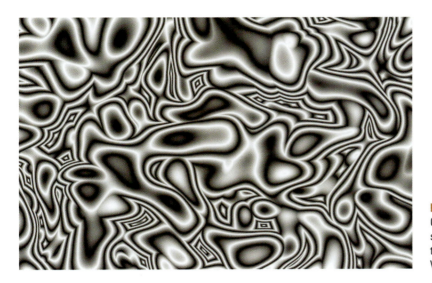

Figure 12.36 Taking the Contrast value to 1100, you can see the product of changing the Overflow drop down to Wrap Back.

This ultra high contrast was only a means to demonstrate the Wrap Back method of overflow. Leaving the Overflow value set to Wrap Back, take the Contrast value to 130, and adjust the Brightness value to 60. Then, open up the Transform area. Deselect Uniform Scaling, and then take the Scale Width value to 170, and the Scale Height value to 20. We now have a texture that looks a little like grayscale water.

Now all that's left is to add color. This time, I'm going to colorize this by applying the Color Balance effect. I'll take all of the red values to –100, and increase some of the green and blue values to taste. After playing with these values for a while, I determined that there was too much brightness. So, I reduced the Brightness value in the Fractal Noise effect to –20. Notice how the Wrap Back setting creates realistic highlights on the crests of the waves in our final result.

Figure 12.37 The grayscale water texture.

Figure 12.38 The result of the water texture, after colorizing it with the Color Balance effect and reducing its brightness.

Fractal Noise is just so flexible. All you have to do is apply another color correction effect (like Curves) to turn this water into billowy satin sheets.

Creating Seamless Loops of Fractal Noise

One of the greatest features of the Fractal Noise effect is its ability to create seamlessly looping patterns. These options can be found in the Evolution Options area towards the bottom of the effect. The steps used to recreate looping were covered in Chapter 9, when we looked at the very similar Cell Pattern effect.

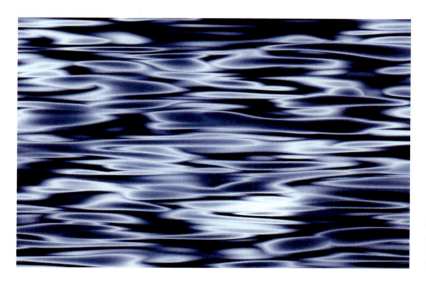

Figure 12.39 Adding additional color adjustments can create satin sheets from our water texture.

Included Animation Presets

In the exercise files folder included on the disc that accompanies this book, I've created a folder called Animation Presets. This folder contains animation presets I've created for you to use and experiment with. Most of these presets were created with Fractal Noise. Remember that you can also use these like little tutorials—apply them and see the settings I used to achieve a particular effect. Here's a sample of some of the Fractal Noise presets that I've created that are included with this book.

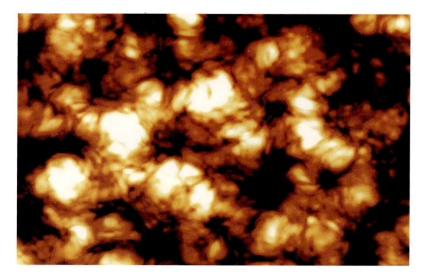

Figure 12.40 Another fiery texture; this time, an explosion.

Figure 12.41 By setting the Noise Type to Block and increasing the Scale Height value, you can create this popular animated bars look.

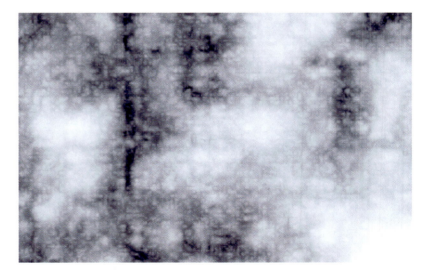

Figure 12.42 It's difficult to see in a still frame, but this an animated 3D city flyover. Using Perspective Offset, you can create what appears to be multiple animated layers of noise.

Figure 12.43 Creepy textures like this are a common use for Fractal Noise.

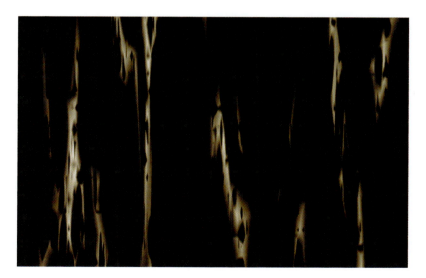

Figure 12.44 Another creepy texture. This one would be great as a Luma matte.

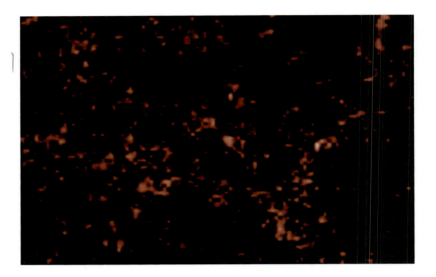

Figure 12.45 Spattered mud or blood.

Figure 12.46 Smoke and fog are textures that are often created with the Fractal Noise effect.

Fractal Noise in Action

I've recently had the privilege of working on a sci-fi series called *Causality* (www.watchcausality.com). It's a really well written show, a brilliant idea, and has really high level production value. The producers of the show (Ulterior Motives Productions) have given me special permission to use footage from the show in this book, as well as to distribute the project files along with the exercise files. Thank you *Causality* team!

So with this, I just wanted to show you a real world example of Fractal Noise in action. The tools and methods will be familiar to you, although the application might not be.

If you open the Causality.aep project from the Chapter 12 folder of the exercise files, you'll see the Fractal Noise in Action comp which contains a visual effects shot from the show.

Figure 12.47 A visual effects shot from *Causality* using Fractal Noise.

You can see the Fractal Noise effect in the vertical lines coming down and scanning the body of the actress. I decided to use Fractal Noise here because it would be a quick way to make streaks of light (by increasing the vertical scale in the Transform area in the Effect Controls panel). And I could also use the Evolution parameter to give life to the scanning waves. I liked the result and the producers were happy.

Note that I included a segment of the actual project files I used for this show in the exercise files. For this shot, I also used a couple of third-party effects, such as Particular and Optical Flares from VideoCopilot.net. So, if you don't have these effects installed, you'll get a notice from After Effects indicating the same, and your results won't look quite like mine. But the rest of the project will be there for you to take apart if you're interested (I also thought the color correction was pretty interesting, if you're interested in seeing what I did there).

The Match Grain Effect

The Match Grain effect is another Noise & Grain powerhouse. Like the Add Grain effect, the purpose here is to create noise (film grain). The difference is that the Match Grain effect takes that a step further to try and analyze the grain on another layer and recreate it on the current layer.

Open the Match Grain.aep project from the Chapter 12 folder of the exercise files. This is a project revisited from Chapter 2.

Figure 12.48 The Match Grain.aep project.

If you went through the effects in Chapter 2, you might remember that we made a sandwich of sorts with this comp. We have the video of my friend Paavo on his unicycle in the center (depth wise), and half of the garage scene in front of him, and the other half of the garage scene behind him. Ideally, we'd apply the Match Grain effect to the elements in front of Paavo, and behind him. But for now, we'll just apply the Match Grain effect to the garage scene behind him (aka layer 3). Because this grain is difficult to see, I'm going to zoom in to 400%. I'm also going to move the Preview Region over to the teal colored post next to Paavo. There is default noise applied, but it doesn't really match the video noise on the Paavo layer. Although, it does already look like a better composite because it adds some real world dirt to our pristine 3D garage scene. But the noise applied here is just too much.

The options here in the Match Grain effect are exactly the same as those we saw in the Add Grain effect earlier in this chapter. Because of that, I won't cover them again here. The big difference is the Noise Source Layer drop down. This is where you choose a layer with the noise you want the current layer to match. We've applied the Match Grain effect to the clean garage scene in the hopes of applying to it the same noise from the paavo balancing layer. So, from the Noise Source Layer drop down, choose the

Figure 12.49 Zoomed in, you can better see the default noise.

Paavo Balancing layer. Even though the Paavo layer doesn't have film grain (it has video noise and compression artifacts instead), it still applies the same type of noise to the garage scene. The effect is subtle splotchy effect, but most grain additions should not be blatant or obvious. This creates a more acceptable composite.

Figure 12.50 The garage scene with the grain matched to the noise on the layer with Paavo. The effect is subtle, but it is much better than a perfectly clean post.

The Median Effect

The Median effect might do a little better in the Stylize category. It basically looks at pixels in a given radius, and makes them all the average (median) color. The result can smooth noise,

I guess. But it really just makes things look smoother in an artsy kinda way.

Open the Median.aep project from the Chapter 12 folder of the exercise files. This project contains the fountain video we looked at earlier.

Figure 12.51 The Median.aep project.

The only property here is the Radius value. Take it to 3 to create an artistic stylized effect.

Figure 12.52 The results of applying the Median effect and increasing the Radius value to 3.

That's basically what the effect does. But one of the things that interesting about this effect is what happens when you take the Radius value really high (like 50). It blurs the image, but keeps the basic structure, including color, intact. This could be a great effect for a quick background if you have a photo, video, or even copyrighted footage with great colors. With a Radius value of 50, only the basic composition of the footage remains, along with the colors.

Figure 12.53 Taking the Radius value to 50 creates a cool blur effect that leaves colors and basic form intact.

The Noise Effect

The Noise effect should be familiar to most Photoshop users. It basically just adds noise. This noise can be used in a way similar to the grain created by the Add Grain effect—to add noise to footage. This effect renders so fast that it's almost imperceptible, but it also doesn't allow you much control over the noise like the Add Grain effect does. The noise created by the Noise effect can also be used for TV noise, because it auto-animates. It can also be used as the foundation for textures. Note that Fractal Noise can also be used for these purposes. However, although Fractal Noise will give you more control over properties, the Noise effect is much faster to setup and render.

Let's start fresh with a new composition. Create a new black solid layer, and apply the Noise effect to it. By default, the Noise effect doesn't make any obvious changes to your layer. To add noise, increase the Amount of Noise value. If you're adding noise to simulate film grain, this should be a very low number—perhaps

10 or less. So that the results are obvious, I'm going to take the Amount of Noise value to 100%.

Figure 12.54 The result of applying the Noise effect, and increase the Amount of Noise parameter to 100%.

I only use colored noise on rare occasion with this effect. Even when simulating film noise (which often has color in it), it just feels a little too colorful. You can create noise that is only black and white by deselecting the Use Color Noise checkbox. Now it's starting to look more like TV static. If you were to play this comp back now, you would see that this noise is randomly generated every frame, which creates an auto-animated result.

Figure 12.55 Black and white noise is created when the Use Color Noise checkbox is deselected.

The results are a little lackluster. We could add a Levels or Curves effect to increase contrast. Or, we could simply deselect the Clip Result Values option, which will make the noise more intense.

Figure 12.56 Deselecting Clip Result Values creates more contrasty noise.

Let's see how the Noise effect does at creating film grain. I'm going to import the Herbie in the Movies.jpg image from the Images folder in the Media folder of the exercise files. I'm going to apply the Noise effect directly to this image. I'll increase the Amount of Noise value to 8%, and leave the other settings as they are. This will create color noise, but at this low Amount of Noise value, the colored noise will provide the perfect amount of variation in the noise.

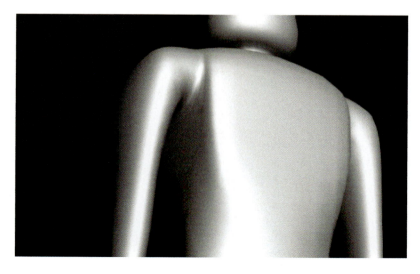

Figure 12.57 Applying the Noise effect at low noise levels can create fairly believable film grain.

Next, let's use the Noise effect to create animated TV noise. I have an image here of some kids next to a TV that is turned off.

Figure 12.58 The image of kids and a TV.

Next, I'll create a new black solid layer and apply the Noise effect to it. We're putting it on a separate layer so that we can distort it to be the size of the TV. In the Noise effect settings, increase the Amount of Noise value to 100%, deselect Use Color Noise, and deselect Clip Result Values. This creates a result identical to that seen in Figure 12.55. Next, apply the Corner Pin effect. Grab the 4 corner effect control points in the Corner Pin effect, and drag them in to match the 4 corners of the TV set.

Figure 12.59 Distort the edges of the noise layer with the Corner Pin effect, so that the noise layer roughly matches the TV screen.

I realize that this looks pretty weak. We're going to go for a quick fix here. Just take the noise layer into the Overlay blend mode (in the Timeline panel). Notice that this still creates noise over the head of the boy in front. If I were going to add finishing touches to this, I would precompose the noise layer, apply the Bezier Warp effect to apply a pincushion distortion to the edges of the noise layer (so that it more fully matches the edges of the TV), and then create a mask on the precomposed noise layer to remove the parts of noise that overlap the boys head.

Figure 12.60 Taking the blend mode of the noise layer to Overlay blends it into our scene, and allows the highlights in the TV to show through.

Finally, we can use the Noise effect to generate patterns. First apply the Noise effect to a black solid layer, increase Amount of Noise to 100%, and deselect both Use Color Noise and Clip Result Values. Next, apply the Directional Blur effect with the Direction value at 90 degrees, and the Blur Length value at 120. Polish this off with a Curves or Levels adjustment, if desired. When complete, you should have a standard brushed metal texture.

We can also create a cool looking star vortex with the same settings in the Noise effect. With the Directional Blur effect deleted (or turned off), apply the CC Radial Fast Blur effect (the default settings are fine). Then increase the amount of black and white in this result using Levels. Finally, polish it off with the Glow effect and a Color Balance effect with lowered blue values.

The Noise effect is often neglected because the results aren't very compelling when the effect is used by itself. But when used in conjunction with other effects, Noise becomes a valuable tool because of its flexibility and impressive render speed.

Figure 12.61 The brushed metal texture created with the Noise effect.

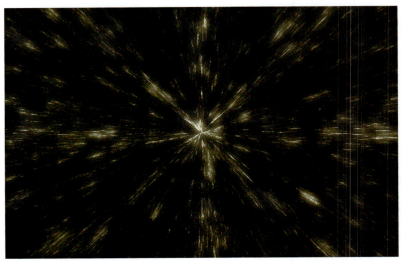

Figure 12.62 The galactic results using the Noise effect.

The Noise Alpha Effect

The Noise Alpha effect is another noise effect, but it allows you to add noise which adjusts the alpha channel. This is great for adding wear and tear to objects.

Open the Noise Alpha.aep project from the Chapter 12 folder in the exercise files. This contains a familiar ghost that I created in Illustrator, against a red solid background. The ugly contrast is intentional, so that the Noise Alpha effect results are more obvious.

Figure 12.63 The Noise Alpha.aep project.

Apply the Noise Alpha effect to the Ghost Body layer. You might notice that the Fast Blur effect has been applied to this layer as well. Just ignore that for now. With the Noise Alpha effect,

Figure 12.64 The Noise Alpha effect results after increasing the Amount value to 50%.

nothing happens until we bump up the Amount value. I'm going to start with a value of 50%. I'm also going to zoom in to 200%, so the results are more apparent in the following screenshots.

At first glance, this effect might appear to just add noise. But it's really creating holes in the layer's alpha channel, showing through to the red solid beneath.

The Noise drop down at the top specifies the type of noise. More importantly, it also specifies how the noise will animate, once it has been animated with the Random Seed/Noise Phase value.

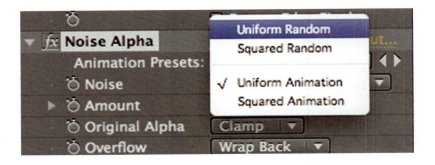

Figure 12.65 The options in the Noise drop down.

You'll notice that the top two settings end in "Random" and the bottom two settings end in "Animation." Both have a uniform option, and a squared option. Uniform noise has less contrast, while selecting a squared noise option adds contrast. The squared options are like deselecting the Clip Noise Values option in the Noise effect.

When one of the Random settings is chosen, the noise can be animated by using the Random Seed option at the bottom of the effect. Animating Random Seed creates new, random noise on every frame. If you select one of the Animation settings from the Noise drop down, the Random Seed value morphs into the Noise Phase value. Animating the Noise Phase value produces a much smoother interpolation, almost like the Evolution parameter in Fractal Noise. Note that opening the Noise Options area gives you access to noise cycling options to create seamlessly looping animations of noise. These function similarly to the cycling/looping options in Fractal Noise and Cell Pattern.

The other option that gives you a lot of control in the Noise Alpha effect is the Original Alpha drop down. These settings give you control over how the effect affects the layer's alpha channel. The default value is Clamp, which is very similar to Scale, only that Scale usually decreases the opacity of the layer. Take the Original Alpha value to Add to have noise in the alpha channel as well as noise on opaque pixels, too.

Figure 12.66 Changing the Original Alpha value to Add allows the Noise Alpha effect to put noise in the alpha channel of the layer.

The other option worth covering in this drop down is Edges. This allows the alpha channel to be reduced by noise, but only in the semi-transparent edges of the object. Currently, our layer doesn't have any semi-transparent edges. So, turn on the Fast Blur effect (already applied for you), and then change the Original Alpha value to Edges. You can then see the transparent noise in the edges of the layer. This can be really useful for creating edge effects like an animated corona around an object.

Figure 12.67 After blurring the layer with the Fast Blur effect and changing the Original Alpha value to Edges creates alpha noise in the edges of the layer only. Note that the layer here is zoomed in to 400%.

The Noise HLS Effect

The Noise HLS effect resides somewhere between the power and features of the Add Grain effect, and the simplicity and ease of use of the Noise effect. HLS stands for Hue, Lightness, and Saturation. This represents the parameters you can change to control the noise created by this effect. Another great advantage of this effect is that it allows you to control the size of the noise.

Open the project Noise HLS.aep from the Chapter 12 folder of the exercise files.

Figure 12.68 The Noise HLS.aep project.

Apply the Noise HLS effect (not the Noise HLS Auto effect) to this bird image. Notice that there isn't a simple noise amount slider to adjust here. The way that we add noise with this effect is to add noise to the hue of the image (with the Hue property), or to the lightness of the image (with the Lightness property), or to the saturation of the image (with the Saturation property). Put more simply, increase the Hue value to create colored noise, increase the Lightness value to create grayscale noise, and increase Saturation to boost the saturation of the hue noise. In this example, I'll increase both the Hue and Lightness values to 5. This will add a moderate amount of noise, balanced between black and white noise, and colored noise. You can add as much noise in each channel as you'd like (up to 1000%).

As with the Noise Alpha effect, there is a Noise drop down. The default is Uniform, but you can also select Squared, which creates

Figure 12.69 Increasing the Hue and Lightness properties to 5 creates a small amount of noise that has an even smaller amount of colored noise.

noise with more contrast. The third option in this drop down is Grain. This creates larger splotches of noise that are more like the grain seen in film.

Figure 12.70 Taking the Noise drop down to Grain creates larger granules of noise.

Once you've selected Grain as the Noise value you can then adjust the size of the noise using the Grain Size parameter. The noise can also be animated by setting keyframes or using expressions with the Noise Phase property.

The Noise HLS Auto Effect

The Noise HLS Auto effect is exactly the same as the Noise HLS effect, except that the Noise HLS Auto effect auto-animates. If you're looking for TV static noise, for example, you can apply this effect. And, as soon as you add any noise by increasing the Hue, Lightness, and/or Saturation values, the noise will automatically change every frame. You can control the speed of the noise by adjusting the Noise Animation parameter.

The Remove Grain Effect

The Remove Grain effect is cut from the same cloth as the powerful Add Grain and Match Grain effects that we looked at earlier in this chapter. The difference here is obviously that the purpose is to remove grain. Even though this effect can be time consuming to render, the results are quite impressive. The

Figure 12.71 The image in the Remove Grain.aep project.

Remove Grain effect can be particularly helpful when cleaning up noisy video footage.

Open the Remove Grain.aep project from the Chapter 12 folder of the exercise files. This project contains the image we saw earlier in this chapter of some kids standing next to a TV set.

When you zoom in to this image—say, to 100% of this very large image—we can see a lot of noise. This photo was taken with an ISO value of 1600—a colossal value that introduces a lot of noise.

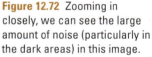

Figure 12.72 Zooming in closely, we can see the large amount of noise (particularly in the dark areas) in this image.

Apply the Remove Grain effect to this image. As with Add Grain and Match Grain, the render times for this effect are quite long, and so the effect only makes changes to the pixels in a preview region.

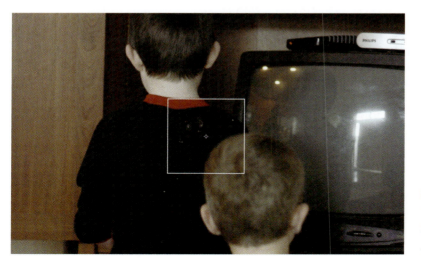

Figure 12.73 The results of applying the Remove Grain effect at the default settings. The results are only visible in the preview region.

Also, as with Add Grain and Match Grain, there are loads of parameters. We'll cover the essential ones. First off, know that the Remove Grain effect removes grain by examining certain points of your image. By default, it selects those sample points for you automatically, but if there are other places in your layer that are more noisy (dark areas, for example), you may wish to move the sample points around. To see the sample points (there are 8 by default), change the Viewing Mode to Noise Samples. The noise samples will show up on your image in the Composition panel as little white squares. At the bottom of the effect options in the Effect Controls panel, you can open up the Sampling area to adjust sample parameters. You can set your own sample points by changing the Sample Selection drop down in this area from Automatic to Manual. You can then change the values from 1 to 10 in the Noise Sample Points area.

Figure 12.74 The image with the Noise Samples visible (the little white squares).

Because of the way that noise typically gets stored in channels, you will probably want to reduce noise from channels independently. You can access this by opening the Noise Reduction Settings are, and then opening up the Channel Noise Reduction area inside. If you are getting varied results over time, you can adjust the properties in the Temporal Filtering area.

Another interesting and helpful feature of this effect is that it has its own built-in Unsharp Mask effect. It even has the same parameters as the Unsharp Mask in After Effects that we covered back in Chapter 4. Open up the Unsharp Mask area in the Effect Controls panel to restore details that were lost by the noise removal. As with Add Grain and Match Grain, change the Viewing Mode to Final Output to see the results of the effect on your entire image. Although I could've done more with sharpening and fine tuning to preserve details, even the rough results are very impressive.

My Favorite Noise Reducer

If you're serious about getting rid of noise and grain (isn't everyone, really?), then I highly recommend the Reduce Noise plugin from Neat Video (neatvideo.com). It probably has the best noise reduction I've ever seen. It takes a custom profile of your footage, keeps edges and details sharp, and also has its own sharpening, which looks fantastic. Be aware though that as of the last time I checked, there were many hosts for the Neat Video noise reducer (e.g. Premiere, After Effects, etc.), but they were all separate licenses (read: purchases).

Figure 12.75 The final result after removing grain from the image.

The Turbulent Noise Effect

The Turbulent Noise effect, introduced in After Effects CS4 is almost exactly like the Fractal Noise effect. It was created to have a more advanced noise pattern so that the results were more organic. When using this effect for the first time, After Effects veterans may notice how much faster it renders than Fractal Noise. That is because this effect is GPU accelerated. However, in After Effects CS4, the Fractal Noise effect was updated to be GPU accelerated as well.

The biggest difference between the Turbulent Noise effect and the Fractal Noise effect is that Turbulent Noise does not allow you to create seamlessly looped patterns. The ability to cycle evolutions is one of the most useful features of the Fractal Noise effect, and the lack of a similar feature in Turbulent Noise is a big deal breaker for me. From what I understand, the math behind the scenes with the Turbulent Noise effect is supposed to be much more advanced. Perhaps I need more time with this effect, but at the time of this writing, I haven't seen much to write home about. For most pattern generating tasks, I still turn to Fractal Noise as my texture maker of choice.

13

THE OBSOLETE EFFECTS

In After Effects CS4, a new effects category was created called Obsolete. Several old effects that are considered outdated were dumped in this desolate wasteland of an effects category. How can you recover from such a social stigma?

While the Obsolete effects may not be invited to the other effects' Christmas party, they might still serve a purpose. We'll cover them briefly in this chapter, just to be complete in covering every effect. But that doesn't mean that they're worthless. For most professionals, there are much better choices out there to accomplish everything that these Obsolete effects do. But if you find certain aspects of After Effects intimidating (such as the often daunting text animation engine), then you might actually find some help in the ghetto of After Effects' Obsolete effects.

The Basic 3D Effect

The Basic 3D effect (formerly in the Perspective category) was created before layers could exist in 3D space. It is used to simulate 3D motion. If you'd like to follow along, open the Basic 3D.aep project in the Chapter 13 folder, and apply the Basic 3D effect to the solid layer in the Grid comp. This solid contains only the Grid effect. Adjust the Swivel property to simulate rotation around the Y axis.

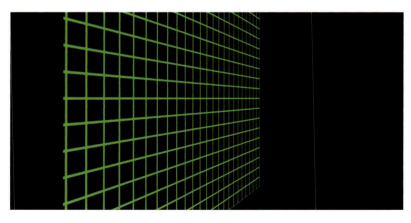

Figure 13.1 After adjusting the Swivel property with the Basic 3D effect.

Similarly, the Tilt value is the equivalent of X Rotation, and the Distance to Image property controls Z position. There are also a couple of other properties to fake what happens in 3D. Show Specular Highlight adds a tiny glint of light (that you can't control), and Draw Preview Wireframe shows a wireframe outline of the layer when the layer is in Draft quality.

While some of the effects in this category can still be helpful to new users because of their simplicity, the Basic 3D effect deserved its demotion in my opinion. It's just as easy to convert a 2D layer to a 3D layer in the Timeline panel, and use the 3D features there.

The Basic Text Effect

Another Obsolete effect with "basic" in its title—this can't be good. Actually, the Basic Text effect can be beneficial to those that find simple text animation in After Effects to be challenging. In the same way that Basic 3D was the only way to create 3D movement many moons ago, Basic Text used to be the only way to create text in After Effects.

Create a new project, a new comp, and a new solid. Unlike real After Effects text, Basic Text is an effect which must be applied to an existing layer. Though this can be of benefit in certain circumstances (such as when creating a luminance map to control an effect, and you want text to be a part of the map and you don't want to precompose), more often than not I like my text to be an independent layer. That way, I'll have access to blend modes, individual animation parameters, and more.

When you first apply the Basic Text effect, as well as many other effects in After Effects that deal with text, you are created with an archaic dialog box. This thing should be on display in a museum somewhere.

All joking aside (for the time being), in this dialog box, you enter your text in the large empty field in the area in the middle. Here you can also change the font, style, and alignment. To accept the text and adjust the effect, click OK. And after a while, you'll realize one of the biggest reasons that this effect is obsolete—you can only change this text by clicking the Edit Text … hot text button at the top of the Basic Text effect in the Effect Controls panel.

In the parameters of this effect, you'll find the most basic of basic properties, such as position, color, fill, stroke, and size.

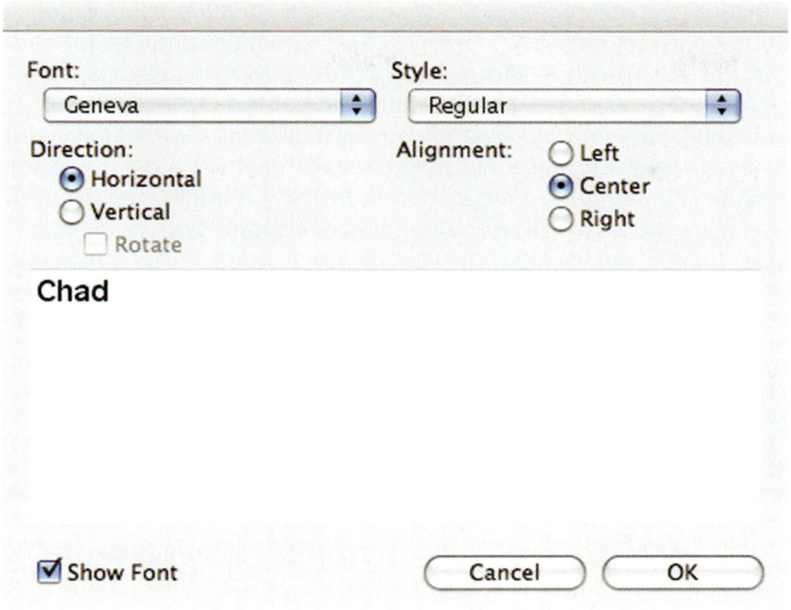

Figure 13.2 The old text entry dialog box, circa late 1990's, still seen in many text effects today. Conservation efforts are needed, as these dialog boxes are near extinction.

So why would you ever want to use this effect? I can only think of one reason. If you want to animate the tracking of a word (the horizontal spacing between all characters), it is a little easier to do with the Basic Text effect than it is with the powerful and complex text animation engine in After Effects. Of course, if you know what you're doing, then the text animation engine will yield much better results because of its amount of controls. But this might be good if you're just getting started.

The Lightning Effect

The Lightning effect creates lightning, as does the Advanced Lightning effect. One of the big differences between them is that Lightning auto-animates, and Advanced Lightning must be animated manually. Another big difference is in the quality of the lightning (the Advanced Lightning effect produces much better results). And the Advanced Lightning effect allows you to use the alpha channel with the lightning it creates. Figure 13.3 shows both types of lightning at their default values.

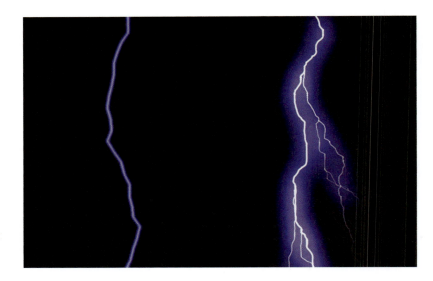

Figure 13.3 The quality of Lightning (on the left) is significantly different than that of Advanced Lightning (on the right).

Obviously the quality of the Advanced Lightning effect is far superior to the Lightning effect when going for realistic lightning. But what if you're going for something else? What about a quick spark? Lightning may be able to get a suitable job done faster, depending on the type of spark you're looking for.

I also like that the Lightning effect animates so wildly. In the Lightning.aep project you'll find in the Chapter 13 folder, I've fiddled around a bit with the Lightning effect. And by now, you've probably guessed that I just love coming up with interesting artistic patterns. So, I'll briefly give you the gist of what I did to come up with the image shown in Figure 13.4.

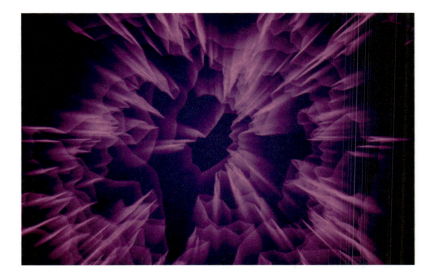

Figure 13.4 This is what happens when you cross too much free time with the Lightning effect.

I started with the Lightning effect and a solid background with a simple radial gradient. In the Lightning effect, I took down the Width and Core Width settings to their minimal values to shrink the lightning. I increase the Segments and Amplitude values to create lines that look more like graffiti than lightning. I duplicated the Lightning effect three times. And moved their Start Point and End Point positions to cover the screen.

Figure 13.5 The lightning project thus far.

I then added a CC Radial Fast Blur effect, followed by a Glow. I really liked the silky texture I got with this. It kind of reminded me of those ribbons of mineral deposits you see in rocks in Las Vegas gift shops.

Figure 13.6 The lightning after CC Radial Fast Blur and Glow.

My beef with the result now is that it is too subtle. It appears faded and washed out. So, to achieve the final result seen in Figure 13.4, I added an adjustment layer, and added a Levels effect, a Curves effect, and a Color Balance effect. These helped to punch the contrast and color.

Even though this looks soft and pretty, the animation built into the Lightning effect will make this jagged and wild. We can smooth it out a little bit by taking down the Speed value, and increasing the Stability value. But those properties only allow you a minimal amount of control. Which brings us to the final point about this effect—in most cases, it's better to use Advanced Lightning (in the Generate category).

The Path Text Effect

Like Basic Text, the Path Text effect used to be in the Text category. Honestly, I'm not sure how I feel about this effect being labeled as obsolete. This is without question the best of the Obsolete effects, and if text animation in After Effects intimidates you, the Path Text effect can be a great asset. It's almost like the Path Text effect is the *Cliff Notes* version of the entire text animation engine, with additional built-in path tools.

When you first apply the effect (again to a layer, like a solid, because it is an effect), you are greeted with a watered down version of the Edit Text dialog box we saw with Basic Text. And, as with Basic Text, you also can only edit text in the Path Text effect by clicking the same Edit Text button at the top of this effect in the Effect Controls panel.

However, after entering text and clicking OK, we quickly see how powerful this effect can be, just by the sheer volume of parameters here. Also, in the Composition panel, we notice that the Path Text has also created a bezier path for our text to exist on. The path also has nice big circles around the anchor points as well as the handles, which are also effect control points.

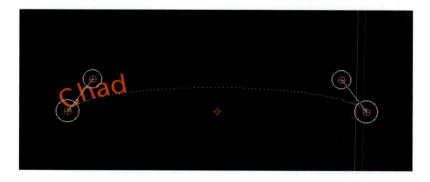

Figure 13.7 The Path Text effect creates its own path automatically.

In the Path Options area, you can change the Shape Type value to a circle or a straight line. Or you can use the Custom Path value in this area to choose a mask that you've created on the layer you've applied the Path Text effect to.

The next several options are fairly self-explanatory, so I'm going to skip down to the Paragraph properties. With the default settings, the Left Margin property determines how many pixels away from the left edge of the path that the text is. Baseline Shift allows you to increase the number of pixels that the text rises up from the baseline (the imaginary line that text sits on).

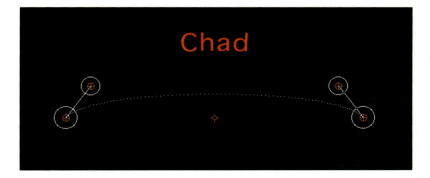

Figure 13.8 Increasing the Left Margin value moves the text to the right, and increasing the Baseline Shift value raises it up from the path.

Open up the Advanced area to really start having some fun with this effect. At the top of this area is the Visible Characters property. This is exactly what it sounds like—it determines how many characters are visible. The default value is a rather high 1024. If I take this value to something like two, then only two of my characters are visible. This is kind of like a really weak version of the Range Selectors found on text layers. You can use this property to animated text appearing, one character at a time.

Finally, we come to the Jitter Settings area. In the world of After Effects, two of my favorite words are jitter and wiggle.

Figure 13.9 My Path Text with the Visible Characters property at a value of 2.

Both words are usually synonyms for randomness, which is a great thing in my book. Jitter (as in the case with Card Wipe and others) can also have the added meaning that it won't wiggle until adjusted. So, if you were to play your composition with this effect at its default settings, there wouldn't be any animation. But if you adjust any of the jitter properties here, they will auto-animate. The number you input for jitter determines the range of how much jittered values are allowed to randomize.

- Baseline Jitter Max—randomizes baseline shift for each character. This is like making all the characters jump up and down independently.
- Kerning Jitter Max—randomizes the kerning of all characters (tracking). Use this to randomize the space between characters, as if your text was caught in a big texty mosh pit.
- Rotation Jitter Max—randomizes rotation for each character. Note that each character rotates around the layer's anchor point. This is another big advantage of text layer animation—each character can rotate around its own anchor point. Such is not the case here.
- Scale Jitter Max—randomizes the size of each character. As with rotation, the characters scale out from the layer's anchor point.

Figure 13.10 shows my final result with this effect after changing the font, the shape of the path, the Paragraph properties, and the Jitter Settings properties.

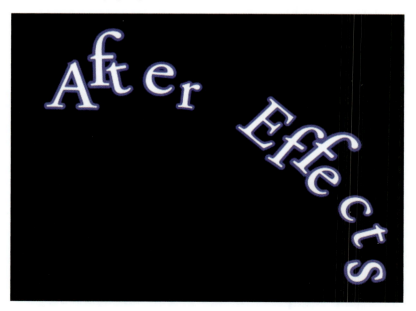

Figure 13.10 After adjusting the jitter values and other properties, my text has a life of its own. And all of this animates without any keyframing!

Look folks, at the end of the day, we all know that the animation on text layers offers far more control and power than anything we could do with the Path Text effect. But many times, we just want to do something very quickly and text layer animation is just too much work. When using text layer animation for simple jobs I feel like I'm powering up a desktop computer to use its calculator to add up my pocket change. It's just a lot more than I need. If you're just trying to create a simple bouncy, random animation with simple text, or if you want it to wrap around an arc that is already created for you, the Path Text effect may not be quite so obsolete after all.

14

THE PERSPECTIVE EFFECTS

The king of the Perspective effects is without question the 3D Camera Tracker effect, introduced in After Effects CS6. It's extremely powerful and remarkably easy to use.

Most of the other Perspective effects attempt to create the illusion of 3D, typically with things like beveled edges and shadows. These effects are somewhat obsolete, especially with the introduction of Photoshop's layer styles in After Effects CS3. Layer styles allow you to add the Bevel and Emboss effect, which is much more powerful (and looks much better) than the bevel effects in this category.

However, the big problem with these layer styles is that they prohibit layers that they are applied to from intersecting in 3D space. So if you're looking for 3D effects to apply to 3D layers, the Perspective effects can come in handy. Also, as we go through this brief chapter, I'll be giving you some pointers for bevels and shadows that will work with either the effect or the layer style. The 3D Glasses and Radial Shadow effects are also quite unique effects that cannot be duplicated with layer styles.

While we're talking about perspective and 3D in After Effects, I should probably bring up the new 3D capabilities in After Effects CS6, which allow you to create truly three-dimensional objects and text. However, this feature can be really clunky and slow, and virtually impossible to use unless you have an Adobe certified, CUDA-enabled Nvidia graphics card.

The 3D Camera Tracker Effect

The 3D Camera Tracker effect is used to examine a shot, and determine what a moving camera was doing. You just apply it to a clip that was shot with a moving camera, and it goes to work. Once it has completed its analysis, it is ready to create an After Effects camera that mimics the real world camera the footage was shot with! Not only that, but you can also use the individual points that the effect used in its analysis to create 3D text layers, solids, nulls, and shadow catchers. It's truly incredible. Let's look at how this works.

Open the 3D Camera Tracker.aep project from the Chapter 14 folder of the exercise files. This contains a shot with a shaky jib, craning up from some children playing, up to the sky.

Figure 14.1 A screenshot from both the beginning and the end of the jib sequence.

Go to the 3D Camera Tracker START comp. There's only one visible layer: the jib sequence. Apply the 3D Camera Tracker effect to this layer. The 3D Camera Tracker begins to get to work right away. But it works in the background, so you're free to work on other layers or comps within After Effects while it does its thing.

When it has completed its analysis, it will move on to the (usually brief) Solving Camera phase. In some rare cases, the camera solving portion might fail. You can usually fix this by giving After Effects more information about your shot. Most shots from professional cameras have a fixed angle of view, meaning that they don't zoom in and out. However, if your shot does, you can change the Shot Type drop down from Fixed Angle of View to Variable Zoom. You might also notice in this drop down that you can specify an angle of view as well. However, I've never found this to be useful because the absolute angle of view changes based on sensor size, which is different from camera to camera. So even if you know the focal length of the lens used, you'll need to do some more calculations in order to get the exact angle of view for your shot. Thankfully, After Effects usually just "gets it" and doesn't need any extra angle of view information on most shots with a fixed angle. If you do need to change the Shot Type value, you'll need to reanalyze the footage if you've already done so.

In the Advanced section at the bottom of the effect in the Effect Controls panel, you can also change the value in the Solve Method drop down to give After Effects more information about your shot. I usually only mess with this setting (or any of these settings, actually) if After Effects can't understand my shot. You might also find that you get better results by checking the Detailed Analysis checkbox, also in the Advanced section of this effect.

Many ways to track

In addition to tracking the camera by applying the 3D Camera Tracker effect, there are a host of other ways to accomplish the same task. For example, you can right click on a trackable layer and choose Track Camera. You could also choose Track Camera from the Animation menu at the top of the interface. And you can also now choose Track Camera from the redesigned Tracker panel, as seen in Figure 14.2. Regardless of the method chosen, the 3D Camera Tracker effect is applied to the layer and the analysis immediately begins.

When your shot has been successfully analyzed and solved, there will be little track points all over the place. These are the points that After Effects has tracked to figure out where the camera is. What's that, you say? You don't see any points? That actually happens all the time, and I used this footage in particular because it creates very small track points. By default, the Show Track Points value in the effect is set to 3D Solved, which essentially means that the points get smaller as they go farther back in Z space. In this case, they're all pretty far away. So, you can either switch the Show Track Points value from 3D Solved to 2D Source (which makes all track points the same size), or you can keep the perspective in the track points by increasing the Track Point Size value. Figure 14.3 shows what these track points look like with the Track Point Size cranked way up to 1200%.

Figure 14.2 You can choose to do a camera track from right inside the Tracker panel.

Figure 14.3 With the Track Point Size value raised to 1200%, you can not only see the track points more clearly, but the tiny track points way in the back are now visible.

Now we're ready to do some cool stuff. With the effect selected in the Effect Controls panel AND with the Selection tool selected, click and drag a marquee around (or shift click) some of those track points. I chose a few along the fence. One of the neatest little features here is that a little target appears to show you the 3D plane that it's thinking that you want. If your target is askew from the way you want it, then whatever you create based on those points will likewise be askew. I kept adding points and/or reselecting until I got a target that was flush with the fence, as seen in Figure 14.4. Note that if your targets are too small (or large), you can adjust their size using the Target Size value in the effect.

The track points' vanishing act!

As you work with the 3D Camera Tracker effect, you'll notice that you'll frequently lose the track points. In order to see them, you'll need to have the EFFECT selected in the Effect Controls panel. Having the layer selected is not enough.

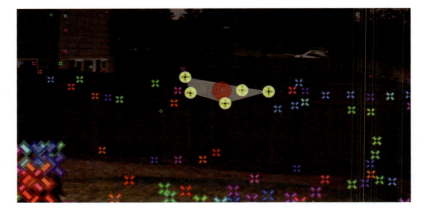

Figure 14.4 After selecting track points, I get a target flush with the fence, letting me know that After Effects "understands" the plane that I want to put some 3D text on.

What we want to do is add some text that sticks to this wall. After getting that target with your track points selected, right click and you'll see all kinds of things that we can do with these points. We can create text, a solid, a null, a shadow catcher, cameras for either of those, and we can also create individual text layers, solids, and nulls for each of those selected track points (five in my case) in one click of a button. For this example, choose Create Text and Camera. I chose to type the text "It was a good day …," but you can choose whatever you want in whatever font you'd like. I also used the RGB values 120,110,110 respectively, but again, feel free to use your own color scheme.

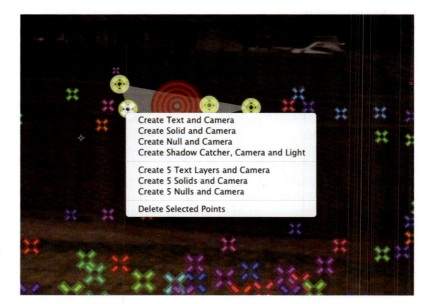

Figure 14.5 With track points selected, right clicking will give you a menu that allows you to create objects that will exist at that same point in 3D space!

Next, you'll probably want to use the Rotate tool (shortcut: W) to set the correct orientation of the text. You can also move the text along either the X axis (side to side) or the Y axis (up and down), but DO NOT move it along the Z axis (towards you and away from you) or it will not appear to be attached to the fence. We could add some lighting (or at least fake it with a gradient) and maybe some motion blur or some defocusing blur (perhaps with the Fast Blur effect), but even as it is, it looks pretty good and tracks extremely well with the fence.

Figure 14.6 As you can see in this frame later in the composition, the text sticks to the fence quite nicely.

I decided to take this a little further and create more text in the latter half of the footage. This time, I used track points in the trees at the end of the sequence. Not that the track points in these trees are only visible with Show Track Points set to 2D Source, as the maximum Track Point Size of 10000% still did not make them visible. I also added a little blur and color correction to these text layers (and converted them to shape layers so you wouldn't have any font issues). You can see my results in the 3D Camera Tracker FINISH comp in this project, if you're interested.

You could use these track points to create a solid that becomes a sign that replaces a billboard. Or you could use these track points to create a null that you attach footage to for compositing. The point is that this effect gives you the tools to stick stuff into video footage to create the illusion that it was there already. And it does a pretty freaking amazing job at that.

The 3D Glasses Effect

The 3D Glasses effect is a unique effect in this category, and it typically caters to a very specific audience, although 3D is becoming more and more common. The purpose of the effect is to create anaglyphic video. Anaglyphic video displays offset red and blue colors and is intended for a viewer wearing 3D glasses, which usually have a blue overlay over one eye, and a red overlay over the other. This forces one eye to see one image, and the other eye to see another, and this creates the illusion of three-dimensional depth. Although you can make 3D motion graphics on your own in After Effects, 3D video is typically created by using two clips from a stereoscopic camera or from footage created with multiple virtual cameras in a 3D application. You can then use this effect to combine those elements into a single stereoscopic file.

So, in this section, I'll show you how to create a quick sample of an anaglyphic video. Even if your workflow doesn't include stereoscopic 3D, this look is so retro and recognizable, you may find it useful. To follow along with me, open up the After Effects project 3D Glasses.aep from the Chapter 14 folder of the exercise files. This project contains a clip from the public domain horror classic, *Night of the Living Dead*. Who better than zombies to teach us about creating anaglyphic video?

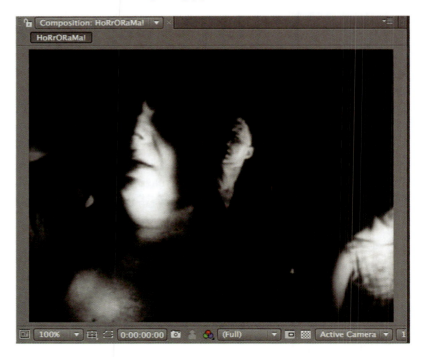

Figure 14.7 The HoRrORaMa! composition in the 3D Glasses .aep project.

There are two copies of the same clip in the HoRrORaMa! composition, simply offset in time. The LEFT layer will become what viewers see out of their left eye, the RIGHT layer will be seen in the right eye. First, select the LEFT layer, and apply the

3D Glasses effect to it. In the Effect Controls panel, change the Left View value to the LEFT layer, and the Right View value to the RIGHT layer. The composition will now appear split with the LEFT layer on the left half of the composition, and the RIGHT layer on the right. This is because the 3D View property in the 3D Glasses effect is set to Stereo Pair. While this view is useful for comparing the left view with the right view, this is primarily a working view only. Change the 3D View property to Balanced Colored Red Blue to complete the effect.

Offsetting the blue and red views

You can use the Convergence Offset property in the 3D Glasses effect to control the offset of the blue and red colored views. Adjust this property if the final result has too much depth (or not enough) after viewing with 3D glasses. Also be aware that the audience's distance from the viewing surface can also affect the 3D depth effect.

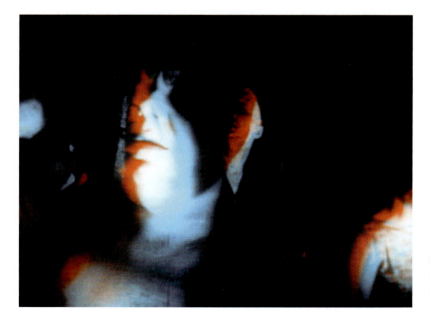

Figure 14.8 The final 3D Glasses settings.

Figure 14.9 After creating the anaglyphic effect. Now you just need some 3D glasses and some popcorn.

The Bevel Alpha Effect

Before we get into the Bevel Alpha and Bevel Edges effects, just remember again that these both pale in comparison to the layer styles in After Effects. They should only be used when you're going for a beveled look to 3D layers that you want to intersect each other in 3D space.

The Bevel Alpha effect creates the illusion of 3D by adding highlights and shadows around the edges of the layer it's applied to. I've created a little project called Bevel Alpha.aep you'll find in the Chapter 14 folder if you'd like to play along here. Essentially all we have here is some text that has been converted to a Shape layer.

Figure 14.10 The Bevel Alpha .aep proejct.

Apply the Bevel Alpha effect to the BEVEL ME Outlines layer. Instantly, you'll notice the highlights and shadows around the edges of the layer that give the illusion of 3D depth.

Figure 14.11 The Bevel Alpha effect applied to the layer.

The four properties this effect has are quite simple. Edge Thickness controls how large the "bevel" is, although the effect starts to kind of fall apart when you increase it too much. The shadows and highlights start to overlap in unnatural ways.

Figure 14.12 After increasing the Edge Thickness value to 6, we see some visual ugliness in the way shadows and highlights overlap.

Light Angle controls what direction the light is shining from. This can be animated to create the illusion that a moving light is being shined on the layer.

Light color controls the color, but it doesn't work too well. It only tints the highlights, and most colors neutralize the shadows, which essentially removes the bevel.

Light Intensity increases the contrast of the highlights and shadows of the bevel. This is good to use when you want to create the illusion that there is brighter light shining on an object.

Tricks with Beveled Layers

Whether you're using the more powerful Bevel and Emboss layer style effect, or one of these bevel effects, the beveling effect is great for subtle text effects like our example here because you can animate something simple like the Light Angle, or maybe use a wiggle expression to control the Light Intensity value. Another idea is to apply a composition light to a layer with a bevel effect. The bevel effect (whether it's an effect or a layer style) will not respond to the light. Normally, this would be terrible, but in this case, areas of the beveled object that are in the dark will still show a subtle highlight. It's a cool effect. See Figure 14.7 for an example of the bevel effect still visible in the dark.

Figure 14.13 The layer with Bevel Alpha and a composition light applied. Notice that the effect does not respect the light, making it glow in the dark.

Making buttons

This chiseled bevel look is great for creating buttons, say for DVD output. This is becoming much more common because Adobe Encore (which integrates with After Effects) can create Flash movies in addition to optical media, such as DVD and Blu-ray.

The Bevel Edges Effect

For the Bevel Edges effect, I'm going to open up the Bevel Edges.aep project in the Chapter 14 folder. It's just a simple rectangular shape layer if you'd prefer to create it from scratch. Once you apply the Bevel Edges effect to this flat rectangle, you'll see that this is a much more intense chisel-type bevel than what we saw with the Bevel Alpha effect.

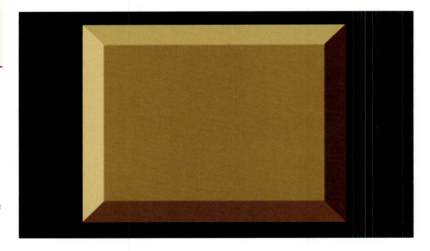

Figure 14.14 A simple rectangle with the Bevel Edges effect applied to it.

The four properties available with the Bevel Edges effect are the exact same properties available with the Bevel Alpha effect and they do the same thing, so I won't recap them here.

But I will point out a significant difference between these two bevel effects. The difference is in their name. Bevel Alpha bevels an object around its alpha channel. The Bevel Edges effect curiously bevels the edges of the entire layer. Figure 14.9 shows what happens when we apply Bevel Edges to the text in the BEVEL ME composition (also included in the Bevel Edges project for convenience).

Figure 14.15 Bevel Edges applies a bevel effect around the edges of the entire layer.

The Drop Shadow Effect

If there was a Hollywood Walk of Fame for overused effects, the first effect to win the honor would be, without a doubt, Drop Shadow, followed closely by Lens Flare. The Drop Shadow effect adds a shadow to an object (typically underneath it), to create the illusion that the object is floating off of the surface. Drop shadows in general help an object to stand out from its background.

If you'd like some practice, you can open up the project Drop Shadow.aep from the Chapter 14 folder. Basically we have some green text on a light gray background. These colors are making this text harder to read than it should be.

Figure 14.16 The Drop Shadow .aep project.

So we're going to take this text, and drop shadow it like it's hot. Apply the Drop Shadow effect to the Drop it … Outlines layer. Notice how it instantly makes the text stand out from the background layer.

Differences Between Layer Styles and Effects

In almost every instance, layer styles are significantly more powerful than effects are. So, what are the differences between Drop Shadow the layer style and Drop Shadow the effect? The Drop Shadow layer style adds more blending options, gives you the ability to use Global Lighting, adjust Spread independently of the blur of the shadow, and the ability to add noise to the shadow. However, the Drop Shadow effect gives you the option to view the shadow only. This allows you to duplicate a layer, and have its drop shadow as a separate, autonomous layer. You can then apply warp effects to the drop shadow layer to give the illusion that the shadow of the main object is being cast onto a more complex surface.

Figure 14.17 The same project with the Drop Shadow effect applied with the default settings.

The Shadow Color and Opacity properties are self-explanatory. Direction is easy to grasp, except it's backwards from what you might think (maybe it's just backwards from the way I think). With the bevel effects, the similar angle control determined what direction the light was coming from. In the Drop Shadow effect, the Direction parameter dictates where the shadow is in relation to the layer. Or, in other words, where the light is pointing towards.

The next property is Distance. This controls how far away the shadow is from the layer. As you increase the distance of a shadow from the thing that is supposed to be casting the shadow, it gives the illusion that the object is floating farther off the surface. You can see the result of this in Figure 14.18.

Figure 14.18 The shadow after increasing the Distance value, as well as increasing the opacity and softness of the shadow.

The Softness parameter is like a blur for the shadow. Adjust the color, opacity, and softness of the shadow to create a realistic composite.

The Radial Shadow Effect

The Radial Shadow effect appears at first glance to be the identical twin to the Drop Shadow effect. But in reality, Radial Shadow is more like Drop Shadow's older, cooler pro-snowboarder cousin. Radial Shadow allows you to create a shadow as if it were being created from a three-dimensional light source. This is great for creating a shadow from 3D layers onto 2D objects, because 2D objects won't accept shadows from 3D layers and lights. The Radial Shadow synthesizes another great feature that is reserved for 3D layers: Light Transmission. Light Transmission allows you to create shadows based on the color of a layer. Radial Shadow doesn't quite get that cool, but it will allow you to create color shadows that vary in intensity based on the opacity of the alpha channel.

If you'd like to follow along, I've created the Radial Shadow .aep project in the Chapter 14 folder of the exercise files. This contains a red window with some variations in its alpha channel. Before we apply the effect, let's solo the Art Window layer and choose Alpha from the Show Channel and Color Management Settings drop down at the bottom of the Composition panel (the icon that looks like overlapping red, green, and blue circles). This will show us only the alpha channel of the Art Window layer which will give us a window (no pun intended) into what's happening with the transparency here.

Figure 14.19 The alpha channel of the Art Window layer.

The white areas indicate where the layer is completely opaque. The two rectangles that are completely black indicate where the layer is completely transparent. The three dark, wide bars, and the three light gray rectangles are areas of partial transparency. That's important to remember going forward. You can now change the channel view back to the RGB composite view, and deselect solo from the Art Window layer. Apply the Radial Shadow effect to the Art Window layer.

At first, this resembles the Drop Shadow effect, except that it will not go beyond the boundaries of the layer. To fix this, click the Resize Layer checkbox at the bottom of the Radial Shadow effect in the Effect Controls panel. Note that if you apply this effect to a layer without any transparency, you might not see anything until you check the Resize Layer checkbox.

One of the properties that really makes this effect stick out is Light Source. Instead of giving us only a light direction, we can actually specify exactly where our light source is. This parameter also has an effect control point, which means that we paste tracking data into Radial Shadow. And, because Light Source has both an X and a Y value, we can easily link this property to things that we might use as a light source, such as the Flare Center value of the Lens Flare effect.

The other really exciting property that sets Radial Shadow apart from other shadows is the Render drop down list. Change the Render value from Regular to Glass Edge. This allows the color of the layer to be used in the shadow, depending on the alpha channel of the layer. So, in Figure 14.20, you can see the red

Figure 14.20 Changing the Render value to Glass Edge creates a stained glass effect where there are semi-transparent areas of the layer.

of the layer showing in the shadow where there are semitransparent areas in the alpha channel. This creates the illusion of stained glass. The Color Influence value controls how much color is allowed to be used in the shadow, where a higher value results in more color and a lower value desaturates the shadow.

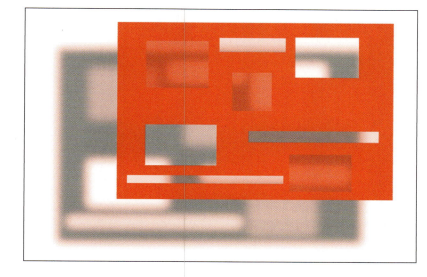

Figure 14.21 Increasing the Softness value while Glass Edge is selected as the Render value adds color to the edges.

One quirk that you might notice with this effect before too long is that when you increase the softness value with Render set to Glass Edge, you'll see the color of the layer in the edges. For those of you that don't find this desirable, I haven't found a workaround for this yet. It's caused because anti-aliased edges have color applied to them under the "rules" of Glass Edge, and added Softness adds more blur to the edges. So, under the eternal decree of Glass Edge, that which hath been blurred, shall be colored, saith the Glass Edge.

15

THE SIMULATION EFFECTS

The Simulation effects are pound for pound the most powerful effects in After Effects. They attempt to create real-world circumstances and behaviors, such as explosions, caustics, and other particle effects. The Simulation effects have a learning curve (and render time) that is usually steeper than most effects in other categories, but these effects can take the art that you produce in After Effects to a whole new level. Because of their overwhelming complexity, we're not going to cover these effects in extreme detail. Effects like Particle Playground could probably have an entire book written about them alone. My attempt here is to spark your creativity, give you a solid foundation, and give you enough information to learn the minutiae (and the extent of the creative possibilities) on your own.

The Card Dance Effect

The Card Dance effect is the more powerful sibling to the Card Wipe effect, discussed later in Chapter 19. For more information on most of the properties here (the ones in common with Card Wipe), consult Chapter 19. And while you're skipping ahead to brush up for the Card Wipe effect, you might also want to jump to Chapter 23 (the chapter on using maps) because the real power and benefit of the Card Dance effect is the way it uses maps to control properties.

The Card Dance effect turns a layer in a bunch of cards. This may seem simplistic or even pointless, but there are such powerful parameters here, that this effect should not be ignored. We can use maps (movies even!) to control how various properties of the cards behave. We can control the width and height (and therefore, the size) of the cards, making them more like tiny dots if we desire.

Another one of the extremely powerful aspects of this effect is that it operates in 3D. As with the Shatter property covered later in this chapter, Card Dance has a built-in camera that you can move around in 3D space, or you can use the comp camera. Also, like Shatter, it has Lighting and Material options as well.

To get some practice with this effect, open up the Card Dance .aep project from the Chapter 15 folder of the exercise files. This project contains an unflattering picture of me that we've looked at in other places in this book.

Figure 15.1 The card dance.aep project.

Equally important is the other layer in this project (in the Card Dance comp), Black and White, which is currently obscured by the Chad layer. The Black and White layer is the map that we'll be using to control Card Dance properties. It doesn't need to be visible, so once you've seen it and know what it looks like, you can click this layer's eye icon in the Timeline panel to turn off its visibility.

Figure 15.2 The black and white layer in the card dance comp.

Apply the Card Dance effect to the Chad layer. The options at the top of the Card Dance effect in the Effect Controls panel allow you to set the total number of cards by adjusting the number of rows and columns. However, you won't be able to see the individual cards until you adjust one of the properties in the position, rotation, or scale areas. And even then, you can't see what's *really* going on. So, let's assign the Gradient Layer 1 drop down to the Black and White layer.

Notice that there are two different gradient layers that you can choose for this effect: Gradient Layer 1 and Gradient Layer 2. All of the position, rotation, and scale values can use an attribute from either of these two gradient layers as a map. Of course my favorite property here is Z position, which creates three-dimensional movement.

Open up the Z Position area. Like all position, rotation, and scale properties in the Card Dance effect, you'll see a Source drop down—where you choose the gradient layer and attribute to use to control the current property, a Multiplier property—which controls how much the Source value affects the current property, and then an Offset value which offsets the values, if needed.

From the Source drop down, you'll see an almost intimidating list of options. Again, you can use any attribute from either gradient layer to control each property. You can use each gradient layer and each attribute as often as you wish. In this case, I'm going to select Intensity 1, which will use the luminance of the first gradient layer. If we were using a second gradient layer, we could control this value with its intensity by choosing Intensity 2.

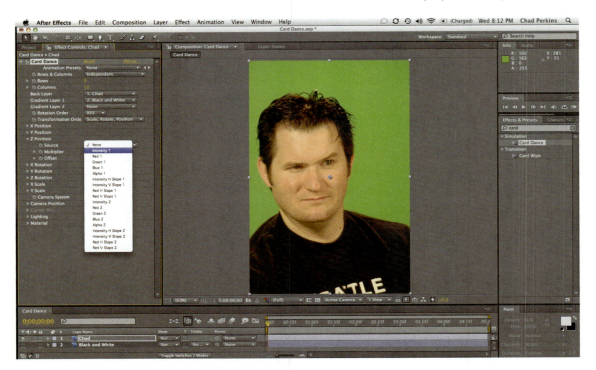

Figure 15.3 The Source drop down, common to all transform properties. This is where you select the gradient layer attribute to use to control this property. The 1 or 2 determines which gradient layer to take the attribute from.

Taking the Source value to Intensity 1 produces an instant result. But what is it doing?

Figure 15.4 The default results of the changing the Z position>Source drop down to intensity 1.

First of all, let's increase the number of cards by increasing both the Rows value and the Columns value to 100. This makes the cards much smaller and appears to create a more organic result. However, the original, lower Rows and Columns value could have created some cool motion graphics as well.

Figure 15.5 Increasing the number of rows and columns makes the cards smaller, almost like increasing the resolution of the result.

OK, so these results are a little creepy. Hang in there just a little longer. To more completely see what's going on here (and to be wowed and dazzled by the Card Dance effect), open the Camera Position controls in the Effect Controls panel, and increase the Y Rotation value to +30. This allows you to see how the cards have been moved in position along the Z axis, based on the brightness values of the Black and White layer. For example, my gratuitous nose is white on the Black and White layer, so the cards over my nose are the front most cards.

Figure 15.6 With the camera rotated, you can see the three-dimensional results of the Card Dance effect.

To make these results more intense, increase the Multiplier value to 1.6. This will create a more intense displacement of these cards along the Z axis.

What if we wanted to move this entire piece back in Z space? That is what the Offset parameter is for. It shifts all of the values

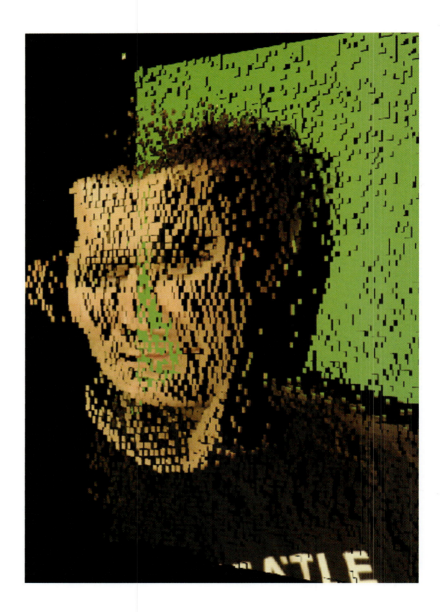

Figure 15.7 Increasing the multiplier makes values more intense.

of a given property (Z position, in this case). I'm going to take the Offset value to about −2.

If we take the Multiplier value to a negative number, the brightest pixels in the Black and White map will become the farthest away. In Figure 15.9, I've used a Multiplier value of −10, and an Offset value of −4. I've also reset the Camera Position>Y Rotation value to 0 degrees.

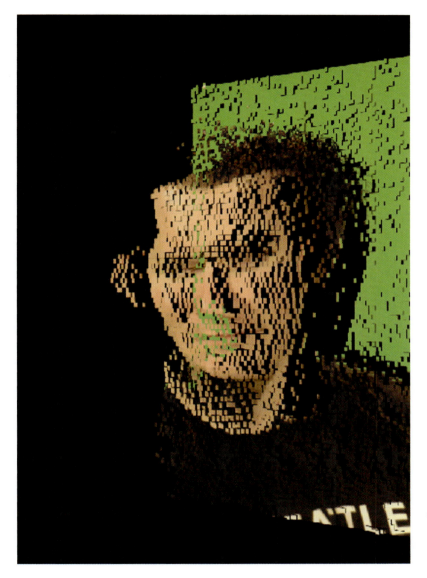

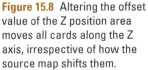

Figure 15.8 Altering the offset value of the Z position area moves all cards along the Z axis, irrespective of how the source map shifts them.

Card Dance is capable of creating some really spectacular visual effects. As with Card Wipe, we can create a grid of images, and then use the same number of rows and columns to distribute each image on a separate card. We can also create stunning motion graphics by having footage explode into a flurry of cards, or we can animate a huge, chaotic field of cards to have them gather into an image.

Figure 15.9 Negative multiplier values can displace pixels in the opposite direction.

The Caustics Effect

Have you ever been inside an indoor pool? Aside from shelter from the elements, one of the coolest features of indoor pools are those dancing strings of light on the walls, created by reflections from the water. These reflections are called caustics. The Caustics effect attempts to simulate the surface of water, or other fluid. It does this by allowing you to specify a map for the floor of the water's surface, a map for the displacement of the water's surface, and a map for a sky, reflected in the water's surface.

The Caustics effect was designed with the Wave World effect in mind. Due to the alphabetical ordering of effects, we're going to cover Caustics first. If you don't know a thing about Wave World, you'll be fine because I've already created the Wave World maps for you. If you want to know how I created these maps, you can jump to the end of this chapter when we look at the Wave World effect.

Open up the Caustics.aep project from the Chapter 15 folder of the exercise files. As tempting as the Chocolate Caustics comp might sound, we're going to start in the Caustics Start comp. This comp contains a solid layer that we'll apply Caustics to, and it also contains three layers that we'll use as maps. Apply the Caustics effect to the Caustics Solid layer.

The default settings don't make a significant change to this blue solid layer. A layer of a different color would appear to be tinted blue. This is because the Caustics effect uses the layer it is applied to as the map of the bottom of the virtual pool, and also uses blue by default for the surface of the water. So, what may just seem like a slight blue tint, is actually a little more complex.

This effect can feel a little overwhelming, but it's actually organized really well. There are three main areas: Bottom (which

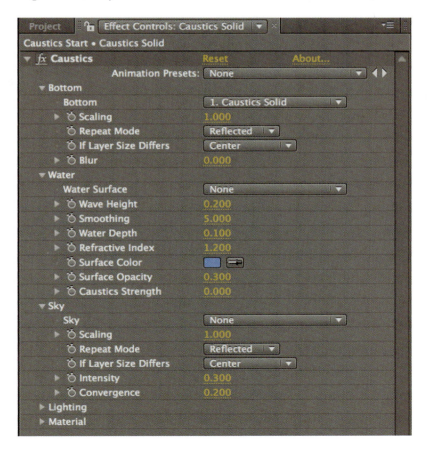

Figure 15.10 The well-organized Caustics Effect controls in the Effect Controls panel.

determines the texture on the bottom of the water), Water (which controls the water's surface), and Sky (which can simulate a sky reflected on the surface of the water). There are also Lighting and Material controls to fine tune the end results.

Let's start at the top. Change the Bottom value in the Bottom area to the Seattle ferry layer. This creates the illusion that the Seattle ferry image is at the bottom of the body of water that we are viewing from the top, or at least it tries to. The results aren't quite believable until we change the surface of the water.

Figure 15.11 Using a map for the Bottom value doesn't really look convincing until other settings are adjusted.

We have some light options for the bottom floor of our water, such as scaling, tiling, and blur options. But let's skip ahead to the surface of the water, which is the most important component in this effect. For the surface of the water, we're going to be using the Wave World Precomp layer, which is an animated texture created with the Wave World effect, covered later in this chapter. This layer is a grayscale texture that appears as though someone is dragging their finger through gray water.

To use this animation to displace the water's surface, go to the Water area in the Caustics effect and change the Water Surface drop down from None to Wave World Precomp. Then we'll see something that resembles rippling water, although we still have a ways to go before using this professionally.

With the surface of the water set up, let's now go back to the bottom of our water and fix that. First, let's reduce the Scaling value to 0.1, which will shrink the texture. If the Repeat Mode

Figure 15.12 A frame from the Wave World Precomp layer.

Figure 15.13 The initial result after changing the surface of the water.

value is still set to its default value of Reflected, the texture will repeat and reflect as it shrinks.

There's still way too much detail here. We want this bottom texture to look like the texture at the bottom of the pool. With this much detail, it seems that our water is either an inch deep, or that it's the purest water known to man. I'm going to increase the Bottom>Blur value to 10. Now this is starting to look a little like something that could pass for water.

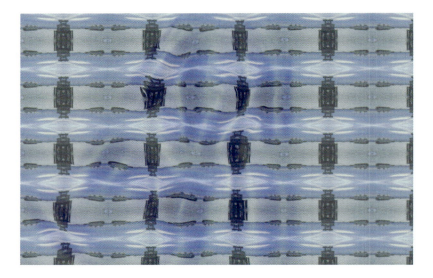

Figure 15.14 The bottom texture scaled down and reflected.

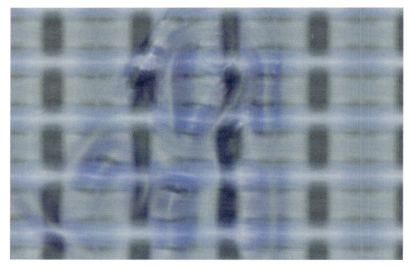

Figure 15.15 The bottom texture blurred to its full capacity (10).

This bottom texture is still too opaque and distracting, but there's not much else we can do for it in the Bottom section. In order to improve the results, we must now adjust the water surface by adjusting the controls in the Water area. The biggest offense here to me is that this water seems so shallow. You might think that we could adjust this with the Water>Water Depth value, but the Water Depth value just increases the contrast of the water ripple. We're going to increase the illusion of deeper water by increasing the opacity of the water. Increase the Water>Surface Opacity value to 0.8, which means that it will be 80% opaque.

This makes it seem like the water is deeper because there is more water between the surface and the bottom.

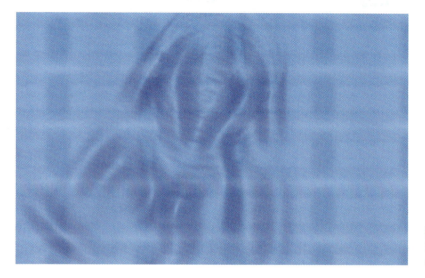

Figure 15.16 The result of increasing the opacity of the surface of the water.

So, the bottom is looking good, but now the water is too vibrant. Unless radioactivity is involved, water usually isn't that intensely blue. So, I'm going to change the Surface Color of the water to a more muted, realistic blue. I used the RGB values 60, 120, 200.

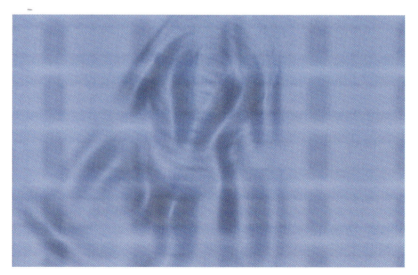

Figure 15.17 After toning down the blue in the surface color color swatch.

For the surface of our water, all that's left is to tweak the other settings to taste. I'm going to increase the Caustics Strength value very, very gently. Even a value of 1 is a high value.

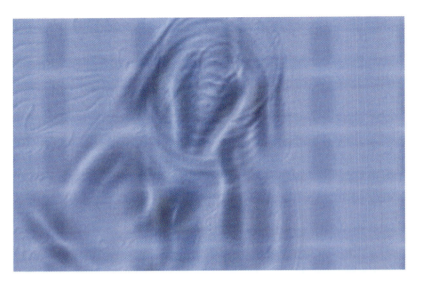

Figure 15.18 The water texture with the Caustics Strength value at 1.

After increasing the Caustics Strength value, you may want to also increase the Smoothing value to smooth out some of the ugly details.

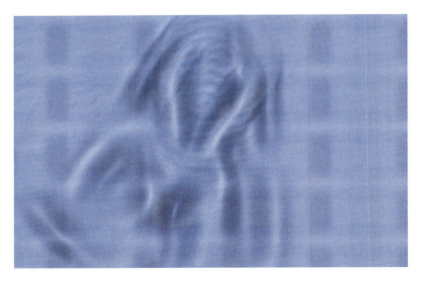

Figure 15.19 The result of increasing the smoothing value to 7.5.

You can now adjust the Wave Height, Water Depth, and Refractive Index properties until you get the wave you're looking for.

Now let's see what adding a sky looks like. In the Sky area, change the Sky drop down to the Seattle Sunset layer. Change the If Layer Size Differs drop down to Stretch to Fit, as the Seattle Sunset layer is considerably larger the this solid.

Figure 15.20 After adding the Seattle Sunset layer as the sky.

You can decrease the opacity of the sky by lowering the Intensity value. I'm going to take my Intensity value to 0.15. If you want to increase the amount of distortion in the sky reflection, increase the Convergence value. I'll set mine to 2. To really appreciate the beauty of the result here, you must play back this animation. A still frame doesn't quite do justice to the quality of this effect.

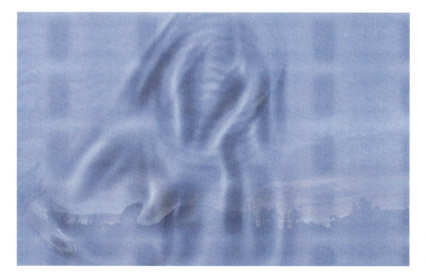

Figure 15.21 After altering the intensity and convergence values.

With that out of the way, we're ready to proceed to dessert. Hop on over to the Chocolate Caustics comp. This comp contains a similar bluish solid, but the animated displacement map is very different. The Chocolate Goodness layer is another pattern created with the Wave World effect. Again, you must play this back to really appreciate this, but it contains the text CHOCOLATE with ripples of liquid flowing over it. We're going to use this to make us some chocolate.

Figure 15.22 The chocolate goodness displacement layer.

Apply the Caustics effect to the Cyan Solid 2 layer. Change the Bottom layer to None. Change the Water Surface drop down to Chocolate Goodness. Because chocolate isn't really transparent, increase the Surface Opacity value to 1, which will make the surface completely opaque. Then change the Surface Color from blue to a chocolaty brown. I used the RGB values 60, 30, 0.

Figure 15.23 After only adjusting a few settings, we turned water to chocolate. There's a movie reference joke in there somewhere. Or perhaps a religious one.

The Wave World effect sometimes creates these ugly artifacts around sharp edges. These are causing some rough edges that should be oily smooth. Increase the Smoothing value to 10 to achieve our final delicious result. Again, you've really got to play this back to appreciate how truly chocolaty and organic this looks.

Figure 15.24 The final chocolate result, after increasing the smoothing value.

The Foam Effect

At the most basic level, the Foam effect creates bubbles. If you're like me, you've never ever needed bubbles in a professional setting before. I'm sure it can come in handy often—for bath tub scenes for animations on TV shows for kids, visual flatulence jokes, bubbling soda, or boiling cauldrons.

There is a limit to how helpful bubbles can be. But the Foam effect is far more important and helpful than for just creating bubbles. The Foam effect is one of my favorites in After Effects because of how intuitive and versatile it is. We can use it to make snow or a multitude of other effects because it allows us to replace the bubbles with textures of our own. It is more powerful than any of the other particle generators in After Effects, other than Particle Playground. But Foam renders far more quickly and is much easier to set up than Particle Playground. I can honestly say that the Foam effect is my native particle effect of choice in After Effects.

Open the Foam.aep project from the Chapter 15 folder of the exercise files. This project contains a few comps because I really want to convey how versatile this effect can be. We'll start out in the Using Foam comp, which demonstrates the Foam effect in its native habitat (as foamy bubbles).

The Using Foam comp contains a shot of a little kid in the bathtub, as well as a solid layer.

Figure 15.25 The kid in the tub layer in the Using Foam comp.

The Foam effect completely replaces the content of the layer it's applied to, so it's usually a good idea to apply this to a solid. So, apply the Foam effect to the blue solid layer. The good news is that Foam auto-animates. Preview this comp to watch bubbles fly out all over the place. The bad news here is that the default results leave something to be desired. Note that if you're not seeing bubbles, you might need to move your current time indicator a little later in time.

Figure 15.26 The default results of applying the Foam effect to the solid layer in the Using Foam comp.

The Foam effect is a little old, and used to render more slowly on old machines. With most modern machines, Foam renders fast enough at full quality. From the View drop down at the top of the effect, choose Rendered. Although the current bubble colors don't mesh well with our project here, it certainly looks more realistic than the default settings do!

Figure 15.27 The bubbles look more realistic after changing the view drop down to Rendered.

Let's start at the top of the effect options in the Effect Controls panel and work our way down, covering the highlights. Open the Producer area to control the system that is creating the particles. In particle systems like Foam, Shatter, and Particle Playground, you don't (and usually can't) control the individual particles, you only control the system making the particles. The Producer Point is the exact spot that is creating the bubbles. You can change its width by adjusting the Producer X Size value, or its height by adjusting the Producer Y Size value. We'll use these later when we make snow with the Foam effect.

Rotate the foam producer by adjusting the Producer Orientation value. Increase the amount of bubbles (or, more precisely, the speed at which they are created) by increasing the Production Rate value. I'm going to increase the Production Rate value to 9.

Open up the Bubbles area to adjust aspects of the bubble. I'm going to decrease the size of my bubbles by lowering the Size value to 0.2.

Figure 15.28 Increasing the production rate value creates more bubbles.

Figure 15.29 Lowering the bubbles>Size value reduces the size of the foam.

The Size Variance parameter adjusts the randomness of size. This may be mildly important with bubbles, but may be hugely important when working with your own custom textures. Lifespan controls how long the bubbles exist before they are popped and disappear. Many of the parameters in this effect—particularly those in the Physics area—pertain to bubbly things. These are properties not seen in most other particle effects.

This includes such things as Wobble Amount, Pop Velocity, and Stickiness.

Also in the Physics area, I want to call your attention to one of the reasons I am so devoted to the Foam effect. You'll notice that there are Initial Speed and Direction values, and Wind Speed and Direction values. This is so that you can have bubbles generated in one direction (the Initial values), and then have it acted upon by a secondary force (the Wind values). I love that.

Towards the bottom of the effect, you'll see a Flow Map area. This section allows you to use a gradient layer to control how the bubbles flow. A flow map can restrict bubbles from going to certain areas. For more information on using maps to control effect properties, check out Chapter 23.

Pound for pound, the Rendering settings are perhaps the most important in the Foam effect. These parameters determine what the bubbles will look like. From the Rendering>Bubble Texture drop down, change the value from Default Bubble to Amber Bock for example.

Figure 15.30 With the bubble texture value changed to amber bock.

Create a lighter bubble (and a grosser one) by using the Spit texture. Or, perhaps, to Algae.

You can also usually get a better composite by adding a slight reflection to the bubbles. To do this, you first need to select the layer that the bubbles will reflect. In the Environment Map drop down (still in the Rendering area), change the value to the kid

Figure 15.31 With the Bubble Texture value changed to spit.

Figure 15.32 With the Bubble Texture value changed to algae.

in the tub layer. Then, to add reflections from this layer to the bubbles, increase the Reflection Strength value. Here, I used a Reflection Strength value of 0.6 with the Spit Bubble Texture.

Now that we understand something of the technical aspects of Foam, let's look at some more practical (i.e., nonbubble) uses for the Foam effect. Switch over to the Creating Snow composition. This comp just contains another simple solid layer and a single, somewhat ugly layer that will be used as a snowflake.

Figure 15.33 The bubbles blend better with the background when they reflect the background layer slightly.

Figure 15.34 The Snowflake layer in the creating snow comp.

The effect is already set up for you in this comp. Make sure the Snowflake layer is turned off, and that the solid layer that contains the Foam effect is turned on. Preview the comp to see the final results.

With this comp, we're going to start with the end result and deconstruct it. The big question is—how did we get rid of the bubbles? In the Rendering area in the Foam effect controls, I changed the Bubble Texture to User Defined. Then, in the Bubble Texture Layer drop down, I selected the Snowflake layer.

Figure 15.35 This snow is courtesy of the Foam effect.

To make the snow fall, I increased the Producer X Size value to make the producer wide. I then placed the Producer Point above the comp, so that the snow would not start from the middle of the screen.

The other key to achieving this effect was to adjust the Initial Direction value to 180 degrees. This pushed the snowflakes downwards from the moment that they were created. The final result is quite impressive when animated.

Finally, let's look at the Making Sparkles composition. We're basically looking at the same effect in this comp, except that instead of using a still image as the Bubble Texture Layer, we're going to be using a movie. The sparkle movie in this composition contains a simple shape that wiggles slightly and changes color over time.

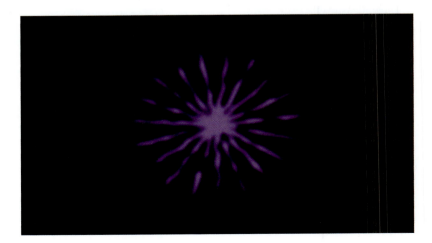

Figure 15.36 The sparkle.mov layer in the making sparkles comp.

As with the snow comp, this example has already been created for you. The only thing that is interesting that we haven't looked at yet is that I've animated the Producer Point. This leaves behind an interesting trail of bubbles, or sparkles in this case. Also, as with the snow, I've already gone into the Rendering area of the Foam effect controls and changed the Bubble Texture to User Defined, and changed the Bubble Texture Layer to the sparkle layer. Because the sparkle movie changes colors over time, the Foam sparkles that use it as a texture will also change colors over time.

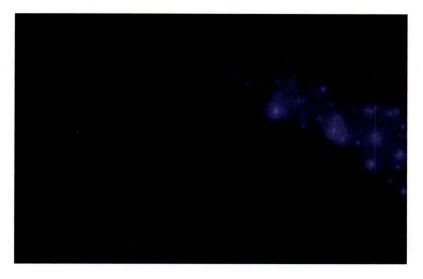

Figure 15.37 The making sparkles composition, at frame 0;00;00;23.

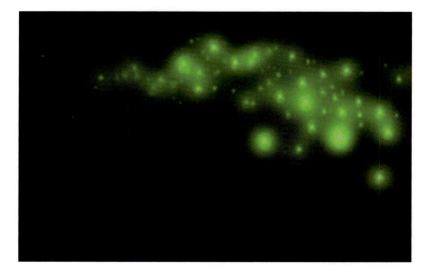

Figure 15.38 The making sparkles composition, at frame 0;00;01;08.

The Particle Playground Effect

The Particle Playground effect is probably the single most powerful and confusing effect in all of After Effects. Like the Foam effect, the Particle Playground effect produces particles that you control through particle generating systems. It has very organic physics simulations, original options (such as repel and wall), and is capable of some really spectacular things. However, its confusing interface, unintuitive workflow, and ridiculously slow render times offset the benefit of using Particle Playground for many tasks. If you love the power of Particle Playground and what it can do, then I strongly recommend purchasing Trapcode Particular.

Open up the Particle Playground.aep project from the Chapter 15 folder of the exercise files. This is by far the largest and most complex project that we will look at in this entire book. Because there are a whopping seven compositions, I've numbered them for you. We'll start in the number 1 composition, Particle Playground Intro. This comp consists of a simple solid with the Particle Playground effect applied to it. Particle Playground auto-animates, so preview the composition to see its default particle fountain-style settings.

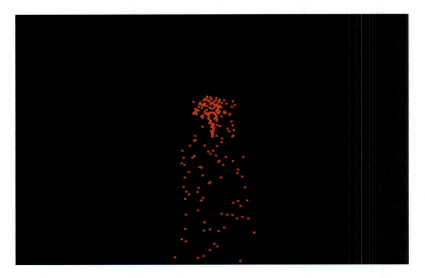

Figure 15.39 The particle playground intro comp, at 0;00;03;24.

Don't worry for now that this looks like an old Atari game exploded. Remember that we can replace these little squares with whatever we want later on.

The Particle Playground effect creates particles using one or more particle generators. There are four particle generators in Particle Playground, and they can be seen as the top four categories of properties at the top of the Particle Playground effect in the Effect Controls panel—Cannon, Grid, Layer Exploder, and Particle Exploder. By default, only one generator is turned on, but you can have as many of these generators simultaneously generating particles as you want.

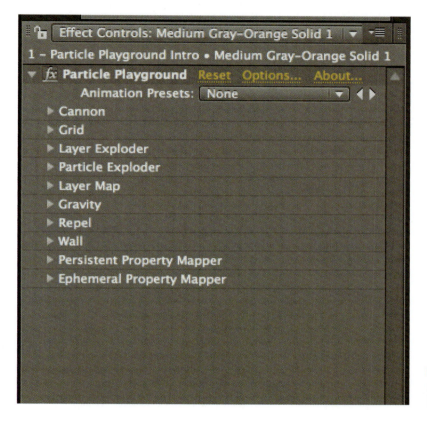

Figure 15.40 The categories of effects in the Particle Playground effect.

Let's look first at some simple examples as we get acquainted with the particle generators. Then, we'll look at the more practical examples in the other compositions in this project.

In short, the Cannon emits particles from a single point, and it is the default emitter. All others are turned off. Like all emitters in Particle Playground, it can emit several different types of particles. It can emit the simple particles created in Particle Playground, it can emit other layers, and it can emit text (which also can be done by the Grid particle generator). We'll look at how to use each of these as we go through this section.

For now, we'll stick to Cannon to go over some Particle Playground basics. Open up the Cannon area in the Effect Controls panel. First off, let's adjust the Direction value so it's easier to see our adjustments. I'm going to take this value to 30 degrees, which shoots particles out to the right.

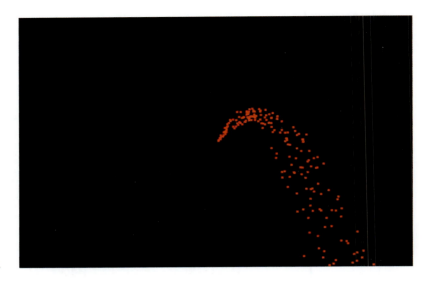

Figure 15.41 Taking the direction value to 30 degrees shoots out particles to the right.

The Barrel Radius value increases the size of the imaginary barrel shooting out these particles. This is helpful when creating things like a waterfall that have a wider source than just a single point.

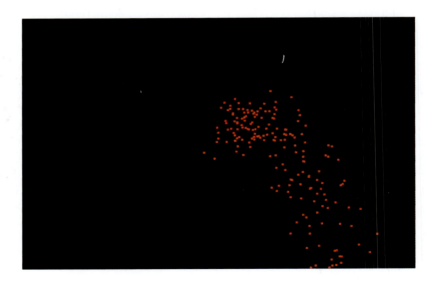

Figure 15.42 The results after increasing the barrel radius value to 40.

Note that the Barrel Radius is much different than the Particle Radius, which increases the size of each particle. Here I took the Particle Radius value up to 11.

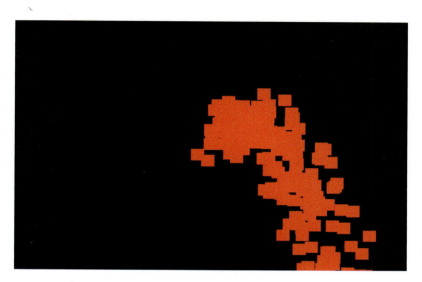

Figure 15.43 With a particle radius value of 11, the particles (squares) become much larger.

Before we go any further with Particle Playground, we need to be aware of the importance of the Info panel with this effect. When the Particle Playground effect is selected in the Effect Controls panel, the Info panel will display the current number of particles on screen that After Effects is having to render. There is no way to overstate how helpful this is, especially when working with other emitters such as Grid.

Next up is the Grid. Before we see what the Grid emitter does, we should probably turn off the Cannon. We can turn off the Cannon by taking the Cannon>Particles Per Second value down to 0. Then we must turn on Grid by increasing either the Particles

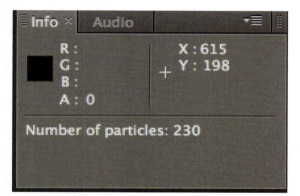

Figure 15.44 The info panel displays the number of particles currently on screen when the particle playground effect is selected.

Across or Particles Down value. The Grid emitter actually creates a grid of particle emitters that emit a new particle every frame. It is so important to be careful with these values because they can obliterate your render time. Let's say that you used a fairly modest value of 10 for the Particles Across and Particles Down values. After 4 seconds, you would have over 12,000 particles on screen. The Grid emitter is great for generating areas of particles, such as a tidal wave or a large fire. Spread out the particles in the grid without increasing their numbers by using the Grid>Width and Height values.

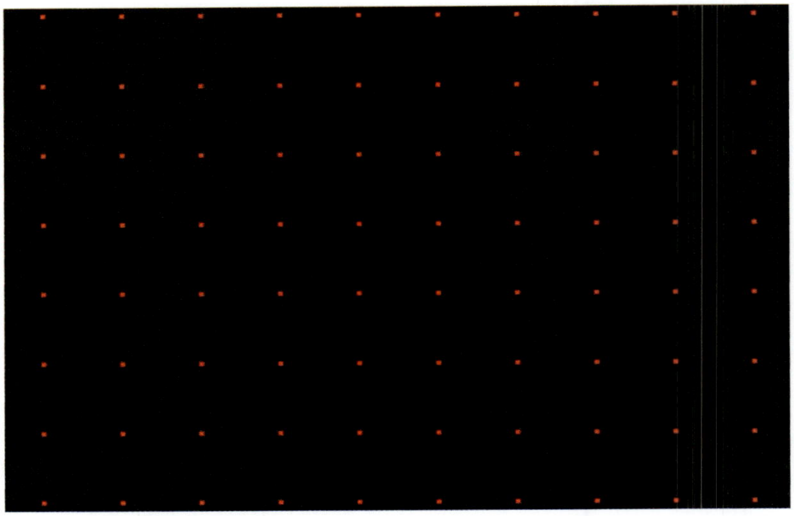

Figure 15.45 The Grid emitter with 10 particles across and down, and the width and height values each set to 650.

The Layer Exploder breaks up a layer, similar to the way the Shatter effect does (which we'll look at next). The Particle Exploder also blows up a layer, but it also allows the particles to be exploded as well.

So, how do you turn these emitters on and off? I've created a handy chart for you in the #2 comp—Particle ON/OFF Rules. These contain cheat sheets on how to handle the various Particle Playground emitters.

Now that we have enough knowledge to be dangerous, let's look at some more practical examples as we dig deeper into

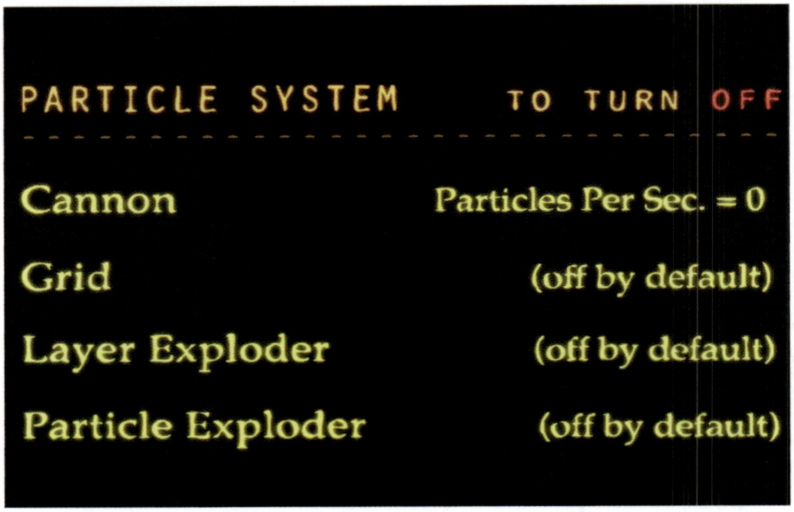

PARTICLE SYSTEM	TO TURN OFF
Cannon	Particles Per Sec. = 0
Grid	(off by default)
Layer Exploder	(off by default)
Particle Exploder	(off by default)

Figure 15.46 How to turn off the various particle generators in Particle Playground.

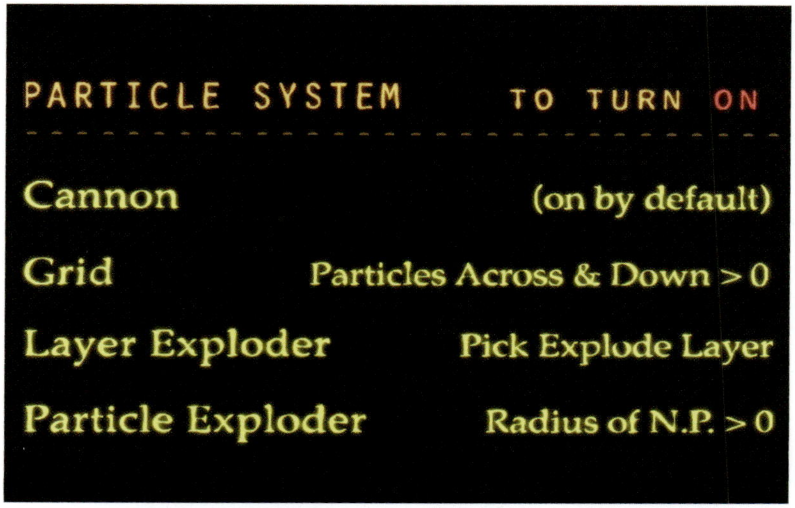

PARTICLE SYSTEM	TO TURN ON
Cannon	(on by default)
Grid	Particles Across & Down > 0
Layer Exploder	Pick Explode Layer
Particle Exploder	Radius of N.P. > 0

Figure 15.47 How to turn on the various particle generators in Particle Playground.

Particle Playground. Switch over to the third composition, Grid Waterfall. This comp contains a simple waterfall I created using the default square particle in Particle Playground. Here, I use both the Cannon and Grid emitters. The Grid emitter is creating the actual waterfall. I've set the Particles Down value to 1 so that there is only a single grid line creating these particles. Even then, it still renders too slow for my liking. I added the Cannon emitter with a fairly high Barrel Radius value (25) to create a pale splash at the top of the waterfall. It's subtle, but it adds a nice touch. I finished off the results by applying the Fast Blur effect with a Blurriness setting of 2.5. Fast Blur does a great job smoothing out the squares generated by Particle Playground.

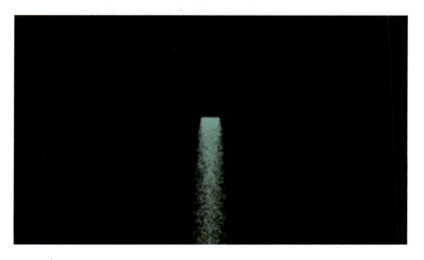

Figure 15.48 The grid waterfall comp.

Now let's move into more advanced territory. Go to comp #4—Layer Exploder Fizz to get an idea of what the Layer Exploder can do, as well as to use controller layers with this effect. We're going to use the Layer Exploder to dissolve this text like it were soda fizz. This comp contains two layers. The first layer is some super sweet retro text that is a logo for a fictitious soda company.

Figure 15.49 The text in the Layer Exploder fizz comp.

The other layer is an animated gradient. It looks like a light wave moving upwards through darkness. Wow. That was almost poetic.

Figure 15.50 The gradient in motion layer.

Apply the Particle Playground effect to the fizz text. Make sure that the gradient layer is turned off. The first thing we need to do with this effect is to turn off the Cannon. Do that by opening the Cannon controls and taking the Particles Per Second value down to 0.

Now we need to turn on the Layer Exploder. Before we do that, I heartily recommend moving the current time to the first frame. The reason why I say that is because the Layer Exploder will turn the selected Explode Layer into particle generators. That means that every particle of this entire layer will generate a new particle every frame. To give you an idea of how intense this can get, if your current time indicator were only 14 frames in, you would have over 91,000 particles on screen. Once you're at frame 0, open the Layer Exploder parameters and change the Explode Layer drop down to the PRECOMP fizz layers (the fizzy text).

Here's our solution to the plethora of particles dilemma. Click the stopwatch for the Radius of New Particles property in the Layer Exploder area. Then advance to the next frame and take this value to 0. This will allow us to use all of the particles generated on the first frame only, and no new particles will be created.

If you preview this animation now, it appears that all of the particles just sink; like a lead brick. That's not very fizzy. So, open up the Gravity area of parameters and change the Direction from 180 degrees (straight down) to 0 degrees (straight up).

The fizz is now moving upwards, but all particles are moving at the same speed. That looks way too robotic. In the Affects area in the Gravity area, we can use a map to control how gravity is applied to the particles. In the Gravity>Affects>Selection Map drop down, select the Gradient in Motion layer. This will create a much more fizzy layer explosion.

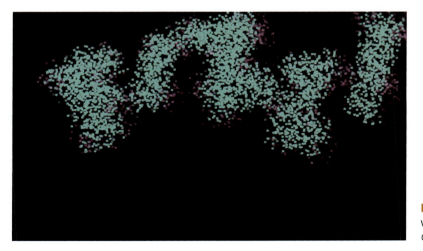

Figure 15.51 The final results with the fizz gravity being controlled by our Gradient layer.

The ability to have particles repel each other is another great feature of Particle Playground. In the number 5 comp, Repel Starfield, I've taken the Repel>Force value to –0.5 and the Force Radius to 10. This causes the particles to repel away from each other, which I've used to create a zooming starfield effect. Radial Blur and Glow have been added to enhance the effect.

Figure 15.52 The repel starfield comp.

As I mentioned, I really don't use Particle Playground all that much. But when I do use it, I'm usually after the Wall properties. These allow you to create a mask on the layer and use it to deflect particles. It is so easy to set up and use to create spectacular results, such as those seen in comp #6, Wall Tornado. In this comp, I've created a tornado-shaped mask. Then, I change the Wall>Boundary value to the mask I created. Once you've done that simple step, the particles bounce off of the sides of the mask, and in this case, create a really cool swirling effect. Note that the mask must be on the same layer that Particle Playground is applied to in order for the effect to see and use it.

Finally, let's go to the last comp—Text Blown Dust. This comp uses text, which we haven't looked at yet.

Although this comp is already set up for you, we're still going to look at how the text was created. Unfortunately, you cannot use a text layer as a source for the particles. To use text as particles, click the Options button at the top of the effect in the Effect Controls panel. As with many older effects that use text, a dialog pops up allowing you to input text. Depending on whether you

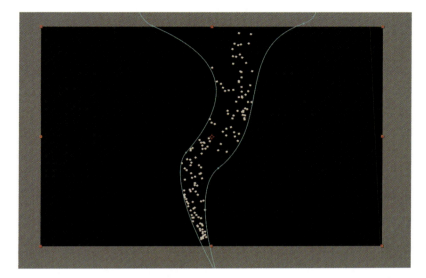

Figure 15.53 The wall tornado comp, with the mask active.

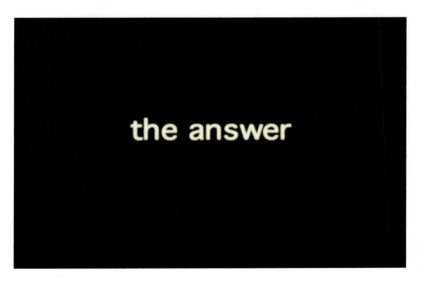

Figure 15.54 The text blown dust comp.

want to create text for the Cannon or Grid, click the appropriate button.

I've also increased the Radius of New Particles value in the Particle Exploder area to turn it on. Then, as before, I've changed Particle Exploder> Affects> Selection Map to the gradient layer to create a more natural and random dissipation of particles. After adding some Fast Blur and Glow, the results are beautiful.

Figure 15.55 The Particle Playground text entry dialogs.

Figure 15.56 The blown dust text. Get it? The answer, my friend, is blowing in the wind. Ha!

The Shatter Effect

Ah, yes. The Shatter effect. Officially, the purpose of the Shatter effect is to blow stuff up (seriously, click the About button at the top of the effect in the Effect Controls panel if you don't believe me). But the magic of the Shatter effect is that when it shatters a layer, it makes it fully 3D in the process. There's just so many cool tricks that we can do with the Shatter effect. Even if violence, mayhem, and explosions aren't your thing (I'm sure it totally is, but let's just pretend that it isn't), the Shatter effect still has a lot to offer.

Open the Shatter.aep project. Let's start in the Shatter Start comp. This comp only contains a simple green solid. As with other effects in this chapter, we're going to start off simple to get acquainted, and then we'll look at more practical examples. Apply the Shatter effect to this green solid. You'll see that the default view can be a little perplexing at first.

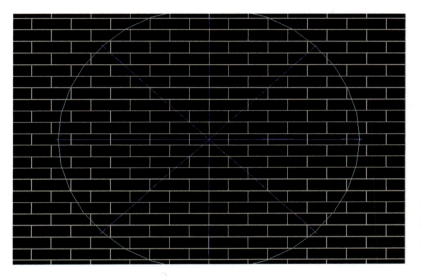

This view is merely a working view to help you work better with Shatter. Before we talk about this lo-fi wireframe view, let's look at the full blown Shatter results. Take the View drop down at the top of the effect to Rendered. Then preview your composition to watch your layer explode. Yes, one of the joys (and frustrations) of the Shatter effect is that it auto-animates, blowing up

An Easier Shatterer

If you're interested in blowing stuff up, but the Shatter effect is a little more complicated and powerful than what you're looking for, check out the Cycore effect CC Pixel Polly, covered in Chapter 21. It basically blows up your layer, but without all of the power, 3D flexibility, learning curves, and complexities of Shatter. It also renders really fast, and it's easy to get the explosion to start later in time.

Figure 15.57 The default results after applying Shatter.

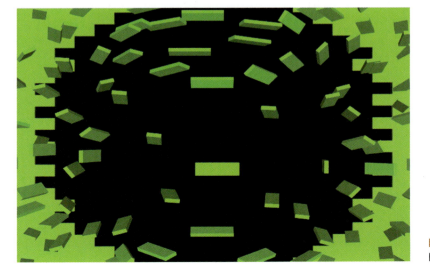

Figure 15.58 The exploding layer.

your layer starting on frame 1 (frame 0 is left alone). We'll look at how to delay the explosion in just a moment.

To really understand the power of this effect, go down to the Camera Position area, and adjust the Y Rotation value to –60 degrees. Now you can see that Shatter is actually making your layer three-dimensional, which means that the blocks that it shatters are also 3D. Oooooooooh …

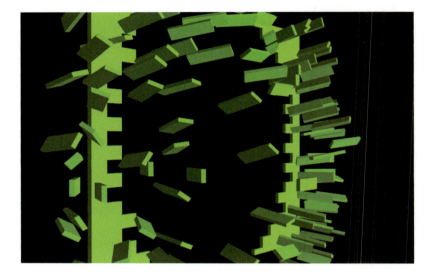

Figure 15.59 Rotation the virtual camera in the Shatter effect allows us to see our layer's recently acquired third dimension.

Let's now go back to the View drop down at the top, and change this value from Rendered back to Wireframe + Forces.

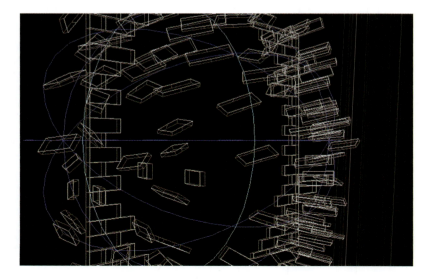

Figure 15.60 The wireframe + forces view with the rotated camera.

Understanding this mess is critical to mastering the Shatter effect. That big blue wireframe sphere that you're seeing is the force (insert tired Star Wars joke here). Only objects that come into contact with this force can blow up. So, let's talk about adjusting this force. Open up the Force 1 properties in the Effect Controls panel. Note that there is also a Force 2 area. Force 2 is turned off by default, but if you needed an additional explosion, you could use Force 2 for that.

The Depth parameter in the Force 1 area controls the Z position of the force. You'll notice that as I take this value to 0.4, it barely touches the layer. And again we see that only parts of the layer that touch the force will blow up. So then, if you want to delay the blowing up of a layer, simply animate the Depth parameter. The Radius value determines the size of the force, and the Strength value can be used to adjust the intensity of the blast. If a child threw a baseball through a window, it would have a lower Strength value than, say, a wrecking ball coming through the same window.

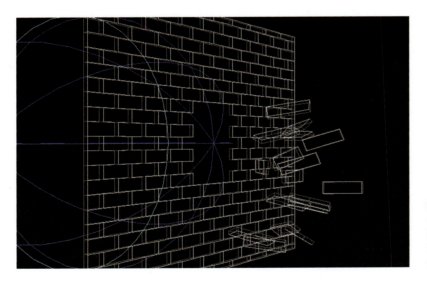

Figure 15.61 With the depth value at 0.4, less of the layer blows up because less of the layer comes into contact with the force.

Click the Reset button at the top of the effect. Change the View drop down to Rendered, and move out in time a few frames.

When you animate the Position property in the Force 1 area, it creates an interesting gopher-like trail. This can be used to remove parts of the layer to reveal a logo, or to create a logo from the negative space created by exploded pieces.

For this, I'm going to go out to frame 13. I'm also going to take the Force 1>Radius value to 0.1 to create a smaller force. I'll then adjust Force 1>Position to be in the upper-left-hand corner of the layer, and then click the stopwatch.

Figure 15.62 The project with a smaller force radius and an adjusted force position.

I'll then move in time and lower the position.

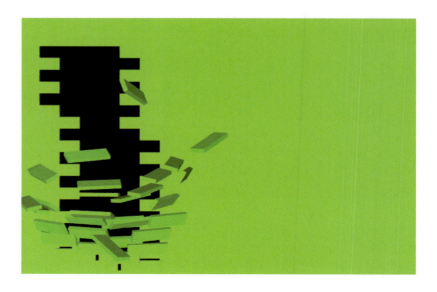

Figure 15.63 After moving in time and lowering the force position.

Finally, I'll move to later in time again, and move the force position to the upper right.

Figure 15.64 The result of moving in time and moving the force position again.

I really like this animation, but I'm not so crazy about the shape of our bricks. At the top of the Shatter effect in the Effect Controls panel, you'll find a Shape area. Open that up to see all kinds of properties that we can use to customize the shape and look of the shattering. The Shape>Pattern drop down is a great place to start. Open that drop down to see a huge slew of patterns that you can use as shatter maps. My favorite is the standard Glass setting.

Figure 15.65 The Shatter effect with the pattern drop down in the shape area set to glass.

This glass is looking too clunky. Increase the Repetitions value to create smaller pieces. This basically shrinks the shatter pattern down and repeats it.

Figure 15.66 Increasing the Repetitions value (taken to 50 here) creates smaller pieces.

The Extrusion Depth value creates thicker pieces, which will come in handy in the next example. Switch over to the 3D pieces composition. In this comp, you'll find a shape layer that I created in the shape of a fish.

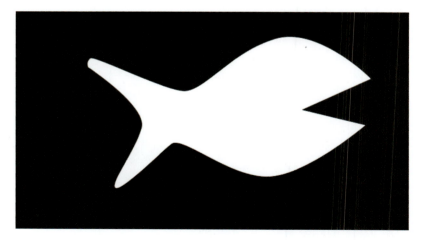

Figure 15.67 The ugliest fish you've ever seen.

One of the lesser known gems about this effect is that it allows you to create your own custom shatter maps using grayscale layers. And because the Shatter effect makes 3D pieces, you can use this trick to create 3D text or other simple objects! As you can see in the underwater layer, this has already been done for you.

Figure 15.68 The 3D fish, thanks to the Shatter effect.

To use the fish shape layer to make a 3D fish, I applied the Shatter effect to the underwater image (NOT the fish shape). Then, in the Shape area of the Shatter effect, I changed the Pattern drop down to Custom, and then changed the Custom Shatter Map value to my black and white fish layer. It's as simple as that.

In the Blown Dust comp, you'll see another trick with the Shatter effect. This comp contains a movie with an octopus revealed by blown dust.

Figure 15.69 The blown dust comp.

The blown dust is created by adjusting two properties. First, crank up the Repetitions value as high as it will go. This will create the smallest possible dust fragments. Then, open up the powerful Physics area in the Shatter effect.

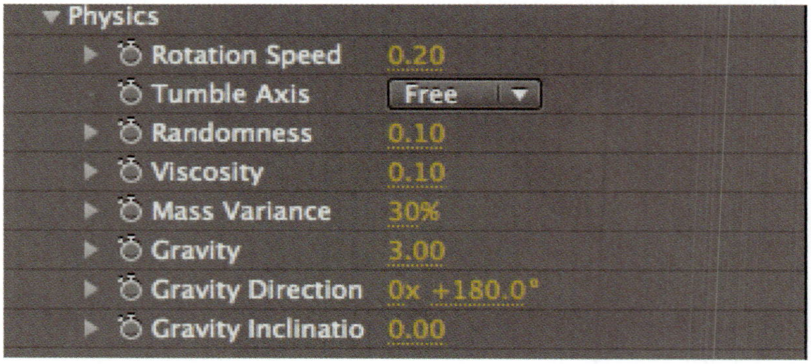

Figure 15.70 The physics area in the Shatter Effect controls.

In this area, you can set options like gravity and viscosity. Viscosity refers to the thickness of the air, which is great for blowing things up underwater or in space. What we're after here, though, is the Gravity property. Set the Gravity Direction in the direction you want the wind to blow. Then increase the Gravity parameter to increase the speed at which the shattered pieces move in that direction.

Finally, go to the Shatter Map composition. We're going to look at how to selectively shatter an object using grayscale maps. We have here this beautiful shot of a stained glass window. This is the layer that will be shattered (no offense if this is your church).

Equally important is the map that will be used to shatter this stained glass. Pay particular attention to the five white circles at

Figure 15.71 The stained glass image in the Shatter Map comp.

the top, the black background, and the gradient that covers the remaining glass.

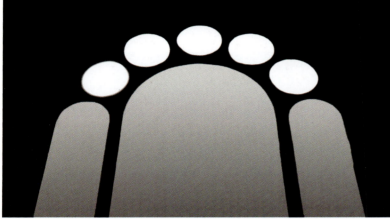

Figure 15.72 The grayscale map that I painted in Photoshop. We'll be using to control the shattering.

As with other complicated examples in this chapter, I've already set this up for you. Here's how I did it. I first changed the Pattern to Glass and increased the Repetitions value pretty high to create smaller pieces. This is important so that it seems like the windows are shattering and not the walls. I probably should take it even higher than I did.

In the Gradient area of the Shatter effect, I selected the grayscale map layer I painted in Photoshop. Then—and here's the key—I animated the Shatter Threshold value. As you increase the Shatter Threshold value, it uses more of the gradient, starting with light areas and moving towards dark areas. In this case, because I painted the five circular windows at the top white, they shatter first.

Figure 15.73 Areas that correspond to the white areas on my Gradient layer blow up first.

If I were to leave the Shatter Threshold at a low value, nothing else would blow up. But I animated the Shatter Threshold value so that as it increases the other windows shatter from top to bottom. I never let the Shatter Threshold value get high enough to blow up the walls.

Figure 15.74 Increasing the shatter threshold value more allows darker colors in our gradient map to blow up additional pixels on our layer.

The Shatter effect is just so awesome. It renders quickly, it's extremely powerful, but also easy to use. And the vast array of options makes this a very versatile effect, indeed. Remember that the Shatter effect has 3D camera, lighting, and material options. You can even choose to use a comp camera and/or a comp light with Shatter as well.

The Wave World Effect

The Wave World effect is another effect that often scares away unfamiliar users. Its default results are perhaps more confusing than the default results of any other effect. And even when you do surmount that obstacle, you come to the realization that the Wave World effect is completely useless on its own. But don't discount it just yet. The Wave World effect simulates real-world water waves and ripples that can be used as maps for other effects, such as Displacement Map. Ultimately, the Wave World effect is supposed to be used in conjunction with the Caustics effect, covered earlier in this chapter.

Open the Wave World.aep project in the Chapter 15 folder of the exercise files. We'll start in the Wave World Start comp, which consists only of a plain solid layer. Apply the Wave World effect to this layer. When first applied the Wave World effect shows you a working view, like the default view that we just saw with the Shatter effect.

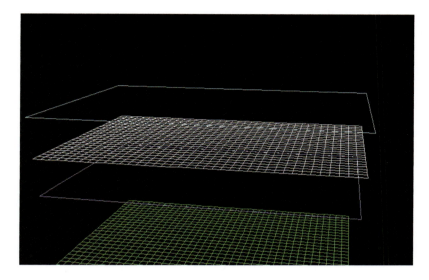

Figure 15.75 The default view of the Wave World effect.

The green bottom grid represents the floor of the water. The white grid represents the surface of the water. Additionally, there are also two other rectangular helpers. Before we discuss those, let's play back this composition. As we do, we'll see a 3D representation of the auto-animated waves created by this effect.

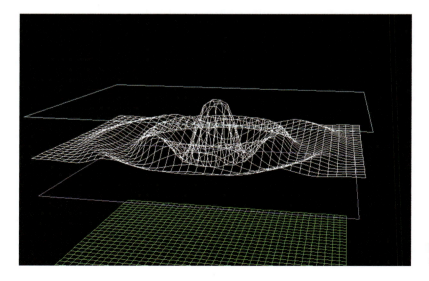

Figure 15.76 The animated waves.

As stated previously, this view is only a working view. Its only purpose is to help you better visualize the end result of the Wave World effect. Remember that the end result of the Wave World effect is only to create a grayscale map. That's all that can be done here. To see that grayscale map, change the View drop down from Wireframe Preview to Height Map.

Figure 15.77 The height map.

Now it will be more clear what the rectangles were for in the wireframe view. The top rectangle shows you the white clipping area and the lower rectangle shows you where the shadows will clip. Generally speaking, you don't want to create displacement maps with clipped highlights or shadows, unless you're purposely intending to do so for some reason.

The Wireframe Controls area allows you to control your view of the wireframe waves, and that is all. None of these settings have any bearing on the final result whatsoever.

The Height Map controls are almost like a built in Levels effect. Normally, that wouldn't be very important, but in an effect like Wave World, these controls become very helpful in creating the exact final product that you're looking for.

The controls in the Simulation area are overall controls. The Grid Resolution setting controls the smoothness of the final result. The default value of 40 is great for working quickly, but not for smooth, final output. I usually use a value between 100 and 150 for output. The results are noticeably smoother.

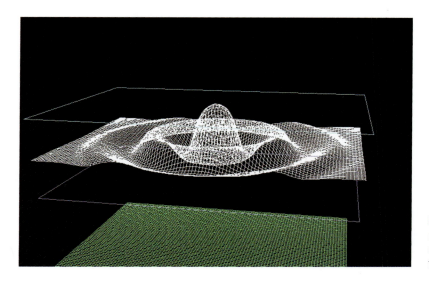

The Reflect Edges value in the Simulation area creates reflections along certain edges of your choosing. For demonstration purposes, I'm going to take this value to All, which will create reflections along all edges. Then, when waves bump into edges, waves will be reflected back, simulating the way real waves bounce back from surfaces.

Figure 15.79 With reflect edges set to all, waves that move to the layer's boundaries are reflected back. This is especially noticeable on the top and bottom edges.

In the Simulation area, you can adjust the speed of the waves (using Wave Speed), or you can adjust Pre-roll (seconds) to eliminate the period at the beginning of the animation where the wave is starting up.

Next we come to the Ground controls area. We'll look more closely at these in a moment. Until we use a map to control this property, however, the only value that does anything is Height. The more shallow water is, the softer its waves will be. So, as we increase the Height value (which represents the height of the water floor), the softer the waves will be.

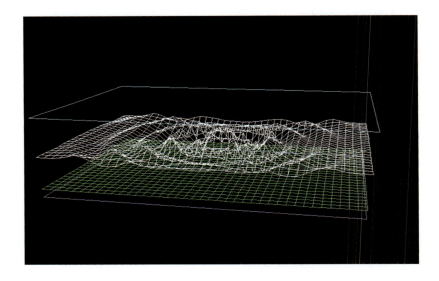

Figure 15.80 Increasing the ground>Height value to 0.45 reduces the intensity of the waves.

Lastly, we come to the Producer 1 controls. Here's where things get fun. Most of these controls are self-explanatory. But the Producer 1>Position value is one of the more important properties in the entire effect. This is the property that we animate to create the illusion that something is disrupting the surface of the ocean. I'm going to place the Position value in the upper left corner and create a keyframe, then move in time and move the position, then move in time and change position again until I've created a U shape. Even a still frame in black and white is beautiful.

Now let's look at the Chocolate Goodness comp. In this comp, I've created a very simple layer with text and a slight blur.

I used this layer as the ground in the Wave World effect to create the illusion of flowing chocolate when we covered the Caustics effect, earlier in this chapter. When you use a grayscale map as a ground layer, it allows the water to be displaced by it.

Figure 15.81 The result of animating the producer 1> position value.

Figure 15.82 The chocolate outlines layer in the chocolate goodness comp.

Imagine a shallow stream that is moving. If you put your hand in it, the water will flow over your hand—the flow has been displaced by the objects underneath. And that's exactly what a ground layer does.

This project has already been set up for you. Make sure that the outlines layer (layer 1) is off, and that the Solid layer (layer 2) is turned on. To use a layer as a ground layer, go to the Ground controls in the Wave Warp effect. Change the Ground value (in the Ground area) to the Ground layer, which is CHOCOLATE Outlines in this case. The Steepness and Wave Height values can be used to control how the water interacts with the ground. If you take the View to Wireframe Preview, you can see how the ground is now severely displacing the surface of the water.

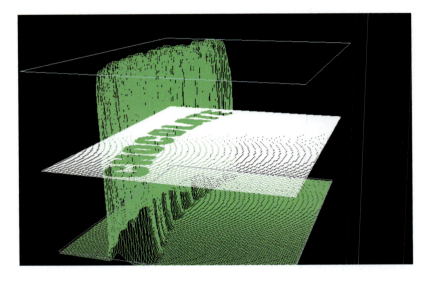

Figure 15.83 The wireframe preview of our chocolate text displacing the surface of the water.

I realize that even the final height map here isn't much to look at. But Wave World produces such high quality maps that when they are used with the Caustics effect, the results are amazing. Be creative here. Not only can this be used with water and chocolate, but for paint, flowing metal or lava, or any other liquid. And the ground plane doesn't have to be simple text, it can be a company logo or any other shape.

16

THE STYLIZE EFFECTS

Many of the effects in After Effects (particularly those we just looked at in Chapter 15) require lots of brain sweat to study and master. For the most part, the effects in the Stylize category are just simple creative tools. If you're reading this book straight through, this will be a nice creative recess.

The Stylize effects are the most like the artsy filters in Photoshop. Many of them create visually interesting patterns out of the pixels in a layer. For my money, the most important Stylize effect by far is the Glow effect. I rarely create a motion graphics project that doesn't use the Glow effect somewhere, and I often use it more subtly in color correction to enhance the beauty of a shot.

The Brush Strokes Effect

The Brush Strokes effect attempts to create a painted look from footage. It gives you a lot of control over the brush strokes used to create the final result. This effect also creates strokes that auto-animate.

To experiment with this effect, import the KS103.mov file from the Artbeats folder in the Media folder of the exercise files.

Apply the Brush Strokes effect to this footage. The results instantly change, and previewing this footage will see that these brush strokes auto-animate. The results here remind me a little of the Scribble effect we covered in Chapter 9.

The first thing I'm going to do is increase the Brush Size value to 5, which is its maximum value. Although this setting is usually too high, as it loses a great detail from our original footage, it will make it more obvious in the upcoming screenshots when we make changes to other properties.

Let's also increase the Stroke Length value to 15 to make the brush strokes that create this image a little longer.

These settings are pretty ridiculous, but we're using them so that we can see what's going on here. In your own projects, you will probably want values that are more subtle. Now that the strokes that are creating this image are a little more obvious,

Figure 16.1 The KS103.mov clip from Artbeats.

Figure 16.2 The Brush Strokes effect at the default settings.

we can see the results of adjusting other properties. Take Stroke Angle value, for instance. This controls the directions of the brush strokes. Taking this value to 270 degrees creates the appearance that the brush strokes were created by dragging the brush from left to right.

By default, when this effect applies paint strokes, it applies them on top of the original layer. Change this by going to the Paint Surface drop down and selecting Paint On Transparent. This will remove the background from the paint strokes. To see

Figure 16.3 Increasing the Brush Size value to 5 gives us larger paint strokes.

Figure 16.4 The results of making the brush strokes longer by increasing the Stroke Length value to 15.

the difference here, reduce the Stroke Density value to 0, so that the paint strokes are more spread out. This allows the transparency beneath to show through.

I have one last trick for you with this effect. Believe it or not, we're going to use this cute little video clip of girls running and playing on a sunny day to make a wall of animated lights, like something you might see on a control panel in a science fiction movie. First, decrease the Stroke Randomness value all the way to 0. Take the Stroke Length value to 1. This creates a

Figure 16.5 Changing the Stroke Angle value to 270 degrees makes this image look like it was painted from a different angle.

Figure 16.6 With Paint On Transparent selected in the Paint Surface drop down, we can see holes in the brush strokes when we reduce the Stroke Density value. Here the Stroke Angle value is taken back to its default.

series of dots, instead of long strokes. Because these strokes auto-animate, they all appear to randomly flicker.

And, because I'm not one to leave well enough alone, I'm going to apply the Hue/Saturation effect to adjust the hue and reduce the lightness. Then I'll apply the Glow effect (covered later in this chapter) to add to the illusion that these dots are lights. Play back the footage for even more sweet sci-fi action. It's hard to believe that this result started off with two little girls running in a field.

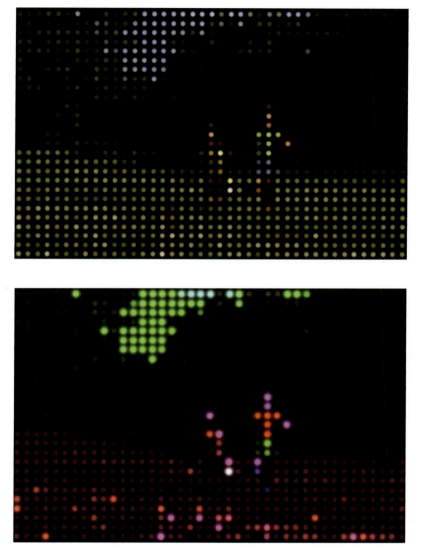

Figure 16.7 The sci-fi control panel effect, created with the Brush Strokes effect.

Figure 16.8 The final sci-fi control panel. Oh yeah.

The Cartoon Effect

Introduced in After Effects CS4, the Cartoon effect creates a stylized look that is intended to resemble vector art. A few years ago, a few commercials for the financial company Charles Schwab showed real video of interviews, but it had a cartoonish look to it. Full length movies like *A Scanner Darkly* and *Waking Life* have also taken advantage of such looks. The Cartoon effect attempts to stylize footage in the same way. Also, because of the way that the

Cartoon effect simplifies and smoothes footage, you can also use it to try and get rid of video noise and other small blemishes.

Open the Cartoon.aep project from the Chapter 16 folder of the exercise files. This project contains two comps—Cartoon Start, and Cartoon Final. First, let's start with the Cartoon Start comp. This comp contains some footage of Paavo jumping around on his unicycle onto a bench.

Figure 16.9 The Cartoon Start comp in the Cartoon.aep project.

Apply the Cartoon effect to this footage. In my opinion the default results don't really encourage me to use this effect. At first glance it appears that the Cartoon effect applies a really bad Photoshop filter effect to our footage; something that might have been popular in the mid-1990s when most people didn't have computers.

The Cartoon effect has two main components: Fill and Edge. For the Fill side of things, the Cartoon effect looks at areas of color and tries to make them cartoony by averaging their values to create areas of flat color. The Edge aspect looks for the edges in the image to overlay them with black outlines, like a cartoon. From the Render drop down at the top of the effect in the Effect Controls panel, you can select to view Fill & Edges, or just Fill, or just Edges. Even if Fill & Edges is your desired end result, you may want to isolate just the fill or just the edges to get a clearer picture of what is going on with them. For now, we'll leave this setting set to Fill & Edges.

Figure 16.10 The default results of the Cartoon effect hurt my feelings and drain me of my will to live.

Figure 16.11 The Cartoon effect with the Render drop down set to Fill. This shows us the Cartoon effect in the fill only.

Beneath the Render drop down, we have two detail settings—Detail Radius and Detail Threshold. These properties affect the entire image. The good news is that these properties are essentially the Bilateral Blur effect that we learned about in Chapter 4. The bad news is that soft, fuzzy blurs like the kind we find in the Bilateral Blur effect, aren't really very cartoony. Like Bilateral Blur, the Radius value determines the amount of blur, and the

Figure 16.12 The Cartoon effect displaying only the edges.

Threshold value determines how the effect defines an edge. A lower Threshold value keeps more details, while a higher Threshold value simplifies and smoothes areas of colors more.

In the Fill area, you can do a lot to create a cartoon look quickly. This is my favorite area of the effect. Reduce Shading Steps to posterize the image more, creating more flat areas of color. Decrease Shading Smoothness to create even harder lines between colors. Figure 16.13 shows and example with the two values in the Fill area significantly reduced. The cement path looks especially cartoonish.

Figure 16.13 Reducing the values in the Fill area simplifies color areas.

In the Edge area, increase the Threshold property to increase the amount of edges that are covered in an outline. You can also adjust its width, softness, and opacity. Fine tune edges with the properties in the Advanced area.

Figure 16.14 The image with increased Threshold value.

I have a love/hate relationship with the Cartoon effect. I love the way that vector art looks (and, by implication, what the Cartoon effect is trying to do), but I really have a tough time getting the Cartoon effect to look even half way decent. The Cartoon Final comp contains my best attempt at an actual cartoon look.

First, I started with some video footage of Mt. Rainier.

Figure 16.15 My original footage in the Cartoon Final comp.

I then added the Levels effect to help bring out contrast, so that the Cartoon effect would have an easier time detecting edges.

Figure 16.16 The Mt. Rainier footage after applying the Levels effect to boost contrast.

Next I applied the Cartoon effect. My settings are found with the result in Figure 16.17.

Figure 16.17 The result and settings that I used with the Cartoon effect on this footage.

Finally, I added the Color Balance effect to bring out some blues in the darker tones, and warm tones in the highlights. Also, I'm kind of addicted to Color Balance, so much so that my wife is jealous.

Figure 16.18 My final results with the Cartoon effect. It's not much, but it's the best I could do with this effect.

The Color Emboss Effect

The Color Emboss effect is basically a simplistic version of the Bevel and Emboss layer style, except that it actually examines the entire layer instead of just the outside edge. As we'll see in the following example, this can be used to bring out details in the highlights of an image.

Open the Emboss.aep project from the Chapter 16 folder of the exercise files. This contains a beautiful vector dragon created by Yo Gabba Gabba artist/animator Will Kindrick, who has supplied much of the medieval art we'll be using in this chapter. Thanks, Will.

Apply the Color Emboss effect to the dragon. Instantly, you can see the added highlights and shadows that create the illusion of depth. The results are obvious, but to make them more pronounced, I'm going to increase the Relief value to 1.5, and the Contrast value to 150. The Relief value somewhat determines how deep the embossing is. Be careful that you don't take this too high, because the highlights and shadows in the embossing will begin to appear to float away. The Contrast property will brighten the emboss highlights and darken the emboss shadows to make the effect more pronounced (or less so, if you reduce it).

Figure 16.19 The Emboss.aep project.

Figure 16.20 After increasing the Relief value to 1.5 and the Contrast to 150, the effects of Color Emboss are more obvious.

Now that we see the embossed results, we can change the Direction value to adjust the angle of the simulated light that is creating this emboss effect. By default the light is coming up from the bottom left towards the upper right. Change the Direction value to –90 to change the light to come from the right side of the layer, pointing to the left. The effect is especially noticeable in the inside details of the wings (which, by the way, would not be changed at all by the Bevel and Emboss layer style in After Effects).

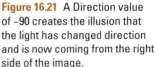
Figure 16.21 A Direction value of −90 creates the illusion that the light has changed direction and is now coming from the right side of the image.

The Emboss Effect

The Emboss effect is just like the Color Emboss effect, but it only returns grayscale results. To get this result to have color, you'll need to add it to the top copy of a layer's duplicate, and then blend using one of the overlay blend modes (e.g., Overlay, Soft Light, Pin Light, etc.). The settings in the Emboss effect are exactly the same as those in the Color Emboss effect.

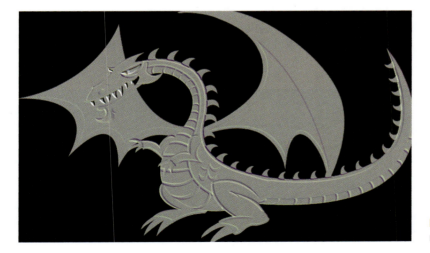

Figure 16.22 The Emboss effect results.

The Find Edges Effect

The Find Edges effect only creates these weird (dare I say ugly?) patterns by exaggerating edges, and brightening and fading nonedge pixels. This is not an effect that you should approach without your creative hat on. But used intelligently, can yield interesting results.

Import the video clip CJ121.mov from the Artbeats folder in the Media folder of the exercise files. This footage contains some sweet CG motion graphics.

Figure 16.23 The CJ121.mov clip, at 0;00;01;16.

Apply the Find Edges effect to this footage. It will be desecrated temporarily, but have faith. We shall overcome this visual vulgarity soon enough.

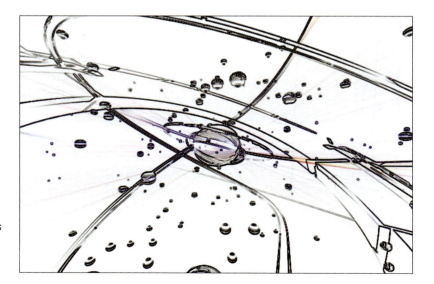

Figure 16.24 The default results from applying the Find Edges effect. Hopefully you haven't eaten recently.

There really aren't any settings here, other than Invert and Blend With Original. There isn't a tolerance or threshold property to change the limits of what After Effects sees as an edge.

Okay, I think I've looked at this as long as I can stand. Duplicate this layer in the Timeline panel, the delete the Find Edges effect on the bottom copy. Select the layer copy on the top in the layer stack in the Timeline panel (the one with the Find Edges effect still applied), and change its layer blend mode to the Overlay blend mode. This removes the junk and blends the enhanced edges back into itself, creating a cool effect. The result is a little intense, so you may want to temper it by lowering the opacity of the top layer just a tad.

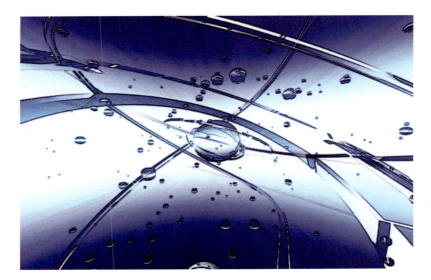

Figure 16.25 After blending the Find Edges effect with the Overlay blend mode, the edges are enhanced and the ugliness goes away. Like I always say, "If Overlay can't fix it, it's broke!"

In this way, Find Edges can be really useful in working with footage that needs more contrast in its edges. But we can also use it for creative purposes when combined with other effects. We're now going to create a quick massive video screen look using Find Edges. I'm going to delete (or turn off the visibility of) the top layer, leaving only the layer on bottom that doesn't have the effect applied. Then apply the Mosaic effect to this layer. We'll look at the Mosaic effect later in this chapter.

Next, apply the Find Edges effect to this layer. The Find Edges effect is finding (enhancing) the edges of the Mosaic effect.

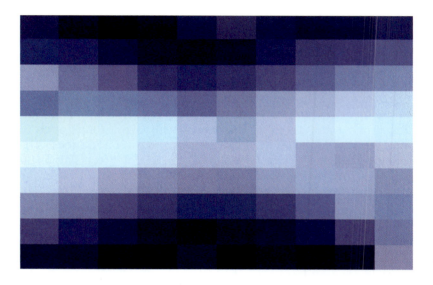

Figure 16.26 The results of applying the Mosaic effect to our footage.

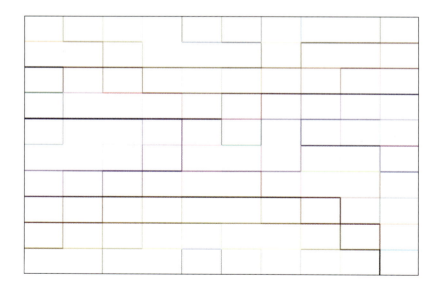

Figure 16.27 The result of applying the Find Edges effect after the Mosaic effect.

Now all that's left to do is to duplicate this layer, and remove the effects applied to the copy on the bottom. Then take the layer on top (the one with the effects) into the Multiply blend mode in the Timeline panel. This will remove the highlights in the Find Edges effect and darken the mosaic lines. This creates an organic grid like a large video screen, or a series of tiles.

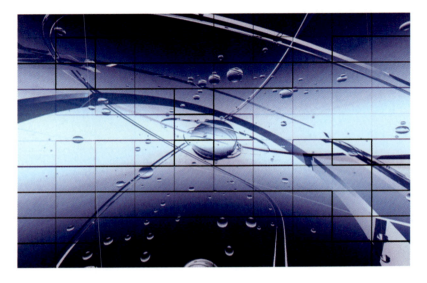

Figure 16.28 Our final results after blending the results of the Find Edges and Mosaic effects.

The Glow Effect

The Glow effect is without question my favorite Stylize effect, and is one of my top five effects in all of After Effects. The Glow effect obviously adds a glow to a layer, but it's not the same glow that you would find in Photoshop. The glow effects you find in Photoshop (and After Effects) layer styles create an outer or inner glow around a layer's transparency. In contrast, the Glow effect creates contrast and brightens highlights and can even add blur to the glow to exaggerate it further. If you want to create effects with light or anything glowing, you will almost certainly want to try out the Glow effect.

Open the Glow.aep project from the Chapter 16 folder of the exercise files. This project contains 3 comps to help you master and appreciate the Glow effect. Let's start in the Glow Start comp.

The Glow Start comp contains a render from the 3D application, 3DS Max. Renders from 3D applications have a tendency to look really dull and lifeless. This image is supposed to be glowing fiery lava, and instead it looks like a cheeseburger that got run over by a truck. Apply the Glow effect to the lava layer.

The results when the Glow effect is first applied probably look worse than what we started with. Let's fix this. There are a lot of parameters in the Glow effect, but the 3 that I use most often by far are Glow Threshold, Glow Radius, and Glow Intensity. The Glow Threshold parameter specifies the tolerance for what brightness levels will glow. Take the Glow Threshold value down to 28% to apply glow to more of the areas with lava in this image.

Figure 16.29 The Glow Start comp in the Glow.aep project.

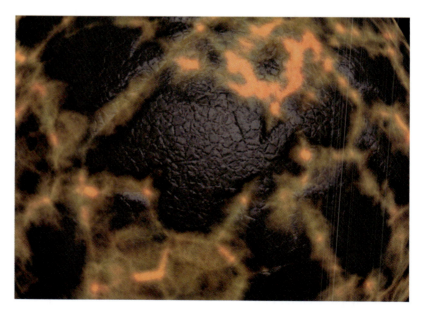

Figure 16.30 The default results after applying the Glow effect to the lava image.

Now, the areas we want to have glow are glowing, but the glow is too concentrated. The Glow Radius value determines the radius of the blur around the glowing areas. Increasing this value can make the glow dissipate a little, while still keeping the lava glowing. I'm going to increase the Glow Radius value to 73.

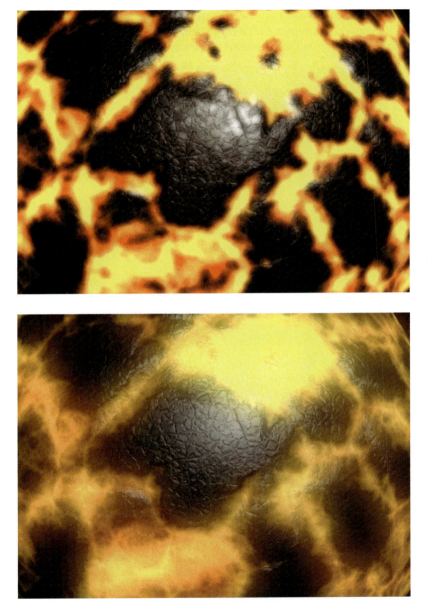

Figure 16.31 The result of decreasing the Glow Threshold value to 28%.

Figure 16.32 The result of increasing the Glow Radius to 73.

This is looking better, but the glow is a little too intense. The glowing areas are creating a haze over the entire image, which is brightening our shadows in effect. That makes the glowing areas less potent and vibrant. We need to reduce the intensity of the glow, which we can do by decreasing the Glow Intensity value. The Glow Intensity value is very sensitive, often returning noticeably different results when adjusted even one-tenth in either direction. In this case I'm going to take down the Glow Intensity value to 0.5. That creates a glow that we can be proud of.

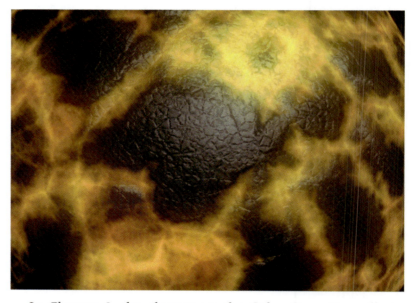

Figure 16.33 The final result of adding glow to our lava layer.

In Chapter 6, the chapter on the Color Correction effects, we looked at several different ways to colorize an object. Interestingly enough, the Glow effect is also another tool that we can use to colorize footage or patterns. Switch over to the More Glow composition. This comp contains a pattern I created with Fractal Noise and Radial Blur. It is still grayscale.

Figure 16.34 The grayscale pattern in the More Glow composition.

Apply the Glow effect to this texture. By default, when the Glow effect works its magic, it does so by glowing the original colors of the layer. Thus, in the case here, the Glow effect just creates a white glow. The first step in creating a colored glow is to change the Glow Colors drop down from Original Colors to A & B Colors. What are A & B Colors you ask? They are the colors in the Color A and Color B values at the bottom of the effect in the Effect Controls panel. These colors create a gradient, which is then used as the glow colors.

I'm going to change my Color A value to a bright pink (with an RGB value of 248, 52, 255), and the Color B value to a bluish color (43, 116, 226).

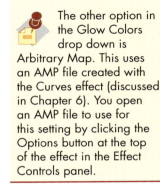

Pointless Trivia

The other option in the Glow Colors drop down is Arbitrary Map. This uses an AMP file created with the Curves effect (discussed in Chapter 6). You open an AMP file to use for this setting by clicking the Options button at the top of the effect in the Effect Controls panel.

Figure 16.35 The colors used for the Color A and Color B values.

Usually, when changing the Glow Colors value from Original Colors to A & B Colors, the glow results change dramatically. To get a better looks with the A & B colors, I lowered Glow Threshold to 10%, increased Glow Radius to 55, and reduced Glow Intensity to 0.8. This produces a colorized result that is pretty impressive.

Figure 16.36 After adjusting the glow settings, the A & B colors produce an appealing colorization of our initial texture.

To see one other example, click on the Glow Final comp tab in the Timeline panel. This contains another grayscale texture created with a series of strokes made with the Vegas effect (discussed in Chapter 9) and the Directional Blur effect (discussed in Chapter 4).

Figure 16.37 The Glow Final comp.

Since this texture was created using 4 layers together, I created an adjustment layer above the 4 layers, then applied the Glow effect to the adjustment layer to affect the entire composition simultaneously. Turn on the visibility of the adjustment layer to see the results I created with the Glow effect, using the techniques we've looked at.

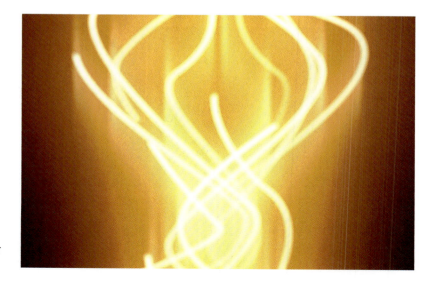

Figure 16.38 The Glow Final comp with the adjustment layer with the Glow effect turned on.

If you're interested in seeing the settings I used here, you can see them in Figure 16.39. You'll notice in this figure that I've also tweaked the Color Phase and A & B Midpoint values. These determine how the A & B colors are balanced, in case you want more of one of the two colors in your image.

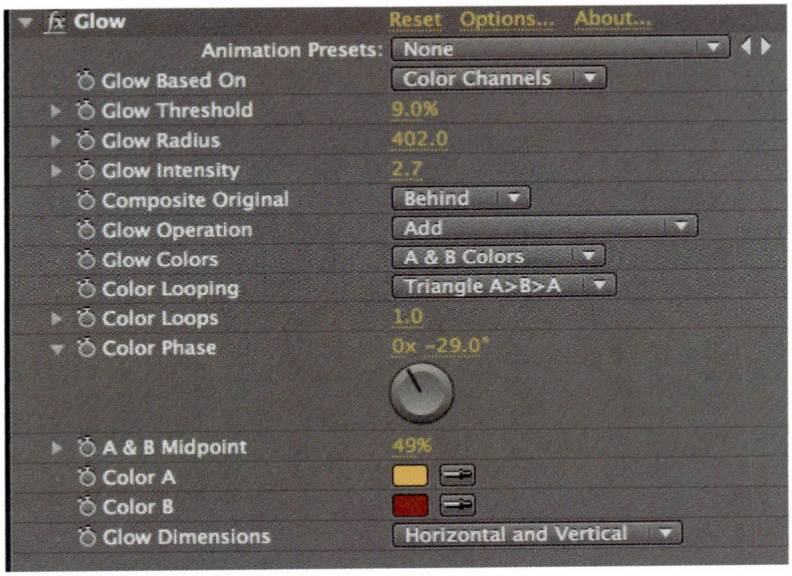

Figure 16.39 The settings I used to create the glowing results.

The Mosaic Effect

The Mosaic effect turns your footage into a series of shaded rectangles, based on the colors of your footage. It can be used to turn detailed footage into a generic background, or for obscuring details, as we'll see in the upcoming examples.

Open the Mosaic.aep project from the Chapter 16 folder of the exercise files. This project contains two comps, which we'll use for two different purposes with the Mosaic effect. First, we'll start in the Dragon Fight comp.

Apply the Mosaic effect to this footage. As you can see, it uses the original colors of the layer to create a grid of rectangles with flat color.

Sometimes, the results are a little lackluster by default. We could apply an effect like Levels or Curves to increase the intensity of these colors. But the Mosaic effect has a built in option that increases the contrast and intensity of these colors without any additional help. Select the Sharp Colors option to intensify these colors.

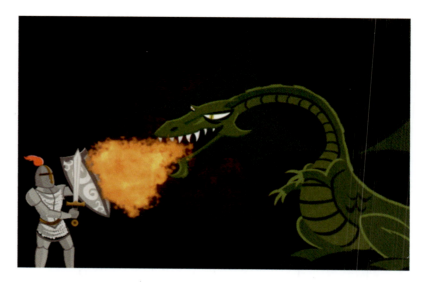

Figure 16.40 The Dragon Fight comp.

Figure 16.41 After applying the Mosaic effect, we have a mosaic based on the colors in our footage.

The Mosaic effect can be great if you have copyrighted footage (or other footage that you don't have permission to use), but you really like the color scheme. You can apply the Mosaic effect to completely obscure the details and reuse the color scheme, and no one is the wiser.

We can increase or decrease the resolution of the mosaic by adjusting the Horizontal Blocks and Vertical Blocks options. Look how cool the results are when we make the blocks three across

Figure 16.42 The Sharp Colors option makes the colors more intense.

(by taking the Horizontal Blocks value to 3) and 20 high (by taking the Vertical Blocks value to 20).

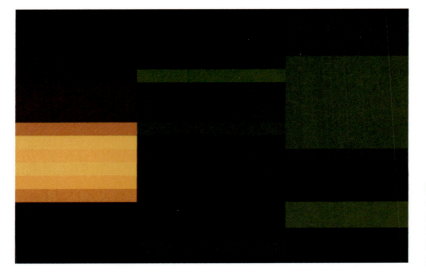

Figure 16.43 We create an entirely new pattern that looks nothing like a standard mosaic by altering the Horizontal Blocks and Vertical Blocks properties.

Let's now switch over to the Offensive Face comp. This comp contains some footage of me, duplicated once. On the top copy, I've isolated my face using a mask.

One of the more common uses of the Mosaic effect is to blur out details. You might have footage of someone being interviewed that doesn't want their identity revealed, or you might not have permission to show someone in your video.

Figure 16.44 The Offensive Face comp. We're actually seeing two layers here—one of my face isolated with a mask, and also the background version, which contains the entire clip.

This technique is also used to obscure offensive, obscene, or trademarked elements in footage.

I have a face only a mother could love (and even that is questionable), so we're going to use the Mosaic effect to make this footage less offensive. Turn on the visibility of the top copy of this layer, which already has the Mosaic effect applied and set up for you. Here, the Horizontal Blocks and Vertical Blocks values have been increased to 50 each. The higher the block numbers, the more resolution can be seen. We still want it to be clear that we are blocking out a face, so I used relatively high numbers for these values.

Figure 16.45 The result of applying the Mosaic effect to the layer that contained only my face.

The Motion Tile Effect

The Motion Tile effect is just like the Offset effect, but it is far more powerful. It also allows you to repeat a layer multiple times, but gives you more control over the adjustment of those duplicates. Because of this extra control, the Motion Tile effect is great for patterns, or for creating a multitude of something.

Open the Motion Tile.aep project from the Chapter 16 folder of the exercise files. This simple project contains one comp with a tank I created in Illustrator. Apply the Motion Tile effect to this tank.

Figure 16.46 The Motion Tile .aep project.

The Tile Center property at the top of the effect in the Effect Control panel is akin to the offset value. Taking the X dimension of the Tile Center value to 650 shows how this effect functions like the Offset effect. It allows you to create an apparently endless loop of your layer. If we animated this property high enough, we would create a large armada of tanks traveling in one direction.

The Tile Width and Tile Height values are a little misleading, but they're also two of the more powerful properties in this effect. Think of these two values like scale values. And, with an effect like Motion Tile that repeats elements, making something smaller—in either dimension—will create more copies. Take both the Tile Width and Tile Height values to 20. This scales down the tanks, creating many more of them. Because the Tile Width and Tile Height values are the same, the tank scales down proportionately. If these values were different, it would create a non-uniform scale of our object.

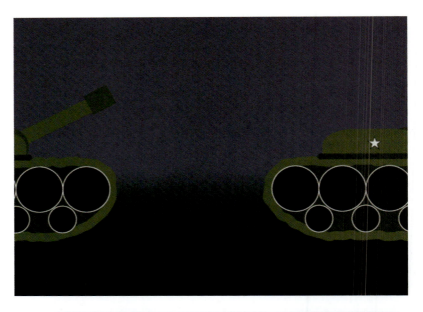

Figure 16.47 The Tile Center value is like an offset property.

Figure 16.48 Reducing the Tile Width and Tile Height values shrinks down our tank(s), but it also creates several more of them.

The Output Width and Output Height values are essentially horizontal and vertical masks for this effect. If I reduce the Output Width value to 60, for example, then the left and right sides are cropped off. This is similar to duplicating the layer and applying a mask to it, but it saves you a step. Let's say that you had a lower third or some other area in which your seamless patterns had to be confined. These output options would be quite handy.

Figure 16.49 The result of reducing the Output Width value to 60, which reduces the width of the layer to 60% of its original size.

Taking the Output Width value back to its default (100), I'm going to select the Mirror Edges option. This causes every other copy in both directions to flip. So, every other vertical copy flips vertically, and every other horizontal copy flips horizontally. You can now start to see the great power of this effect in generating repeating patterns, and its advantages over the Offset effect.

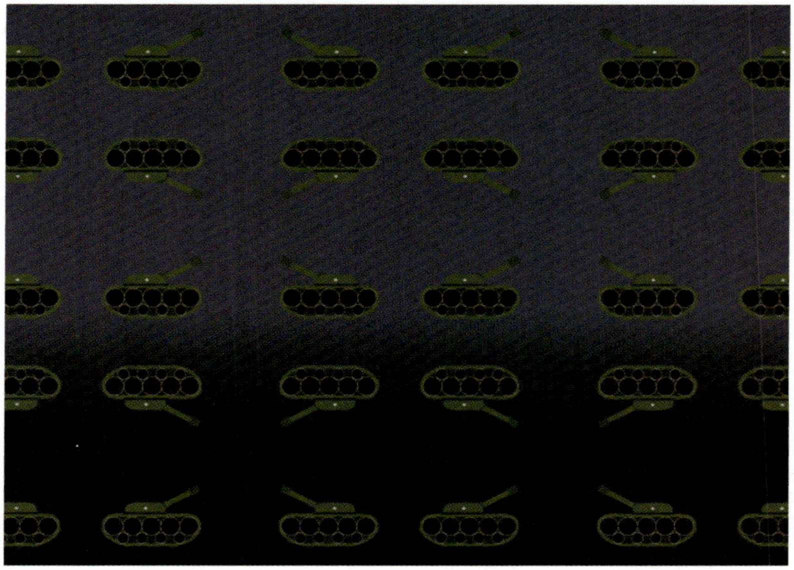

Figure 16.50 Selecting Mirror Edges inverts every other instance of the tank.

Perhaps my favorite parameter here is the Phase parameter. The Phase value shifts every other vertical line of copies, like in a casino gambling machine. You can shift every other horizontal line of copies by selecting the Horizontal Phase checkbox. In Figure 16.51, I left Horizontal Phase unchecked, and changed the Phase value to 180 degrees. Again we see the great versatility of this effect to create patterns and large numbers of objects from a single object.

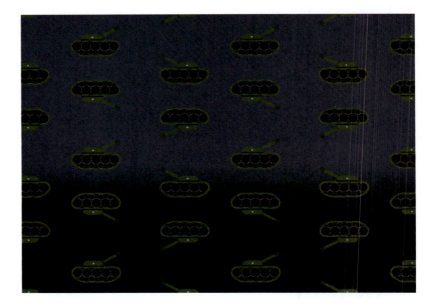

Figure 16.51 With the Phase value at 180 degrees, every other column shifts vertically, creating more randomization.

The Posterize Effect

The Posterize effect reduces the numbers of colors in an image, which often creates hard transitions between colors. When I first started learning digital arts, this was usually a very bad thing. But in modern times, edgy lo-fi art is very popular. Often, art in this style is vector based, like the art created in Adobe Illustrator. In this example, we're going to use the Posterize effect to help us create some trashy, urban, street style art with apparently flat color. For an even more dramatic effect, check out the Threshold effect at the end of this chapter.

Import the CED113.mov clip from the Artbeats folder in the Media folder of the exercise files. This clip contains a high quality aerial shot of a big city—perfect fodder for posterized, edgy graphics. I'm going to drag the Current Time Indicator out to 7 seconds and 14 frames (0;00;07;14).

Figure 16.52 The CED113.mov clip at 0;00;07;14.

Apply the Posterize effect. While the default results apply some degree of posterization, it's not nearly enough. The default results remind me of bad web graphics from the late 1990s. So let's adjust the Level value, which is the only parameter

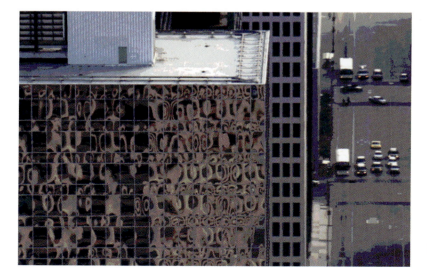

Figure 16.53 The default results of applying the Posterize effect.

in this effect. With the Posterize effect, high Level values create a smoother result, eventually making the posterized image resemble the original footage. Ironically, reducing the Level value actually increases the amount of posterization by reducing the number of colors used.

My only complaint with the Posterize effect is the way that the Level effect is set up. While the property only displays integer values, it actually is capable of recognizing fractions in the hundredths. So, values of 2.51 through 3.49, for example, get rounded off and displayed as 3. The value I'm looking for here is 3 exactly, so click and type in the number 3 for the Level value. Don't scrub to this value, or you could achieve different results, not realizing that the value is not exactly on 3.

Figure 16.54 After taking the Level value to 3, the results are less smooth.

It's important to note here that the Level value does not refer to the exact number of colors, per se. Although, you reduce the number of colors in the image by lowering the Level value, the Level value does not specifically refer to the total number of remaining colors.

We need to add one final step here. Apply the Tritone effect (discussed in Chapter 6) to this result, which will force all colors to become one of three colors. I used a pale yellow color for the Highlights value, a deep red for the Midtones value, and left the Shadows value at black. The results look like edgy Illustrator art that you might find on an urban poster.

Figure 16.55 The final results after applying the Tritone effect.

The Roughen Edges Effect

If you're currently unfamiliar with the Roughen Edges effect, it might possibly be the best thing that you get out of this book. The Roughen Edges effect, well … roughens edges. But this comes in handy so much, as we'll see.

It's important to realize what's going on behind the scenes with this effect. It's basically distorting the edges of a layer (or sometimes its contents, depending on your settings) by using a fractal pattern, similar to Fractal Noise (from Chapter 12). Because of this, the Roughen Edges effect has many important parameters (such as Complexity and Evolution) that are similar to Fractal Noise and other effects like it.

Open the Roughen Edges.aep project from the Chapter 16 folder of the exercise files. First we'll start in the Roughen Edges comp, which contains some text on a shape layer.

Apply the Roughen Edges effect to the GINGIVITIS Outlines layer (the text). Instantly after applying the Roughen Edges effect, you can see the result on the text. The text already seems to have more life and character, even without changing any parameters or animating anything! This plain, boring font has been transformed into creepy text, befitting of a dreaded gum disease.

Increasing the Border value probably has the most significant results. The Border value determines how many pixels the rough-

Figure 16.56 The Roughen
Edges comp.

Figure 16.57 The default results
after applying Roughen Edges.

ened edges get to dig into the layer. Even taking the Border value
from 8 to 15 makes an extreme change.

At the very top of the effect in the Effect Controls panel,
you'll notice an Edge Type drop down. This specifies how the
edges will be roughened. There are a lot of options here worth
exploring. You can select Roughen Color, for example, which
uses the Edge Color value as part of the roughening. This creates
a realistic rust effect with the default color value. But you could

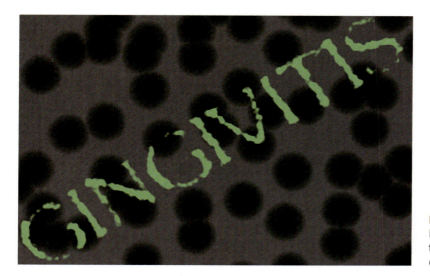

Figure 16.58 Increasing the Border value allows more of the edge of the layer to be eroded.

also use this to create fiery edges, or other results. All values in the Edge Type drop down that have the word color in their title (e.g., Rusty Color, Photocopy Color) use the Edge Color value in their results.

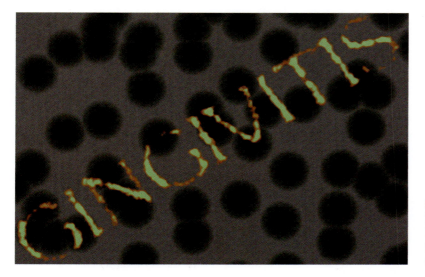

Figure 16.59 Selecting Roughen Color as the Edge Type allows the Edge Color to be added in the roughened edges.

The Spiky edge type is another unique value. This can create ornate, spiky edges that be used for spiky, fiery, or electric edges.

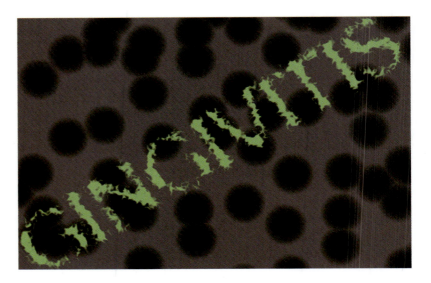

Figure 16.60 The text with the Spiky edge type.

Some of the edge types, such as Rusty and Photocopy, actually leave the edges perfectly intact, and instead erode the layer itself. Why these options are in an effect called Roughen Edges (and selectable in a parameter called Edge Type) is beyond me, but they're really interesting, so I'm not complaining! The Rusty Color edge type is great for making objects look rusty and old. It actually eats away at the transparency of the layer. The Photocopy edge type creates random worn areas in the center of the layer, which creates the illusion of damage or wear.

Figure 16.61 The text with the Rusty Color edge type.

Figure 16.62 The text with the Photocopy edge type.

Using a Border value of 3, the Photocopy edge type can create the illusion that our layer has only an outline, without a core.

Figure 16.63 The result of lowering the Border value to 3 with the Edge Type value set to Photocopy.

The remaining properties are self-explanatory if you remember that these edges are being distorted with a fractal pattern. For example, the Scale property scales the noise pattern, creating tighter or larger edges. And, as with Fractal Noise and Cell Pattern, these edges can come alive with the Evolution parameter. You can also create the illusion that there is a force (like wind) acting on these edges by animating the Offset (Turbulence) parameter.

Now, let's go over to the Dragon Fire FINAL comp. This comp contains some great Will Kindrick art that we've seen a few times in this book. The difference is here, that the fireball isn't complete yet. I must confess that there was a time in my life when I was an Adobe Certified Instructor in After Effects, and yet I couldn't make a decent fireball. How can this be, you ask? It was a dirty shameful secret that even my family didn't know about. If I hadn't found the answer in Roughen Edges, my wife probably would have left me for another After Effects trainer that knew how to make fireballs.

Figure 16.64 shows the Dragon Fire FINAL comp with the fireball in its original state. This fireball is created with a solid with the Fractal Noise effect applied. A simple mask is also applied to create the approximate fireball shape. The obvious problem here is that fireballs don't have smooth edges.

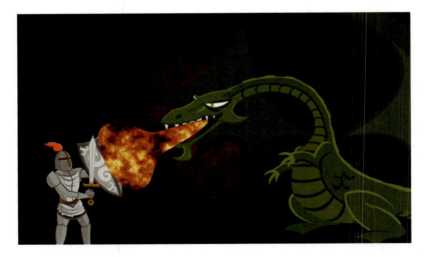

Figure 16.64 The Dragon Fire FINAL comp.

At the lowest point in my life (when I couldn't make a decent fireball), I tried to fake it by feathering the mask. There are several problems with this method. We're colorizing this fire with the Colorama effect, which acts on the alpha channel after masks are applied. So, feathering the mask only makes a larger fireball because Colorama also colorizes the semitransparent pixels and makes them completely opaque. The results ain't pretty.

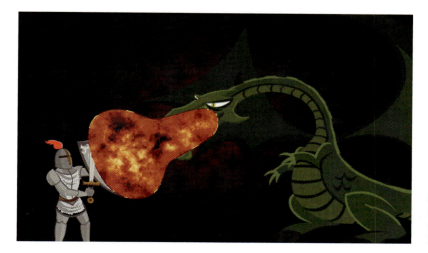

Figure 16.65 The result of increasing the feather of the mask applied to the fireball layer.

I realize that we could fix this by precomposing the layer, then applying a mask with feather to the nested precomp. But even that doesn't make a decent enough fireball to convince my wife to stay with me. We need something more here. We need the Roughen Edges effect. Apply it to the fireball layer, and take the Border value up to 50. That makes a fairly decent fireball right there. You can add more detail to the edges of the fireball by reducing the Scale property and/or by increasing the Complexity value.

To make the fireball shown in Figure 16.66, I set the Edge Type to Spiky, increased the Border value to 70, decreased Edge

Figure 16.66 Roughen Edges help me create the fireball that saved my marriage.

Sharpness to 0.2, decreased Fractal Influence to 0.7, increased Scale to 180, and increased Complexity to 3. After seeing this fire, I also went back to Fractal Noise to reduce the Complexity to 3, to go more with my newfound sexy edges. I've also increased the zoom magnification to 200% to make my changes more visible.

The Scatter Effect

The Scatter effect breaks up layers into many tiny fragments. It's definitely not a high end tool, but it can create quick and simple animations.

Open the Scatter.aep project in the Chapter 16 folder of the exercise files. This project contains the tank graphic we saw earlier in this chapter, but it also has a smooth yellow area created with a yellow solid layer with a mask applied to it.

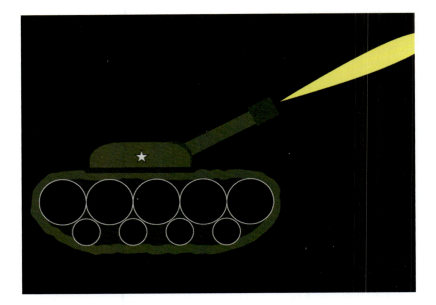

Figure 16.67 The Scatter.aep project.

Unless this tank is fighting an enemy that is allergic to banana pudding, this isn't the most persuasive ammo to be shooting. Apply the Scatter effect to the yellow solid layer. Increase the Scatter Amount value to 150 to scatter the pixels of the layer. You can choose a dimension of the scatter in the Grain drop down (not sure why it's called the Grain parameter). And if you want to have the scattered pixels of the layer flicker and animate, select the Randomize Every Frame checkbox at the bottom of the effect.

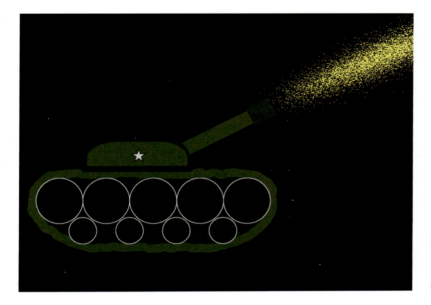

Figure 16.68 The result of applying the Scatter effect and increasing the Scatter Amount value.

The Strobe Light Effect

The Strobe Light effect is another obscure effect that can actually come in handy in several ways. It creates a strobe effect by either flashing a color on the layer, or by making it transparent. It will be a little challenging demonstrating in print, so I heartily recommend following along with the project in the exercise files.

Open the Strobe Light.aep project from the Chapter 16 folder. This project contains two comps—Strobe Light Start, and Strobe of Lightning. We'll start in Strobe Light Start. This comp contains a simple red solid, just so you can see the results of the Strobe Light effect.

Apply the Strobe Light effect to the red solid square. The results aren't obvious until you preview the composition, at which point you'll see that the Strobe Light effect is creating a white flash on the layer. The Strobe Light effect has a number of parameters you can change, including the color of the strobe, its duration, frequency, and more.

One of the best aspects of this effect is the Strobe drop down. By default, it is set to Operates on Color Only. This creates a flash of color on the layer. I don't find this option all that useful, frankly. Perhaps it can be beneficial for creating twinkling lights or something of that nature.

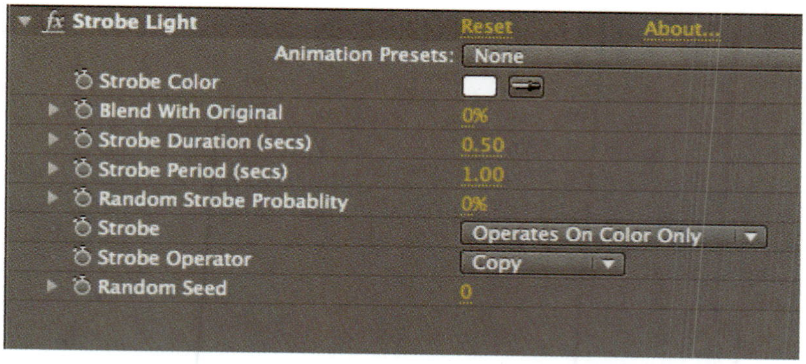

Figure 16.69 The Strobe Light effect options.

However, the effect becomes much more helpful when the Strobe drop down is changed to Makes Layer Transparent. This can make layers flash on and off. The benefit of this will be readily seen as we go over to the Strobe of Lightning comp. This contains an animated instance of the Advanced Lightning effect.

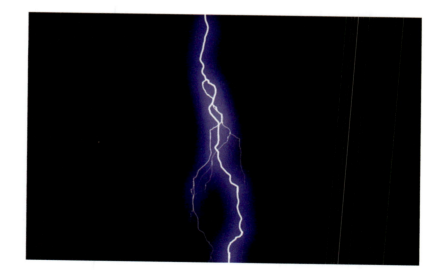

Figure 16.70 The Strobe of Lightning comp.

The Strobe Light effect has already been applied for you in this comp, with the Strobe value set to Makes Layer Transparent. This turns several seconds of continuous lightning into several lightning strikes. This is the quickest way that I've found to create a flashing layer. You could even apply a wiggle expression to the Strobe Period value to create more random timing in the strobes.

The Texturize Effect

The Texturize effect would probably be more descriptive if it were called the Watermark effect, because that's essentially what it does. It takes one layer, and makes a transparent version of it applied to a layer. You can use it to create a logo "bug" (the little station identifier at the bottom right hand corner of the screen that constantly and annoyingly reminds you what station you're watching). Or, you can use it to create a protective, and yet non-obstructive mark on footage to prevent others from using it professionally.

Open the Texturize.aep project from the Chapter 16 folder of the exercise files. This project contains a comp with some video footage of Seattle with loads of effects applied (some from this chapter, some from Chapter 6), and it also contains a vector logo.

Figure 16.71 The Texturize comp.

The first thing to do is to turn off the visibility of the logo layer (Static Logo for AE). This is the texture we're going to apply to the Seattle footage, and we don't actually want to see this layer. Apply the Texturize effect to the seattle.mov layer. In the Effect Controls panel, change the Texture Layer drop down to the logo layer. This creates a tiled arrangement of the semi-transparent version of the logo all across the Seattle footage.

Figure 16.72 The results of applying the Texturize effect and using the logo as the Texture Layer value.

You can change the Light Direction and the Texture Contrast with the properties of the same names. You can use these properties to make the texturized logo more pronounced, or less so. You can also change how the texture is placed in the footage using the Texture Placement drop down list. For instance, you can center the layer instead of tiling it.

If you were really using this effect to create a logo bug, you'd probably want to apply the Texturize effect to the logo, and use the footage as the texture. That way, you'd have control over where your logo is placed, as well as its size and other properties.

Figure 16.73 The result of centering the logo texture and lowering the Texture Contrast to 0.5.

The Threshold Effect

The Threshold effect is another favorite from Photoshop. It does nothing more than convert every single pixel to pure white or pure black. This might seem pointless, but it does have a useful purpose, and an artistic one as well.

Open the Threshold.aep project from the Chapter 16 folder of the exercise files. This project contains two comps. We're going to start in the simple comp, Threshold Start. This contains a simple gradient.

Figure 16.74 The Threshold Start comp in the Threshold.aep project.

Apply the Threshold effect to this gradient. Every pixel will be turned pure white or pure black.

Figure 16.75 The default results of applying the Threshold effect.

We can only change one property: Level. This setting determines the cutoff as to which pixels turn white, and which ones turn black. Increase this value to 200 to turn more pixels black. If you were to decrease this value, more pixels would be turned white. This effect is great for tweaking the grayscale maps that you might use to control effect properties.

Figure 16.76 Increasing the Level value to 200 causes more pixels to be converted to black.

Now let's use the Threshold effect in a more practical scenario. Switch over to the Edgy Example comp.

Figure 16.77 The Edgy Example comp in the Threshold.aep project.

Figure 16.78 The final result, after applying the Threshold effect to the background video clip.

Like we discussed earlier in this chapter with Posterize, sometimes damaged or grungy graphics are exactly what you're looking for. Let's say we want to create an intro for an edgy music video. This comp contains a grungy logo, and a sugary sweet video clip of Mt. Rainier. The colors and textures are not conducive to a music video like this, but it's all we have available. No worries. Just apply the Threshold affect, and adjust to taste. This will instantly create the street cred we're looking for.

17

THE TEXT EFFECTS

Back in the old days when I started learning After Effects, the effects in the Text category were essential. However, in After Effects 6.0 Adobe added the most powerful text animation engine anyone had ever seen, and the Text effects became largely forgotten. In After Effects CS4, half of the Text effects were removed, stripped of their ranks, and discarded into the Obsolete category. So, who are the two effects that dodged the bullet? The Numbers and Timecode effects. And as you'll see, they deserve to stick around. Although simple, they can both come in handy for different purposes.

The Numbers Effect

The Numbers effect generates numbers; numbers of all kinds. Numbers can generate random numbers (including numbers with multiple decimal places), animate numbers counting forwards or backwards, it can generate time passing, the current timecode, the date, and more.

Applying the Numbers Effect

Go ahead and create a new composition. I used the NTSC DV preset with a length of 5 seconds. Also, create a new solid at the comp size. The color of the solid doesn't matter because Numbers will completely replace it. Then apply the Numbers effect to this solid.

When you first apply this effect, you're immediately greeted by a reminder how old school this effect is. This reminder comes in the form of a dialog box that pops up.

From this dialog, you can change the font size, style, and alignment. You can also choose whether to align the text horizontally or vertically in your comp. Figure 17.2 shows this effect with the Vertical option selected.

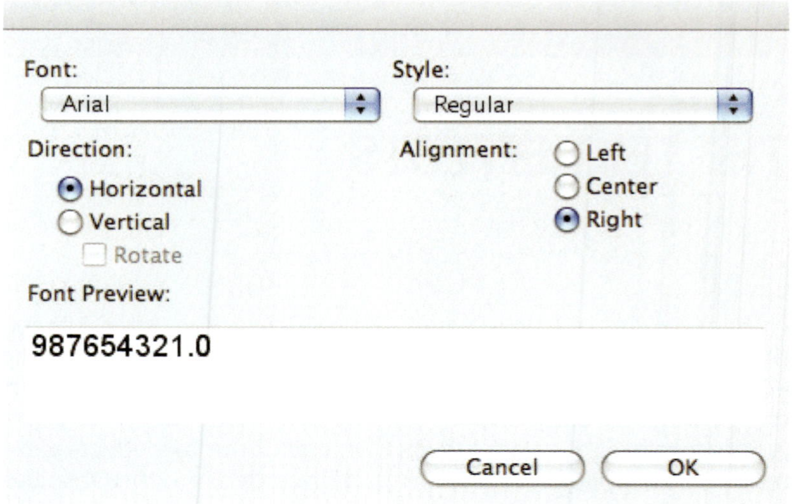

Font:
Arial
Style:
Regular

Direction:
⦿ Horizontal
◯ Vertical
☐ Rotate

Alignment:
◯ Left
◯ Center
⦿ Right

Font Preview:

987654321.0

Cancel   OK

Figure 17.1 The Numbers effect options dialog box.

Figure 17.2 Numbers with the Vertical direction chosen.

Notice how the characters have the same orientation as they would if you would've chose a horizontal direction. However, in the Numbers options, if you select the Rotate check box, the character will be rotated 90 degrees. See Figure 17.3 for the difference.

For now, just leave this dialog box alone (horizontal direction, et al.) and click OK. At any time, you can get back to this dialog box by clicking the Options button at the top of the effect in the Effects and Presets panel.

The Format Properties

Without a doubt, the most important properties in this effect are in the Format area at the top of the effect. The Type property drop down list at the top of the effect specifies what type of numbers are created. The default setting is just "Numbers." This means that only regular numbers will be created. The cool thing about this is that you can set keyframes from one number at one frame, to another number at another frame, and the Numbers effect will interpolate this difference. Let's say for example that you've got some footage of a rocket launching. You can set a keyframe for the Numbers effect to display the number 10 ten seconds before the rocket launches. You can then set another keyframe when the rocket launches to display the number 0, and then the Numbers effect will

Comparing Numbers to the Timecode Effect

Also be aware that from the Type drop down list, that you can chose three different types of timecode displays- 30 fps for NTSC, 25 fps for PAL, and 24 fps for film. The Timecode effect does the same thing, but gives you far more control over timecode options (such as drop frame timecode, and so forth), but it also gives you significantly less control over the appearance of the timecode. If you want to add a live timecode to your footage, and you want to be able to change the font or add a stroke, then use the Numbers effect.

interpolate the countdown. I'll show you how to do that momentarily. From the Type drop down list, you can also choose various displays of date, time, and a hexadecimal number.

Another one of the critical properties of this effect is the Value/Offset/Random Max value. This is where you can specify an exact number to display, if your Type value is set to Numbers. This is how you would specify 10 and 0 if you were animating the rocket launch countdown. Or, if you're using another Type value, such as timecode, time, or date, this value becomes an offset. For example, if you have the Type value set to Numerical Date, you'll see something like 1/1/95. If you increase the Value/Offset/Random Max value from 0.0 to 1.0, the date will display as 1/2/95. Again, we see another use for this effect as an indication of time or date passage, as with a time lapse.

If you've selected the Random Values option, then the Value/Offset/Random Max value sets a limit of how much the Numbers effect is allowed to randomize. It's a little kooky, though, because a value of 0 actually means "go crazy, Numbers effect." It really doesn't start limiting the randomization until you input a value of greater than 0. In effect, then, a value of 1.0 would create the smallest amount of randomization, while a value of 0 would create the most randomization.

Figure 17.3 Numbers with the Vertical direction and the Rotate option checked.

Figure 17.4 Click the Options button to get back the dialog that will allow you to change the font and other properties of the Numbers effect.

Does the Numbers effect auto-animate?

The Numbers effect does not auto-animate. However, if you simply check the Random Values option immediately below the Type drop down list, the Numbers effect will return randomly generated values on each frame automatically.

Fixing a big Numbers problem

One of the biggest pet peeves I have with the Numbers effect is that it appears to wiggle as it animates. Seriously. Try it yourself. Select Random Values and then preview it. Argh! Why is that the default? That is so annoying! The way to solve the problem is by deselecting the Proportional Spacing option at the bottom of the effect.

Changing the Appearance of Numbers

The remainder of the properties for the Numbers effect pertain to the appearance of the numbers. For the most part these are self-explanatory, and are similar to other what we've seen these properties do in other effects. You can add a stroke, adjust the stroke, display only the stroke, adjust fill and stroke colors, and composite the numbers on the original layer.

The Size property makes the characters larger or smaller. You can also increase (or decrease) the Tracking property to increase (or decrease) the space between all numbers. It is not possible to adjust the kerning, or in other words, the space between two characters while maintaining the space between the other characters.

Recreating the *24* Intro

Because I am a huge fan of the Jack Bauer power hour, one of my favorite tricks with the Numbers effect is to recreate the logo animation from the TV show *24* (R.I.P.). In this logo, a series of random numbers are generated, eventually stopping on the key numbers, 24. In the following mini-project, we'll recreate a similar logo using the Numbers effect.

For this exercise, I'm going to be using an LCD type font. I don't have the rights to distribute this font with this book, but you can Google LCD fonts and find plenty of places online to download LCD type fonts for free if you'd like to follow along exactly. Just remember that you'll have to restart After Effects if it was open when you installed the font. If you don't have an LCD style font, any font with numbers will do.

The first step is to have a blank comp with a solid layer at comp size, and then apply the Numbers effect to it. Change the font from the drop down list in the upper left hand corner of the Numbers options dialog box to the LCD font mentioned above, or another font of your choosing, and click OK. Then change the Value/Offset/Random Max value to 42 (so we don't get sued for using the number 24), and the Decimal Places value to 0. Then uncheck the annoying Proportional Spacing parameter at the bottom of the effect. I'll also increase my Size value to make these characters larger. I'm using a Size value of 320, but that will change depending on the font you've selected. After all this fiddling, you might also want to adjust your Position value to center the numbers. Figure 17.5 shows you what I have so far.

The next part will be a little trickier than you might think. In order to recreate this logo animation accurately, we need

Figure 17.5 This is my 42 logo so far. It's not much to look at yet, but have patience.

both characters to animate randomly and then stop on the number 42. However, once we select Random Values, then we lose control over the display of exact numbers because the Value/Offset/Random Max value becomes only a limit for randomness. So, how do we pull this off? There are actually a few solutions. We could create a Wiggle expression on the Value/Offset/Random Max property, connect the magnitude value of the Wiggle expression to an expression control, and then animate the expression control. But that's way too much work.

A much simpler way to get the job done is to simply animate the Random Values property. So, go out to about 3 seconds in your timeline, and click the stopwatch for the Random Values property with the checkbox unchecked. This tells After Effects that at 3 seconds, we want randomization off, and to display the value 42. Now, hit the Home key on your keyboard (or use another method) to get to the first frame of the comp. Then click the checkbox to turn on Random Values. We're not going to animate the Value/Offset/Random Max property.

Making the Logo Even More Awesome

So, we're essentially done with the part of the tutorial that uses the Numbers effect. Now, we're going to finish the job by making this look more like the *24* logo. We'll do that by adding an additional effect.

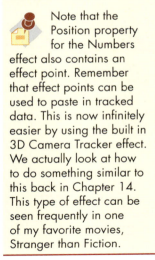

Tracking and the Numbers Effect

Note that the Position property for the Numbers effect also contains an effect point. Remember that effect points can be used to paste in tracked data. This is now infinitely easier by using the built in 3D Camera Tracker effect. We actually look at how to do something similar to this back in Chapter 14. This type of effect can be seen frequently in one of my favorite movies, Stranger than Fiction.

Animating the Random Values Property

Typically we don't animate properties that only have on/off options. This is because they don't interpolate well. In this case, that's exactly what we want. Just know that this is an exception.

Apply the Glow effect from the Stylize category. We'll change values from the top of the effect to the bottom. Change the Glow Threshold value from 60% to 10%. This allows more of the numbers to be subject to the glow. Then change the Glow Colors value from Original Colors to A & B Colors. This tells the Glow effect that instead of using the default red color from the Numbers effect as the glow color, we're going to be choosing two of our own colors to use. Click the color swatch for the Color A property and select a yellow-orange color. I used the RGB values of 220, 220, 0. Finally, change the Color B value to white, and you're done!

Figure 17.6 The final 42 logo.

If you wanted to take this project to the next level, here are a couple suggestions. You could apply the Transform effect and adjust the Skew Axis to 90 degrees, and take the Skew value to about 5 or so. This will create a faux italics if you don't have an italicized version of the font you're using. You could also apply and animate a blur effect to have it blur the randomized characters, and then stop blurring when the logo comes to a stop at 24. For an even greater effect, you could add an additional Directional Blur effect (on top of the other blur effect), and then duplicate that layer and apply the Add blend mode to the top layer. Feel free to play with any combination of color correction effects, blurs, and layer tricks, such as adjustment layers, blend modes, and layer duplication.

If you'd like to examine my completed project, I've created an aep file for you called 42 project.aep. You'll find it in the Chapter 17 folder of the exercise files.

Figure 17.7 The logo after adding a few extra touches.

The Timecode Effect

The Timecode effect is actually very similar to the Numbers effect with one of the Timecode options selected. It essentially just displays the timecode of the current frame. The difference here is that the Timecode effect gives you a lot less control over the appearance of the timecode, but a lot more control over the format.

So, it goes without saying that the Timecode effect is purely utilitarian. It's not intended to be displayed on a final project. It's meant to be used for things like collaboration on visual effects shots.

Let's briefly cover the differences here between this and the Numbers effect. For one, your timecode display with the Timecode effect can be used to display the film standard of feet and frames. You can also select the Drop Frame option to display drop frame timecode if desired. The Time Units property allows you to manually input the number of frames per second. All of these parameters are important because the Timecode effect does not change its defaults based on the composition it is applied to. Everything must be input manually.

The Starting Frame value serves as an offset. You may have received footage from a 3D artist with a few seconds of blank space at the beginning, and you might want to adjust the display of the timecode to start at zero once the action begins. Thus, you would use the Starting Frame value to adjust the timecode

Guide Layers and the Timecode Effect

If you wanted to keep the Timecode effect visible while you're working, but you don't want it to render, consider applying the effect to an adjustment layer or a guide layer. You can convert any layer into a guide layer by right clicking it in the Timeline panel and selecting Guide Layer. Unless manually specified to do so in the Render Settings in the Render Queue, guide layers do not render.

value to start when the action in the 3D file started. Note that you can also change the starting timecode of the composition in the Composition Settings dialog box, which would automatically make the Timecode effect display the correct, adjusted timecode.

It's also important to note that the default setting for Time Source is Layer Source. This takes the timecode from the layer it's applied to, which might not match the composition timecode (which is almost always what I want this effect for). So, change the Time Source drop down from Layer Source to Composition in order to display the timecode of the current comp.

18

THE TIME EFFECTS

The effects in the Time category all fiddle with time. Some of them, like Echo and Time Displacement, can create some really interesting visual effects using time tricks. Time Difference is a huge help for visual effects and color correction.

The powerhouse effect in this category is of course, Timewarp. Timewarp allows you to speed up and slow down time, to control the quality of the end result, and to apply motion blur to footage that has already been rendered.

The Echo Effect

The Echo effect creates copies (echoes) of a layer by adding duplicates from different places in time.

In the Echo.aep project you'll find in the Chapter 18 folder of the exercise files. In Figure 18.1, we see the original video clip without the Echo effect applied. This clip shows my friend, Paavo—a video editor at lynda.com—doing some of his sweet unicycle tricks.

Figure 18.1 The original footage of Paavo doing a stair jump on his unicycle. Don't try this at home, kids.

Where won't Echo work?

The Echo effect only works on layers that change over time, but the motion must be either rendered or precomposed. Still images that are animated in the current composition won't do much with the Echo effect.

Apply the Echo effect to the stair jump PRECOMP layer in the stair jump composition. The default results in this case don't look all that great. To get a better idea of what Echo is doing, change the Echo Time (seconds) value to −0.35, and change the Echo Operator value from Add to Minimum. Also, take the Number of Echoes to 8. Then you'll see what's really going on here.

Figure 18.2 After applying the Echo effect, we can see a composite of multiple frames from this layer.

The Echo effect creates echoes in time by blending frames from different times together into one composite. This creates a visual "echo" as the frames ripple into one another. Echo works well for those times when you want to really exaggerate an action in video, and slow motion just doesn't pack a big enough punch. It also can create visually interesting motion graphics because the echo effect creates a trail. In this example, Paavo's stair jump was in a beautiful and natural arc, which looks awesome when echoed.

The Echo Time (seconds) parameter determines where, in time, that the echoes come from. A negative value will create the echoes from the past, and a positive value will take create echoes from the future. Remember that this value is the time between echoes in seconds, not frames. Figure 18.3 shows the Echo Time value at −0.15, which is much shorter than what we saw in Figure 18.2. Notice how the echoes are now much closer together.

In Figure 18.4, I've adjusted the Echo Time value to a positive number. Both Figures 18.3 and 18.4 show the exact same frame. Thus we see how negative values take previous frames to make echoes, which causes the current frame to be the beginning of the trail. A positive value causes echoes to be from upcoming frames, which causes the current frame to be the caboose in a choo-choo train of echoes.

Use a tripod!

One of the things that really helped with this trick is that the camera operator was using a tripod. If the camera had been shaky, the echoes would have been off center and the results would not have aligned so well.

Figure 18.3 The layer with an Echo Time value of − 0.15.

Figure 18.4 When Echo Time is taken to a positive value, the echoes come from future frames.

Creating a Video "Smear"

To create the illusion of a smear, take the Echo Time value to a very small number (positive or negative) such as 0.1 or lower, and take the Number of Echoes to 1. You can also soften the effect by decreasing the Starting Intensity or Decay values. This effect is great for creating a delirious effect, such as when someone is waking up from a serious injury and you're showing their point of view in the shot.

The Number of Echoes parameter is self-explanatory, as it controls the number of duplicates it creates. Note that if you're not seeing all echoes created by this value, it's probably because your Echo Time value is too far away from 0, which indicates that your echoes haven't started yet, or they've already gone off screen.

The Starting Intensity and Decay properties are very similar, and they're also connected. The Starting Intensity value controls the opacity of the current frame. Easy enough. The Decay value controls the opacity of the echoes. However, it is based on the Starting Intensity value, and then each echo decays more, based on the Decay value. For example, if your Starting Intensity is 1, that is the equivalent of 100% opacity, or completely opaque. If you take the Decay to 0.5, this is the equivalent of an opacity value of 50%. The first echo would be at 50% opacity, the second echo would be at 25% opacity (50% of the second echo), and the third would be half of that. If the Starting Intensity value were 0.5 and the Decay value were set at 0.7, the first copy would be 70% of 50%. The next copy would be 70% of that, and so on. As you can see, there's a lot of control here.

Figure 18.5 The footage with lowered Starting Intensity and Decay values, as seen in the Effect Controls panel.

Finally, the Echo Operator property controls how the echoes blend together. Remember that we're dealing with transparency here, so if we want to combine multiple frames—at least with this video—then we'll need to use a blend mode of some type. And that's what the Echo Operator allows us to do. Most of the modes, such as Add, Screen, and Maximum will return a much lighter result. These are great for creating ghost-like effects, or other soft, ethereal or angelic effects. We've been using Minimum as it returns a dark result, which works well with this footage that has a lot of blown out highlights.

The Posterize Time Effect

The Posterize Time effect is as simple as it gets. The purpose of the effect is to conform a video layer to a specific frame rate. The only parameter for this effect is Frame Rate, which is the absolute frame rate. This effect is useful for conforming video to a film frame rate (24fps, which is also the default value for this property).

You can also achieve this same result with a little more effort by precomposing a video layer, and in the Composition Settings dialog box, change its frame rate in the Basic tab, and the click the Advanced tab and select the option with one of the longest names of all time: Preserve frame rate when nested or in render queue. This will allow the contents of the precomp to play at any frame rate, regardless of the frame rate of the parent composition.

I honestly haven't found much use for this effect. While I do use mixed frame rates, I'm typically combining higher frame rate footage into my 24p comps in order to get slow motion. But Posterize Time doesn't do that. Using the Posterize Time effect to conform 60 frame per second footage to 24 frames per second basically does the same thing that After Effects already does when you put 60fps per second into a 24fps composition.

Although, I will say that if you ever wanted to simulate one of the most popular video effects from the 1990s, take the Frame Rate value of the Posterize Time effect to around 8.

The Time Difference Effect

If you're familiar with the Difference blend mode, you know that one of the uses of it is to be able to compare the pixels of two layers to see where they differ. Hence the name. The Time Difference effect does the same thing, but it allows you to compare frames from different places in time on the same layer. Now, before you go skipping on ahead to Time Displacement, let me tell you that this effect has some pretty useful features, especially for color correction and visual effects workflows.

To start out, let's open the Time Difference.aep project from the Chapter 18 folder, and apply the Time Difference effect to the Chad with Hand Dot layer. This is just a video clip of me being a goon in front of a green screen. So, when you first apply this effect and the screen goes gray, my sense of embarrassment subsides.

The reason the screen goes gray is because blending things in the Difference blend mode is meant to compare things. When two identical objects are compared, the result is a solid color.

With Difference the layer blend mode, identical layers become black. With the Time Difference effect, identical frames become gray. And by default, the Time Difference effect compares the current frame with the current frame.

Before we go any farther, let's actually adjust this effect so that we can see something more than just gray here. Change the Time Offset (sec) value to 0.2. You will then visually see where these frames are different, because the difference (the non-identical pixels) will not be gray.

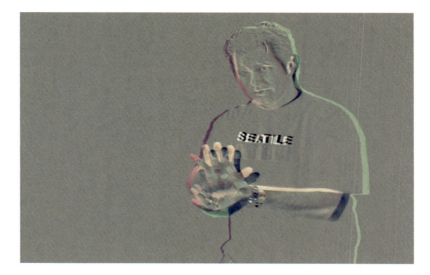

Figure 18.6 With the Time Offset value changed to 0.2, we can compare the current frame with the frame 2/10 of a second ahead.

As has been our tendency throughout this book, let's look at the properties in this effect from the top down. The first parameter is Target. This drop down controls which layer is being compared to the current layer. It defaults to the layer the effect was applied to, but it can be any layer, and the layer doesn't even have to be visible to be used as a Target.

The Time Offset value is the amount, in seconds, that the Target layer is offset from the current time. To compare the same frame, keep this at zero. Contrast increases the intensity of the difference.

The Alpha Channel value is very interesting. It allows you to change the Alpha Channel of the result, which opens up a lot of doors. Here's the gist of what each option does:

- Original—No change to the alpha.
- Target—Uses the alpha channel of the layer chosen with the Target property.
- Blend—blends the alpha channels of both the target layer, and the layer the effect is applied to.

Making Time Difference Behave

If you want to make Time Difference behave like Difference the blend mode, select the Absolute Difference option, which will change the gray caused by identical pixels to black.

- Max—Uses whichever alpha channel is more opaque between the target layer and the effect layer.
- Full On—Forces the alpha channel to be completely opaque.
- Lightness of Result—This is where it starts getting interesting. Lightness of Result will create a new alpha channel that is based on the difference result only. This option creates an alpha based on the lightness of the result.
- Max of Result—This is similar to Lightness of Result, but the result is usually brighter.
- Alpha Difference—Uses the difference between the alphas of the target layer and the effect layer.
- Alpha Difference Only—This returns the same alpha channel as Alpha Difference, except that the entire RGB result becomes white.

So what can you do with this wackiness? One of the great purposes of this effect is to compare color adjusted frames and instantly see their differences.

Another great purpose is to use the end result for visual effects. Let's use this example, and say I wanted to create some fire around my hands a la that guy in Fantastic Four. I could rotoscope my hands as they move around. But it would be much easier to simply use Time Difference to create a layer with an alpha channel that was roughly my moving hands, as in Figure 18.7.

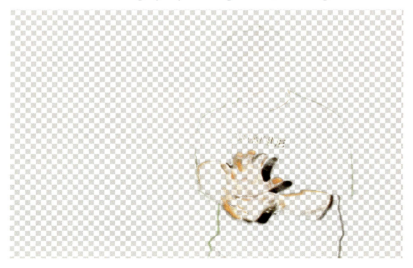

Figure 18.7 Because my hands are the only thing moving much here, we can use Time Difference to create a layer with just my hands, complete with transparency.

In this example, I set Time Offset to a small 0.07, enabled Absolute Difference, and took the Alpha Channel result to Max of Result. There's some extra pixels around the edge of me, but we could easily mask that out. The point is that we've isolated the hands for the most part, with a modicum of effort. We can then add an effect like Particle Playground and use the Layer Exploder to create the illusion that my hands are on fire. What else can be done with Time Difference? The potential is pretty big with this one.

The Time Displacement Effect

As we saw back in Chapter 7 when we looked at the Displacement Map effect, you can use the lightness values in an image as a controller to shift pixels. Similarly, we can use the lightness values in a map as a controller with the Time Displacement effect, only the map will not shift pixels spatially. The map will shift pixels *in time*.

To see some hot displacement action, open up Time Displacement.aep from the Chapter 18 folder. Apply the Time Displacement effect to the stairsdock PRECOMP layer in the stairsdock composition. As with almost any displacement effect, when you first apply it, it attempts to use itself as a displacement map, and it looks terrible.

If you solo the grayscales.tga layer, you'll see a grayscale map I've created to control this effect.

Figure 18.8 The grayscales.tga layer.

Change the Time Displacement Layer value to the grayscales .tga layer. You'll then see that the white area of the displacement map shifts the footage pixels forward in time, the gray area has no effect, and the black area shifts the pixels back in time.

Figure 18.9 The result of having the grayscales.tga layer control the time displacement of the stairsdock footage.

The only parameter we really need to be concerned with here is Max Displacement Time [sec] which controls the maximum amount of time from which pixels will be taken. At the default value of 1, white pixels in the controller will shift those areas of the footage ahead 1 second. Black areas in the controller will shift those areas back 1 second. Other values will adjust in between those values.

To see another example, solo the fractal noise PRECOMP layer.

Figure 18.10 The fractal noise PRECOMP layer.

Next change the Time Displacement Layer value on the stairsdock PRECOMP layer to the fractal noise PRECOMP layer. Figure 18.11 shows the result (showing a frame that is more illustrative of what is happening).

Figure 18.11 A result of using the fractal noise PRECOMP as the displacement layer.

The Timewarp Effect

The Timewarp effect is one of the more powerful effects in After Effects. We can use it to slow down and speed up time, and we also have control over the speed/quality of how that is done. As we'll see, the Timewarp effect can also add motion blur to footage that is already rendered. It also has features similar to the time controls in the Stretch column of the Timeline panel, except that the Timewarp effect allows us to also animate speed changes. For practice with this effect, you can open the Timewarp.aep project from the Chapter 18 folder.

Many of the settings in this effect (such as motion blur, time stretching, and frame blending) can also be seen in different forms in the Timeline panel, although the Timeline and the Timewarp effect act independently of each other.

First we need to talk about the Method drop down, because this is one of the greatest aspects of this effect. When footage is slowed down, it creates a serious dilemma. Let's say you have a piece of footage that is 30 fps. If you slow it down to 50% of its original speed, then it will be twice as long. Because it is twice as long, After Effects will have to do something for all those extra frames. Think of this like typing in a Word document. If I type:

12345

and then I decide to stretch those fives across the width of the document, I'll have to do something to fill in the gaps. I can duplicate the numbers:

1111111111112222222222223333333333333333344444444444
44555555555555

I can also place spaces between them:

1   2   3   4   5

The point is, that something has to fill the gaps between them. Frames in time work the same way.

The Method drop down is key because it determines how After Effects will stretch the footage. Whole Frames renders the fastest, but also the lowest on the quality totem pole. Whole Frames just duplicates frames to fill the gaps. If you slow down your footage a great deal, the footage will seem to stutter during playback. The Frame Mix option is essentially a cross dissolve transition from frame to frame. The "real" frame will fade out over time until the next "real" frame completes the process of fading in. If you have something with linear motion, such as a race car going from one side of the screen to the other, this could do the trick. It takes longer to render than Whole Frames, but also looks better (usually).

The other Method deserves its own paragraph. The Pixel Motion method is nothing short of digital magic. Pixel Motion attempts to create vectors or paths that connect pixels in one frame to pixels in the next frame. In effect, it attempts to recreate brand new frames. This is very helpful when you need details and a cross fade, like that in Frame Mix, won't help. Say for example, you have some footage of a fight scene. Pixel Motion can help you get the most detail out of the slow mo shot. And in most instances, it works remarkably well. Also, you'll notice that once Pixel Motion is selected, several other properties of the Timewarp effect become selectable.

Let's see the digital magic of Pixel Motion in action. For this example, we'll use a crystal clear video clip from Artbeats.com. Import the file CJ121.mov from the Artbeats folder in the Media folder of the exercise files. Make a new composition with this footage and apply the Timewarp effect to it. I'm going to leave the Speed value at the default 50, which will play this clip back at 50% of the speed of the original clip. Figure 18.12 shows two adjacent frames of the video in Whole Frames mode, so After Effects has not changed the original content. When the video footage is slowed down, the small difference between these two frames will seem like a much larger jump.

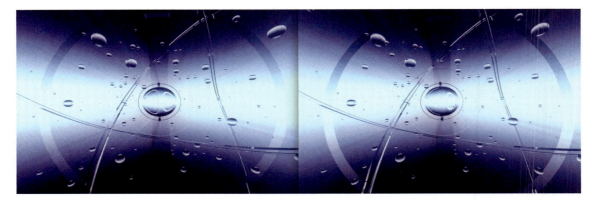

Figure 18.12 Two adjacent frames of video. They seem very similar, but when played back slowly, the difference between them is obvious.

Just by way of comparison, let's see what these frames look like when blended using Frame Mix. You can see hard edges and other visual stutter effects caused by Frame Mix's cross dissolve-type blending.

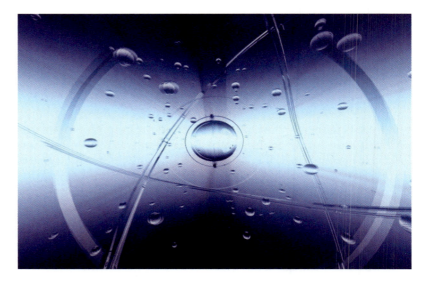

Figure 18.13 Blending the frames using the Frame Mix method.

Next, we'll change the Method value to Pixel Motion. This causes After Effects to create an intermediate frame in between these two frames. Figure 18.13 shows the frame that After Effects created to transition between these two frames. Not bad!

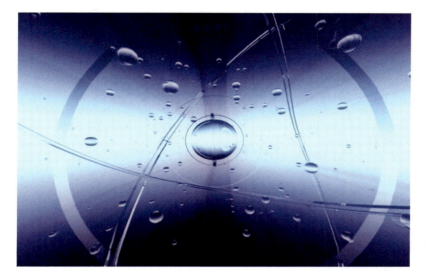

Figure 18.14 The frame that After Effects created to create a smooth transition between the two frames seen in Figure 18.12.

The Speed property controls the speed of the clip. I'm not sure I understand why there isn't a % sign here, because that's exactly what this value indicates. If Speed is set to 100%, then the clip will play back at regular speed. If the Speed value is higher, the clip will play faster, and if it is less than 100, it will slow the clip down. The ability to animate this property adds a lot of power to this effect. For example, if you had footage of an athlete doing a long jump, you could play the footage at regular speed until the athlete started their jump. At that point, you could animate the Speed value to slow the motion to accentuate the jump.

One of the problems that you'll run into with Timewarp is layer duration. For instance, if you had a two-second clip that you wanted to play at half speed, you would expect that clip to then play for four seconds. Unfortunately, that's not the case. Timewarp would actually play the first two seconds of your clip at half speed, and then when the duration of the source layer ended, it would stop playback (so you'd only get the first half of your clip). What can you do?

Well, the solution to this problem is to precompose the layer in a precomp that is as long as you need. In this hypothetical example, you would create a precomp that is four seconds long (consisting of your original two seconds of footage, and then two extra blank seconds). Apply the Timewarp effect to the precomp in the parent comp, slow it down to half speed, and enjoy the heck out of that magic.

Also note that Timewarp really likes being the center of attention, and doesn't like sharing the spotlight. If you have other

Timewarp and Interlaced Footage

According to the After Effects Help, the Timewarp effect won't work on fields in interlaced footage. If you want to use the Timewarp effect on interlaced footage, Adobe suggests doubling the frame rate of the composition in the Composition Settings dialog box, and then when it's time to render, changing it back to the correct frame rate in the Render Queue.

effects applied to your layer, regardless of what the effects do (from blurring to keying) or what order they are placed in, the Timewarp effect will often turn off those other effects. The solution here, as before, is to precompose the layer with the desired effects, and then apply Timewarp to the precomposed layer in the parent comp.

The Motion Blur property is another one of the very impressive items on the resumé of the Timewarp effect. We know that After Effects can add motion blur to layers that you animate. This simulates the blur that is created by quickly moving objects when filmed with a real camera.

But what happens when you get some footage that is already rendered, such as a render from a 3D application or a clip of stock video footage, and the motion in the video doesn't match the motion blur of the rest of the composition? By selecting Enable Motion Blur in the Timewarp effect, After Effects will look at the footage, and by using the same system of vectors it used to create the intermediate Pixel Motion frames, it will analyze the motion in the video, and add motion blur. You can even adjust the Shutter Angle property to control how much blur is added! For someone who works often with 3D artists, I can tell you that this is a lifesaver when you need it. Because of how much computer brain sweat goes into analyzing already rendered footage to apply motion blur to it, this property will slow down your render time considerably. But for those times when you have a video that wasn't rendered with enough blur for your liking, this parameter is worth the wait.

19

THE TRANSITION EFFECTS

Transitions are most often used in NLE (video editing) programs, as one video clip cuts to the next. Because transitions are such a huge part of video editing, in most NLE's, such as Adobe Premiere Pro, you simply drag and drop transitions to apply them. Most transitions also auto-animate.

In After Effects, it's a slightly more manual process. Most transition effects have a Transition Completion value that you need to animate from 0% to 100% in order to have the transition completely replace the clip. Also, while most NLE programs automatically handle audio, you must manually adjust audio for transitions in After Effects.

The transitions in After Effects are also a little more, well … After Effectsy. They are a little more showy and over the top in most cases. They all create transitions to the next clip (i.e., the layers beneath them) by removing parts of the top layer until it is completely removed.

Noticeably absent from the After Effects transition video roster is the most popular of video transitions, Cross Dissolve, which is a soft crossfade between clips. So make sure that you use these transitions with tact. Don't be like Homer Simpson who, when doing some video editing of his own, would only use the gaudy and anti-subtle star wipe transition between clips. When petitioned by his daughter Lisa to try a different transition, his response was "Why eat hamburger when you can have steak?" So, be sure that there is an aesthetic or artistic link to your video content and the transitions you use.

That's not to say that you can only use transitions for transitioning between clips. For crying out loud, this entire book is about using effects for purposes other than what they were intended for. Try applying a transition to a solid layer, then take the Transition Completion value to a given number and use that layer as an alpha matte for another layer. Or try recreating the famous James Bond intro sequence with the Iris Wipe effect without animation. We'll also use a transition effect to animate a flower blooming. There's a horde of possibilities here.

Faking Cross Dissolve

If you wanted to fake a Cross Dissolve effect, you can simply fade the Opacity value of the layer on top. Remember that you must also animate the audio separately if you don't want the audio to cut off abruptly.

One effect in this category stands out above all the rest—Card Wipe. This effect splits up a layer into a series of cards that can flip and move in three dimensions. Card Wipe is quite powerful (especially for a transition), allowing you to control the navigation of the effect with composition cameras and lights, and control how the cards react to light with material options. It's also the last effect that we'll be looking at that was designed by After Effects guru and legend Brian Maffitt.

Throughout this chapter, when looking at the simple transitions (i.e. everything except Card Wipe), we'll be using a couple

Figure 19.1 The Seattle clip. This clip will be the clip on top; the layer being removed by the Transition effects.

Figure 19.2 The Artbeats clip of children running. This clip will be on bottom, and will show through the transparent holes in the Seattle clip.

of simple contrasting solids so it's clear what each transition is doing. The green solid will be the layer on the bottom, or in other words, the layer we'll be transitioning to. The magenta solid will be the layer on top, and it's the one that we'll be applying the transition effects to. We'll also be using two video clips to test these transitions—the one on top is of Seattle, and the video clip below is from Artbeats, and depicts two children running.

You can find a project already set up if you'd like to follow along by opening the Transitions.aep project from the Chapter 19 folder of the exercise files. The solids are in the comp called Basic, and the video clips are in the comp called Video.

The Block Dissolve Effect

The Block Dissolve is fairly simple, but it needs a little help to be useful. Its default settings look like a layer using the Dissolve blend mode (that's bad). The purpose of this effect is to transition to transparency by removing the layer in blocks. There are only a few settings, but they can create a variety of looks. We can probably categorize them into two groups: settings that control the size of the blocks, and settings that control the softness of the edges of the blocks.

If we adjust width and height independently, we can create fractal/turbulent noise-type transitions.

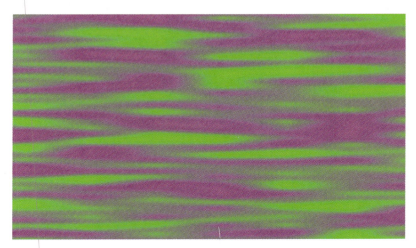

Figure 19.3 With the Transition Completion halfway complete, I took the Block Width value to 100, Block Height to 5, and Feather to 10 to create this Fractal Noise looking transition.

If you want to produce hard-edged blocks with this effect, you'll need to deselect the Soft Edges option. By so doing, you can create fractal bars and other interesting patterns. This could also be good if you're looking for a venetian blinds effect, but don't like uniform look created by the included Venetian Blinds effect.

Figure 19.4 Using the same settings as those in the previous figure on the seattle layer in the Video comp. Notice that you can see the most prominent features of both clips. Cool.

Figure 19.5 By deselecting the Soft Edges option, the blocks created by this effect get hard edges. Here, my settings are 10% for Transition Completion, 5 for Block Width, and 500 for Block Height.

The Card Wipe Effect

Card Wipe is by far the most powerful of the transition effects, and really stands in a class all its own. Similar to the slightly more powerful Card Dance effect we looked at in the Simulation effects category, Card Wipe breaks up a layer into a group of cards. Although Card Dance gives you more control with the use of maps, Card Wipe still allows you to control card movement in 3D space, randomize the motion, control when they flip over, control what the image is on the backside of the cards, and much more.

Figure 19.6 Using the same settings as Figure 19.5, but with 85% Transition Completion.

Figure 19.7 Using the same settings as Figure 19.6, but with the layers in the Video comp.

The original purpose of this effect is to reenact those times in major sporting events when large groups of people all hold up signs for a company, and then flip them over. As if you could ever get a rowdy crowd at a sporting event to ignore the sporting event to praise their cell phone service provider. Hence, this effect was created to simulate the cards that those people would have held up and flipped over. But it's even more common to use this effect to create a 3D postcard effect, as we'll see later in this section.

First let's open up the Card Wipe.aep project from the Chapter 19 folder. There is a comp here called Simple Card Wipe, which is similar to the comp found in the Transitions.aep project we've been working with in this chapter. Let's apply the Card Wipe effect to the magenta solid, just to get the idea of what's going on. Then we'll move into deeper waters.

After applying the Card Wipe effect, the Transition Completion value is bumped up a little for us, just so we can see what's going on with this effect. As with Shatter, Fractal Noise, and other effects, the default settings here don't really tell the whole story of what this effect can do.

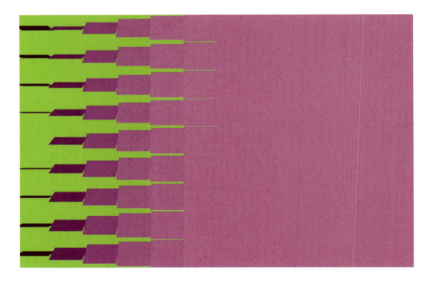

Figure 19.8 The Simple Card Wipe comp with the Card Wipe effect applied with the default settings.

What's really going on here is that Card Wipe is turning the magenta solid into a sea of cards. The ones on the left side of the screen have started flipping over, or transitioning. This is very similar to what we saw in Chapter 16 with the Card Dance effect. However, I find that the Card Wipe effect is much easier to understand and control than the Card Dance effect. Card Wipe also has several easy-to-use features that Card Dance does not have. Let's look at the highlights from the top of the Effect Controls panel down.

Transition Completion functions here the same as it does in every other effect. But what about Transition Width? Transition Width determines how wide the area of flipping cards is. If you want a single strip of cards flipping at once, reduce the Transition Width value considerably. Likewise, if you want all of the cards to flip at once, increase this value to 100%.

As with Card Dance, we can specify how many rows and columns of cards we want. We'll use this to our advantage later in this section, when we create the ever popular 3D postcard effect.

Flip Axis, Flip Direction, and Flip Order all allow you to control how these cards flip. Flip Axis has a really interesting value. By default, the flip axis is the X axis, meaning that the cards rotate around the X axis when transitioning. You can also set Flip Axis to Y, which makes the cards flip around the Y axis when transitioning. Note that the cards can still transition from left to right (or any other order you choose from the Flip Order drop down), but the cards themselves will spin on their own individual Y axis. But the Flip Axis drop down also allows you to select Random, which causes each card to randomly flip along the X or Y axis. The results are actually quite chaotic and artistic. You can also have more control over how your cards flip by using a gradient layer to control the flip order. To do this, select Gradient from the Flip Order drop down, and then choose the gradient layer from the Gradient Layer drop down. Note that if you create the gradient using effects, layer styles, or shape layers, you might have to precompose the layer before it can be used as a map for effects.

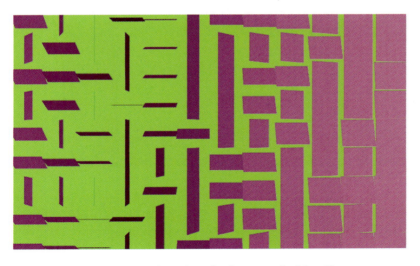

Figure 19.9 With the Flip Axis drop down set to Random, each card randomly flips around it's own X or Y axis.

Like many effects we've already discussed, this effect operates in 3D space. There are camera controls, as well as lighting and material options. And as with Shatter, and other such 3D effects, you can animate the camera built into the effect, animate the perspective using Corner Pins, or control the 3D movement with a camera in the composition. Choose your method of movement from the Camera System drop down.

The last two properties are perhaps the most special of the features in Card Wipe. You might have noticed that Card Wipe does not auto-animate. However, if you do want to add some random animation to these cards, the developers of Card Wipe have made it so that you don't have to even set keyframes (or use expressions) to generate random motion. Open up the Position Jitter and Rotation Jitter groups. Remember that "jitter" is often Adobe's way of saying "randomness." At first, this may seem like there's a lot going on. But really, there are just two properties each for X, Y, and Z position and rotation jitter.

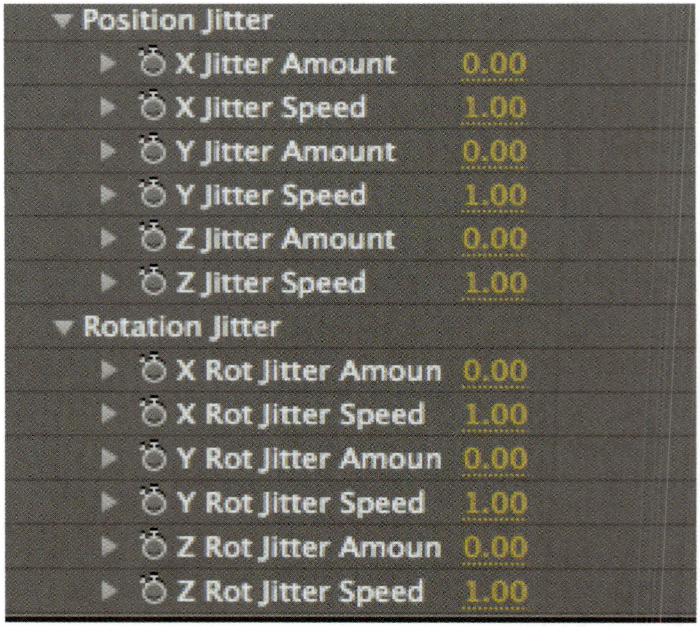

Figure 19.10 The Position Jitter and Rotation Jitter controls in the Effect Controls panel.

Those two properties are jitter amount and jitter speed. Note that all jitter amount properties have been set to 0 and all jitter speed properties have been set to 1. As soon as you adjust the jitter amount value for any property, that property auto-animates randomly. No keyframes are necessary because of the jitter speed value. If you were to take the jitter speed value to 0, the property would not animate. Say for example that you wanted to have these cards pulsate towards the camera randomly. You would increase the Z Jitter Amount value, and that's all. If you wanted the cards to randomly move in Z space and just stay there without motion, you would increase the Z Jitter Amount value, and decrease the Z Jitter Speed value to 0. Adjusting these jitter values can create an entire world of beautiful randomness.

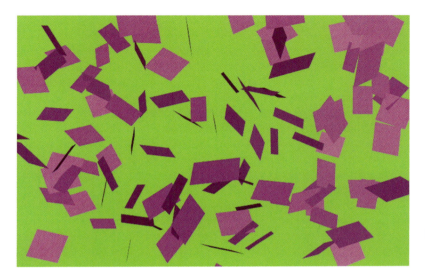

Figure 19.11 After increasing jitter amount values, these cards go all over the place.

Creating the 3D Postcard Effect

Now that we know what it does, let's see a more practical example of the Card Wipe effect at work. We're going to create a myriad of postcards flying in 3D space that gather and then flip to become a logo. In the Card Wipe.aep project, I've provided a few versions of the project start points, in case you felt like doing more (or less) work on your own.

This project takes advantage of the ability that Card Wipe gives you to adjust the size of your cards. What I did first is to start out in Photoshop, creating a large PSD file that has 36 photos of animals that my wife and I have taken, divided up into a 6 × 6 grid. Note that this file was imported as Merged Footage, and so all of these images exist on one flat layer.

Figure 19.12 The Photos .psd file in the Card Wipe.aep project.

3D Postcards and Size

You might notice that this is a colossal comp, created from a colossal PSD file. When creating PSD files to be used as 3D postcards, you might want to consider creating images much larger than necessary (this PSD file is 3600 pixels wide). That way, when you zoom your camera in and around these images, they still maintain their quality.

Now, if we were to have all 36 of these images as separate files, it would be extremely annoying to position them in 3D space and animate them individually. Using the Card Wipe effect, we can makes these squares separated, automatically animate these squares, and control all of them from one simple interface (the Effect Controls panel).

Apply the Card Wipe effect to the Photos.psd layer in the Card Wipe Photos comp. Then take both the Rows value and the Columns value to 6, to correspond to the grid I created in the Photoshop document. Because the two grids match (the Card Wipe grid and the PSD grid), the pictures appear to all be separate cards now.

So, technically, we've already created the 3D postcard effect. But what really enhances this is taking the Transition Completion value to 0%, then increasing Z Jitter Amount (in the Position Jitter area at the bottom of the effect's options in the Effect Controls panel), and reducing the Z Jitter Speed value to 0, so they don't fluctuate forwards and backwards. Then you are free to animate

Figure 19.13 Creating the same grid size in both the source footage and in the Effect Controls panel with the Card Wipe effect causes each picture to exist on its own card.

the camera position to navigate through the "postcards" to create an interesting animation. This effect is seen often in National Geographic shows, and travel related TV programs. In the 3D Postcards comp, I've added some a comp camera, a comp light, and some animation.

The animation includes a reduction of the Z Jitter Amount property to make these cards gather back together again. The purpose of this is to then flip the gathered cards over, and have the logo for the TV show be on the backside of the cards. In the Card Wipe effect controls on the Photos.psd layer, make sure that the Back Layer value (which determines what is on the backside of the card) is set to the Animal Discoveries comp

Figure 19.14 The 3D Postcards comp, which has an added spot light.

layer. It's best to leave the visibility of the actual layer used as the back layer off in the Timeline panel. Then, when the cards have gathered, animate the Transition Completion value from 0% to 100%. When it's all said and done, you have a cool show opener. Note that in this comp, I've also allowed the slightest amount of position jitter by taking the jitter speed values to 0.1 for all dimensions. This setting will allow these cards to slowly wiggle randomly. This creates the sense that these cards are wild and untamable, like animals.

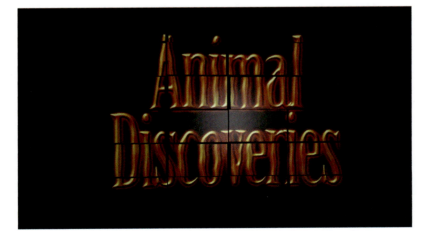

Figure 19.15 After the cards have gathered, you can flip them to the Animal Discoveries logo by selecting it as the Back layer and animating the Transition Completion property.

The Gradient Wipe Effect

The Gradient Wipe effect uses a gradient to determine in what order pixels are removed from the top layer to reveal the bottom layer. Because you can actually create some innovative transitions using the Gradient Wipe effect, I've created a project for you to use to experiment with this effect. It's called Gradient Wipe.aep, and you'll find it in the Chapter 19 folder of the exercise files.

This project contains the same basic magenta and green solids we'll be looking at in this chapter, and it also contains a couple of layers that we'll use to control the transition. The first control layer we'll use is a simple gradient created with the Ramp effect (discussed in Chapter 9).

Figure 19.16 The gradient on the Ramp layer. We'll be using this to control the transition.

Next, apply the Gradient Wipe effect to the magenta solid. In the Gradient Layer drop down, choose the Ramp layer. The luminance (brightness) values of the Ramp layer will now determine how the magenta solid layer transitions to the layers beneath it. Darker values are removed first. Figure 19.17 shows the transition at about 30% complete. You can soften the hard edge seen here by increasing the Transition Softness value.

Now, this was just a simple example to get the gist of what this effect is doing. Now let's push the envelope here a little bit. At the bottom of the layer stack in the Timeline panel, you'll find a layer called Rad Rockets.mov. This is a render from a 3D program, and also contains movement.

One of the ways we can create very unique results with the Gradient Wipe effect is by using video as the gradient layer! In this case, we don't even need to animate Transition Completion to get movement in the magenta and green solid layers. The

Figure 19.17 With the Transition Completion parameter at 30%, you can see how the Gradient Wipe effect is removing the pixels on the magenta solid based on the brightness values of the Ramp layer, seen in figure 19.12.

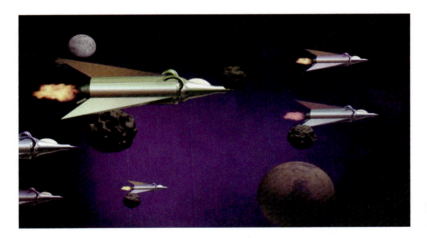

Figure 19.18 The Rad Rockets .mov layer.

movement in the gradient layer can create the motion for us because the Gradient Wipe effect is constantly updating, based on the changes in the gradient layer. The Gradient Wipe effect is like Card Wipe, in that it can do far more than just create a transition from one layer to another.

Note that every pixel seen in Figure 19.20 is either from the Seattle clip or the Artbeats clip of children. We're not seeing any of the actual pixels of the Rad Rockets clip. The Rad Rockets clip is only being used to determine what pixels are seen from which layer.

Figure 19.19 The Gradient Wipe effect, using the Rad Rockets movie as the gradient layer. Here, the Transition Completion property is at 30%, the Transition Softness value is at 50%. Try previewing this comp without animating Transition Completion.

Figure 19.20 Using the same settings as Figure 19.19, but with video clips.

The Iris Wipe Effect

The Iris Wipe effect is quite unusual. It creates a transition by essentially creating a transparent geometric shape on the top layer. Once the shape is larger than the layer, the transition is complete. This is the only Transition category effect that doesn't have a Transition Completion value, and as a matter of fact, no talk of transitioning in this entire effect. The parameters make it look more like a Generate category effect. The difference here is that the effect is not generating a shape, it's creating a hole in the layer.

To explore this effect, we'll be using the Transitions.aep project in the Chapter 19 folder. Apply the Iris Wipe effect to the magenta solid in the Basic comp. To see any of the features of the Iris Wipe, you'll need to increase the Outer Radius value. This creates a triangle-shaped hole in the layer. To fully transition to the layers beneath, just increase the size of this shape until it completely removes the layer it is applied to.

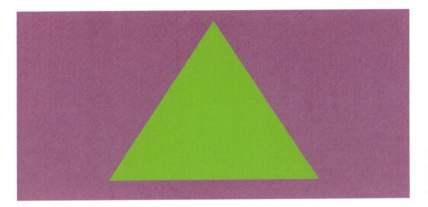

Figure 19.21 The Iris Wipe effect, at the default settings, except for the Outer Radius value, which is at 200.

Figure 19.22 Using the same settings as those seen in Figure 19.21, except with the layers in the Video comp.

Another important characteristic of the Iris Wipe effect is the Inner Radius. However, the Inner Radius value is not used until you select the Use Inner Radius checkbox. You can increase the number of points to create a star by increasing the

Iris Points value. You can rotate the shape, move it around, or feather it (using the Rotation, Iris Center, and Feather values, respectively).

Figure 19.23 The Iris Wipe effect with two other Artbeats video clips. Here, the Iris Points value is 12, Outer Radius is at 560, Use Inner Radius is selected with an Inner Radius value of 60, and a Feather value of 50. Here, I'm going for a subtle result with a not-so-subtle effect, but you can see the 6-pointed star, centered in the layer.

Transitions that Don't Transition

As we saw with Gradient Wipe, some of these transitions create interesting effects, even without animation. Although their names imply transition, you don't have use them for transitions only. Again, the whole theme of this book is to create illusions by using effects for purposes other than those for which they were intended. You can use transitions that don't transition for vignettes, POV shots (say, through a rifle scope), to do split screens, and much more. Don't let the name of the effect category limit your creativity.

The Linear Wipe Effect

The Linear Wipe effect is one of the most simple effects in this category, but it's also one of the most useful effects for actual transitioning. Transitioning with a linear wipe is usually the least tacky kind of wipe. Linear wipes can be seen extensively in all of the Star Wars movies. George Lucas used these to show the great distances of time and space between scenes.

For this example, I'm again using the Transitions.aep project from the Chapter 19 folder. The Linear Wipe effect transitions between clips with a simple line. You can change the transition completion, alter the angle of the line, and feather it, and that's it.

But it is the simplicity here that makes it so appropriate. Just like the way it was used by George Lucas, use this to create a harder transition than a simple cut between shots. It can also be used to transition with movement in the shot. If you had footage of someone opening a door, for example, you could use the Linear Wipe transition to create the illusion that they were opening the door to the next clip.

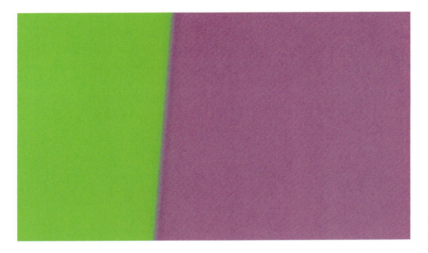

Figure 19.24 The Linear Wipe effect with the Transition Completion property at 40%, Wipe Angle at 94 degrees, and a Feather value of 20.

Figure 19.25 Using the same settings as Figure 19.24, but with the layers in the Video comp.

The Radial Wipe Effect

The Radial Wipe effect creates a wipe that goes around a layer, like the hands of a clock. Because of this, it is often used to communicate the passage of time. Let's say you had a nervous father pacing in a hospital waiting room, waiting to hear about the birth of his child, you might show different shots of him pacing, separated by a radial wipe.

But when used with motion graphics instead of as a video transition, Radial Wipe actually does come in handy quite often as a cool way to reveal graphic elements. We'll look in a moment at how to use Radial Wipe to reveal a flower blossoming, for example.

Before we jump into that, let's just make sure we're clear what Radial Wipe does. Again using the Transitions.aep project, apply the Radial Wipe effect to the magenta solid in the Basic comp. Figures 19.26 and 19.27 demonstrate the purpose of the effect, with only the Transition Completion value altered.

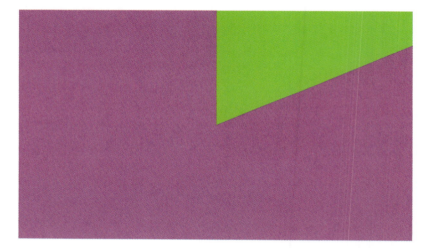

Figure 19.26 The Radial Wipe effect with the Transition Completion value at 18%.

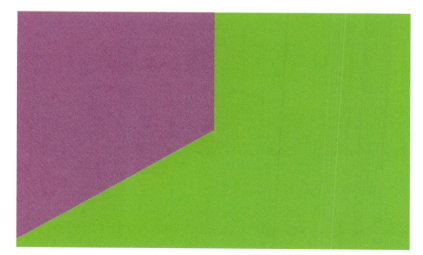

Figure 19.27 The Radial Wipe effect with the Transition Completion value at 66%.

Figure 19.28 Using the same settings as those seen in Figure 19.27, but with the layers in the Video comp.

You can change the Start Angle value, which is the equivalent of an offset value. You can move the center of the wipe with the Wipe Center property. You can soften the edges with Feather. You can also adjust the direction of the wipe with the Wipe drop down. The default setting is Clockwise. You can also choose Counter Clockwise. Or, you can choose both, which creates an interesting result, as if someone were waving both arms (like when doing jumping jacks). This could also be used for a dramatic reveal, or to create a searchlight effect.

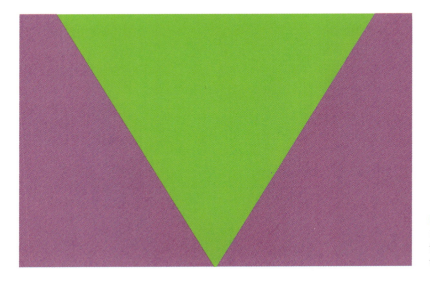

Figure 19.29 The Radial Wipe effect with the Wipe value set to Both, and the Wipe Center at the bottom of the comp.

Now, let's look at what this baby can really do. Open the Radial Wipe.aep project from the Chapter 19 folder of the exercise files. We're going to use Radial Wipe to make the petals disappear, and then appear.

Figure 19.30 The Radial Wipe .aep project.

Apply the Radial Wipe effect to the petals layer (the only visible layer in the Timeline panel, as the other layers are hidden). Nothing happens. Increase the Transition Completion value to 100%. This will make the petals completely disappear.

Figure 19.31 Once you apply the Radial Wipe effect and increase the Transition Completion value to 100%, the petals are "transitioned away."

Now the magic. Animate the Transition Completion value from 100% to 0%, which makes the petals appear to blossom. In this case, I didn't like where the flower was being split by the Radial Wipe effect. So, I adjusted the Start Angle value a bit (to a value of –5 degrees). And then I softened that a little bit by adding a smidgen of feather (2 pixels worth). When animated, ESPECIALLY when echoed by duplicates, this kind of animation just works and is eye-catching.

Figure 19.32 After tweaking a few settings, the flower appears to grow.

It's a really cool effect. Radial Wipe can also be used to replicate the motion of a radar scan, or to animate the growth of a ring created with the Polar Coordinates effect, as described in Chapter 7.

The Venetian Blinds Effect

The Venetian Blinds effect mimics the look of venetian blinds, turning the layer into slats. Other than Transition Completion, you can adjust the direction, width, and feather of the blinds. To play with this effect, you can open the Transitions.aep project from the Chapter 19 folder.

Honestly, I can't think of a good reason to use the Venetian Blinds effect as a transition. Unless you had a time machine back to the 1980s (or were simulating video created then), this effect will be too tacky to use as a transition for most projects.

However, that doesn't mean that you can't use the effect in other ways. Without animating this effect, you can obviously make static venetian blinds, especially those inbetween the camera and the subject. But you can also quickly and easily make bars, like the

Figure 19.33 The Venetian Blinds effect, with the Transition Completion value set to 30%.

bars of a jail cell. Figure 19.34 shows an image of an African dog in a cage. The cage was created by a black solid with the Venetian Blinds effect applied with the Transition Completion value set to around 70%, and the Width set to about 80. To enhance the effect, I've applied the Bevel and Emboss layer style to the black solid layer. This creates the look of roundness on the bars.

Figure 19.34 The Venetian Blinds effect after being applied to a black solid layer with the Bevel and Emboss layer style, on top of a layer that contains a photo of an African dog.

20

THE UTILITY EFFECTS

As the name implies, the Utility effects are utilitarian in purpose. Nothing showy or flashy here. These effects, generally speaking, will be more useful to those in more professional workflows, including those working with film, managing color, and using HDR color. The exception here is the Grow Bounds effect, which is useful for all After Effects users. Interesting factoid: the Utility effect category is the only effects category in After Effects that contains visual effects that all work at 32 bit (unless you count the Expression Controls; Blur & Sharpen is almost there).

The Apply Color LUT Effect

A color look-up table (often abbreviated "LUT" and pronounced phonetically as if to rhyme with "glut") is a file used to convert a set of colors into another set of colors. This is typically used when storing color corrections for reuse or for sharing, or to bring files into compliance with known standards.

If you were working for a company doing a color grade on a complex or critical scene, it might be a good idea to store a LUT of your color adjustments so that you could apply that shift in colors at a later time. However, LUTs are a standard practice, used by most professional coloring tools. So you could not only apply them again in After Effects, but in Adobe SpeedGrade, or in a number of other professional color correction apps. Or you could pass those LUT files back to the client to store for later use, in case they wanted to get that same effect later.

As mentioned, LUTs can also bring your files into conformity with known standards. I recently worked on a project that was shot on the ARRI Alexa camera, using a flat mode called Log C. Whenever shooting with professional digital cameras, it's always a good idea to shoot "flat," meaning that there is plenty of room in the shadows and highlights before they blowout. This is great for post production flexibility, but producers get really nervous because it doesn't look so great. The Log C setting on the ARRI Alexa produces especially ugly raw files, but especially beautiful files after color correction. For this project, we just quickly applied a LUT created for the ARRI Alexa Log C profile and our footage looked beautiful in an instant.

The Apply Color LUT is a simple effect, so simple in fact that there aren't any controls. And if you don't have a LUT to apply, there's nothing you can do with it. Let's see how this puppy works. Import the R3D file cigarette guy.R3D. This is a 4k raw file from the RED Scarlet camera. Drag the file to the Create a new Composition button at the bottom of the Project panel to create a new 4k comp for this file.

Figure 20.1 The original cigarette guy image. Please note that this is not a real cigarette. My mom (and my doctor) would be disappointed.

In this unprocessed image, we see this "flatness" that I was referring to earlier in this section. The shadows and highlights are washed out, and the colors really aren't saying anything. It just looks like real life instead of a film. So let's apply a LUT and magically fix this image.

Apply the Apply Color LUT effect to this layer. As soon as you do, you'll get a browser window asking you to select a LUT file. So navigate on over to the Misc folder in the Media folder in the exercise files. There, you'll find a LUT file called LUT for cigarette guy.look.

Where My LUTs At?

In case you're curious, I created the LUT that we're using here in Adobe SpeedGrade. But you can also create them from right here in After Effects using Synthetic Aperture's Color Finesse which ships with After Effects CS6.

Figure 20.2 The image with the LUT applied.

Once you apply this effect, you'll see the image change drastically thanks to the LUT we applied. Basically, the LUT is remapping all of the colors in the image to other colors. In this case, the warm shadow and darker midtone values have been remapped to cooler values and in general, saturation and redness have been removed a bit from the entire image. And all of these specific instructions were stored in the LUT.

Because this is how LUTs work (i.e., by remapping colors), they will not work the same on each image. Here, the result is pretty cool, but if you were to apply this same LUT to another clip, the results might not look so great. Hence, it's good to either use simple LUTs (that just do basic exposure adjustments, such as with the ARRI Alexa Log C mentioned earlier) or if you're going to do specific, more complex looks, they can work well with other clips shot with the same camera at the same location, or other shots for the same scene.

The Cineon Converter Effect

To understand the Cineon Converter effect, we first need to back up a little and look at the Cineon file format. Cineon files (CIN) are most commonly used as a file format for scanned film. Let's say that someone has shot a movie using a film camera. This film can be taken to a production facility, where the film can be scanned and digitized. Note that the Cineon file format has been largely superseded by the DPX format, which includes additional metadata for timecode, sampling rate, etc.

Now, there are a lot of issues here with the color space of film (and the Cineon format) and the color space of video that are beyond the scope of this book. But you do need to know that CIN files have a different way of working with color than video does. CIN understands color in the logarithmic color space, while video exists in the linear color space. Or, stated more simply, the colors in Cineon files are condensed to allow a wider dynamic range. The darks in the CIN file are brighter than the original film, and the highlights appear darker than the original. This explains why Cineon files often look washed out, or blended with gray.

Note that CIN files are 10 bits of color per channel. This allows for more colors than 8 bits per channel (the After Effects default). To get the most out of the color space of Cineon files, make sure your After Effects project is in 32 bpc mode. You can put your project into 32 bpc mode by holding the Alt(Win)/Opt(Mac) key while clicking the 8 bpc button at the bottom of the Project panel. Click once to enter 16 bpc mode, then Alt/Opt click again to change your project to 32 bpc.

Should You Use the Cineon Converter Effect?

Adobe recommends that in "most cases," you should not use the Cineon Converter effect. You should instead convert the colors in Cineon files by using After Effects's color management features. Among other things, this allows for better compositing with Cineon files. We'll still cover the basics of the format and the effect here, for the sake of completeness.

The Nature of Cineon Files

The Cineon file format is a still image format. To playback frames of Cineon files as a movie, they must be imported as an image sequence.

Import the file Cineon.cin from the Images folder in the Media folder of the exercise files if you'd like to follow along with me. I've also created a comp using this file, and have applied the Cineon Converter effect.

Figure 20.3 The Cineon.cin file, without the Cineon Converter effect.

Perhaps the most important option in this entire effect is the first property, Conversion Type. Selecting Linear to Log will take a regular file and make it more like a Cineon version. Adobe suggests that this is useful for applying to 8 bpc linear proxies so that they more fully resemble the original Cineon files. Selecting Log to Linear will convert a regular (non-Cineon) logarithmic 8 bit file for when you're outputting to a Cineon sequence.

The remainder of the settings in this effect are almost like a mini-Levels adjustment. Note that the 10 Bit Black/White Point values are set to the correct levels for 10 bit color, by default. Highlight Rolloff controls what happens to bright highlights. Increasing this value can smooth out over exposure in the highlights.

The History of Cineon

For those of you interested in knowing the extra technical details, a brief history of the Cineon file format is presented. The Cineon file format was created by imaging giant, Kodak. Initially, the term Cineon referred to the hardware; the equipment that actually scanned the film. Manufacturing of the equipment didn't last very long, as the hardware—and the software that went with it—was abandoned in the mid 1990's. Although the days of the hardware were short lived, the Cineon file format persisted, and is still in use to this day.

The Color Profile Converter Effect

The Color Profile Converter effect is a renamed version of the Color Profile effect, which was used prior to After Effects CS3, when a color management system was introduced. Although the settings available in this effect are similar to the ones available in the application's color management system, the color management settings are superior and preferable to the Color Profile Converter Effect. The color management settings are available by going to the flyout menu of the Project panel and choosing Project Settings, and then changing the Working Space to anything besides None. You choose a color profile to describe the color space of the layer, and then you choose settings to control conversion to that profile. Again, it's typically recommended that you avoid using this effect in favor of the native color management tools in After Effects.

The Grow Bounds Effect

The Grow Bounds effect is useful for all After Effects users. It is almost like the Collapse Transformations switch for nested comps. You can use the Collapse Transformations switch to expand the boundaries of layers in nested compositions that are larger than the boundaries of the nested comp layer. Grow Bounds works in the same way, but it works on regular layers. If you'd like to follow along with the example given here, open the Grow Bounds.aep project in the Chapter 20 folder. Figure 20.4

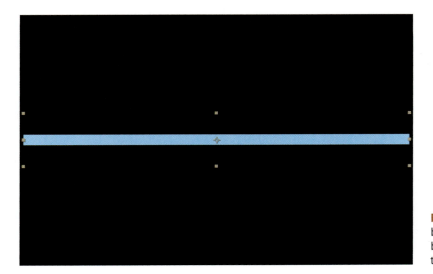

Figure 20.4 Notice that this bar exists on a layer that has boundaries only slightly larger than the bar.

shows a simple solid layer from this project. Notice the bounding box around the layer, and how the size of the layer is only slightly larger than the solid itself.

Next, I'm going to apply the Wave Warp effect to this layer, and I'm going to take the Wave Height value to 100. This warps the solid blue bar a great deal, causing the tops and bottoms of the wave to go beyond the boundaries of the layer. This results in the pixels being cut off.

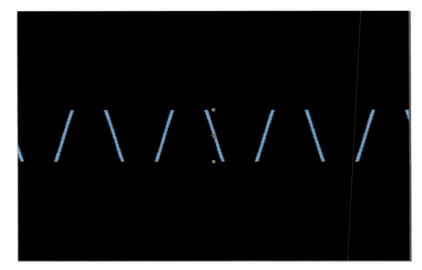

Figure 20.5 After applying the Wave Warp effect, the bar is distorted, resulting in lost pixels because they go beyond the layer's edges.

Enter the Grow Bounds effect. The Grow Bounds effect extends the boundaries of the layer so that pixels that fall outside the layer's boundaries are revealed. However, after applying the effect in this case, nothing appears to happen. In this instance, the problem is found in the stacking order of the effects. We must drag the Grow Bounds effect before (i.e., above, since effects are processed from top to bottom) the Wave Warp effect in the stack of effects in the Effect Controls panel. That way, the layers boundaries can "grow" before they are warped. Increase the Pixels value to determine how many pixels beyond the layer's boundaries that pixels are allowed to extend. I took my Pixels value to 70.

You might be wondering why the Grow Bounds effect is useful, especially when compared with the Collapse Transformations switch which appears to do the same thing. For starters, Collapse

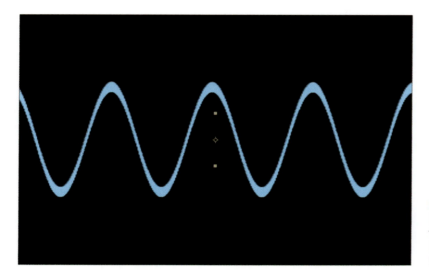

Figure 20.6 After using Grow Bounds before Wave Warp, the layer is allowed to distort beyond the boundaries of the layer.

Transformations doesn't help in situations like those seen in Figure 20.6, where the effect causes the pixels on a layer to go beyond the layer's boundaries. The Grow Bounds effect is useful for working with individual layers, not just compositions. For example, Grow Bounds is a very common solution when blurs or glows are applied to layers, and the boundary of the layer clips the blur or glow.

The Pixels parameter allows you precise control over how much the layer extends beyond its boundaries. And also, Collapse Transformations also changes blend modes and other properties, which you might not want changed.

The HDR Compander Effect

The purpose of the HDR Compander effect is to allow you to use 8-bit effects in a 32-bit project. The HDR Compander effect sounds technical, but it's actually quite helpful, and easy to understand. The word compander, created in the 1930's, is an amalgam of two words: compressor and expander. To understand why this effect is important, let's first look at life without it.

Figure 20.7 shows the HDR.aep project from the Chapter 20 folder of the exercise files. This is a 32-bit project, and the letters are actually shape layers using HDR color (super white), which has been possible since After Effects CS4.

Figure 20.7 The HDR.aep project.

When browsing through effects in the Effects and Presets panel, the little number next to the plugin icon for each effect indicates the highest bit depth that the effect can process.

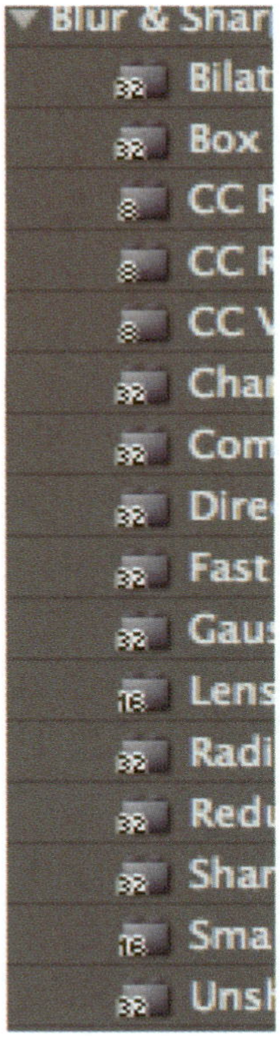

When you use an 8-bit effect in an HDR project, the natural looking light effects are lost because the color of the layer is squished back to 8 bits. The same is true for 16-bit projects. Realistic light behavior is only possible in 32 bit. So, when we apply an 8-bit effect like CC Radial Fast Blur, for example, the power of the color is lost. This is because the color in the HDR layer was created by using super white values; values that were whiter than white. When the super white values are all smashed to 8-bit values, it all becomes the same value of white.

The HDR Compander allows us to use 8-bit effects—like CC Radial Fast Blur—and keep the color in 32-bit colors. But here's the deal. You need to apply one instance of the HDR Compander effect *before* the 8-bit effect(s), and another instance of the HDR Compander effect *after* the 8-bit effect(s). Think of it like an HDR Compander sandwich; or rather, an 8-bit sandwich on HDR Compander bread.

Figure 20.8 The numbers next to each effect indicate the bit depth, which determines the number of colors the effect can recognize.

Figure 20.9 After applying an 8-bit effect, we lose our 32-bit color.

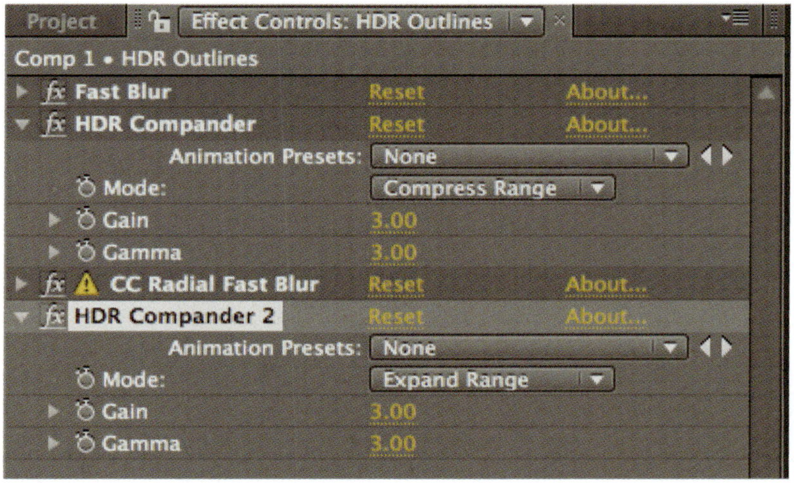

Figure 20.10 The Effect Controls panel with the "HDR Compander sandwich." Note that Fast Blur does not need to be part of the "sandwich" because it operates at 32 bits.

On the instance of the HDR Compander effect applied before 8- or 16-bit effects, set the Mode value to Compress Range. Set the Gain value to the highest brightness value on the layer. For this HDR layer, my red value is set to 3, so I set the Gain property to 3 as well. You can also use the Gamma property to adjust the levels and luminance a little.

Then you apply another instance of the HDR Compander effect, and stack it after all 8-bit and 16-bit effects. This time, set the Mode value to Expand Range. Set the Gain value to the same number you used for the compressing version of the HDR Compander effect. In my case, I'm going to use a Gain value of 3. When you're done adding these instances of the HDR Compander effect, your HDR color will return.

Figure 20.11 After applying two instances of the HDR Compander effect on either side of the CC Radial Fast Blur effect.

Now, I realize these results are not without flaw. Some of the original subtle nuances are lost through this process. Although we would get much better results if all effects could process in 32 bit, this effect is a valuable workaround until that day comes.

The HDR Highlight Compression Effect

The HDR Highlight Compression effect is very simple. It compresses 32-bit color values to conform to 8-bit color values. That's it. There is an amount slider that basically functions as a Blend with Original parameter that we see in so many other effects. But it does pay to note that the values really do become 8-bit values. If you put your cursor over super white pixels after applying this effect, you'll see in the Info panel that 1.0 (standard white) is the brightest pixels are allowed to go.

21

THE CYCORE EFFECTS

Ah, the Cycore effects. I love these things. I believe it was back in After Effects CS3, this collection of third-party effects started being included with After Effects as a free bonus. It's a collection of over SEVENTY (!) effects that are a great addition to the native After Effects effects.

When I wrote the first edition of this book, I figured that Adobe would soon remove this blessed collection. It was just too good to be true. Thankfully, I was really, really wrong. And as a matter of fact, not only are the Cycore effects still included as of CS6, but starting with CS6, the Cycore effects have been upgraded to the CycoreFX HD collection, which adds 12 new effects (such as CC Block Load, which is a great progressive download simulator, and a completely revamped and improved CC Snowfall), makes every effect at least 16 bpc compatible (with most 32 bpc, so you can now finally have your HDR Mr. Mercury and CC Particle Systems II), as well as support for After Effects lights and native motion blur in several effects.

So, with the blessing of my wonderful publisher (thank you, Focal Press), it's now my pleasure to add an in-depth intro to the Cycore effects to this book. Because there are 73 effects, I won't be able to cover each effect individually. But I decided it would be better anyway to share with you the Cycore effects that I use the most, other Cycore effects which might come in handy for you, and the Cycore effects that add the most to the After Effects toolset. One of the best things about the Cycore effects is that there's something for everyone, whether you're a compositor, a motion graphics artist, or a visual effects person, and whether you're a beginner with After Effects or a more experienced user.

So, we're going to look at my "Cycore Top 10" (kind of) in this chapter, in no particular order. In this chapter, we'll look at how to create quick-rendering 3D objects, liquid metal, the best particle system in After Effects, the fastest way to create a star field, snow, rain, incredibly beautiful ornate background shapes, all kinds of cool lighting tricks, and more—all courtesy of these amazing Cycore effects.

Which Effects are Cycore Effects?

You can tell that an effect is part of the Cycore collection if it has a "CC" in front of its name (e.g., CC Snowfall, CC Radial Fast Blur, etc.). Because the Cycore effects are spread through all of the After Effects effects categories, the best way to see them all at once is to do a search for "cc" in the Effects & Presets panel.

CC Sphere

CC Sphere instantly turns a flat 2D image or video clip into a 3D ball. Watch what this little dude can do. We're going to even start from scratch here. Create a new 1920 × 1080 comp (with square pixels). Make a new solid that matches the comp size. Apply the Fractal Noise effect. Change the Fractal Type to Subscale. Change the Contrast to 60, the Brightness to –20, and inside the Transform area, increase the Scale value to 150%.

Figure 21.1 The Fractal Noise layer after our changes. This is going to get cool. Just hold on.

Next, I applied the Tritone effect and changed the Midtones RGB value to 140, 170, 185 just to add a little coolness to this.

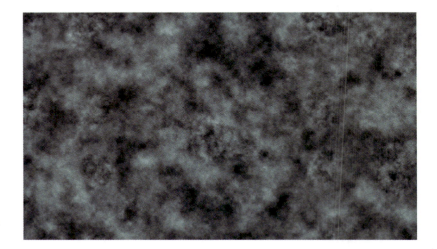

Figure 21.2 The Fractal Noise texture with a slight color shift with the Tritone effect.

Okay. Nothing amazing so far. But apply the CC Sphere effect, and even with its default settings, we have something that looks like a planet.

Figure 21.3 After applying CC Sphere, our Fractal Noise gets wrapped around an imaginary 3D ball. Amazing.

But not only does it just *look* like a 3D ball, it behaves like one, too. Open up the Rotation area and adjust the Rotation Y property. It causes your planet to rotate on its axis!

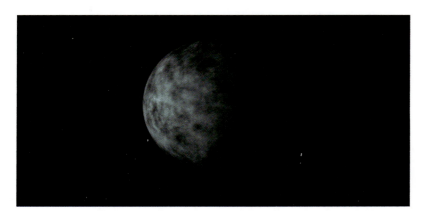

Figure 21.4 It might be hard to see in this screenshot, but this is rotated around its axis significantly. Good night, other side of my planet!

The CC Sphere effect is great for creating spherical objects like this—Christmas tree ornaments, balls, etc. Its other controls let you adjust its size (Radius parameter), whether you're seeing inside the bubble (Render drop down), as well as all kinds of lighting and shading options, including reflection. You could use these settings to create the look of semi-transparent spheres or reflective objects or both.

And for best results with CC Sphere, you'll want to make sure that the layer you're applying it to has an aspect ratio of about 2:1 (it's twice as wide as it is tall). This ensures that you have all the resolution you need as the map (aka the source layer) is stretched spherically.

Note that there's also a CC Cylinder effect that does the same thing, except that it wraps your layer around itself (like a cylinder without caps on the ends). I find this a lot less useful, but CC Cylinder is a 3D effect, meaning that it will respond to After Effects cameras (but not AE lights). CC Sphere does not respond to either lights or cameras.

CC Star Burst

Hey, while we're looking at nerdy space things, let's create some stars to go with the planet that we just created. We'll pick up where we left off by using the CC Star Burst.aep project in the Chapter 21 folder of the exercise files. This project is basically the planet we just made (albeit slightly larger, thanks to the Radius value in CC Sphere), as well as a planet surface in the foreground, and some slight, spacey glows behind both. It looks OK, but it's missing stars. Bad.

Figure 21.5 Like a low-budget indie movie, this scene really doesn't have any stars in it, but it needs some.

So go ahead and apply the CC Star Burst effect to the Star Burst layer I've created for you, which is just a black solid.

HA! Tricked you! I created this solid as a black solid intentionally, because the CC Star Burst effect takes the colors of its stars from the colors of the layer it's applied to, and there's no way to change that in the effect. So if you're not careful, you'll have black stars on a black background and you will pull out your hair trying to figure out what's wrong. Of course that's never happened to me. That bald patch is from something completely unrelated.

Change the color of the Star Burst solid layer by selecting it and pressing Ctrl+Shift+Y(Win)/Cmd+Shift+Y(Mac). Change the color of the solid to white. Ah! There are our stars! They look like crap, but we can see them!

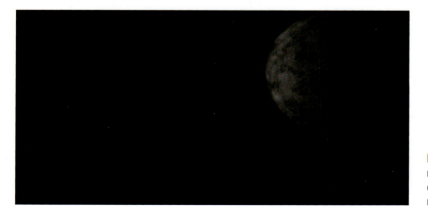

Figure 21.6 We can finally see our "stars"! They certainly need a lot of help though.

Not only do these stars look terrible with their default settings (which are probably set that way so that you can clearly see them), but they also animate way too fast, so let's fix that first. The "Chad default" for the Speed value is a very tiny 0.005. This causes a nice drift in the stars that makes you feel like you're in space. You could take this to zero of course, but I think a little movement adds a lot, especially because the CC Star Burst recognizes that larger stars appear closer and should therefore move faster than smaller, more distant stars.

To change the appearance of the stars, I reduced the Size value to 25. When these stars get small enough, they auto-twinkle in the background, which you may or may not like. Realistic or not, it's pretty hardcore. So, I'm going to spread my stars out more by taking up the Scatter value to about 350. Looking pretty good.

Figure 21.7 The first iteration of my stars after spreading them out, slowing them down, and reducing their size.

Maybe I want a different look. The Grid Spacing value can be thought of almost like a zoom for the "galaxy" being created here, where high Grid Spacing values zoom in, and lower values zoom out. I tried a Grid Spacing value of 1, which makes a more distant sea of stars. But it was a bit small, so I increased the Size value to 50.

Figure 21.8 My stars after "zooming out" by reducing the Grid Spacing value.

It's a little challenging to balance good settings in the real world versus settings that show up in printed screenshots. In real life, this is probably still too many stars. So if this were a real scene, I might raise the Scatter value up to 2000 to reduce the number of stars, and then compensate a bit by increasing the Size value to 80.

I also decided to add a lens flare from VideoCopilot's Optical Flares, and tweak the light settings in CC Sphere accordingly. I also added a slight Curves adjustment. The stars definitely add a lot to the scene here.

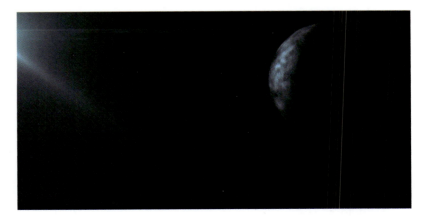

Figure 21.9 My final galaxy scene after adding a little extra pizzazz.

CC Radial Fast Blur

CC Radial Fast Blur is one of my favorite and most oft used blur effects. It creates a zoom style blur, like that found in the Radial Blur effect in After Effects (or Photoshop, for that matter). Like most of the Cycore effects, it renders FAST. If you've ever tried to use the Radial Blur effect in either Photoshop or After Effects, you're probably still waiting for it to render. And with an effect like this, part of its magic is that it's interactive and renders quickly, so you can play with it and see how it would benefit your project.

Continuing again with our planetscape project, open the CC Radial Fast Blur.aep project from the Chapter 21 folder of the exercise files. Apply CC Radial Fast Blur to the Star Burst layer. Note that these stars are a little too big so that we can play with them with CC Radial Fast Blur. You can see the results. The stars streak as if we're warping through hyper space.

Now, let's enhance this effect with a unique setting. The Zoom drop down in the Effects Controls panel allows you to change how these blurry streaks interact with each other. Change this value to Brightest, and then increase the Amount value to 90. NOW we're going through hyper space.

Let's say goodbye to our space scene and see how this effect works in another type of project. Go over to the Cinematic Text START comp, still in this same project. It's basically white text on a black background. Simple. We're going to take this simple text and make it a horror title.

Let's make it look more cinematic. Select the PRECOMP text layer and press Ctrl+D(Win)/Cmd+D(Mac) to duplicate it. On the top copy, apply the Fill effect and change the color to black.

Figure 21.10 The image after applying CC Radial Fast Blur to the stars.

The white copy below should now be invisible (except for some white anti-aliasing around the edges). Next, apply CC Radial Fast Blur to the bottom (white) copy of the text. The blurred white text turns the top, black text into a spooky silhouette.

Figure 21.11 Warp speed, Captain! Uh-oh. Stop! Watch out for that planet!

Figure 21.12 Oh, ok. Nothing creepy about that.

Figure 21.13 Oh yeah. That's what I'm talking about.

Finally, let's animate this by taking Center value in the CC Radial Fast Blur effect over to the left of the text. Then, move in time and move it to the right of the text. If you wanted to take this further, you could also animate the Zoom amount, and possibly even the opacity of the whole layer, to animate on and reveal the text and then disappear.

Figure 21.14 With the Center of the Radial Fast Blur offset to the left of the text, the light rays (aka blur) come from the left side of the image. This looks great when animated.

CC Particle Systems II

The Cycore effects add two all-purpose particle generators: CC Particle World and CC Particle Systems II. Considering that the only other all-purpose particle system in After Effects natively is the dinosaur known as Particle Playground, these additions are most welcome.

While Particle World and Particle Systems II share a lot of common parameters, and a similar look and feel, there are notable differences between them. Most importantly, Particle World is a 3D plugin, responding to After Effects cameras. Additionally, Particle World can use other layers as custom particles (called "textures" in Cycore-speak), while CC Particle Systems II is confined to the particle shapes that are native to it.

That being said, for the sake of ease we're going to look at CC Particle Systems II. Particle Systems II is the perfect primer for those intimidated by other particle effects and plugins; it's like a particle system with training wheels. After getting the hang of this effect, it will be a cinch so upgrade to CC Particle World.

Open the CC Particle Systems II.aep project from the Chapter 21 folder of the exercise files. Go to the CC Particle Systems II Intro comp in this project, which contains just a plain ol' black solid. Apply CC Particle Systems II to this layer. You might need to move forward in time a few frames to see the results, but it's already spitting stuff out. The default settings look a little like bad fireworks, but they render very quickly, and are very helpful in understanding what your particles are actually doing.

Figure 21.15 The default settings for CC Particle Systems II create a fast rendering fountain of particles.

We're going to make some smoke in another comp in a minute, but for now let's just play a little bit with this. Like most particle systems, the paradigm here is that of an emitter that we control that gives "birth" to cute little baby particles, and we get to determine things about the life of those particles. This is very similar to what we see in Foam and Trapcode Particular.

Take the Longevity (sec) value down to 1.0 so the particles don't live quite as long. Show 'em who's boss. Then, in the Producer area, increase the Y position to 720 so that the particle generator sits at the bottom of the comp. In that same area, increase the Radius X to 100 to widen the emitter, and take Radius Y to 0 to flatten it. In the Physics section, we can change the way the particles emit. Try changing the Animation drop down to Vortex so that the particles swirl around like a tornado after being born. Double the Velocity value to 2 so the particles cover more ground faster after birth.

Next, we can adjust the look of the particle itself in the Particle section. Change the Particle Type drop down to Star. Change the Birth Size to 0.06 so that they're smaller when they are created, and take the Death Size way down to 0.16 so they're smaller when they die. There really isn't an overall size value, per se. It's really a balance between Birth Size and Death Size. Increase Size Variation to 100% to get some randomness in size. Make these particles a little brighter by increasing Max Opacity to 100%.

Finally, I changed Birth Color to a purple color, and the Death Color to a bright green so that over time, the particles are purple when they are born, and then gradually change to green.

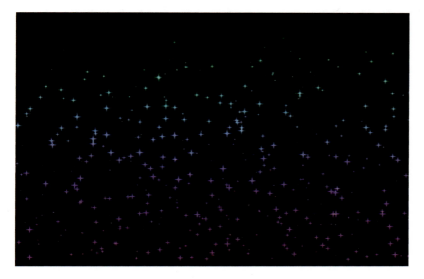

Particle Animation

Now these are just the settings I used to play around with, but when played back, this doesn't look that great. You can make less particles by reducing the Birth Rate, slow the particles down by reducing the Velocity, or play with the direction they travel by adjusting Gravity, Resistance, and Direction.

Figure 21.16 Quick and easy sparkles.

You can get so much mileage out of this particle generator. Even a simple change of Particle Type from Star to something like Cube can totally change the feel of the piece, and be inspiration for another project, or a background to use for later.

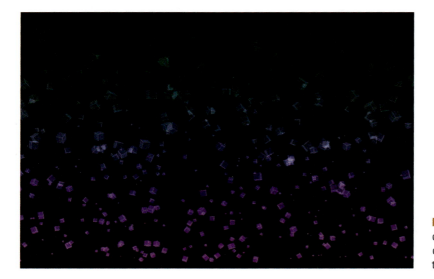

Figure 21.17 Changing the object in a particle generator can make all the difference in the final result.

Now let's look at an interesting example. We're going to play with this effect until we create some cool smoke that trails out of a UFO. Go over to the Cycore Particles START comp in this same project. We've got this UFO flying around, and I've already animated the Position value of the Producer so that it matches up with the UFO, but that's all I've done for you here. Notice how just animating the position of the particle producer creates this really cool trail of particles.

Figure 21.18 Our next little project here, with the Producer>Position value animated.

Now, different people go about setting up particle systems in different ways. Some people start with the particle and some people start with getting the emitter set up right. I hate to be all politically correct about it, but for me, it all depends on what I'm doing. In most cases, I'll probably set up the animation, physics, birth, death, and so on of the particles first. Sometimes, when you have a great looking particle, it's easy to get distracted by it, and take your eye off the ball when it comes to the physics and the movement of the particles.

But in this case, I want to start with the particle first because we're making smoke. When making something where the particles blend together like this, every setting has a dramatic effect on the end result. With a star for example, the particles pretty much always look like stars, so it doesn't have much of an advantage to start there.

So, let's take the Particle>Particle Type drop down to Shaded Sphere. Looks alright, but the dark edges of the Shaded Sphere make each particle too distinct. So fix this by changing the

Transfer Mode from Composite to Screen. Note that this affects how the particles blend with each other, not with the source layer. Looking better, but not quite smoke just yet. We're going for a really stylized, kinda goofy smoke to go with our equally goofy UFO. So the smoke is going to go from blue (the Birth Color) to red (the Death Color).

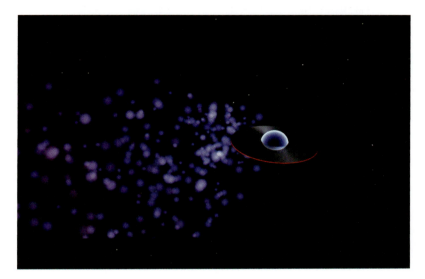

Figure 21.19 After changing some of the settings, we're getting closer. Making good looking particles always takes a little extra fiddling.

Next, let's just add a bunch more particles in there. Smoke doesn't appear to be a bunch of disparate elements, and that's kinda what we have so far. So crank up the Birth Rate value really high, say to like 25. Ah, much better. Another problem with this smoke is that we're not seeing much red and, therefore, not seeing these particles fade out. Reduce the Longevity of the particles by taking the Longevity (sec) value down to 0.5. Now we're getting something that looks much more like smoke.

Notice that the bottom of the smoke is cut off because the layer was elevated while I was animating the particle producer. But I'm not worried about that. It's an easy fix if we wanted to fix it, but our final smoke won't be going that low, so we're OK in this case.

To make our last changes, change Physics>Animation to Direction Normalized. Increase Velocity to 2.0 so that the particles come out faster, and the Inherit Velocity to 11% so that the particles pick up a little of the emitter's velocity. Take the Gravity to 0 so they're not influenced by it. Change the Direction to about 270 degrees so that the particles trail the UFO.

Our particles are spread out a little too much. Let's decrease the Extra value to 0.2. The Extra value increases the randomness

Figure 21.20 Reducing the Longevity (sec) value is now finally making this look a little like smoke.

in the particles (where the higher the Extra, the more the particles are little rebels). The Extra parameter is weirdly named, and it's just as hard to describe/understand. It affects each type of Animation differently, and with some Animation types (such as Explosion), Extra has no effect.

So we're pretty much there. You can adjust Birth Size and Death Size to taste to control the size of the particles, Size Variation, and Max Opacity to taste. And there you have our smoke particles, created from scratch pretty quickly with this simple and versatile Cycore effect.

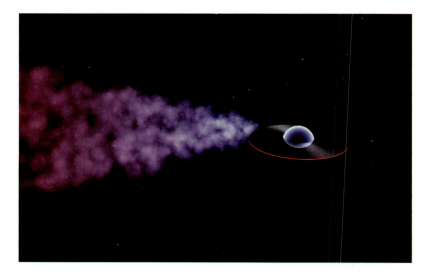

Figure 21.21 The final smoke. For a laugh, go to the Cycore Particles FINAL comp and do a RAM preview to watch this entire animation, along with some great sound effects!

CC Kaleida

OK. I'm going to try to make this brief. But I LOVE CC Kaleida. Unfortunately, I don't think you'll like it as much as I do, but because it's probably the Cycore effect I might use the most often, I just have to include it.

CC Kaleida gets its name from a kaleidescope, which creates these really weird, psychedelic shapes and images. But CC Kaleida actually creates beautiful patterns so easily, that I find myself using it all the time for backgrounds. I can't tell you how many times I've worked for a client that just wants to see their logo in a simple, but beautiful environment. Putting a logo on boring old black can be really lackluster these days. For me, CC Kaleida is almost always the place I go first. I love it.

To follow along, go to the CC Kaleida START comp in the CC Kaleida.aep project in the Chapter 21 folder of the exercise files. Here, I've set up some text, a vignette, and a purple background. Nothing special. Sometimes, a project calls for this level of simplicity. But today is not that day.

Figure 21.22 A typical client logo in front of a boring background.

Before we apply CC Kaleida to this purple background (which actually wouldn't do anything), we need to apply something else. CC Kaleida is in the Stylize category, and like other Stylize effects, it alters (stylizes) content that is already there. So first apply Fractal Noise to the purple solid layer. What's really fun about CC Kaleida as we'll see is that Fractal Noise can feed CC Kaleida infinite patterns to work with. This is fun.

First, at the bottom of the Fractal Noise effect, take the Blending Mode drop down to Overlay to make our background purple and black. Take the Fractal Type (back at the top) to Dynamic. Increase Contrast to 150, and in the Transform section, take Scale down to 35. And just to make things render a bit faster, let's take Complexity down to 4.5. And I think our Fractal Noise is ready to be kaleided.

Figure 21.23 Our final Fractal Noise pattern.

Now apply the CC Kaleida effect to this same purple solid layer. Already, it takes the mush of the Fractal Noise pattern and turns it into a very ornate pattern.

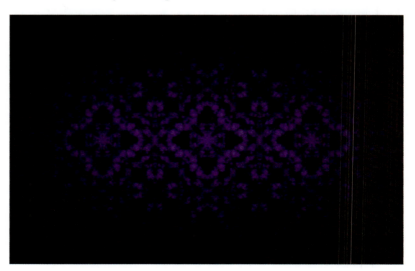

Figure 21.24 The pattern after applying CC Kaleida, with the text layer turned off for better visibility.

Don't like it? Try turning the Evolution value in the Fractal Noise effect one full rotation so that the value reads 1× +0.0. The pattern is completely different.

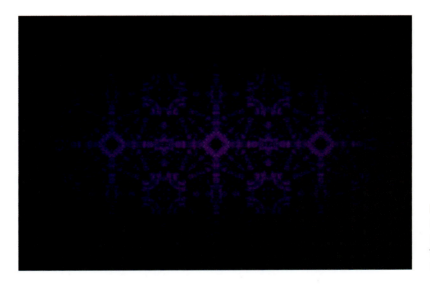

Figure 21.25 After a full revolution of the Evolution property in Fractal Noise, the pattern has completely changed.

Still not happy? Try going to the CC Kaleida effect and reducing the Size value to 5.5. And we've created yet another beautiful ornate pattern that could easily pass for antique wallpaper.

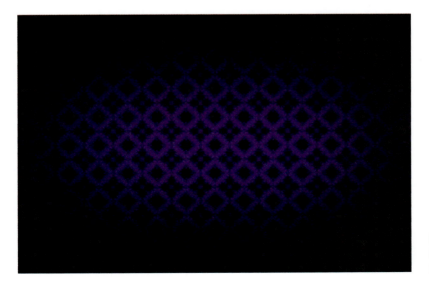

Figure 21.26 Playing with the Size value in CC Kaleida always mixes things up a lot.

Of course, any of these parameters can be animated to create a psychedelic effect, but if we don't animate them, they remain a beautiful background. Let's keep playing with this.

Let's leave the CC Kaleida effect alone and go back to Fractal Noise. Let's try changing the Fractal Type. Try Max.

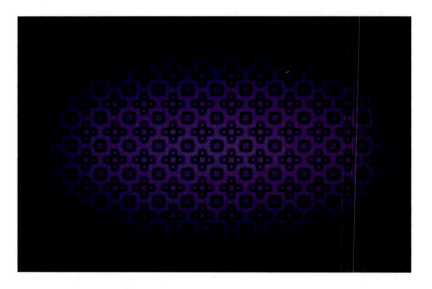

Figure 21.27 The pattern with the Max Fractal Type.

Try Smeary.

Figure 21.28 The pattern with the Smeary Fractal Type.

Try Rocky.

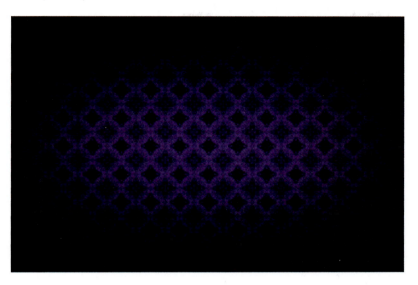

Figure 21.29 The pattern with the Rocky Fractal Type.

Try Threads.

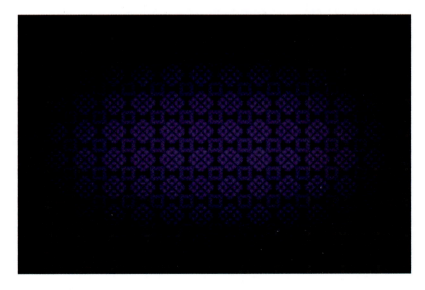

Figure 21.30 The pattern with the Threads Fractal Type.

Are you seeing how amazing this is and why I love it so much? It's hard to create a pattern that ISN'T beautiful with this effect, or rather I should say, effect combination. After playing around with duplicates and glows, this is my final result. I like this much better than our original example.

Note that there are also "shapes" with the CC Kaleida effect. I think Flower (and perhaps Starlish) are the best, but you might try experimenting with other selections from the Mirroring drop down menu in the CC Kaleida effect.

Figure 21.31 The final result with my (not so) boring client logo.

CC Ball Action

The CC Ball Action effect is included in this list because it represents some of the really offbeat effects in this collection. Like so many other Cycore effects, I don't know that I've found the perfect use for CC Ball Action. But it gives you so much additional power, that we are almost obligated to look at it.

The CC Ball Action effect is aptly named, because it basically turns a layer into a grid of 3D balls. The controls of the effect allow you to manipulate these balls by twisting them into interesting 3D shapes. It can be used for everything from creating 3D DNA strands that a camera can fly through, to creating interesting particle transitions that are much easier to set up than they would be with a particle system, to creating a quick and easy array of stage lights.

Open the CC Ball Action.aep project from the Chapter 21 folder of the exercise files. Let's start with the CC Ball Action 1 comp. This contains just a single solid layer with some fractal fire on it. The layer is tactfully named I NEED SOME BALL ACTION.

Fulfill the desires of this layer by applying the CC Ball Action effect to it. The default settings look like a quilt or something, but these are actually little individual spheres.

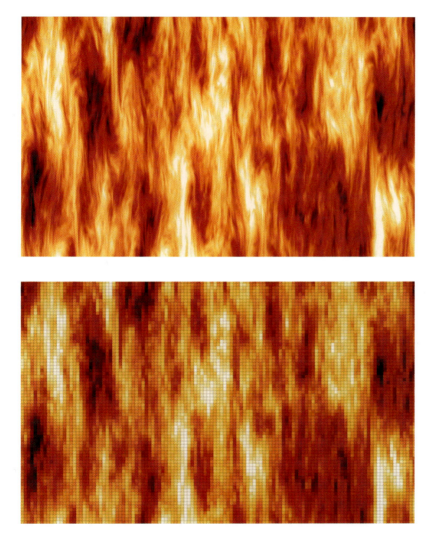

Figure 21.32 The I NEED SOME BALL ACTION layer.

Figure 21.33 The default settings of the CC Ball Action effect.

In order to see the results of our adjustments to this effect, I'm going to create a new camera (50mm is fine) and zoom out and pan around just a little bit so I can see what's going on. This also shows off the 3D capabilities of this effect. Note that the layer that CC Ball Action is applied to needs to remain a 2D layer.

Let's first look at the Grid Spacing and Ball Size parameters. They are closely related. The Grid Spacing value determines the size of the grid, where a larger number increases the spacing of the grid, which makes the grid bigger, but less spaces, and fewer balls to fill those spaces. It also increases the size of the balls. Reducing the Grid Spacing value has the opposite result.

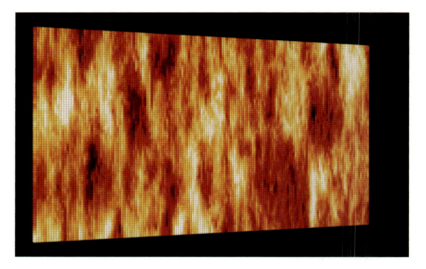

Figure 21.34 After creating a camera in the same comp, zooming out, and rotating the camera a bit so we get a clearer (and more 3D) picture of what's happening here.

The Ball Size value is easier to understand—a larger value increases the size, while a reduction in the value reduces the size of the balls. If the balls get too large, they will get truncated by the cell next to it, and there really isn't an overlap/blend mode/transparency option here.

To get a feel for this, let's play around with it a bit. I'm going to increase my Grid Spacing to 50, which creates a grid with fewer spaces in it, and increases the size of the little spheres. So, I'm going to take the Ball Size value down to 30. A slight adjustment to this (and a little glow) could make this a great wall of light for stage lighting, especially with how each light has a distinct color.

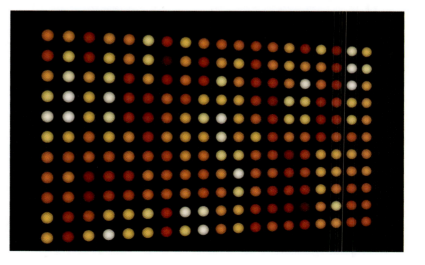

Figure 21.35 With Grid Spacing at 50 and Ball Size at 30.

Now let's switch it. Let's reduce the Grid Spacing value to 4, and increase the Ball Size value a little to 40. Notice how we have a lot more balls with the lower Grid Spacing value. This will be a good resting spot for these values while we experiment with other properties.

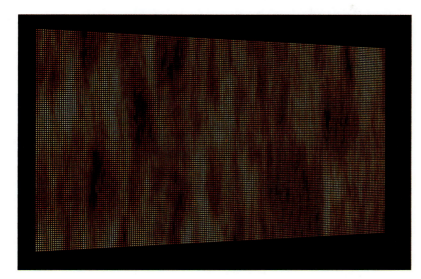

Figure 21.36 With Grid Spacing set to 4 and Ball Size at 40.

Now let's get to the good stuff. This effect really comes alive with the Twist Property and Twist Angle parameters. Increase the Twist Angle value to 180 degrees. Now things are getting interesting.

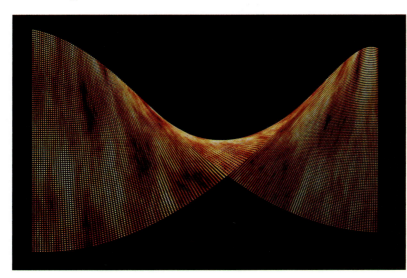

Figure 21.37 The Twist Angle value allows this effect to essentially fold on itself in 3D.

With the Twist Angle value still at 180 degrees, let's adjust the Twist Property to see what else can be twisted.

Change the Twist Property drop down to Y Axis. This creates an almost tunnel-like effect.

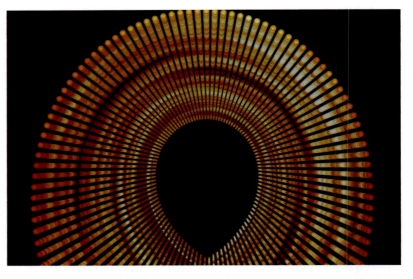

Figure 21.38 With the Twist Property set to Y Axis, this wraps the array of balls around, creating a tunnel. Shown here after rotating and zooming in the camera.

We could stay here all day playing with the different Rotation Axis and Twist Property settings. But I just want to show you one more before moving on to another example. I'm going to reset my camera back to where it was, and then take the Twist Property to Brightness. I also took the Twist Angle down to about 30 degrees so it's clear what's happening here. What CC Ball Action is doing is actually looking at the content of the layer and displacing the balls based on their brightness values. You can also do this based on the red, green, or blue color information as well. When combined with the trick we're about to look at next, this would allow you to create interesting transitions and distortions of images.

Now let's move over to the CC Ball Action 2 comp in this same project for one other cool trick. This comp contains a background (with CC Kaleida! WOO!), a camera, and a 3D render of some text with CC Ball Action already applied. You might notice that this has been precomposed. The reason is that CC Ball Action really doesn't like semitransparent pixels, and will only make balls out of areas in your footage that are completely opaque.

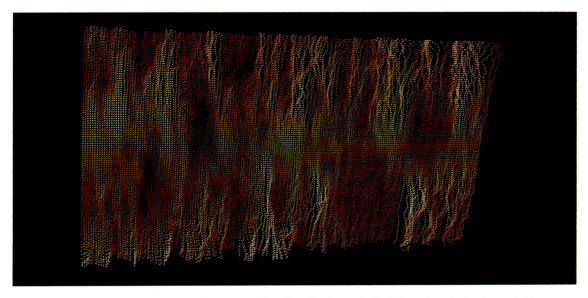

Figure 21.39 With Twist Property set to Brightness, the effect displaces the balls based on the luminance of the source layer.

Figure 21.40 The CC Ball Action 2 comp.

On the Freezing Text layer, go to CC Ball Action and increase the Scatter value to 80. This causes the pixels to go all over the place. Note that you might need to apply the Grow Bounds effect before CC Ball Action if your scattered balls get cut off from the edges of the layer.

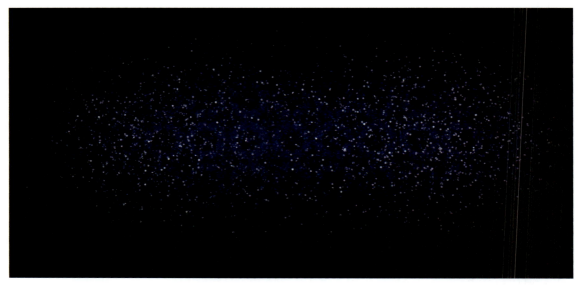

Figure 21.41 When the Scatter value is raised to 80, the balls scatter everywhere.

Now that the Scatter value is bigger than zero, we can play with the Instability State parameter to add more randomness if we wanted to. But what I want to do is actually animate the Scatter property from 80 at frame 0, to 0 at about 3 seconds in

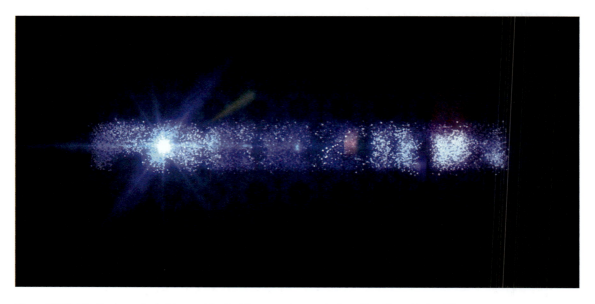

Figure 21.42 My final results (mid-transition) with some glow and a lens flare from Optical Flares.

time. We've now created a really cool reverse shatter effect where the particles of the icy text gather together. We could accent this with an additional lens flare, or by playing with the 3D space with a camera move, and we could trim the layer with CC Ball Action, or add a glow, and place a layer without the CC Ball Action effect on it to be visible after the transition is over.

That concludes our look at CC Ball Action. I would just like to point out that I went through this entire section full of references to ball action and ball size without making any inappropriate jokes. So, I'm feeling pretty good about myself and I thought you should know.

CC Pixel Polly

Shatter is one of my favorite plugins of all time. But it is quite a beast. And one of the problems that people have with Shatter when first applying it is that it kind of just automatically blows up, and it takes some know how to change that.

Enter Pixel Polly. Like many of the Cycore effects, Pixel Polly presents us an easier (albeit less powerful) way to do some of the same things that native After Effects effects do, like CC Bubbles versus the native After Effects Foam.

In this case, Pixel Polly blows up a layer. The good news is that it's much easier than Shatter. And like Shatter, you just apply it and it automatically blows up. However, there is a very intuitive Start Time (sec) value that you can use to choose when in time

Figure 21.43 The CC Pixel Polly effect laying waste to an innocent green solid.

you want the explosion to occur. That's so nice. You don't even have to set a keyframe for that. Just set it and forget it. There are also controls to set the power of the explosion (Force), as well as Force Center, and a few parameters to adjust the physics of the explosion, such as Gravity, Spinning, and so on.

The real bad news in my opinion is that the exploded shards are 2D, and you can basically just choose between squares or triangles. Still, in some instances, this can get the job done with a lot less effort (and processing power) than Shatter.

CC [Weather Systems]

For this section, I'm going to give you a very quick demo of several weather effects, namely CC Drizzle, CC Rainfall, and CC Snowfall. For this let's just create a new comp that's 1920 × 1080 with square pixels. Create a new solid layer that's dark blue. I used the RGB values of 0, 15, 25.

First, let's look at CC Drizzle. This effect is basically used to create the look of raindrops hitting the ground. This effect gives you all kinds of controls over the size, shape, and frequency of the drips, as well as control over lighting and shading. It even lets you use After Effects lights so that it composites better with your scene. The only challenge with this effect is that you can't change the angle of view. But if you ever needed to look straight down onto falling raindrops, this is the effect for you.

Figure 21.44 Falling raindrops, courtesy of CC Drizzle.

While we're looking at rain, let's delete the CC Drizzle effect and apply CC Rainfall. This is actually a really cool effect, but it doesn't look that great when initially applied, especially on a still frame.

Figure 21.45 The default result of applying CC Rainfall to a solid.

What I love about this effect is that it's a significant improvement over the last Cycore rain effect included with After Effects. The effect used to be called CC Rain, and it was an 8-bit effect with limited parameters.

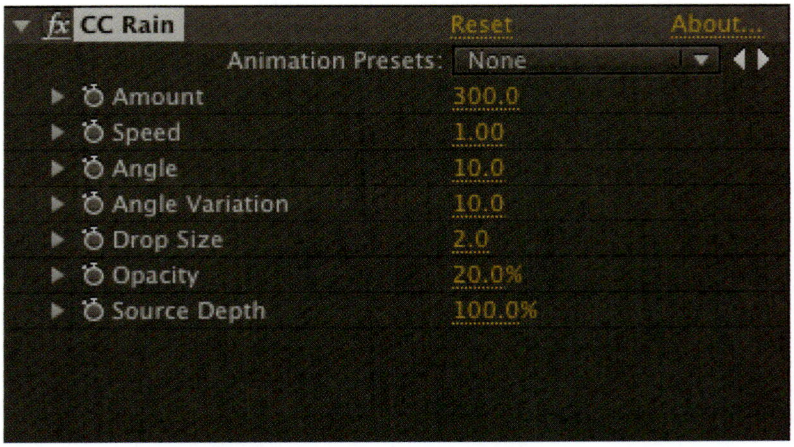

Figure 21.46 The properties of the old CC Rain effect didn't give you much control.

Now, however, we have all kinds of great control over things like wind, color, and reflection and refraction of a background. Try increasing the Wind value to 1500 and the Variation % (Wind) value to 20. Things are looking more realistic.

Figure 21.47 The rain looks better with a little wind.

For some final touches here, I decreased the number of Drops to about 2000, increased Scene Depth to about 8000 (so that there are less drops in the world, and so that those drops appear to go back farther into the distance). I also applied the Fast Blur effect and increased Blurriness to 4 because those raindrops were just too sharp. The results look good when animated.

Note that we're doing this against a dark solid so that you can see what's going on. This effect is difficult to see in a still frame when applied to real footage (as it should be). If you'd like to play with this effect using a more real world example, import the oregon coast.jpg image from the Images folder in the Media folder of the exercise files.

Figure 21.48 The final result with CC Rainfall.

Let's also take a quick look at CC Snowfall, which is very similar to CC Rainfall, but is obviously used for snow. Delete CC Rainfall and apply CC Snowfall. Note that in these screenshots, I've reduced the Flake Flatness % to zero, just so it's a bit more visible in the screenshots.

Figure 21.49 The default results of CC Snowfall.

This is pretty good when animated. Just like CC Rainfall, the CC Snowfall effect replaces the old 8-bit CC Snow effect that was in versions of After Effects before CS6. And like CC Rain, CC Snow really didn't give us much control.

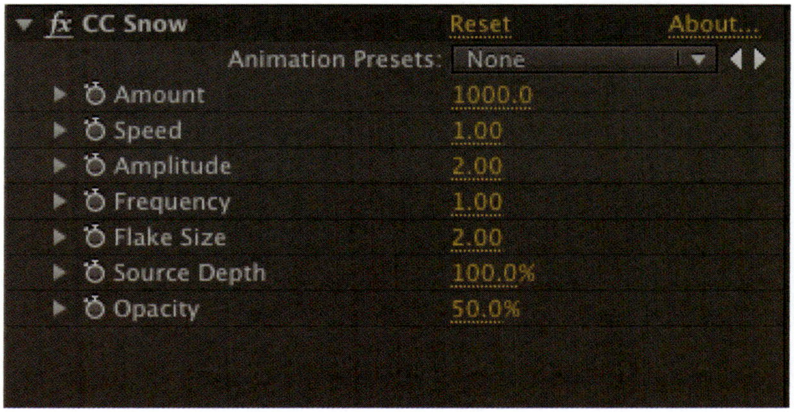

Figure 21.50 The controls in the old CC Snow effect.

So, like CC Rainfall, CC Snowfall is a welcome addition. Because snow is so light and typically has such a lack of density, it's really important that you have control over the wind for the utmost realism. CC Snowfall gives us control over the wind, as well as a series of controls that allow us to control the randomness (Wiggle) of the particles. Just like CC Rainfall, however, I think CC Snowfall benefits from just a smidgen of Fast Blur. But that's just me. Again, this effect shows up best in screenshots against a dark solid background, but if you'd like to play around with this, I've included a snowy background for you to play with. It's called skyrim.jpg and it's in the Images folder of the Media folder in the exercise files.

CC Light Sweep

How many times have you animated a logo spinning on, and need some little extra flashy thing to happen afterwards, like a visual post script? The CC Light Sweep effect is perfect for that. It basically adds a little diagonal streak of light across the front surface of an object. This kind of glint is great also for just adding a subtle emphasis to something.

Open up the CC Light Sweep.aep project from the Chapter 21 folder of the exercise files. This contains a familiar comp.

Figure 21.51 The CC Light Sweep project; pre-CC Light Sweep.

Now apply the CC Light Sweet effect to the freezing 3D text layer. The default settings are actually really good, but just so that it's easier to see for now, I'm going to bump up the Sweep Intensity value to 350. This just makes the streak of light brighter.

Figure 21.52 The CC Light Sweet effect applies a cool streak of light to the front surface of a source layer.

To make this effect come alive, you'd typically animate the Center value to go across an object (say, from left to right) and be done with it. Boom.

But there are a lot of parameters here for doing that. One that might not be so obvious is that CC Light Sweep is capable of creating a light bevel around the edge of your object. This can be really cool on text to make it appear more three dimensional. Still, with all of these controls, this is an ideal effect. It has a simple purpose, it's intuitive, it has all of the controls you need, and it works very well.

CC Mr. Mercury

No look at the Cycore effects would be complete without at least a perfunctory glance at the oddity and hot mess that is CC Mr. Mercury. CC Mr. Mercury is a particle effect like no other, as it specializes in creating flowing liquid type effects.

To get a feel for what's going on here, let's just make a new 1920 × 1080 comp, and a new brightly colored solid. Like CC Star Burst, CC Mr. Mercury uses the colors of the source layer. So if you apply it to a black solid, you won't see much. The default settings look like cartoon goop.

Figure 21.53 The default settings after applying CC Mr. Mercury to a red solid.

Most of the other settings are identical to what we see in Particle Systems II, so we won't cover them here. But I want to show you a cool trick. Apply the Fractal Noise effect to this layer as well, but drag it ABOVE the CC Mr. Mercury effect so that After Effects processes the Fractal Noise effect first. The Fractal Noise grayscale pattern (even just the default settings) creates a mercury type effect now. Note that we didn't even have to precompose!

Figure 21.54 When we apply CC Mr. Mercury to a layer that has Fractal Noise applied to it, the noise pattern creates a liquid metal (i.e., mercury) look to it.

In another example (in the CC Mr Mercury.aep project in the Chapter 21 folder of the exercise files), I tinted the Fractal Noise gold, and then animated the Mr. Mercury Producer in order to create a dollar sign.

Figure 21.55 When animating the Producer point in CC Mr. Mercury, we can create shapes.

CC Mr. Mercury is not one of those effects that you use very often. But it's good to know that liquid particles are a possibility.

Honorable Mentions

There are a couple of other effects worth mentioning. They're great effects, but they're also indicative of more of the benefit of the Cycore effects in general.

CC Bend It

CC Bend It is just a simple bending effect. And that doesn't sound like that big of a deal until you realize how freaking hard it is to do a simple bend without it! With all of the myriad After Effects distort effects, you think it would be easier to do a simple bend.

Open the CC Bend It.aep project from the Chapter 21 folder of the exercise files. There's just some text here.

Apply the CC Bend It effect to the WOO HOOO!! text layer. Let's make this little guy happy. Unfortunately, the default settings cut off the layer. We need to fix the Start and End points. The Start point is almost like an anchor point and the End point is the point that will move.

I put the Start point on the left of the text (at about 260, 720) and the End point on the right of the text (at about 1600, 715). Now increase the Bend value to taste. I used a value of –36. Now come on. It doesn't get any easier than that. Many of the Cycore distort effects provide fast rendering, easy distortions like this.

Figure 21.56 The CC Bend It project.

Figure 21.57 Look at that happy little fella go!

CC Block Load

CC Block Load simulates the progressive download that images on the internet used to have, like 20 years ago. But it's still helpful. You could be doing visual effects on a spy movie where you need to track in footage to a handheld device. This progressive download could also be a great storytelling tool as you build anticipation by not giving the viewer information as quickly as they want it.

Open the CC Block Load.aep project from the Chapter 21 folder of the exercise files. This contains a sweet shot of model Bitsy Rini at an airport, playing a spy sneaking around planes.

Figure 21.58 The spy footage.

Apply the CC Block Load effect. The footage immediately goes dark. Even though it feels like it, this isn't technically a transition effect. It's a stylize effect. But I just wanted to point out that in both the stylize and transition categories, the Cycore effects add a big arsenal of helpful tools.

With the CC Block Load effect, what you're doing is using the Completion value to progressively increase the quality of your footage. The Scans value determines how many passes it takes to download your footage. I'm going to bump up Scans to 10. See Figures 21.59 through 21.61 for progressive stages of this effect as we increase the Completion value. Note that the "blocks" load from top to bottom, as seen mid-scan in Figure 21.61.

Figure 21.59 With the Scans value at 10 and the Completion value at 5.

Figure 21.60 With the Scans value at 10 and the Completion value at 15.

Figure 21.61 With the Scans value at 10 and the Completion value at 21. Notice how this scan is about halfway through her jacket.

You can see how cool this would look when animated, especially if it were motion tracked to be "downloading" to a HUD or handheld spy device.

22

USING MULTIPLE EFFECTS TOGETHER

This chapter, along with the few to follow, can best be thought of as an appendix to the book. Here, I just want to underscore some of the concepts that we've lightly breezed through in the book that deserve greater emphasis.

In this chapter, we're going to be looking at using multiple effects together. No matter which effect you're going for, the final results are almost always enhanced by another effect. Throughout this book, we've seen numerous examples of this. We've used the Strobe Light effect with the Advanced Lightning effect to create lightning strikes. We've used the Roughen Edges effect with the Fractal Noise effect to create a fireball. But we don't have to apply just two. We can apply as many effects to a layer as our system can handle. Let's look a little more closely at using effects together.

Using Multiple Effects for Utility

The possibilities are endless when we use effects together. But it's not only a matter of creative possibilities—the quality of effects is also greatly increased when using them together. The quality (and photorealism) of effects is often increased a great deal by adding one of the Color Correction effects. When keying footage, the Minimax effect or one of the Matte effects can often help you fix edge problems. When creating maps for other effects (as we'll discuss in the next chapter), many of the grayscale pattern generators—such as Ramp, Fractal Noise, or Wave World—can save you from having to go back to Photoshop to create those maps.

Using Multiple Effects for Creativity

There are so many times as a motion graphics artist when you are asked to create an original background or texture in an instant. When using effects for creative and artistic purposes, using multiple effects is critical. To help you create artsy textures,

I've created a couple formulas to help you get started, or in case you ever encounter a mental block and need some inspiration.

Some Sample Formulas

To create artistic textures from scratch, try starting with an effect from the Generate category, or by using any other effect that creates a pattern from scratch, such as Fractal Noise or Turbulent Noise.

Figure 22.1 Start the formula with a texture created from scratch with effects. In this case, I used the Lens Flare effect.

Next, apply an effect from either the Distort, Blur, or Stylize category, or some from each.

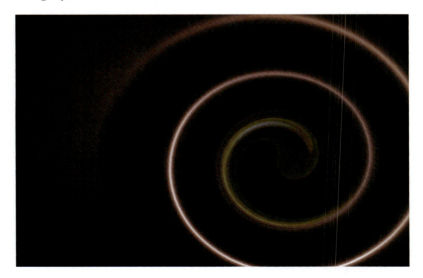

Figure 22.2 The Lens Flare, after distorted with the Twirl effect from the Distort category.

Then finish up with either the Stylize>Glow effect, or another Color Correction effect, or both.

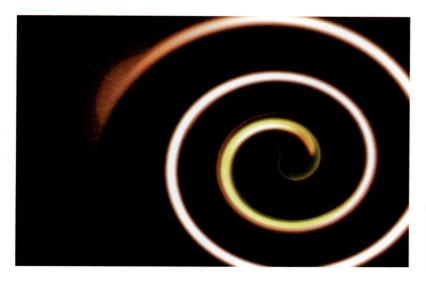

Figure 22.3 Here, I added the Glow effect from the Stylize category. Then I enhanced the Light effect by adjusting colors using the Levels effect.

Here are a few other quick samples I created from randomly grabbing effects in this order. These aren't perfect, nor are they exemplary art. But they are fairly decent patterns created very quickly.

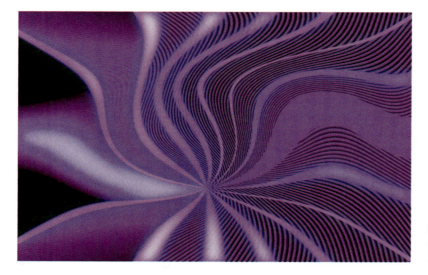

Figure 22.4 A pattern created with Radio Waves, Turbulent Displace, and Glow.

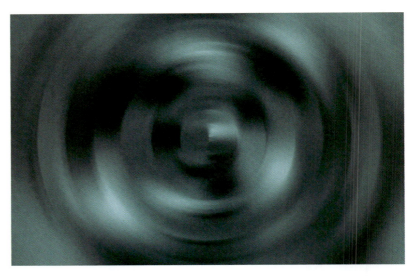

Figure 22.5 A pattern created with Turbulent Noise, Mosaic, Radial Blur, then levels. I also added some color with color balance.

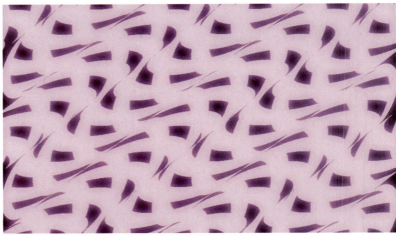

Figure 22.6 A pattern created with Grid, Wave Warp, and Glow.

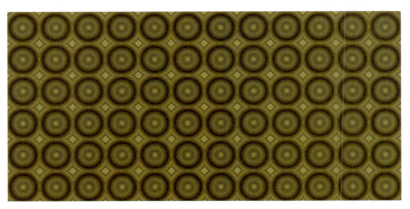

Figure 22.7 A pattern created with Cell pattern, Find Edges, and Colorama.

Figure 22.8 A pattern created with Fractal Noise, Ripple, and Glow.

Remember that you can also create animation presets that store the effects that comprise these patterns. If you find yourself with free time (hey, it could happen), you might consider creating your own library of patterns to use in a pinch.

Also, as mentioned back in Chapter 1, After Effects ships with a large library of animation presets that are not only great jumping off points for use in your own work, but they can also be educational. They can help you see the possibilities available when using multiple effects. And, because the presets are actually "live" applications of effects settings, you can go back to the effects after applying these presets to play CSI and figure out what the original settings were. This is an absolutely phenomenal way to get acquainted with After Effects and the creative potential there.

Playing CSI with Animation Presets
The way to Sherlock an animation preset after you've applied it is to select the layer and press UU (that's the letter "U" pressed two times in a row). This super sweet keyboard shortcut reveals every property that has been changed from its default in the Timeline panel.

23

ENHANCING THE ILLUSION WITH MAPS

Many of the more powerful effects in After Effects have properties that can be controlled with other layers. Some effects, such as Displacement Map, absolutely require these controller layers in order to work correctly. These layers that are used as controllers are often referred to as maps. Once you're familiar with an effect, mastering maps is what you need to take them to the next level. In this chapter, we're going to look at a few options that might help you when controlling effect properties with maps.

Making Maps in After Effects

Frequently, maps are made right here in After Effects. And it makes sense, as there some great tools for the job. There are gradient creators like 4-Color Gradient, Ramp, and the Gradient Overlay layer style. There are grayscale pattern generators like Fractal Noise and Cell Pattern. There is also a very powerful painting engine, which shares many features with the painting features in Adobe Photoshop.

Precomposing Maps

When making maps in After Effects, it is often (though not always) necessary to precompose the layers that the effects or painting are on. If this is not done, effects will often ignore the map layer's effects, painting, and layer styles and instead look at the layer's source content. This is because of the order in which objects are rendered. To "bake" the effects, layer styles, and painting into a layer, precompose it by selecting the layer, and going to the Layer menu and selecting Pre-compose (at the bottom). You can also use the handy shortcut Ctrl+Shift+C (Win)/ Cmd+Shift+C (Mac). You'll also want to make sure to choose the second option (Move all attributes into the new composition) in the Pre-compose dialog box. Note that you can also "bake" After Effects elements in a layer to use its effects as a map by rendering and reimporting it.

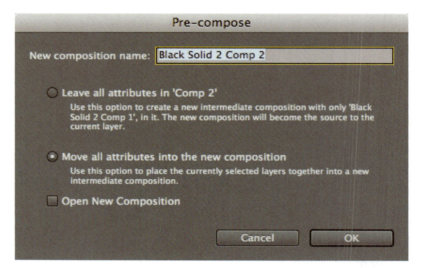

Figure 23.1 The Pre-compose dialog box.

Once precomposed, the results of effects (like Fractal Noise) can be used as maps by other effects (such as Displacement Map). In Figure 23.2, I've created a solid layer with Fractal Noise applied with the default settings, and then precomposed it. I then applied Displacement Map to the precomposed Fractal Noise. By default, the Displacement Map effect uses the layer

Figure 23.2 Precomposing the Fractal Noise effect allows us to use it as a displacement map layer in the Displacement Map effect. Kinda looks like mountainous terrain.

it is applied to as the Displacement Map Layer. I changed both the Use For Horizontal Displacement and Use For Vertical Displacement drop down menus to Luminance, and changed both the Max Horizontal Displacement and Max Vertical Displacement values to 5.

Making Maps Externally

While making maps in After Effects is the quickest way to go, it doesn't always allow for the most possible control in map creation. For detailed maps (such as those created for photorealistic character displacement with the Displacement Map effect), I usually use an external program, such as Adobe Photoshop. Obviously, you can't go wrong using Photoshop with After Effects. These two applications are brothers from another mother. However, there are a few additional issues (and tips) we need to be aware of when traversing this path.

Layer Size and Map Size

Many effects that use maps have built-in contingency plans for how to handle maps that are a different size than the layer. These settings typically allow you to center the map, tile it, or something along those lines. However, if you're using maps to create a specific and detailed result, then these might produce undesirable results. This is usually the case with maps—such as shatter or displacement maps—that often have to line up perfectly with the layer with the effect applied to it.

For this reason, I almost always import such Photoshop documents as a Composition, not as Composition—Cropped Layers. This guarantees that the size of the layer to be affected, and the size of the map layer are imported at the exact same size. I find that this is the best way to achieve consistent results with maps that must line up perfectly with the layers they will adjust.

I realize that the Center option in effects that use maps will align the centers of both layers. But if the edges of one of the layers is off just a little, then the effect might treat them as different sizes, which can throw off your final results.

Editing Maps Created Externally

If you have a map created in Photoshop that you need to edit, a shortcut has been created for you in After Effects. First, select the footage in the Project panel. It must be the actual footage itself, NOT a composition or a folder containing the footage.

Then, select Edit>Edit Original from the top of the interface, or use the keyboard shortcut Ctrl+E (Win)/Cmd+E (Mac). This will launch Photoshop (if it's not already open), and it will open the selected document in Photoshop for editing.

Actually, this will not necessarily launch Photoshop per se, but it will launch whatever program your operating system has associated with Photoshop files. If you have Adobe Bridge (or the Mac's Preview application, or the QuickTime Player, etc.) associated with PSD files, then that's what gets launched. Change your operating system preferences for PSD files if you want After Effects' Edit Original command to open Photoshop.

Reloading Maps Edited Externally

Instead of launching Photoshop from After Effects, you may make adjustments in Photoshop without using the Edit Original command. In that case, you may be frustrated to find that your changes in Photoshop are not reflected in After Effects. Don't worry about this. Seriously. You don't need to reimport your footage and start your work on that file over from scratch.

After Effects has a built-in feature to access the current version of an imported file, and use that version instead of the one that After Effects is using. This also works for any type of imported footage, not just Photoshop documents. To reload a piece of footage, you must first find the original footage in the Project panel. As with the Edit Original command, you must find the actual footage, and not a composition or folder. Once you've found it, right click on it and choose Reload Footage. This will force After Effects to access the file again, and update the file with any changes that have been made to it.

24

WHERE DO I GO FROM HERE?

Naturally, after having such a great experience digging into native effects in After Effects and using them creatively, you might be curious as to what other effects are out there. I thought that I would take just a few words to whet your whistle about the third-party effects that are included with the current version of After Effects, as well as some other great effects companies out there.

The Included Third-Party Effects

Every version of After Effects for the last several years has included a group of free plugins from third-party vendors (the term "third-party" just means a company other than Adobe). These change from version to version, which is one of the reasons that we've decided not to include detailed coverage of all of these effects in this book, as we've done with the other effects. Still, many users are left scratching their heads as to what these extra effects do. If it makes you feel any better about your purchase of After Effects, these third-party effects alone are worth thousands of dollars, which is significantly more than you paid for your copy of After Effects. Note that if you're using an older version of After Effects you might have to go back to the original software disc or the download site to make sure that you've installed all of the included goodies.

Synthetic Aperture's Color Finesse

Color Finesse (in the Synthetic Aperture category) is a color correction powerhouse.

After applying the effect, you'll see a button in the Effect Controls panel that says Full Interface. Click that to open the real Color Finesse effect. As you can see, this is a color adjustment juggernaut, complete with scopes and all manner of color tools.

It's really slow to launch and render in the timeline, so I honestly never use it. But it is the only place to get scopes in After

Effects without an additional plugin. And it definitely is the most advanced color correction tool in After Effects on top of that. Another reason that I didn't use it is that it required a separate serial number from After Effects. I always lose mine and it's just too annoying to keep fiddling with.

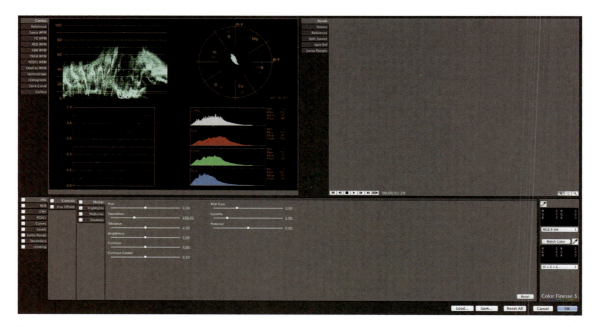

Figure 24.1 The full interface of Color Finesse. Notice that there is no footage in the corner. There actually is on my screen, but it doesn't show up in screen captures.

Other Third-Party Effects

What if you want to go even further? Well, in that case, there are loads of After Effects plugin companies that would love to take your money. I've tried most After Effects plugins out there, and I'll share with you some of my favorites.

Trapcode Plugins

If you only purchase one third-party effect, then it absolutely must be Trapcode Particular. Particular is a particle system of the highest order. It's intuitive and renders quickly, but its loads of options can almost be overwhelming. It's almost like having a second After Effects within After Effects. Particular is famous not just for sparkles and such, but for all kinds of cool effects, such as the ever popular light streaks.

Note that all Trapcode tools are marketed by Red Giant Software (redgiantsoftware.com), which is great because Red Giant is one of the best companies out there. They have phenomenal customer service, they're staffed by artists who love what they do, they're based in the Pacific Northwest (HOLLA!), and they give out free tutorials and presets (and even free plugins) like they're candy.

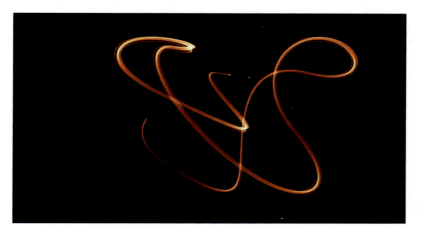

Figure 24.2 The Particular light streaks.

Similar to Particular, Trapcode also makes Form, which is like Particular, except that the particles just take the shape of an object, even a 3D object based on a 3D model imported from a 3D application.

Figure 24.3 The bubble this fairy is living in was created with Trapcode Form.

Another recognizable plugin is the Shine effect. This effect creates volumetric light that appears to shine out from objects. You can see this in the McDonald's logo in some of their old commercials, as well as a financial company logo, and a rum company logo that I can't remember the names of. Shine is relatively inexpensive, renders quick, looks great, is easy to setup, and has some great options for experimenting.

Trapcode also creates an entire suite of effects, almost all of which are quite impressive, and greatly add to the effects in After Effects. If the Cycore plugins are the watered down versions of After Effects effects, the Trapcode effects might be thought of as the super charged versions of After Effects effects.

The Keying Suite

This is a collection of tools (again by Red Giant Software) for keying and adjusting mattes. There are so many valuable tools in this collection, that I almost feel powerless when I have to go to a client facility and work without them. They are an extra purchase (and there are great tools in After Effects that work in this arena), but to me, it's worth it. It's almost like buying a good recliner, or eating at a great sushi restaurant, or taking the kids to Disneyland. Does it cost more? Yeah. But it's such a great experience, it's well worth the money.

Magic Bullet

The Magic Bullet set of plugins (also marketed and sold by Red Giant Software) was created by After Effects master Stu Maschwitz. This suite of effects was created to make video look more like film, which includes changing frame rate, colors, and more.

And Stu knows all about that. He co-founded a successful effects company called the Orphanage, and is quite the movie maker himself. He's also written one of my favorite books on filmmaking, *The DV Rebel's Guide*.

Magic Bullet has now turned into a suite of (mostly) color correction tools and apps. Magic Bullet also makes a growing suite of apps for the iPhone, iPad, and other devices. Mojo is a plugin that quickly adds a cinematic look. Magic Bullet Looks is a full featured color correction studio that allows you to select from premade looks, or construct your own look with a host of real world and intuitive tools. The popular Colorista color correction tool is now free from the Red Giant website, as it's been replaced by the even more powerful Colorista II. If you're into creating cinematic images and love color correction tools, these are definitely things to check out.

Optical Flares

Created and sold by Andrew Kramer at VideoCopilot.net, Optical Flares is one of the best investments you can make for After Effects. If you can only afford one plugin for After Effects, make it Trapcode Particular. But if you can afford two plugins for After Effects OR if you can't afford Particular, then get Optical Flares. It's an extremely powerful lens flare creation tool that adds production value and magic to everything it touches.

Figure 24.4 A still from my award-winning short film *GODLIZZA,* where I used Optical Flares to enhance the power of a baby destroying a city.

Neat Video Noise Reduction

As mentioned in Chapter 12, the noise reduction plugin from Neat Video (neatvideo.com) is one of the best noise reduction tools I've ever seen. You have to pay per host (e.g., Premiere, After Effects, etc.), but it's worth it. This plugin takes a custom profile of each clip, and removes noise in such a way that your footage isn't damaged. There's also built in sharpening that works wonders. I do this with all of my footage before I send it out for final render.

And the Rest ...

Of course, there are hundreds of other plugin makers out there. And perhaps there's a third-party plugin out there that can save your life and sanity that I didn't cover here. This is by no means a comprehensive list, or even a comprehensive list of the good third-party plugins. These are just some of my favorites and some of the more popular ones. There are also entire websites out there devoted solely to the topic of After Effects plugins. Keep your eyes peeled and your mind open to plugins that can solve your problems.

INDEX